W9-BNA-221

THE ANALYSIS OF PUBLIC OUTPUT

NATIONAL BUREAU OF ECONOMIC RESEARCH

UNIVERSITIES—NATIONAL BUREAU CONFERENCE SERIES

1. Problems in the Study of Economic Growth (in mimeograph)
2. Conference on Business Cycles
3. Conference on Research in Business Finance
4. Regularization of Business Investment
5. Business Concentration and Price Policy
6. Capital Formation and Economic Growth
7. Policies to Combat Depression
8. The Measurement and Behavior of Unemployment
9. Problems in International Economics
10. The Quality and Economic Significance of Anticipations Data
11. Demographic and Economic Change in Developed Countries
12. Public Finances: Needs, Sources, and Utilization
13. The Rate and Direction of Inventive Activity: Economic and Social Factors
14. Aspects of Labor Economics
15. Investment in Human Beings
16. The State of Monetary Economics
17. Transportation Economics
18. Determinants of Investment Behavior
19. National Economic Planning
20. Issues in Defense Economics
21. The Role of Agriculture in Economic Development
22. The Technology Factor in International Trade
23. The Analysis of Public Output

THE ANALYSIS OF
PUBLIC OUTPUT

EDITED BY
JULIUS MARGOLIS
The Fels Institute of Local and State Government
The University of Pennsylvania

A Conference of the
Universities — National Bureau Committee
for Economic Research

1970
NATIONAL BUREAU OF ECONOMIC RESEARCH
NEW YORK

DISTRIBUTED BY
COLUMBIA UNIVERSITY PRESS
NEW YORK AND LONDON

Copyright © 1970 by the National Bureau of Economic Research, Inc.
All Rights Reserved

Library of Congress Card Number: 78-119997
ISBN: 0-87014-220-8

Printed in the United States of America

NATIONAL BUREAU OF ECONOMIC RESEARCH

OFFICERS

rthur F. Burns, *Honorary Chairman*
heodore O. Yntema, *Chairman*
alter W. Heller, *Vice Chairman*
hn R. Meyer, *President*
homas D. Flynn, *Treasurer*
ouglas H. Eldridge, *Vice President-Executive Secretary*

Victor R. Fuchs, *Vice President-Research*
F. Thomas Juster, *Vice President-Research*
Hal B. Lary, *Vice President-Research*
Robert E. Lipsey, *Vice President-Research*
Edward K. Smith, *Vice President*

Joan R. Tron, *Director of Publications*

DIRECTORS AT LARGE

seph A. Beirne, *Communications Workers of America*   David L. Grove, *IBM Corporation*
rthur F. Burns, *Board of Governors of the Federal Reserve System*
Walter W. Heller, *University of Minnesota*
allace J. Campbell, *Foundation for Cooperative Housing*
Vivian W. Henderson, *Clark College*
win D. Canham, *Christian Science Monitor*   John R. Meyer, *Yale University*
obert A. Charpie, *The Cabot Corporation*   J. Irwin Miller, *Cummins Engine Company, Inc.*
olomon Fabricant, *New York University*   Geoffrey H. Moore, *Bureau of Labor Statistics*
ank W. Fetter, *Hanover, New Hampshire*   J. Wilson Newman, *Dun & Bradstreet, Inc.*
ugene P. Foley, *Dreyfus Corporation*
James J. O'Leary, *United States Trust Company of New York*
arion B. Folsom, *Rochester, New York*
Robert V. Roosa, *Brown Brothers Harriman & Co.*
i Goldston, *Eastern Gas and Fuel Associates*   Boris Shishkin, *AFL-CIO*
awford H. Greenewalt, *E. I. du Pont de Nemours & Company*   Lazare Teper, *ILGWU*
Donald B. Woodward, *Riverside, Connecticut*
Theodore O. Yntema, *Oakland University*

DIRECTORS BY UNIVERSITY APPOINTMENT

oses Abramovitz, *Stanford*
ary S. Becker, *Columbia*
harles H. Berry, *Princeton*
ancis M. Boddy, *Minnesota*

R. A. Gordon, *California*
Robert J. Lampman, *Wisconsin*
Maurice W. Lee, *North Carolina*
Lloyd G. Reynolds, *Yale*
Robert M. Solow, *Massachusetts Institute of Technology*
om E. Davis, *Cornell*   Henri Theil, *Chicago*
tto Eckstein, *Harvard*   Thomas A. Wilson, *Toronto*
alter D. Fisher, *Northwestern*   Willis J. Winn, *Pennsylvania*

DIRECTORS BY APPOINTMENT OF OTHER ORGANIZATIONS

milio G. Collado, *Committee for Economic Development*
Douglas G. Hartle, *Canadian Economics Association*
homas D. Flynn, *American Institute of Certified Public Accountants*
Walter E. Hoadley, *American Finance Association*
athaniel Goldfinger, *AFL-CIO*   Douglass C. North, *Economic History Association*
arold G. Halcrow, *American Agricultural Economics Association*
Murray Shields, *American Management Association*
eorge Cline Smith, *National Association of Business Economists*
Willard L. Thorp, *American Economic Association*
W. Allen Wallis, *American Statistical Association*

DIRECTORS EMERITI

rcival F. Brundage
Gottfried Haberler

Albert J. Hettinger, Jr.

George B. Roberts
Joseph H. Willits

SENIOR RESEARCH STAFF

Gary S. Becker
harlotte Boschan
Phillip Cagan
lfred H. Conrad
ames S. Earley
olomon Fabricant
filton Friedman

Victor R. Fuchs
Raymond W. Goldsmith
Jack M. Guttentag
Daniel M. Holland
F. Thomas Juster
C. Harry Kahn
John F. Kain

John W. Kendrick
Irving B. Kravis
Hal B. Lary
Robert E. Lipsey
John R. Meyer
Jacob Mincer
Ilse Mintz

Geoffrey H. Moore *
M. Ishaq Nadiri
Nancy Ruggles
Richard Ruggles
Anna J. Schwartz
Robert P. Shay
George J. Stigler

Victor Zarnowitz

* On leave.

RELATION OF NATIONAL BUREAU DIRECTORS TO PUBLICATIONS REPORTING CONFERENCE PROCEEDINGS

Since the present volume is a record of conference proceedings, it has been exempted from the rules governing submission of manuscripts to, and critical review by, the Board of Directors of the National Bureau.

*(Resolution adopted July 6, 1948,
as revised November 21, 1949, and April 20, 1968)*

UNIVERSITIES—NATIONAL BUREAU COMMITTEE
FOR ECONOMIC RESEARCH

This committee is a cooperative venture of universities and the National Bureau. Its guiding objective is the encouragement of economic research on problems susceptible of objective treatment and of sufficiently broad scope to merit attention by institutions serving a scientific and public interest.

Participating universities and their present representatives are:

Buffalo,* *Daniel Hamberg*   New York, *Bruno Stein*
California (Berkeley), *John M. Letiche*   North Carolina, *Henry A. Latané*
California (Los Angeles), *J. C. La Force*
                                          Northwestern, *Richard B. Heflebower*
Carnegie-Mellon, *Norman Miller*   Ohio State, *Jon Cunnyngham*
Chicago, *Robert J. Gordon*   Pennsylvania, *Almarin Phillips*
Columbia, *Phillip Cagan*   Pittsburgh, *Janet Chapman*
Cornell, *George J. Staller*   Princeton, *Albert Rees*
Duke, *David G. Davies*   Queen's,† *David C. Smith*
Harvard, *John V. Lintner*   Rochester, *Richard N. Rosett*
Illinois, *John F. Due*   Stanford, *Moses Abramovitz*
Indiana, *Robert W. Campbell*   Texas, *Ray Marshall*
Iowa State, *Dudley G. Luckett*   Toronto, *D. C. MacGregor*
Johns Hopkins, *Carl F. Christ*   Vanderbilt, *James W. McKie*
Massachusetts Institute of Technology, *Richard S. Eckaus*
McGill, *A. Deutsch*   Virginia, *Richard T. Selden*
Michigan, *Harvey E. Brazer*   Washington (St. Louis), *Werner Hochwald*
Michigan State, *Carl E. Liedholm*   Washington (Seattle), *Richard W. Parks*
Minnesota, *James M. Henderson*   Wisconsin, *Leonard Weiss*
New School for Social Research, *Thomas Vietorisz*   Yale, *Richard Ruggles*

The National Bureau of Economic Research representative is
Robert E. Lipsey.

Members at large are:

Daniel Creamer   George Jaszi   Julius Shiskin
S. A. Goldberg   Rudolf R. Rhomberg   George J. Stigler
                        Walter S. Salant

The officers of the Universities–National Bureau Committee are: Carl F. Christ (Johns Hopkins University), Chairman; Walter S. Salant (Brookings Institution), Vice Chairman; and Robert P. Shay, Secretary. The members of the Executive Committee are: Moses Abramovitz (Stanford University), Carl F. Christ, James M. Henderson (University of Minnesota), Robert E. Lipsey (National Bureau of Economic Research), Almarin Phillips (University of Pennsylvania), and Walter S. Salant.

* Michael Gort, alternate for 1970–71. † M. C. Urquhart, alternate for 1970–71.

Funds for the economic research conference program of the National Bureau of Economic Research are supplied by the National Science Foundation.

CONTENTS

Introduction JULIUS MARGOLIS xi

Political and Economic Evaluation of Social Effects and Externalities
KENNETH J. ARROW 1
Comment SIDNEY S. ALEXANDER 24

Local Decentralization and the Theory of Optimal Government
JEROME ROTHENBERG 31
Comment GORDON TULLOCK 65

Uncompensated Nonconstruction Costs Which Urban Highways and Urban Renewal Impose Upon Residential Households
ANTHONY DOWNS 69
Comment BURTON A. WEISBROD 107

Administrative Decision Making and Pricing: Externality and Compensation Analysis Applied OLIVER WILLIAMSON 115
Comment PETER O. STEINER 136

An Efficiency Basis for Federal Fiscal Equalization
JAMES M. BUCHANAN and RICHARD E. WAGNER 139
Comment MARTIN S. FELDSTEIN 159

Changing Roles of Different Levels of Government
GEORGE F. BREAK 163
Comment MANCUR OLSON 210

Assessing the Role of Systematic Decision Making in the Public Sector
HENRY S. ROWEN 219
Comment WERNER Z. HIRSCH 228

Cost Functions and Budgets (Cost Considerations in Systems Analysis) G. H. FISHER 231
Comment EDWIN S. MILLS 264

Systematic Errors in Cost Estimates for Public Investment Projects
MAYNARD M. HUFSCHMIDT and JACQUES GERIN 267

Externalities in Public Facility Use: The Case of Highway Accidents
WILLIAM VICKREY 317
Comment MARTIN J. BAILEY 336

The Value of Output of the Post Office Department JOHN HALDI 339
Comment WILLIAM M. CAPRON 381

Index 389

INTRODUCTION

JULIUS MARGOLIS

University of Pennsylvania

In recent decades the field of public finance has become transformed and, with inputs from several other fields, has given birth to an as yet unnamed field which we shall call public economics. An early preoccupation with the incidence of taxes and taxing institutions has been replaced with a focus on the behavior of governments. This change is not based upon the internal logic of the discipline but is responsive to the dramatic growth of government and an involvement of economists with the operations of government programs. The papers of this conference do not fully represent this new field, but it is clear that many of them have been influenced by the developments in public economics.

The government, though it has accounted for a huge share of economic activity and regulated an even larger share, has traditionally been considered exogenous to the economy. Some economists are reluctant to extend economic analysis to the workings of government since they believe that the political process does not exhibit the properties of a market, but at the same time many economists recommend that the government adopt policies which they believe economically optimal. Unless such advice is given with no account to possible implementation, it is implied that there is a mechanism in government which heeds and responds to these exhortations for economic rationality. Certainly the characteristics of government are relevant to the shaping of a program. There is no wisdom in urging a government program to overcome a market failure due to informational deficiencies if it is itself encumbered by similar inadequacies. Nor would it be wise to press the government to correct an efficiency in the market and as a consequence create an unacceptable redistribution. Too often we are made painfully aware of outcomes not anticipated by the legislative architects. The indifference to government structure in design of policy or programs can lead to frustration.

The planners of the conference sought to produce a progress report on the applications of economic analysis in the formulation and im-

Introduction

plementation of public programs. We designed an orderly structure
and we convinced an impressive panel of authors of the value of the
product, but the output of independent scholars is a chancy thing.
Though some authors performed according to expectations the resultant product has large, unplanned elements. Possibly this is to the
good—the working scholars, in resisting our restraints, may better reflect the state of analysis than a committee of planners. In any case,
the papers do provide a valuable set of contributions about the public
economy.

A decade back Universities-National Bureau Conference 12 dealt
with the general field of public finance. The links between the two conferences are strong. Some papers continue arguments begun then;
others apply the analysis to specific problems; some break new ground
reflecting the growth of the field. The conference planners did not refer
back to the older plan but it is clear that, despite dramatic changes in
the real world, continuity in science is strong.

The conference papers fall into four categories: theory of market
failure and public action, the distributional aspects of public decisions,
intergovernmental fiscal relations, and a set of applications of analysis
to specific problems and general approaches. The division is artificial
and there are important classifications which cut across the groupings.
Political analysis, for example, falls into at least one paper of each
category.

Kenneth Arrow's contributions lie in the analytical underpinnings of
the analysis of the public sector. Studies in this area have stressed two
related themes: the determinants of public intervention in the economy
and the design of rules for optimal public behavior. Both sets of problems share a common theoretical base which is Arrow's concern. His
paper does not deal with the forms of public behavior; it is a basic
reappraisal of the analysis of the failures of the market that give rise
to the necessity of intervention. His approach is "natural" to economists—a perfectly competitive utopia which fails and therefore necessi-
tates the sinful tampering by government. In Arrow's paper, externalities retain their central role of confounding the market but he general-
izes them to the more ubiquitous phenomena of transaction costs. Since
transaction costs are universal, almost all private commodities become
potential candidates for public intervention; of course the possible
advantages of public supply or regulation will be subject to evaluation
in terms of the same private, and often other public, transaction costs
which may exist even in government decision making.

Arrow turns to other questions (e.g., political process, social codes), but the analysis is always in the context of economic theory. Individuals, though they are acting in the political sphere, are the same individuals who are purchasing goods and working for wages. Rather than partitioning their behavior into separate worlds he suggests that a general theory would be applicable. This section of analysis in the paper is little more than a suggestion though it is highly illuminating. Sidney Alexander, in discussing the paper, took exception to this conventional approach which relies on the preferences of individuals and instead appealed to a very different frame of reference for public policy—the choices of reasonable and moral men with information adequate to judge among alternative states. The different approaches to public action are drawn sharply in the paper and discussion; they are less visible in the many other debates about public policy but nevertheless they are present.

Jerome Rothenberg's paper deals with a specific problem, decentralization of government within a metropolitan area; however it presents a useful foil to Arrow's very general, theoretical paper. Instead of the unitary government assumed in the body of theory, Rothenberg applies the analytical concepts of externalities and welfare economics to the set of local governments. The units of government are specified by fixed territories, their service areas and tax bases are confined within their territories, but transactions flow across borders, and residential and business populations move in response to economic advantage and the decisions of government. The shift of orientation to the behavior of a set of governments, rather than the single government with minimum organizational characteristics, opens a whole new direction of research.

The problem of an objective function takes a very different form when individuals can choose residence among territories with different packages of services and taxes. Redistributional functions can be dealt with in greater richness by considering the incentives and barriers to the movement of population of different income levels. Though Rothenberg focuses on the spatial division of a metropolitan area into a set of governments, the extension of the arguments to deal with special function and higher level governments not only adds realism to the model but it may prove to be an appropriate mechanism by which to incorporate the political and moral elements suggested in the Arrow paper.

The next two papers, by Williamson and Downs, deal with that most difficult of subjects—the distributional aspects of public behavior. Anthony Downs is concerned with the "damages" imposed on individuals by a government program involving a forced sale as for urban highways or urban renewal. An exhaustive listing of possible harmful consequences yielded the impressive number of twenty-two categories, ten of which he believes should be compensated for and only two of which are actually compensated. The inequity is aggravated by the selectiveness of the two programs which focus on the dilapidated slum housing surrounding the inner core of the city and occupied by low-income minority groups. The criteria by which to judge whether a damage should be compensated are not formally developed; however they provide usable guides to administrators and they are suggestive for the more formal treatment in Williamson.

While Downs appeals unabashedly to a concern with equity, Oliver Williamson casts his arguments in terms of allocative effects. Uncompensated damages, in his framework, can cause severe efficiency losses because of the demoralizing effects on the potential recipients. Their investment patterns may be inhibited by fears of arbitrary public acts, they may resort to political restraints on government, even be driven to political disorder. The analysis does not conclude that all damages should be compensated but that an efficiency calculus should be made of the gains and costs of compensation. It would be intriguing to extend his arguments to the more general problem of distribution policy. In that case the redistributive aspects of a program would not be the reflection of a social welfare function but a cost to the system in order to achieve acceptance of its general structure. Distributional rules would be comparable to institutions for enforcing contracts and preventing monopoly—procedures whose merits are judged by their consequences for efficient output. Of course one need not reject any role for equity judgments in order to explore the role that self-interest may play in a willingness to redistribute.

The papers of Buchanan-Wagner and Break deal with intergovernmental relations; they continue the debate of the conference a decade back and it is clear that the issues will remain of lively interest in the coming decade. Buchanan-Wagner examine the possible efficiency bases for the introduction of equalizing elements into a program of bloc or unconditional grants. Their analysis bears a relationship to the Rothenberg paper; they also assign a major role to migration and to externalities. Individuals respond to average tax costs and public benefits in making their locational decisions but the averages diverge from the marginals, therefore leading to misallocations in population. They do not analyze the many forms of intergovernmental fiscal relations, but they focus on general policies.

George Break's paper places the policy alternatives about intergovernmental fiscal relations in an historical perspective. He examines the record of expenditures by function and level since the turn of the century. The analysis of the trends is the basis of his evaluation of the likely developments in intergovernmental fiscal structures and the choice among them of those it would be sensible to encourage.

The last set of papers are applications of economic analysis to a set of problems of the public sector. Three of them deal with general phenomena and the remaining two examine one agency and one program in depth. Henry Rowen, on the basis of experiences in the Bureau of the Budget and RAND, evaluates the sectors where systematic analysis is likely to be successful. Dimensions like knowledge of technological process, prominence of distributional objectives, ignorance of users, availability of data, and fragmentation of administrative responsibility are considered in providing guides to the areas amenable to the PPBS framework. It would be instructive to subject Rowen's judgments to the analytical concepts developed by Arrow. Will the transactions costs which create inefficiencies in the private market have a counterpart in the public sector which create even greater inefficiencies?

Fisher provides a very useful survey of the conceptual framework and the practical problems involved in establishing cost analysis capabilities. Where Rowen's paper deals with the strategy of systematic analysis Fisher summarizes the techniques used to overcome the many problems facing the analyst. He does not solve any new problems, but he illustrates the techniques with hypothetical and military problems.

Hufschmidt addresses a problem which repeatedly crops up—an assumed underestimation of costs of public investment projects. He finds that the bias towards underestimation was true in earlier decades, but it has been disappearing; improvements in planning procedures have had desirable consequences. The critics of engineering agencies have assumed a bureaucratic bias to strengthen their position before budgetary authorities and Congressional committees. Hufschmidt's results imply that this cynical approach to the engineering agencies is too simple. An extension of the investigations to other public works and a more detailed study of the errors will go far to overcome these problems.

Vickrey's paper greatly broadens the concept of public service. He deals with the public highway and with the accidents which arise with congestion but his analysis is not restricted to conventional tools of increasing capacity, changing geometry, imposing driving rules or tolls. Instead he ingeniously treats of alternative insurance and tax schemes by which to discourage accidents.

Haldi's paper on the postal services was commissioned because we wanted an example of the influence of political and social criteria on the output of a commodity which most closely approximated a commercial good. We were not disappointed. Haldi demonstrates many of the "inefficient" practices and certainly these are attributable to political factors. Are these political influences the signs of a venal government responding to special interests? Are they clues to the public goods aspects of the postal services? Are they the results of a log-rolling process where postal services enter as one of many trading items? Should the monopoly position of the postal services be chopped and will the ensuing competition lead to more efficient production and pricing? Haldi argues, after surveying cost and demand data, that a corporate structure for the Post Office and competitive supply would lead to an increase in social utility; that there exists no public goods features in the Post Office though its facilities have been means by which other social values have been furthered. Capron takes exception to some of Haldi's conclusions, and though debate did not lead to a reconciliation of views, it is clear that a continued systematic analysis of this service will permit us to resolve the policy issues being debated.

The set of papers touch on theory and policy, speculation and fact, economics and politics. They do not make a neat, integrated set of arguments, but they do reflect the range of analysis and studies now pursued in public economics.

The text was prepared for publication by George Santiccioli. The charts were drawn by H. Irving Forman.

THE ANALYSIS OF PUBLIC OUTPUT

POLITICAL AND ECONOMIC EVALUATION OF SOCIAL EFFECTS AND EXTERNALITIES

KENNETH J. ARROW
Harvard University

Introduction

The concept of public goods has been developed through successive refinement over a long period of time. Yet, surprisingly enough, nowhere in the literature does there appear to be a clear general definition of this concept or the more general one of "externality." The accounts given are usually either very general and discursive, difficult to interpret in specific contexts, or else they are rigorous accounts of very special situations. What exactly is the relation between externalities and such concepts as "appropriability" or "exclusion"?

Also, there is considerable ambiguity in the purpose of the analysis of externalities. The best developed part of the theory relates to only a single problem: the statement of a set of conditions, as weak as possible, which insure that a competitive equilibrium exists and is Pareto-efficient. Then the denial of any of these hypotheses is presumably a sufficient condition for considering resort to nonmarket channels of resource allocation—usually thought of as government expenditures, taxes, and subsidies.

At a second level the analysis of externalities should lead to criteria for nonmarket allocation. We are tempted to set forth these criteria in terms analogous to the profit-and-loss statements of private business; in this form, we are led to benefit-cost analysis. There are, moreover, two possible aims for benefit-cost analysis. One, more ambitious but theoretically simpler, is specification of the nonmarket actions which will restore Pareto efficiency. The second involves the recognition that the instruments available to the government or other nonmarket forces are scarce resources for one reason or another, so that all that can be achieved is a "second best."

Other concepts that seem to cluster closely to the concept of public goods are those of "increasing returns" and "market failure." These are related to Pareto inefficiency on the one hand and to the existence and optimality of competitive equilibrium on the other; sometimes the discussions in the literature do not adequately distinguish these two aspects. I contend that market failure is a more general category than externality; and both differ from increasing returns in a basic sense, since market failures in general and externalities in particular are relative to the mode of economic organization, while increasing returns are essentially a technological phenomenon.

Current writing has helped bring out the point that market failure is not absolute; it is better to consider a broader category, that of transaction costs, which in general impede and in particular cases completely block the formation of markets. It is usually though not always emphasized that transaction costs are costs of running the economic system. An incentive for vertical integration is the replacement of the costs of buying and selling on the market by the costs of intrafirm transfers; the existence of vertical integration may suggest that the costs of operating competitive markets are not zero, as is usually assumed in our theoretical analysis.

Monetary theory, unlike value theory, is heavily dependent on the assumption of positive transaction costs. The recurrent complaint about the difficulty of integrating these two branches of theory is certainly governed by the contradictory assumptions made about transaction costs. The creation of money is in many respects an example of a public good.

The identification of transaction costs in different contexts and under different systems of resource allocation should be a major item on the research agenda of the theory of public goods and indeed of the theory of resource allocation in general. Only the most rudimentary suggestions are made here. The "exclusion principle" is a limiting case of one kind of transaction cost, but the costliness of the information needed to enter and participate in any market, another type of cost, has received little attention. Information is closely related on the one hand to communication and on the other to uncertainty.

Given the existence of Pareto inefficiency in a free market equilibrium, there will be pressure in the system to overcome it by some sort of departure from the free market, i.e., some form of collective action. This need not be undertaken by the government. I suggest that in fact there is a wide variety of social institutions—in particular, generally accepted social norms of behavior—which serve in some means as compensation for failure or limitation of the market, though each in turn involves transaction costs of its own. The question also arises of how the behavior of individual economic agents in a social institution (especially in voting) is related to their behavior on the market. A good deal of the theoretical literature of recent years seeks to describe political behavior as analogous to economic, and we may hope for a general theory of socio-economic equilibrium. But it must always be kept in mind that the contexts of choice are radically different, particularly when the hypotheses of perfectly costless action and information are relaxed. It is not accidental that economic analysis has been successful only in certain limited areas.

Competitive Equilibrium and Pareto Efficiency

A quick review of the familiar theorems on the role of perfectly competitive equilibrium in the efficient allocation of resources will be useful at this point. Perfectly competitive equilibrium has its usual meaning: households, possessed of initial resources, including possibly claims to the profits of firms, choose consumption bundles to maximize utility at a given set of prices; firms choose production bundles so as to maximize profits at the same set of prices; the chosen production and consumption bundles must be consistent with each other in the sense that aggregate production plus initial resources must equal aggregate consumption.[1] The key points in the definition are the parametric role of the prices for each individual and the identity of prices for all individuals. Implicit are the assumptions that all prices can be known by all individuals and that the act of charging prices does not itself consume resources.

A number of additional assumptions are made at different points in the theory of equilibrium, but most clearly are factually valid in the usual contexts and need not be mentioned. The two hypotheses frequently not valid are *C,* the convexity of household indifference maps and firm production possibility sets, and *M,* the universality of markets. While the exact meaning of the last assumption will be explored later at some length, for the present purposes we mean that

[1] Sometimes this is stated to permit an excess of supply over demand, with a zero price for such free goods; but this can be included in the above formulation by postulating the existence of production processes (disposal processes) which have such surpluses as inputs and no outputs.

the consumption bundle which determines the utility of an individual is the same as that which he purchases at given prices subject to his budget constraint, and that the set of production bundles among which a firm chooses is a given range independent of decisions made by other agents in the economy.

The relations between Pareto efficiency and competitive equilibrium are set forth in the following two theorems.

1. *If* M *holds, a competitive equilibrium is Pareto-efficient.* This theorem is true even if *C* does not hold.

2. *If* C *and* M *hold, then any Pareto-efficient allocation can be achieved as a competitive equilibrium by a suitable reallocation of initial resources.*

When the assumptions of Proposition 2 are valid, then the case for the competitive price system is strongest. Any complaints about its operation can be reduced to complaints about the distribution of income, which should then be rectified by lump-sum transfers. Of course, as Pareto already emphasized, the proposition provides no basis for accepting the results of the market in the absence of accepted levels of income equality.

The central role of competitive equilibrium both as a normative guide and as at least partially descriptive of the real world raises an analytically difficult question: does a competitive equilibrium necessarily exist?

3. *If* C *holds, then there exists a competitive equilibrium.* This theorem is true even if *M* does not hold.

If both *C* and *M* hold, we have a fairly complete and simple picture of the achievement of desirable goals, subject always to the major qualification of the achievement of a desirable income distribution. The price system itself determines the income distribution only in the sense of preserving the status quo. Even if costless lump-sum transfers are possible, there is needed a collective mechanism reallocating income if the status quo is not regarded as satisfactory.

Of course *C* is not a necessary condition for the existence of a competitive equilibrium, only a sufficient one. From Proposition 1, it is possible to have an equilibrium and therefore efficient allocation without convexity (when *M* holds). However, in view of the central role of *C* in these theorems, the implications of relaxing this hypothesis have been examined intensively in recent years by Farrell [1959], Rothenberg [1960], Aumann [1966], and Starr [1969]. Their conclusions may be summarized as follows: Let *C'* be the weakened convexity assumption that there are no indivisibilities large relative to the economy.

4. *Propositions 2 and 3 remain approximately true if C is replaced by C'.*

Thus, the only nonconvexities that are important for the present purposes are increasing returns over a range large relative to the economy. In those circumstances, a competitive equilibrium cannot exist.

The price system, for all its virtues, is only one conceivable form of arranging trade, even in a system of private property. Bargaining can assume extremely general forms. Under the assumptions C' and M, we are assured that not everyone can be made better off by a bargain not derived from the price system; but the question arises whether some members of the economy will not find it in their interest and within their power to depart from the perfectly competitive price system. For example, both Knight [1921, pp. 190–194] and Samuelson [1967, p. 120] have noted that it would pay all the firms in a given industry to form a monopoly. But in fact it can be argued that unrestricted bargaining can only settle down to a resource allocation which could also be achieved as a perfectly competitive equilibrium, at least if the bargaining itself is costless and each agent is small compared to the entire economy. This line of argument originated with Edgeworth [1881, pp. 20–43] and has been developed recently by Shubik [1959], Debreu and Scarf [1963], and Aumann [1964].

More precisely, it is easy to show:

5. *If M holds and a competitive equilibrium prevails, then no set of economic agents will find any resource allocation which they can accomplish by themselves (without trade with the other agents) which they will all prefer to that prevailing under the equilibrium.*

Proposition 5 holds for any number of agents. A deeper proposition is the following converse:

6. *If C' and M hold, and if the resources of any economic agent are small compared with the total of the economy, then, given any allocation not approximately achievable as a competitive equilibrium, there will be some set of agents and some resource allocation they can achieve without any trade with others which each one will prefer to the given allocation.*

These two propositions, taken together, strongly suggest that when all the relevant hypotheses hold, (a) a competitive equilibrium, if achieved, will not be upset by bargaining even if permitted, and (b) for any bargain not achievable by a competitive equilibrium there is a set of agents who would benefit by change to another bargain which they have the full power to enforce.

The argument that a set of firms can form a monopoly overlooks the possibility that the consumers can also form a coalition, threaten not to buy, and seek mutually advantageous deals with a subset of the firms; such deals are possible since the monopoly allocation violates some marginal equivalences.

In real life, monopolizing cartels are possible for a reason not so far introduced into the analysis: bargaining costs between producers and consumers are high, those among producers low—a point made most emphatically by Adam Smith [1937, p. 128]; "People of the same trade seldom meet together, even for merriment or diversion, but the conversation ends in a conspiracy against the public, or in some contrivance to raise prices." *It is not the presence of bargaining costs per se but their bias that is relevant.* If all bargaining costs are high, but competitive pricing and the markets are cheap, then we expect the perfectly competitive equilibrium to obtain, yielding an allocation identical with that under costless bargaining. But if bargaining costs are biased, then some bargains other than the competitive equilibrium can be arrived at which will not be upset by still other bargains if the latter but not the former are costly.

Finally, in this review of the elements of competitive equilibrium theory, let me repeat the obvious and well-known fact that in a world where time is relevant, the commodities which enter into the equilibrium system include those with future dates. In fact, the bulk of meaningful future transactions cannot be carried out on any existing present market, so that assumption *M,* the universality of markets, is not valid.

Imperfectly Competitive Equilibrium

There is no accepted and well-worked-out theory corresponding to the title of this section. From the previous section it is clear that such a theory is needed perforce in the presence of increasing returns on a scale large relative to the economy (hereafter, the phrase "increasing returns" will always be understood to include the prepositional phrase just employed), and is superfluous in its absence.

There are two approaches to a theory of general equilibrium in an imperfectly competitive environment; most writers who touch on public policy questions implicitly accept one or the other of these proto-theories without always recognizing that they have made such a choice. One assumes that all transactions are made according to the price system, i.e., the same price is charged for all units of the same commodity; this is the *monopolistic competition* approach. The alternative approach assumes unrestricted bargaining; this is the *game theory* approach. The first might be deemed appropriate if the costs of bargaining were high relative to the costs of ordinary pricing, while the second assumes costless bargaining.[2]

It cannot be too strongly emphasized that neither approach is, at the present stage, a fully developed theory, and it is misleading to state any implications about the working of these systems. Chamberlin's [1933] purpose was certainly the incorporation of monopoly into a general equilibrium system, together with a view that the commodity space should be considered infinite-dimensional, with the possibility of arbitrarily close substitutes in consumption; Triffin [1941] emphasized this aspect, but the only completely worked-out model of general monopolistic equilibrium is that of Negishi [1960–61], and he made the problem manageable by regarding the demand functions facing the monopolists as those perceived by them, with only loose relations to reality. Such a theory would have little in the way of deducible implications (unless there were a supplementary psychological theory to explain the perceptions of demand functions) and certainly no clear welfare implications.

Of course, whatever a monopolistic competitive equilibrium means, it must imply inefficiency in the Pareto sense if there are substantial increasing returns. For a firm can always make zero profits by not existing; hence, if it operates, price must at least equal average cost, which is greater than marginal cost. Kaldor [1935] and Demsetz [1964], however, have argued that in the "large numbers" case, the welfare loss may be supposed very small. I would conjecture that this conclusion is true, but it is not rigorously established, and indeed the model has never been formulated in adequate detail to discuss it properly.[3]

[2] Within the framework of each prototheory attempts have been made to modify it in the direction of the other. Thus, price discrimination is a modification of the price system in the pure theory of monopoly, though I am aware of no attempt to study price discrimination in a competitive or otherwise general equilibrium context. Some game theorists (Luce [1954, 1955a, b], Aumann and Maschler [1964]) have attempted to introduce bargaining costs in some way by simply limiting the range of possible coalitions capable of making bargains.

[3] Suppose that the degree of increasing returns is sufficient to prevent there being more than one producer of a given commodity narrowly defined, but not to prevent production of a close substitute. Is this degree of returns sufficiently substantial to upset the achievement of an approximately perfect competitive equilibrium, as discussed in the last section?

With unrestricted bargaining it is usual to conclude that the equilibrium, whatever it may be, must be Pareto-efficient for, by definition, it is in the interest of all economic agents to switch from a Pareto-inefficient allocation to a suitably chosen Pareto-efficient one. This argument seems plausible, but is not easy to evaluate in the absence of a generally accepted concept of solution for game theory. Edgeworth [1881] held the outcome of bargaining to be indeterminate within limits, and von Neumann and Morgenstern [1944] have generalized this conclusion. But when there is indeterminacy, there is no natural or compelling point on the Pareto frontier at which to arrive. It is certainly a matter of common observation, perhaps most especially in the field of international relations, that mutually advantageous agreements are not arrived at because each party is seeking to engross as much as possible of the common gain for itself. In economic affairs a frequently cited illustration is the assembly of land parcels for large industrial or residential enterprises whose value (net of complementary costs) exceeds the total value of the land in its present uses. Then the owner of each small parcel whose acquisition is essential to the execution of the enterprise can demand the entire net benefit. An agreement may never be reached or may be long delayed; at positive discount rates even the latter outcome is not Pareto-efficient. It is to avoid such losses that the coercive powers of the state are invoked by condemnation proceedings.

There is, however, another tradition within game theory which argues for the determinacy of the outcome of bargaining. Zeuthen [1930, Chapter IV] had early propounded one such solution. After von Neumann and Morgenstern, Nash [1950, 1953] offered a solution, which Harsanyi [1956] later showed to be identical with that of Zeuthen. Nash's analysis of bargaining has been extended by Harsanyi [1959, 1963, 1966]; variant but related approaches have been studied by Shapley [1953] and Selten [1964]. The analysis has proceeded at a very general level, and its specific application to resource allocation has yet to be spelled out. In the simplest situation, bargaining between two individuals who can cooperate but cannot injure each other except by withholding cooperation, and who can freely transfer benefits between them, the conclusion of the theories is the achievement of a joint optimum followed by equal splitting of the benefits of cooperation net of the amounts each bargainer could obtain without cooperation. Thus, in a land assembly, if the participation of all parcels is essential, each owner receives the value of his parcel in its present (or best alternative) use plus an equal share of the net benefits of the project. Without further analytic and empirical work it is not easy to judge the acceptability of this conclusion.

An elementary example may bring out the ambiguities of allocation with unrestricted bargaining. Since the perfectly competitive equilibrium theory is satisfactory (in the absence of marketing failures and costs) when increasing returns on a substantial scale are absent, the problem of imperfectly competitive equilibrium arises only when substantial increasing returns are present. In effect, then, there are small numbers of effective participants. Suppose there are only three agents. Production is assumed to take place in coalitions; the output of each coalition depends only on the number of members in it. If the average output of the members of a coalition does not increase with the number of members, then the equilibrium outcome is the perfectly competitive one, where each agent produces by himself and consumes his own product. If the average output of a coalition increases with the number of members, then clearly production will take place in the three-member coalition; but the allocation is not determined by the threats of individuals to leave the coalition and go on their own, nor by threats of pairs to form coalitions (for any one member can claim more than one-third of the total output and still leave the other two more than they could produce without him). But perhaps the most interesting case is that where the average output is higher for two individuals than for either one or three, i.e., increasing returns followed by diminishing returns. For definiteness, suppose that one agent can produce one unit, two agents can produce four units, and all three agents together can produce five units. Clearly, Pareto efficiency requires the joint productive activity of all three. Since each pair can receive four units by leaving the third agent out, it would appear that each pair must receive at least four units. But this implies that the total allocated to keep the three-man coalition together must be at least six, more than is available for distribution.[4]

(Theories of the Nash-Harsanyi type arrive at solutions in cases like this by assuming that the economic agents foresee these possible instabilities and recognize that any attempt by any pair to break away from the total coalition can itself be overturned. If each is rational and assumes the others are equally rational, then they recognize, in the completely symmetric situation of the example, that only a symmetric allocation is possible.)

[4] The general principle illustrated by this example has been briefly alluded to by Shapley and Shubik [1967, p. 98, fn. 5].

The point of this lengthy discussion of possible game theory concepts of equilibrium is to suggest caution in accepting the proposition that bargaining costs alone prevent the achievement of Pareto efficiency in the presence of increasing returns, as Buchanan and Tullock [1962, p. 88] and Demsetz [1968, p. 61] assert.

Risk and Information

The possible types of equilibria discussed in the previous two sections are not, in principle, altered in nature by the presence of risk. If an economic agent is uncertain as to which of several different states of the world will obtain, he can make contracts contingent on the occurrence of possible states. The real-world counterparts of these theoretical contingent contracts include insurance policies and common stocks. With these markets for contingent contracts, a competitive equilibrium will arise under the same general hypotheses as in the absence of uncertainty. It is not even necessary that the economic agents agree on the probability distribution for the unknown state of the world; each may have his own subjective probabilities. Further, the resulting allocation is Pareto-efficient if the utility of each individual is identified as his expected utility according to his own subjective probability distribution.

But, as Radner [1968] has pointed out, there is more to the story. Whenever we have uncertainty we have the possibility of information and, of course, also the possibility of its absence. No contingent contract can be made if, at the time of execution, either of the contracting parties does not know whether the specified contingency has occurred or not. This principle eliminates a much larger number of opportunities for mutually favorable exchanges than might perhaps be supposed at first glance. A simple case is that known in insurance literature as "adverse selection." Suppose, for example, there are two types of individuals, *A* and *B,* with different life expectancies, but the insurance company has no way to distinguish the two; it cannot in fact identify the present state of the world in all its relevant aspects. The optimal allocation of resources under uncertainty would require separate insurance policies for the two types, but these are clearly impossible. Suppose further that each individual knows which type he belongs to. The company might charge a rate based on the probability of death in the two types together, but the insurance buyers in the two types will respond differently; those in the type with the more favorable experience, say *A*, will buy less insurance than those in type *B*, other things (income and risk aversion) being equal. The insurance company's experience will be less favorable than it intended, and it will have to raise its rates. An equilibrium rate will be reached which is, in general, between those corresponding to types *A* and *B* separately but closer to the latter. Such an insurance arrangement is, of course, not Pareto-efficient. It is not a priori obvious in general that this free market arrangement is superior to compulsory insurance even though the latter is also not Pareto-efficient because it typically disregards individual differences in risk aversion.

As the above example shows, the critical impact of information on the optimal allocation of risk bearing is not merely its presence or absence but its inequality among economic agents. If neither side knew which type the insured belonged to, then the final allocation would be Pareto-efficient if it were considered that the two types were indistinguishable; but in the above example the market allocation is Pareto-efficient neither with the types regarded as indistinguishable nor as distinguishable.

There is one particular case of the effect of differential information on the workings of the market economy (or indeed any complex economy) which is so important as to deserve special comment: one agent can observe the joint effects of the unknown state of the world and of decisions by another economic agent, but not the state or the decision separately. This case is known in the insurance literature as "moral hazard," but because the insurance examples are only a small fraction of all the illustrations of this case and because, as Pauly [1968] has argued, the adjective "moral" is not always appropriate, the case will be referred to here as the "confounding of risks and decisions." An insurance company may easily observe that a fire has occurred but cannot, without special investigation, know whether the fire was due to causes exogenous to the insured or to decisions of his (arson, or at least carelessness). In general, any system which, in effect, insures against adverse final outcomes automatically reduces the incentives to good decision-making.

In these circumstances there are two extreme possibilities (with all intermediate possibilities being present): full protection against uncertainty of final outcome (e.g., cost-plus contracts for production or research) or absence of protection against uncertainty of final outcome (the one-person firm; the Admiral shot for cowardice *pour encourager les autres*). Both policies produce inefficiency, though for different reasons. In the first, the incentive to good decision-making is dulled for obvious reasons; in the second, the functions of control and risk-bearing must be united, whereas specialization in these functions may be more efficient for the workings of the system.

The relations between principals and agents (e.g., patients and physicians, owners and managers) further illustrate the confounding of risks and decisions. In the professions in particular they also illustrate the point to be emphasized later: that ethical standards may to a certain extent overcome the possible Pareto inefficiencies.

So far we have taken the information structure as given. But the fact that particular information structures give rise to Pareto inefficiency means that there is an economic value in transmitting information from one agent to another, as well as in the creation of new information. J. Marschak [1968], Hirshleifer [unpublished], and others have begun the study of the economics of information, but the whole subject is in its infancy. Only a few remarks relevant to our present purpose will be made here.

(1) As both communications engineering and psychology suggest, the transmission of information is not costless. Any professor who has tried to transmit some will be painfully aware of the resources he has expended and, perhaps more poignantly, of the difficulties students have in understanding. The physical costs of transmission may be low, though probably not negligible, as any book buyer knows; but the "coding" of the information for transmission and the limited channel capacity of the recipients are major costs.

(2) The costs of transmitting information vary with both the type of information transmitted and the recipient and sender. The first point implies a preference for inexpensive information, a point stressed in oligopolistic contexts by Kaysen [1949, pp. 294–95] and in other bargaining contexts by Schelling [1957]. The second point is relevant to the value of education and to difficulties of transmission across cultural boundaries (so that production functions can differ so much across countries).

(3) Because the costs of transmission are nonnegligible, even situations which are basically certain become uncertain for the individual; the typical economic agent simply cannot acquire in a meaningful sense the knowledge of all possible prices, even where they are each somewhere available. Markets are thus costly to use, and therefore the

multiplication of markets, as for contingent claims as suggested above, becomes inhibited.

Externalities Illustrated

After this long excursus into the present state of the theory of equilibrium and optimality it is time to discuss some of the standard concepts of externality, market failure, and public goods generally. The clarification of these concepts is a long historical process, not yet concluded, in which the classic contributions of Knight [1924], Young [1913, pp. 676–684], and Robertson [1924] have in more recent times been enriched by those of Meade [1952], Scitovsky [1954], Coase [1960], Buchanan and Stubblebine [1962], and Demsetz [1966]. The concept of externality and the extent to which it causes nonoptimal market behavior will be discussed here in terms of a simple model.

Consider a pure exchange economy. Let x_{ik} be the amount of the kth commodity consumed by the ith individual ($i = 1, \ldots, n; k = 1, \ldots, m$) and $\bar{x}_k$ be the amount of the kth commodity available. Suppose in general that the utility of the ith individual is a function of the consumption of all individuals (not all types of consumption for all individuals need actually enter into any given individual's utility function); the utility of the ith individual is $U_i(x_{11}, \ldots, x_{mn})$. We have the obvious constraints:

$$(1) \qquad \sum_i x_{ik} \leqq \bar{x}_k$$

Introduce the following definitions:

$$(2) \qquad x_{jik} = x_{ik}.$$

With this notation a Pareto-efficient allocation is a vector maximum of the utility functions $U_j(x_{j11}, \ldots, x_{jmn})$, subject to the constraints 1 and 2. Because of the notation used, the variables appearing in the utility function relating to the jth individual are proper to him alone and appear in no one else's utility function. If we understand now that there are n^2m commodities, indexed by the triple subscript jik, then the Pareto efficiency problem has a thoroughly classical form. There are n^2m prices, p_{jik}, attached to the constraints 2, plus m prices, q_k, corresponding to constraints 1. Following the maximization procedure formally, we see, much as in Samuelson [1954], that Pareto efficiency is characterized by the conditions:

(3) $\lambda_j(\partial U_j/\partial x_{ik}) = p_{jik}$,

and

(4) $\sum_i p_{jik} = q_k$,

where λ_j is the reciprocal of the marginal utility of income for individual *j*. (These statements ignore corner conditions, which can easily be supplied.)

Condition 4 can be given the following economic interpretation: Imagine each individual *i* to be a producer with *m* production processes, indexed by the pair (i, k). Process (i, k) has one input, namely, commodity *k*, and *n* outputs, indexed by the triple (j, i, k). In other words, what we ordinarily call individual *i*'s consumption is regarded as the production of joint outputs, one for each individual whose utility is affected by individual *i*'s consumption.

The point of this exercise is to show that by suitable and indeed not unnatural reinterpretation of the commodity space, externalities can be regarded as ordinary commodities, and all the formal theory of competitive equilibrium is valid, including its optimality.

It is not the mere fact that one man's consumption enters into another man's utility that causes the failure of the market to achieve efficiency. There are two relevant factors which cannot be discovered by inspection of the utility structures of the individual. One, much explored in the literature, is the appropriability of the commodities which represent the external repercussions; the other, less stressed, is the fact that markets for externalities usually involve small numbers of buyers and sellers.

The first point, Musgrave's "exclusion principle" [1959, p. 86], is so well-known as to need little elaboration. Pricing demands the possibility of excluding nonbuyers from the use of the product, and this exclusion may be technically impossible or may require the use of considerable resources. Pollution is the key example; the supply of clean air or water to each individual would have to be treated as a separate commodity, and it would have to be possible in principle to supply it to some and not to others (though the final equilibrium would involve equal supply to all). But this is technically impossible.

The second point comes out clearly in our case. Each commodity (j, i, k) has precisely one buyer and one seller. Even if a competitive equilibrium could be defined, there would be no force driving the system to it; we are in the realm of imperfectly competitive equilibrium.

In my view, the standard lighthouse example is best analyzed as a problem of small numbers rather than of the difficulty of exclusion, though both elements are present. To simplify matters, I will abstract from uncertainty so that the lighthouse keeper knows exactly when each ship will need its services, and also abstract from indivisibility (since the light is either on or off). Assume further that only one ship will be within range of the lighthouse at any moment. Then exclusion is perfectly possible; the keeper need only shut off the light when a nonpaying ship is coming into range. But there would be only one buyer and one seller and no competitive forces to drive the two into a competitive equilibrium. If in addition the costs of bargaining are high, then it may be most efficient to offer the service free.

If, as is typical, markets for the externalities do not exist, then the allocation from the point of view of the "buyer" is determined by a rationing process. We can determine a shadow price for the buyer; this will differ from the price, zero, received by the seller. Hence, formally, the failure of markets for externalities to exist can also be described as a difference of prices between buyer and seller.

In the example analyzed, the externalities related to particular named individuals; individual i's utility function depended on what a particular individual, j, possessed. The case where it is only the total amount of some commodity (e.g., handsome houses) in other people's hands that matters is a special case, which yields rather simpler results. In this case, $\partial U_j / \partial x_{ik}$ is independent of i for $i \neq j$, and hence, by condition 3, p_{jik} is independent of i for $i \neq j$. Let,

$$p_{iik} = p_{ik}, p_{jik} = \bar{p}_{jk} \text{ for } i \neq j.$$

Then condition 4 becomes,

$$\bar{p}_{ik} + \sum_{j \neq i} \bar{p}_{jk} = q_k,$$

or,

$$(p_{ik} - \bar{p}_{ik}) + \sum_{j} \bar{p}_{jk} = q_k,$$

from which it follows that the difference, $p_{ik} - \bar{p}_{ik}$, is independent of i. There are two kinds of shadow prices, a price $\bar{p}_{ik}$, the price that individual i is willing to pay for an increase in the stock of commodity k in any other individual's hands, and the premium, $p_{ik} - \bar{p}_{ik}$, he is willing to pay to have the commodity in his possession rather than someone else's. At the optimum, this premium for private possession must be the same for all individuals.

Other types of externalities are associated with several commodities simultaneously and do not involve named individuals, as in the case of neighborhood effects, where an individual's utility depends both on others' behavior (e.g., aesthetic, criminal) and on their location.

There is one deep problem in the interpretation of externalities which can only be signaled here. What aspects of others' behavior do we consider as affecting a utility function? If we take a hard-boiled revealed preference attitude, then if an individual expends resources in supporting legislation regulating another's behavior, it must be assumed that that behavior affects his utility. Yet in the cases that students of criminal law call "crimes without victims," such as homosexuality or drug-taking, there is no direct relation between the parties. Do we have to extend the concept of externality to all matters that an individual cares about? Or, in the spirit of John Stuart Mill, is there a second-order value judgment which excludes some of these preferences from the formation of social policy as being illegitimate infringements of individual freedom?

Market Failure

The problem of externalities is thus a special case of a more general phenomenon, the failure of markets to exist. Not all examples of market failure can fruitfully be described as externalities. Two very important examples have already been alluded to; markets for many forms of risk-bearing and for most future transactions do not exist and their absence is surely suggestive of inefficiency.

Previous discussion has suggested two possible causes for market failure: (1) inability to exclude; (2) lack of the necessary information to permit market transactions to be concluded.

The failure of futures markets cannot be directly explained in these terms. Exclusion is no more a problem in the future than in the present. Any contract to be executed in the future is necessarily contingent on some events (for example, that the two agents are still both in business), but there must be many cases where no informational difficulty is presented. The absence of futures markets may be ascribed to a third possibility: (3) supply and demand are equated at zero; the highest price at which anyone would buy is below the lowest price at which anyone would sell.

This third case of market failure, unlike the first two, is by itself in no way presumptive of inefficiency. However, it may usually be assumed that its occurrence is the result of failures of the first two types on complementary markets. Specifically, the demand for future steel may be low because of uncertainties of all types: sales and technological uncertainty for the buyer's firm, prices and existence of competing goods, and the quality specification of the steel. If, however, adequate markets for risk-bearing existed, the uncertainties could be removed, and the demand for future steel would rise.

Transaction Costs

Market failure has been presented as absolute, but in fact the situation is more complex than this. A more general formulation is that of transaction costs, which are attached to any market and indeed to any mode of resource allocation. Market failure is the particular case where transaction costs are so high that the existence of the market is no longer worthwhile. The distinction between transaction costs and production costs is that the former can be varied by a change in the mode of resource allocation, while the latter depend only on the technology and tastes, and would be the same in all economic systems.

The discussions in the preceding sections suggest two sources of transaction costs: (1) exclusion costs; and (2) costs of communication and information, including both the supplying and the learning of the terms on which transactions can be carried out. An additional source is (3) the costs of disequilibrium; in any complex system, the market or authoritative allocation, even under perfect information, it takes time to compute the optimal allocation, and either transactions take place which are inconsistent with the final equilibrium or they are delayed until the computations are completed (see T. Marschak [1959]).

These costs vary from system to system; thus, one of the advantages of a price system over either bargaining or some form of authoritative allocation is usually stated to be the economy in costs of information and communication. But the costs of transmitting and especially of receiving a large number of price signals may be high; thus, there is a tendency not to differentiate prices as much as would be desirable from the efficiency viewpoint. For example, the same price is charged for peak and off-peak usage of transportation or electricity.

In a price system, transaction costs drive a wedge between buyer's and seller's prices and thereby give rise to welfare losses as in the usual analysis. Removal of these welfare losses by changing to another system (for example, governmental allocation on benefit-cost criteria) must be weighed against any possible increase in transaction costs (for example, the need for elaborate and perhaps impossible studies to determine demand functions without the benefit of observing a market).

The welfare implications of transaction costs would exist even if they were proportional to the size of the transaction, but in fact they typically exhibit increasing returns. The cost of acquiring a piece of information, e.g., a price, is independent of the scale of use to which it will be put.

Collective Action: The Political Process

The state may frequently have a special role to play in resource allocation because, by its nature, it has a monopoly of coercive power, and coercive power can be used to economize on transaction costs. The most important use of coercion in the economic context is the collection of taxes; others are regulatory legislation and eminent domain proceedings.

The state is not an entity but rather a system of individual agents, a widely extensive system in the case of a democracy. It is appealing and fruitful to analyze its behavior in resource allocation in a manner analogous to that of the price system. Since the same agents appear in the two systems, it becomes equally natural to assume that they have the same motives. Hotelling [1929, pp. 54–55] and Schumpeter [1942, Chapter XXII] had sketched such politico-economic models, and von Neumann and Morgenstern's monumental work is certainly based on the idea that all social phenomena are governed by essentially the same motives as economics. The elaboration of more or less complete models of the political process along the lines of economic theory is more recent, the most prominent contributors being Black [1958], Downs [1957], Buchanan and Tullock [1962], and Rothenberg [1965].

I confine myself here to a few critical remarks on the possibilities of such theories. These are not intended to be negative but to suggest problems that have to be faced and are raised by some points in the preceding discussion.

1. If we take the allocative process to be governed by majority voting, then, as we well know, there are considerable possibilities of paradox. The possible intransitivity of majority voting was already pointed out by Condorcet [1785]. If, instead of assuming that each individual votes according to his preferences, it is assumed that all bargain freely before voting (vote-selling), the paradox appears in another form, a variant of the bargaining problems already noted in Section 2. If a majority could do what it wanted, then it would be optimal to win with a bare majority and take everything; but any such bargain can always be broken up by another proposed majority.

Tullock [1967, Chapter III] has recently argued convincingly that if the distribution of opinions on social issues is fairly uniform and if the dimensionality of the space of social issues is much less than the number of individuals, then majority voting on a sincere basis will be transitive. The argument is not, however, applicable to income distribution, for such a policy has as many dimensions as there are individuals, so that the dimensionality of the issue space is equal to the number of individuals.

This last observation raises an interesting question. Why, in fact, in democratic systems has there been so little demand for income redistribution? The current discussion of a negative income tax is the first serious attempt at a purely redistributive policy. Hagström [1938] presented a mathematical model predicting on the basis of a self-interest model for voters that democracy would inevitably lead to radical egalitarianism.

2. Political policy is not made by voters, not even in the sense that they choose the vector of political actions which best suits them. It is in fact made by representatives in one form or another. Political representation is an outstanding example of the principal-agent relation. This means that the link between individual utility functions and social action is tenuous, though by no means completely absent. Representatives are no more a random sample of their constituents than physicians are of their patients.

Indeed, the question can be raised: to what extent is the voter, when acting in that capacity, a principal or an agent? To some extent, certainly, the voter is cast in a role in which he feels some obligation to consider the social good, not just his own. It is in fact somewhat hard to explain otherwise why an individual votes at all in a large election, since the probability that his vote will be decisive is so negligible.

Collective Action: Social Norms

It is a mistake to limit collective action to state action; many other departures from the anonymous atomism of the price system are observed regularly. Indeed, firms of any complexity are illustrations of collective action, the internal allocation of their resources being directed by authoritative and hierarchical controls.

I want, however, to conclude by calling attention to a less visible form of social action: norms of social behavior, including ethical and moral codes. I suggest as one possible interpretation that they are reactions of society to compensate for market failures. It is useful for individuals to have some trust in each other's word. In the absence of trust, it would become very costly to arrange for alternative sanctions and guarantees, and many opportunities for mutually beneficial cooperation would have to be foregone. Banfield [1958] has argued that lack of trust is indeed one of the causes of economic underdevelopment.

It is difficult to conceive of buying trust in any direct way (though it can happen indirectly, e.g., a trusted employee will be paid more as being more valuable); indeed, there seems to be some inconsistency in the very concept. Nonmarket action might take the form of a mutual agreement. But the arrangement of these agreements and especially their continued extension to new individuals entering the social fabric can be costly. As an alternative, society may proceed by internalization of these norms to the achievement of the desired agreement on an unconscious level.

There is a whole set of customs and norms which might be similarly interpreted as agreements to improve the efficiency of the economic system (in the broad sense of satisfaction of individual values) by providing commodities to which the price system is inapplicable.

These social conventions may be adaptive in their origins, but they can become retrogressive. An agreement is costly to reach and therefore costly to modify; and the costs of modification may be especially large for unconscious agreements. Thus, codes of professional ethics, which arise out of the principal-agent relation and afford protection to the principals, can serve also as a cloak for monopoly by the agents.

References

Aumann, R. J., 1964. "Markets with a Continuum of Traders," *Econometrica*, Vol. 32, pp. 39–50.

Aumann, R. J., 1966. "The Existence of Competitive Equilibria in Markets with a Continuum of Traders," *Econometrica*, Vol. 34, pp. 1–17.

Aumann, R. J., and Maschler, M., 1964. "The Bargaining Set for Cooperative Games," in Dresher, M., Shapley, L. S., and Tucker, A. W. (eds.), *Advances in Game Theory. Annals of Mathematics Study*, Vol. 52, Princeton, pp. 443–476.

Banfield, E. C., 1958. *The Moral Basis of a Backward Society*, Glencoe, Ill.

Black, D., 1958. *The Theory of Committees and Elections*, Cambridge, U.K.

Buchanan, J., and Stubblebine, W. C., 1962. "Externality," *Economica*, Vol. 29, pp. 371–384.

Buchanan, J., and Tullock, G., 1962. *The Calculus of Consent*, Ann Arbor, Michigan.

Chamberlin, E. H., 1933. *The Theory of Monopolistic Competition*, Cambridge, Mass., eighth edition.

Coase, R. H., 1960. "The Problem of Social Cost," *Journal of Law and Economics*, Vol. 3, pp. 1–44.

Condorcet, Marquis de, 1785. *Essai sur l'application de l'analyse à la probabilité des décisions rendues à la pluralité des voix*, Paris.

Debreu, G., and Scarf, H., 1963. "A Limit Theorem on the Core of an Economy," *International Economic Review*, Vol. 4, pp. 236–246.

Demsetz, H., 1964. "The Welfare and Empirical Implications of Monopolistic Competition," *Economic Journal*, Vol. 74, pp. 623–691.

Demsetz, H., 1966. "Some Aspects of Property Rights," *Journal of Law and Economics*, Vol. 9, pp. 61–70.

Demsetz, H., 1968. "Why Regulate Utilities," *Journal of Law and Economics*, Vol. 11, pp. 55–66.

Downs, A., 1957. *An Economic Theory of Democracy*, New York.

Edgeworth, F. Y., 1881. *Mathematical Psychics: An Essay on the Application of Mathematics to the Moral Sciences*, London.

Farrell, M. J., 1959. "The Convexity Assumption in the Theory of Competitive Markets," *Journal of Political Economy*, Vol. 67, pp. 377–391.

Hagström, K. G., 1938. "A Mathematical Note on Democracy," *Econometrica*, Vol. 6, pp. 381–383.

Harsanyi, J. C., 1956. "Approaches to the Bargaining Problem Before and After the Theory of Games: A Critical Discussion of Zeuthen's, Hicks', and Nash's Theories," *Econometrica,* Vol. 24, pp. 144–157.

Harsanyi, J. C., 1959. "A Bargaining Model for the Cooperative N-Person Game," in Tucker, A. W., and Luce, R. D. (eds.), *Contributions to the Theory of Games IV. Annals of Mathematics Study,* Princeton, pp. 325–355.

Harsanyi, J. C., 1963. "A Simplified Bargaining Model for the N-Person Cooperative Game," *International Economic Review,* Vol. 4, pp. 194–220.

Harsanyi, J. C., 1966. "A General Theory of Rational Behavior in Game Situations," *Econometrica,* Vol. 34, pp. 613–634.

Hotelling, H., 1929. "Stability in Competition," *Economic Journal,* Vol. 39, pp. 41–57.

Kaldor, N., 1935. "Market Imperfection and Excess Capacity," *Economica,* Vol. 2, pp. 33–50.

Kaysen, Carl, 1949. "Basing Point Pricing and Public Policy," *Quarterly Journal of Economics,* Vol. 63, pp. 289–314.

Knight, F. H., 1921. *Risk, Uncertainty, and Profit,* Boston and New York.

Knight, F. H., 1924. "Some Fallacies in the Interpretation of Social Cost," *Quarterly Journal of Economics,* Vol. 38, pp. 582–606.

Luce, R. D., 1954. "A Definition of Stability for N-Person Games," *Annals of Mathematics,* Vol. 59, pp. 357–366.

Luce, R. D., 1955a. "Ψ-Stability: A New Equilibrium Concept for N-Person Game Theory," in *Mathematical Models of Human Behavior,* Stamford, Conn., pp. 32–44.

Luce, R. D., 1955b. "K-Stability of Symmetric and Quota Games," *Annals of Mathematics,* Vol. 62, pp. 517–555.

Marschak, J., 1968. "Economics of Inquiring, Communicating, Deciding," *American Economic Review Papers and Proceedings,* Vol. 58, pp. 1–18.

Marschak, T., 1959. "Centralization and Decentralization in Economic Organizations," *Econometrica,* Vol. 27, pp. 399–430.

Meade, J. E., 1952. "External Economies and Diseconomies in a Competitive Situation," *Economic Journal,* Vol. 62, pp. 59–67.

Musgrave, R. A., 1959. *The Theory of Public Finance: A Study in Public Economy,* New York.

Nash, J. F., Jr., 1950. "The Bargaining Problem," *Econometrica,* Vol. 18, pp. 155–162.

Nash, J. F., Jr., 1953. "Two Person Cooperative Games," *Econometrica,* Vol. 21, pp. 128–140.

Negishi, T., 1960–61. "Monopolistic Competition and General Equilibrium," *Review of Economic Studies,* Vol. 28, pp. 196–201.

von Neumann, J., and Morgenstern, O., 1944. *Theory of Games and Economic Behavior,* Princeton, second edition.

Pauly, M. V., 1968. "The Economics of Moral Hazard: Comment," *American Economic Review,* Vol. 58, pp. 531–537.

Radner, R., 1968. "Competitive Equilibrium Under Uncertainty," Vol. 36, pp. 31–58.

Robertson, D. H., 1924. "Those Empty Boxes," *Economic Journal,* Vol. 34, pp. 16–30.

Rothenberg, J., 1960. "Non-Convexity, Aggregation, and Pareto Optimality," *Journal of Political Economy,* Vol. 68, pp. 435–468.

Rothenberg, J., 1965. "A Model of Economic and Political Decision-Making," in Margolis, J. (ed.), *The Public Economy of Urban Communities,* Washington, D. C.

Samuelson, P. A., 1954. "The Pure Theory of Public Expenditures," *Review of Economic Statistics,* Vol. 36, pp. 387–389.

Samuelson, P. A., 1967. "The Monopolistic Competition Revolution," in Kuenne, R. E. (ed.), *Monopolistic Competition Theory: Studies in Impact,* New York, London, and Sydney, pp. 105–138.

Schelling, T., 1957. "Bargaining, Communication, and Limited War," *Journal of Conflict Resolution,* Vol. 1, pp. 19–36.

Schumpeter, J., 1942. *Capitalism, Socialism, and Democracy,* New York, third edition.

Scitovsky, T., 1954. "Two Concepts of External Economies," *Journal of Political Economy,* Vol. 62, pp. 143–151.

Selten, R., 1964. "Valuation of N-Person Games," in Dresher, M., Shapley, L. S., and Tucker, A. W. (eds.), *Advances in Game Theory. Annals of Mathematics Study,* Vol. 52, Princeton, pp. 577–626.

Shapley, L. S., 1953. "A Value for N-Person Games," in Kuhn, H. W., and Tucker, A. W. (eds.), *Contribution to the Theory of Games II. Annals of Mathematics Study,* Princeton, Vol. 28, pp. 307–317.

Shapley, L. S., and Shubik, M., 1967. "Ownership and the Production Function," *Quarterly Journal of Economics,* Vol. 81, pp. 88–111.

Shubik, M., 1959. "Edgeworth Market Games," in Tucker, A. W., and Luce, R. D. (eds.), *Contribution to the Theory of Games IV. Annals of Mathematics Study,* Princeton, Vol. 40, pp. 267–278.

Smith, A., 1937. *An Enquiry Concerning the Causes of the Wealth of Nations,* New York.

Starr, R., 1969. "Quasi-Equilibria in Markets with Nonconvex Preferences," *Econometrica,* Vol. 37, pp. 25–38.

Triffin, R., 1941. *Monopolistic Competition and General Equilibrium Theory,* Cambridge, Mass.

Tullock, G., 1967. *Toward a Mathematics of Politics,* Ann Arbor, Mich.

Young, A. A., 1913. "Pigou's Wealth and Welfare," *Quarterly Journal of Economics,* Vol. 27, pp. 672–686.

Zeuthen, F., 1930. *Problems of Monopoly and Economic Warfare,* London.

COMMENT

by SIDNEY S. ALEXANDER, *Massachusetts Institute of Technology*

Instead of commenting in detail on Arrow's paper, I will address myself directly to the original question. The topic announced is "The Political and Economic Evaluation of Social Effects and Externalities." The key word is evaluation, and Arrow has very carefully avoided treating evaluation. What he has done is to sketch with great virtuosity the relationship of the existence of markets, and the convexity of utility and production possibility sets, to Pareto-efficiency. In particular he has indicated how Pareto-efficiency can fail to be achieved if externalities exist, and how externalities may be regarded as equivalent to the failure of certain markets to exist.

The essence of an externality is that there is an effect on some person of a transaction to which he is not a party. Since the attainment of Pareto-efficiency through the operation of a competitive market is brought about by each party to a transaction adjusting to the price parameters, the fact that there are people affected by the transaction but not parties to it means that the appropriate adjustments will not be made, and the points attained in such a process will not in general be Pareto-efficient. As I construe the topic, the question is how the effects of economic and political transactions which fall upon those who are not parties to the transactions are to be evaluated with a view toward possible public action.

To this question Arrow has furnished only an implicit response, but a very clear one, and one that he shares with the majority of social scientists. It is, in effect, that all value judgments but one are outside the business of the social scientist: the one exceptional value judgment that can be embedded in economic analysis is the so-called "pig-principle," that more is better, so an economist's concern is with efficiency.

Except for an occasional lapse Arrow refers to Pareto-*efficiency* rather than to Pareto-*optimality*. It is there that he parts company with me and with evaluation, for evaluation is normative and efficiency is descriptive. A Pareto-efficient point is one that is undominated from a preference point of view; a Pareto-optimal point is one that is undominated from a welfare point of view. A point is Pareto-efficient if nobody can be *put into a preferred position* by moving to some other attainable point without putting someone else into a less preferred position. A point is Pareto-optimal if nobody can be *made better off* by moving to some other attainable point without making somebody else worse off. The set of Pareto-efficient points will be different from the set of Pareto-optimal points if to be in a preferred position is not the same as to be better off. To say that the two states are the same is a normative statement equating a positive operational state of being preferred to a normative state of being better off. Indeed it specifies a particular form of utilitarianism, a normative doctrine. To talk about Pareto-optimality rather than Pareto-efficiency, then, is to leap the gulf from the *is* to the *ought,* and Arrow has elected not to take the jump but to stay on the *is* side of that gulf. But evaluation lies on the other side.

Arrow recognizes with Pareto that a Pareto-efficient point has a normative claim to make only if the income distribution is appropriate, or, more accurately, if there is an appropriate initial distribution of control over resources. But what makes such a distribution appropriate or inappropriate, good or bad, neither Pareto nor Arrow says. In fact, they both imply that it is something which, if it exists at all, is given from outside the realm of their inquiries. Any complaints can be met by lump-sum transfers, Arrow tells us (p. 4). Whether such complaints are well or poorly grounded, or how to tell whether such a complaint is well or poorly grounded, Arrow does not say. But that is one of the most important problems of evaluation of the operation of the market mechanism, the topic of this discussion. Faced with this problem Little took recourse to Superman to evaluate different income distributions.[1]

If we are to evaluate social effects and externalities we must evaluate income distributions as well, and much more. In fact we must evaluate Pareto-efficiency. My message to you is that you too can be a Superman, that you can make judgments of better or worse in social affairs, not infallible judgments it is true, but to the extent that you err such error can be detected only by another judgment of the same sort.

What do we do when we judge between two possible states of the world? In general, we look to two characteristics, welfare and justice, corresponding to two principal strains in ethical theory, utilitarianism and deontology respectively. Utilitarianism judges between states of the world according as it finds more happiness, by some measure deemed suitable, in one state than in another. From a deontological point of

[1] I. M. D. Little, *A Critique of Welfare Economics,* 1950, p. 87.

view, one state of the world is better than another when it is more the way things should be by some prior standard. Pareto-efficiency makes its normative claim through an implicit utilitarianism that says that people are better off when they have their wants satisfied to a greater extent. The income distribution actually found in practice in our economy is largely based on a deontological notion of justice, that one should not take away from a man that which is his. This may indeed have a utilitarian basis in the long run, but again it may not. When we do use the social coercion of the state to take by taxation from a man what would otherwise be his, we usually justify that action either in terms of distributive justice or in terms of increasing the over-all happiness suitably measured.

A conceptually simple test for both justice and happiness together can be based on a fundamental principle of morality expressed in the question "how would you feel if you were in his shoes?" If we have to make sense of saying that one state of the world is better than another, we can, I submit, do it in the following way. If a reasonable man completely knowledgeable of the conditions in both states is given the choice of taking a chance with equal probability of being anyone concerned in either state A or state B and he chooses state A, we can say that state A is better than state B.[2] This is not given as a *definition* of the word "better" but rather as a proposed positive test of the normative concepts of better or worse in social affairs, it being presumed that "better" has a primitive normative meaning in our language. Whether state A is preferred by the test man because there is more happiness in it or more justice we need not here inquire. The test would presumably test both simultaneously, with trade-offs implicit.

It might be argued on the basis of the reigning attitudes in the social sciences that this "place-taking" test probably appeals to the ethical intuitions of many of us, but the resulting agreement is only a conjunction of personal preferences of those who share common standards. If I say state A is better than state B, it is commonly argued, I am merely saying that I personally would rather take the chance of being anyone in state A than of being anyone in state B. I am saying something more than that, however, and that something is critical. It is the implication that anyone else who thought clearly and was knowledgeable would have a similar preference. I am making an impersonal claim

[2] This test, and the philosophy underlying it, is more fully discussed in my essay "Public Television and the Ought of Public Policy," *Washington University Law Quarterly,* Winter 1968 (to be reprinted in a forthcoming Brookings Institution volume).

as an agent for all reasonable moral men and not just expressing my personal taste.

We need have no deep metaphysical support for this usage. It is simply proposed as what, upon reflection, we mean when we say state of the world A is better than state of the world B.

How do I know that this is a good test? The same way I know that an operational test is a good test, say of the specific gravity of some substance. These are methodological judgments appropriate to the subject in hand. If you agree that this is the right test to use we can proceed with our inquiry. If not, we have to escalate the question to the next higher methodological level of what is a good test, or the meta-methodological level of what is a good method for choosing methods—and the sequence has no end. No discussion at all can take place except among people who agree on something.

There can be hardly any question that if a place-taking test were applied to our current social arrangements as compared with possible alternatives the test man would almost certainly demand a state with more equalization of opportunities than our society affords. How much, if at all, other desirable features of the society would have to be traded off for greater equality of opportunity requires a lot of study. But it would be the greatest of coincidences if the current balance was the best possible world, since there is, apparently, no equivalent of a market process to lead to an optimal trade-off between all desirable characteristics. This is a subject which is simply avoided in social science discussions because of the presumed impossibility of making normative judgments. Deference to that impossibility is perfectly illustrated in Arrow's paper where no attempt is made to treat income distribution except as a boundary condition to be governed from some external position from which complaints are made, or distributions regarded as acceptable.

Suppose that an ideal distribution of income has been achieved, relative to the attainable Pareto-efficient points, and the corresponding Pareto-efficient point attained. Thus, we may assume Arrow's conditions C and M to hold, so that each person is compensated for the smoke nuisance just up to the point which makes him choose the amount of smoke he actually gets and each smoke emitter is charged accordingly. Conditions 3 and 4 (pp. 4–5) will accordingly hold. Would that indeed be heaven, or at least the Good Life? Everybody would be getting what he wants to the extent that is jointly possible given the resource endowment, the conditions of production, and the best possible distribution of ownership of resources. While that would undoubtedly be a far better world than we now have, it need by no means be the Good Life. Whether it would or would not be a Good Life depends on what sort of people it makes of us, and what we get out of the satisfaction of our wants. One does not have to go very deep into philosophy to observe rather tritely with Frank Knight and others that want-satisfaction is not a particularly worthy ethical ideal. The wealthier people in our society do not live such worthy lives that we can follow Hayek in regarding them as pioneers of the Good Life.

That the value of a life depends upon the values served and realized rather than on the extent of want-satisfaction is certainly a trite observation, but the current state of thought in the social sciences so clearly ignores this point that I must remind you of it however trite it may be. If you feel that this is preacher talk and unsuitable for serious social scientists, I must disagree, and give my reasons. We concentrate on Pareto-efficiency because there are many elegant things we can say about it, and because it lies closest to what we can reasonably hope that our economy can achieve through its current institutions. If, then, we delude ourselves into thinking that that which we can analyze is that which we ought to analyze when we seek to evaluate our social institutions, we are making the mistake illustrated by the vaudeville routine of looking for the lost quarter at the corner under the lamp post where the light is good rather than in the darkness of the middle of the block where the quarter was lost.

Arrow recognizes externalities where there is a failure of a market to exist but where the wants do exist so that if a market existed there would be a tendency for the appropriate economic agent to adjust his demand for the "commodity" to its price. There are some externalities, and indeed I think the most important ones, where even if a market should be brought into existence there would be no appropriate adjustment because the element does not enter into the utility function of the person affected. In some cases this might just be a matter of ignorance; if a man knew what was happening to him he would be interested in paying for changing the amount of that particular activity, or in Arrow's term, "commodity." But the pig will not pay to become Socrates. The external effects of our economic, political and social activities which make us what we are are not such that an appropriate balance would be struck if a market were created or established for these "commodities." The value of a good society is not to be measured by how much people in our present society are ready to pay for it. There is a difference between what serves a man's welfare and what enters his utility function if the latter is to be derived from his pattern of preference in the manner called "revealed preference." Perhaps much of the difference between what a man wants and what serves his welfare is just a matter of information. This was certainly argued by Socrates when he claimed that no man knowingly did wrong, that evil came from ignorance. It was also the basis of Mill's argument for poetry's superiority over pushpin in that those who really knew both preferred poetry. But the argument, I think, is unsound. There are, I believe, many of us who knowing the better choose the worse. Here perhaps Dostoevski saw more clearly than John Stuart Mill what the problem is. So, while the imperfection may in part be one of lack of information, there may indeed be a more deep-seated root of evil in man's nature and it may take more than better information to bring us closer to the saints through want-satisfaction. Is it just ignorance that makes a racist, or is he responding to other environmental forces?

But whether the trouble comes from lack of information or lack of desire for the good, the practical problem is the same. There are effects of economic and political transactions whose impact on individuals not party to the transactions are individually negligible but cumulatively determine the very nature of those individuals. These cumulative forces operate outside an optimizing mechanism. They constitute a fundamental challenge to social policy. I maintain that, the positive facts being available, better guidance could be obtained from the place-taking test than from a Pareto-efficiency test. The place-taking test might indeed be a test for Pareto-optimality, in that it is an attempt to measure welfare rather than want-satisfaction.

But the positive facts are not generally available, and their lack is the principal obstacle to the recognition of sound policy. How, for example, can the system be altered to achieve greater equality of opportunity? What would be the effects on output or on other aspects of our life? But recognition of policy and its achievement are two different things. Even were we to gain perfect knowledge of the operation of our social and economic system and have it all in the computer, would our political process, there so well described, realize an optimal point? Surely that self-interest which drives an economic system to a Pareto-efficient point may not drive our political system to a Pareto-optimal one.

If one wishes to operate on that system, one needs a model far more complex than our elegant model of a perfectly competitive market. But complex as the understanding of the positive features of our society are, the normative is relatively simple. The way to evaluate is to evaluate, to judge between two social states the best we can. That means fundamentally to consider in which state a man would prefer to live who was reasonable, moral, well informed as to the nature and consequences of various actions and of how it is to live under the two different regimes. That is hardly the end of evaluation but it is a beginning, and a beginning that leads to something other than want satisfaction as the ideal and the relegation of ideal income distribution to some offstage force which is to supply us with an answer that is beyond our capacity to formulate for ourselves.

LOCAL DECENTRALIZATION AND THE THEORY OF OPTIMAL GOVERNMENT

JEROME ROTHENBERG

Massachusetts Institute of Technology

Introduction

Many of the key issues involved in today's problems about cities focus on local government. Government is a form of group decision making just as is the market and can be analyzed with much the same tools. Structural imperfections in the one can lead to inefficient resource allocation just as in the other. Moreover, much the same criteria of efficiency can be used in both, although evaluation of income distribution is more intrinsic to public sector activities.

In the present paper we concentrate on a welfare evaluation of local government in the typical metropolitan area. We study chiefly the influences on efficient local decision making of (1) population migration into the metropolitan area from outside, (2) suburbanization of a given metropolitan area population, and (3) the fragmentation of local government in the metropolitan area into various nonhierarchical jurisdictions.

Our study suggests that the pattern of local government in modern decentralized urban areas leads to suboptimal resource use in the public sector, and helps thereby to contribute to the severity of problems more popularly blamed on other phenomena.

Some Issues in the Theory of Optimal Government

To discover whether a particular government is inefficient, one must first determine what constitutes efficiency. It is beyond the scope of the present paper to conduct a systematic study of the theory of optimal government. But some important issues involved in specifying optimality for the public sector must be mentioned.

Suppose we have a given population extending over a substantial geographic area. The population establishes a system of markets for private transactions. It wishes to establish a collective decision making system to complement the market system. How shall the apparatus of collective choice be fashioned? In particular, what principles shall guide the distribution of collective powers among political jurisdictions? How much centralization, delegation under hierarchy, and decentralization are desirable? This differs from the comparable problem for a business firm or for the economy as a whole because we assume that collective decisions are to be made by majority rule. In any given choosing situation a majority will outvote a minority, thereby imposing a special form of external diseconomy upon the latter. Different patterns of jurisdictional delegation of power will affect who are included among the majority and the minority on different issues, and therefore what public sector decisions will be made, thus determining the distribution of real well-being among the population.

Assume individualistic welfare criteria apply to the public sector. Then movement from a Pareto-inferior to Pareto-superior position is a sufficient condition for welfare improvement; and Pareto-optimality is a necessary condition for over-all welfare maximization. In this context, the presence of substantial private sector externalities suggests inefficient resource allocation. Indeed, one key rationale for the public sector is to preclude, control or internalize these externalities.

For this purpose, the delegation of power to political jurisdictions should be done in a way that minimizes the redistributional effects of majority rule. The goal is to shape government to be able to carry out efficiently resource decisions which a strong consensus desires collectivized. Given the convention—which could be shown to have efficiency properties—that political jurisdictions be geographically connected spaces, and that political hierarchy be represented as spatial inclusion, the actual U.S. distribution of characteristics and activities over space suggests that majority rule will generate the least "political externalities" in highly homogeneous communities, and that such homogeneity is most nearly approximated at the extreme local level ("home rule").[1] Maximal practical political consensus will call for very small political jurisdictions indeed.

[1] Even the most local level will not have perfect homogeneity, but differences within the community will be substantially smaller than differences between communities of this size.

What size unit would most effectively achieve "home rule" consensus is significant in assaying governmental performance, for consensus, while important, is not the only consideration bearing on efficiency, and the size of the jurisdictional unit affects the achievement of the others.

Economies and diseconomies of scale is one. If public output is produced under substantial scale economies, then a system of many very small jurisdictional units will incur considerably higher costs of producing public output than will a system of a few large units. Savings under the second could adequately compensate individuals who would have preferred the first. Other things being equal, the greater the net scale economies the larger is the size of the optimal political jurisdiction.

Other things are not equal. While the exact magnitudes depend on real world facts, it seems reasonable to surmise that the degree of political decentralization which maximizes consensus generates units considerably smaller than what is efficient for public output production. Some moderate scale economies do very likely exist for particular public functions, and these probably more than offset scale diseconomies in a few other functions so that, aided by constant costs in the bulk of public services, minimum average costs are achieved in the moderate sized jurisdiction, a scale which much exceeds the unit of maximal consensus (probably the neighborhood).[2]

[2] We refer to jurisdictions for *clusters* of public functions, not for single functions. Functions will generally differ in their consensual and scale economy characteristics. Optimal size for consensus and scale will both necessitate compromise among the component function profiles—but a different compromise generally for the two, as the text asserts.

Jurisdictions could be set up for individual functions. Since consensus is more broadly attainable for certain functions, government units for some functions might be formed which were optimal on both home rule and scale economy grounds. The special district represents an accommodation of this sort. But while the existence of a few types of special district in an environment of multifunction jurisdictions may prevent important scale economies from being neglected, a system where all public functions are divided into single-function jurisdictions is quite different, and can be shown to be highly inefficient. First, it would substantially increase total resource costs of public decision making, since such decision making involves important overhead components which would be seriously underutilized. Legislative, executive and judicial bodies set up to perform one function could inexpensively perform related functions as well. Second, it would hamper the rationality of public decision making by preventing the same electorate from considering complementary and substitutive relations among different functions. Compromises (log-rolling) across different functional categories would be unavailable to accommodate intergroup differences in policy preferences.

A further mechanism for minimizing scale economy–home rule discrepancies is claimed to be in the ability of a given multifunction jurisdiction to purchase

Another efficiency consideration arises out of externalities not within, but among, political jurisdictions. If the population affected by the policy of any jurisdiction is larger than that jurisdiction's constituency the jurisdiction will generate externalities beyond its borders. Similarly, if the actions of nonconstituents of a jurisdiction can influence the operation of policies within the jurisdiction, then externalities will be imposed on the jurisdiction from outside. In both instances the externalities are not of the usual economic sort: here the behavior of at least one of the participants involves political action, not economic. What is involved is that the jurisdiction is too small to enable the entire affected population to take the totality of their interaction into account in formulating public policy. Public decision making is faulty insofar as important interactions either cannot be coordinated or must be disregarded.

All other things being equal, the jurisdictional unit should be large enough to include the total population affected by all policies within its purview and all whose behavior affects the character of its policies. Even more than scale economies, this desirability of internalizing all sources of interjurisdictional externality prescribes a local jurisdictional unit considerably larger than what is called for on home rule grounds.

Both scale economies and diseconomies, and interjurisdictional externalities affect the real cost and real output possibilities with existing resources. Changes in unit size toward greater efficiency will result in output gains available to serve as bribes (compensation) to induce general agreement to the direction taken—i.e., they result in Pareto improvements. A third efficiency consideration refers to income distribution alone. Collective choice is not resorted to only to fulfill allocative goals; it is conventionally employed to achieve income distributional goals as well. Indeed, political scientists often devote preeminent attention to the redistributive functions of government, largely ignoring the allocative.

Suppose the population of the system as a whole decides that it wishes the political apparatus to make possible a certain range of redistributional functions. We suppose this is arrived at within the

services from public or private organizations which can more efficiently produce those services. This is possible for some functions, but by no means all. It is likely to be difficult where large, durable, specialized capital installations are associated with provision of the services; where the services are difficult to price on a market; where sensitive direct relations with the electorate as clients are integral; or where the chief production issue is not so much to provide inputs cheaply as to coordinate the planning of a complex service system.

highest governmental jurisdiction of the system, supposing this to be anterior to the various decentralized jurisdictions. The broad principles and direction of desirable redistribution are assumed to be decided here; however, it is desired that they be worked out concretely in ongoing situations close to jurisdictional levels possessing strong consensus. This goal requires forming jurisdictional units which contain both the appropriate donors and beneficiaries and in which majorities and minorities are present that will make the appropriate everyday decisions likely to come to pass. Whereas maximal consensus requires optimal homogeneity, "socially desired" redistributions require optimal heterogeneity. At whatever level of government the redistributive function is desired to be incorporated, jurisdictional units at that level must include the desired constituent mix, whether by spatial extension or by inducements on the locational incentives of private parties. Since the latter device depends on the everyday incentives of existing—and sometimes inappropriate—constituencies, the former is more dependable. Thus, insofar as there may be "socially approved" redistributional goals, and insofar as some of them may be delegated to the local level of government to be fulfilled, the desirable unit is likely to be larger and more heterogeneous than what would be designated on home rule consensus grounds alone.

In sum, we denote four types of criteria with which to evaluate the optimality of local political jurisdictions: (1) minimization of political externalities within each jurisdiction, (2) minimization of political externalities across jurisdictions, (3) minimization of the resource cost of providing public output, (4) maximization of the achievement of social redistributive goals. Of these, the first and fourth rest upon social value judgments about real income redistributions, the second and third rest upon narrower definitions of efficiency in terms of aggregate output levels. Broadly, (1) calls for the greatest degree of political decentralization, (2) and (4) for the least. In general no distribution of political powers is likely to rank uniformly on all criteria. Relative evaluation of alternative distributions will depend on trade-offs across these criteria, whose a priori character is difficult to discern, except in principle for the common aggregate output dimension of (2) and (3)—although the actual empirical magnitudes of these trade-offs are not less difficult to discern.

In the remainder of the paper, we shall examine to what extent the distribution of political powers within a typical metropolitan area meets the various criteria specified here. We shall be most concerned with tensions between home rule and interjurisdictional externalities within this institutional setting, but an examination of a potential conflict between home rule and the redistributive function will precede this. Finally, the strategic opportunities for ameliorating these conflicts inherent in scale economies will be briefly noted.

Constituent Composition and the Collective Redistributive Function

Assume we begin at time t_0 with a metropolitan area in which the "entire" urban population is concentrated in the central city: the "suburbs" are still rural. The population N at t_0, N^0, has a certain total income Y^0 and a certain distribution of that income, of which $\bar{Y}^0 = \dfrac{Y^0}{N^0}$ is the mean, σ^0 the standard deviation, m_3 the third moment, etc.

Given these characteristics of income, in a socio-economic institutional context which we shall assume to remain essentially unchanged throughout the analysis, the collective decision making process—the municipal government—generates a tax system from which we can predict a real-income redistributive flow—a tax-expenditure program providing services which help the poor: a "welfare" program[3]—for each specified tax rate. This productivity of the tax system can be expressed as a percentage of the community's income (k). Further, we may measure each actual flow in a normalized form as the per capita income improvement to the poor. A simple model will be presented to indicate the relationships involved.

(1) $$k^i = k(\bar{Y}^i, \sigma^i \mid T_1 = T_2)$$

$$\frac{\partial k^i}{\partial \bar{Y}^i} > 0, \frac{\partial k^i}{\partial \sigma^i} > 0,$$

where Y^i is the SMSA total income at t^i; $\bar{Y}^i$ is the SMSA per capita income at t^i; σ^i is the dispersion of the income distribution at t^i; T_1 is the central city tax rate for welfare purposes; T_2 is the suburban tax rate for welfare purposes; and k^i is the productivity of the tax system, measured at the city tax rate $T^i = T_2$.

(2) $$W^i \equiv \frac{T_1^{\,i} Y^i}{N_w^{\,i}},$$

---

[3] It is a "welfare" program in a broad sense. It includes public goods enjoyed by the nonpoor as well as the poor.

where $N_w{}^i$ is the number of poor people—beneficiaries of the welfare program—in the central city at t^i, and W^i is the size of the welfare budget per welfare recipient at t^i.

The tax rates in 1 and 2 express only the levies for welfare purposes, interpreted broadly. For simplification we assume that other dimensions of the city and suburban budgets are unaffected by the population shifts involved in the model.

Now we introduce an opportunity for greater home rule. Income recipients above the mean are paying taxes to support welfare services for low-income households. If they moved to a new political jurisdiction in the suburbs where the population was homogeneously concentrated above the poverty line the total redistributive flow necessary to raise through government would be considerably lower—i.e., the suburban welfare tax rate T_2 would be less than T_1. This attraction has to be balanced against a comparison between suburban and city land prices, the greater transportation costs necessitated by a suburban location, and the general tastes for or against the amenities of suburban relative to urban life. Symbolically, the decision to relocate in a suburban political jurisdiction is given in the suburb location function, as follows:

$$(3) \qquad N_2{}^i = \Pi\left(N^0, A, \frac{T_2{}^i}{T_1{}^i}, \frac{q_2{}^i}{q_1{}^i}\right)$$

where q_2 is the price per acre in the suburbs at t_i; q_1 is the price per acre in the city at t_i; A refers to relative amenities in city and suburb and is a general index of tastes for urban vs. suburban life; and $N_2{}^i$ is the number of persons locating in the suburbs at t^i.

We have assumed that at t_0 $N_2 = 0$. Let tastes for suburban life improve among a small group, so that at $\dfrac{T_{20}}{T_{10}}, \dfrac{q_{20}}{q_{10}}$ they are now willing to move to the suburbs. This establishes an initial emigration source. There is also an immigration source. Whenever someone leaves the city an "empty place" is created, and this place is filled by an immigrant from outside the metropolitan area. The latter belongs to a population which is attracted to the higher average income opportunities available in the SMSA than in its place of origin. The immigrant population has a lower per capita income and a higher incidence of poor people. The mean out-migrant income is $(1 + r)\bar{Y}^0$, that of in-migrants, $(1 - r)\bar{Y}^0$; so the mean difference between them is $2r\bar{Y}^0$. The mean difference in incidence of the poor in the two streams is w.[4] Thus:

---

[4] As the two streams proceed, the mean city income drops, so the differential between them decreas᠎s. We assume immigrant incomes to be unchanged, a reflection

(4)
$$\frac{\partial EY_1}{\partial N_2} = -2r\bar{Y}_1^0 \qquad\qquad 0 < r < 1$$

(5)
$$\frac{\partial EN_W}{\partial N_2} = w \qquad\qquad 0 < w < 1$$

where EY_1 and EN_W are expected values of Y_1 and N_W and $\bar{Y}_1^0$ is the original per capita income in the city.

Since immigration into the metropolitan area is assumed to depend on per capita income differences, similar differences between central city and suburb must be assumed to evoke similar desires to suburbanize by lower-income city dwellers, or to prevent the suburbanites from escaping the city's tax jurisdiction. In the present model we assume these desires are frustrated by the incentive and ability of the suburbanizing well-to-do to prevent either of these from occurring. Zoning regulations, high travel costs, and sometimes outright discrimination hamper low-income suburbanization, and home rule sovereignty vetoes political annexation. On the other hand, the central city cannot, or does not, similarly "protect" itself against the flow of low-income migrants. These assumptions are not far from real-world circumstances.

This outflow together with its inflow replacement have the effect of decreasing the city's mean income and income dispersion, and thereby of decreasing the productivity of the tax system, while at the same time increasing the welfare case load (equation 5). The response to this by the municipal government with respect to its welfare tax rate is of real importance. We assume that the tax rate is negatively influenced by the productivity of the tax system, positively by the tax welfare case load, and negatively by the fear of losing high income population to the suburbs. I.e.,

(6)
$$T_1 = T_1(k, N_W, N^0 - N_2)$$

$$\frac{\partial T_1}{\partial k} < 0, \ \frac{\partial T_1}{\partial N_W} > 0, \ \frac{\partial T_1}{\partial N_2} < 0$$

$\partial T_1/\partial k < 0$ because, for a given case load, a greater tax productivity suggests the need for a smaller tax rate to furnish adequate welfare services.

$\partial T_1/\partial N_W > 0$ because, all else being equal, a larger case load induces the production of greater welfare revenues through tax rate increases.

of a very large pool of potential immigrants relative to the specific SMSA being discussed. Thus, when mean city income has fallen to this level, immigration will cease even though suburbanization continues.

$\partial T_1 / \partial N_2 < 0$ because, all else being equal, an increase in T_1 without a comparable increase in T_2 will induce further out-migration of higher-income households with consequent further replacement that lowers $\bar{Y}$, σ, and the productivity of the tax system, while increasing the welfare case load. The intensity of the constraint against tax rate increases from this source is approximated by the size of N_2 (actually $N^0 - N_2$) since this indicates how much migration loss has already occurred, and therefore how important (scarce) the remaining upper income population in the city is. In addition, it suggests roughly the existing extensiveness of the T_2 / T_1 discrepancy in terms of its effect on locational incentives. The larger is N_2 (relative to N^0) the more reluctant will the city be to risk "chasing" more of its inhabitants out by even further tax rate increases.

What then is the effect of the first migration round on the tax rate? From (6) taking into account (1), (4), and (5), and rearranging, we may write:

$$(7) \quad \frac{dT_1}{dN_2} = \frac{\partial T_1}{\partial k} \left[-\frac{2r\bar{Y}^0}{N_1} \frac{\partial k}{\partial \bar{Y}} + \frac{\partial Ek}{\partial E\sigma} \frac{\partial E\sigma}{\partial N_2} \right] + w \frac{\partial T_1}{\partial EN_W} + \frac{\partial T_1}{\partial N_2}$$

Since $\partial T_1/\partial k < 0$, $2r\bar{Y}/N_1 > 0$, $\partial k/\partial \bar{Y} > 0$, $\partial Ek/\partial E\sigma > 0$, $\partial E\sigma/\partial N_2 < 0$, $w\partial T_1/\partial EN_W > 0$, and $\partial T_1/\partial N_2 > 0$, the first two terms are positive and the third is negative. Migration tends to increase the city tax rate insofar as it decreases the tax's productivity while increasing the welfare case load. It tends to decrease the tax rate insofar as it enhances the desirability of the remaining upper-income persons and thereby leads to efforts to forestall further out-migration. The net effect depends on the relative size of the opposing forces.

In the situation at hand with trivial N_2, the increasing forces are likely to prevail and the tax rate will rise. The rise in T_1 will now make location in the suburbs seem more attractive to persons hitherto just willing to stay in the city, persons whose antipathy to suburban living is slight relative to the rest of the population, or whose positive attraction for the suburbs is relatively strong and has been just barely offset by suburban disadvantages like high transportation expenses. Some of these will now therefore move to the suburbs; their places will be taken by others from the same lower-income outside population as before. This will have the same effect on tax productivity, welfare load and very likely, on the tax rate again. So a third and successive round will proceed via this mechanism, until greater and greater personal antipathy to suburban living has to be overcome to induce further migration, and the growing desperation in the city about the loss of higher-income groups prevents the tax rate from rising despite unfinanced growing public service needs. Moreover, in-migration will be shut off when the falling per capita city income reaches the level of the in-migrants.

It is instructive to ask what happens to the level of redistributive aid during this migration process. The analysis is given in (8):

$$(8) \quad \frac{\partial W}{\partial N_2} = \frac{\partial \left(\frac{T_1 Y_1}{N_W}\right)}{\partial N_2} = \frac{N_W \left[T_1 \frac{\partial Y_1}{\partial N_2} + Y_1 \frac{\partial T_1}{\partial N_2} \right] - T_1 Y_1 \frac{\partial N_W}{\partial N_2}}{(N_W)^2}$$

Since the out- and in-migration processes have a stochastic element, we convert to expected values in the appropriate places.

$$(9) \quad \frac{\partial EW}{\partial N_2} = \frac{N_W \left[T_1 \frac{\partial EY_1}{\partial N_2} + Y_1 \frac{\partial ET_1}{\partial N_2} \right] - T_1 Y_1 \frac{\partial EN_W}{\partial N_2}}{(N_W)^2}$$

$$= -\frac{2r T_1 \bar{Y}^0}{N_W} + \frac{Y_1}{N_W} \frac{\partial ET_1}{\partial N_2} - \frac{w T_1 Y_1}{(N_W)^2}$$

The first term represents the tax loss per welfare client due to the changed income composition of the city population; the second is the revenue change per welfare client due to a tax rate change; the third is the result of spreading the original welfare revenues over a larger case load [especially when written as $(T_1 Y_1 / N_W)(w / N_W)$]. The first and third terms are negative; the second depends on the direction of response of the municipal tax rate.

From this formulation we can see what constitutes a dilemma for the city. If the city keeps its tax rate unchanged (its constraint against losing further well-to-do population just offsetting the opposite pressures of tax erosion and heightened expenditure needs), then its per-client welfare benefits will decline, possibly substantially. If it attempts to forestall this by raising its tax rate, then welfare standards will decline anyway unless the tax increase is large enough to offset the other factors. A rate increase large enough to maintain welfare standards $\left[\frac{\partial ET_1}{\partial N_2} = \frac{2r T_1 \bar{Y}^0}{Y_1} + \frac{w T_1}{N_W} \right.$ $\left. > T_1 \left(\frac{2r}{N_1} + \frac{w}{N_W} \right) \right]$ will induce additional out-migration with its attendant replacement by a population that erodes its taxable capacity and expands its needed welfare services: in other words, it simply buys a small amount of time before induced suburbanization brings about the same dilemma, but in even worse degree (because of the further population compositional change). A tax rate decline intended to attract suburbanites back to the city results in a significant worsening of welfare services.

Insofar as the present simplified model (especially with respect to the endogeneity of the in-migration stream[5]) resembles the real world, the option most likely to be chosen is to raise tax rates somewhat, to allow welfare standards to fall somewhat, and to allow some further suburbanization to be pushed—a compromise of sorts.

How is this phenomenon to be appraised in welfare terms? It is sometimes described as a distortion of resource allocation: basic needs hitherto met by the public sector are now going unmet. The public sector, because of shifts in fiscal capacity, becomes less responsive to the needs of its own constituents. A less responsive public sector is a distortion of the purpose of collectivization. So a straightforward welfare loss is encountered as a result of less efficient decision making.

This argument is faulty. The critical error is in carrying out the analysis as though a given population were experiencing an inadvertent loss of control over their own collective instrumentality. In fact, the constituency of the city government changes throughout the process. It becomes, from the welfare point of view, a different decision-making unit. The cut in per-client benefits, the raising of the tax rate, are well understood in these terms: a new group with lower per capita income than the earlier one, faced with a rising cost of welfare per capita of population, *chooses rationally* to purchase a smaller bundle of such services. The higher tax rate expresses the higher cost to the new community, the lower welfare standards express the rational output response by the new decision makers. So long as the new city population differs from the old we cannot conduct a straightforward welfare analysis. No direct normative comparison can be made between the two populations or the relative over-all fulfillment of their respective needs.

An indirect analysis can, however, be made. What has happened must be viewed against the whole of the population affected. The critical, indeed active, agency is the group that migrated to the suburbs to take advantage of the tax benefits inhering in a closer approximation to home rule with selective entry. Their move has resulted in the formation of a community for themselves more nearly homogeneous than they had before, and the transformation of the community they came from into one also more nearly homogeneous than before. In the latter community, this homogenizing has raised the cost of redistributing income

[5] The typical real-world phenomenon is an immigrant stream largely exogenous. It has many of the characteristics we posit here, but its largely uncontrollable magnitude has an active augmenting role, not merely a passive one, in the forces leading to suburbanization.

to any desired recipient level through the collective mode of decision making, as witnessed by the increased tax rate (or perhaps more clearly, by the erosion of tax productivity k). That less recipient redistribution will be purchased when its price rises is to be expected.

Thus, if the population of the over-all system has decided on a certain desirable degree of income redistribution to be achieved at the local level, closer approximation to home rule can induce too little a degree of population mix in each community to bring it about. This decrease in average redistribution might be accompanied by an increase in over-all redistribution if—as is likely—immigrants came from areas in which redistribution was less than the newer lower level at their destinations. Regardless of this, however, even the average degree of redistribution would be greater if, despite physical suburbanization, suburbanites *remained within the same political jurisdiction*. It is not physical but jurisdictional mobility that affects redistributional ease. The home rule option of forming separate, more homogeneous jurisdictions through controlled political entry conflicts with the possibility of maintaining jurisdictions with desirable population mix for redistributional purposes. The unrestricted right to maximize home rule consensus could transform the local community system into a set of homogeneous special privilege preserves established by active segregating groups on the one hand, and a set of residual homogeneous "problem" dumping grounds, passively formed in their wake, on the other. The use of local government for significant redistributional purposes would be significantly compromised.

The welfare evaluation of our model is therefore based on the efficiency of the public sector to produce not income but income redistribution. It depends on the existence of social value judgments concerning the desirable degree and locus of income redistribution. While such decisions are, of course, highly controversial, the structure of the normative analysis that results is the same in the two cases. If we agree on the goals for public decision making we can examine the efficiency with which the particular institutions achieve the redistributional as well as the income level goals. Since ideal resource utilization includes establishment of decision-making instruments that can meet society's broad goals, redistributional inefficiency is a symptom of resource misallocation just as is income level inefficiency.

Analysis of the use of resources to produce decision-making apparatus has been largely neglected, but it represents an extremely important type of production. Collective decision making especially merits new attention, since it has often been accorded an ideological sanctuary akin to that of individual decision making. This paper joins other recent work in attempting to rectify this omission.

A final matter. We see that the goal of unrestricted home rule consensus can conflict with income redistributional goals. One compromise is to restrict the former somewhat in the interest of the latter. Another is to shift the locus of redistributional responsibility to a higher level of government, where adequate population mix is achieved despite local homogeneity. Since the real-world counterpart of our model's inmigration is heavy interregional flows, largely uncontrollable on even a state level, this suggests that the appropriate site of such responsibility is the federal level.

Home Rule, Suburbanization and Interjurisdictional Externalities: A Family of Location-Resource Allocation Models

So far we have dealt with misallocations concerning the income redistributive goal. For the rest of the paper we shall be concerned with the more usual aggregate income level goal. We find public sector transactions that appear to produce resource misallocations in this more usual sense.

The crux is that the ability of economic agents—households and business firms—to proliferate nonhierarchical political jurisdictions within the metropolitan area, and their freedom to relocate among them at will, creates a set of asymmetrical interjurisdictional externalities, especially between the central city and the several suburban jurisdictions taken as a whole. These externalities affect the revenue and expenditure policies of the several jurisdictions and by so doing, have an impact on the decisions taken by the economic units as to where they should locate within the metropolitan area. Each stage of location decisions creates a new balance of interjurisdictional externalities in the system and thereby influences a new stage of impacts on public sector experience and then new location decisions. The allocation of resources to the several units in the public sector, as reflected in the ultimate pattern of intrametropolitan location, can thus be explained in part by the presence of these externalities. As such, they bear the usual stamp of inefficiency stemming from imperfect coordination between wants and opportunities.

Many issues are involved in formulating a complete system. The author has been examining a family of models to incorporate the several factors. We present here only the two simplest ones, in order to throw into boldest relief the kind of impact interjurisdictional externalities have on resource allocation. But it is instructive to summarize the character of other members of the family.

1. A model of residential location. The same homogeneous public good is produced in all political jurisdictions, and the total public output is invariant over different locational configurations. Taxes are levied on income, but all individuals have the same income.

2. The same, but total public output varies with different locational configurations.

3. The same as no. 1, but a separate tax on land and improvements is levied, relative land prices explicitly influence location decisions and are endogenous, and individual income levels differ.

4. A model of residential and business location. An invariant homogeneous public good, a separate tax on land and improvements.

5. The same, but with relative land prices influencing location.

6. A model of residential location. Heterogeneous public output. Differential spillovers as interjurisdictional consumption.

7. The same for residential and business location.

8. The same as no. 6, but differential spillovers are costs of accessibility to the SMSA center.

9. The same as no. 6, but the specialized differentiated public outputs in different jurisdictions are endogenous (functions of locational configurations).

We shall concentrate on models number 1 and 4.

A Model of Residential Location with Interjurisdictional Externalities

Specification of the Model

This first model is notably oversimplified, excluding some important facts of both private and public sector mechanisms and somewhat misrepresenting others. But it illustrates sharply the kind of impact that interjurisdictional externalities have on resource allocation, and the role that home rule distribution of political power—local political fragmentation—plays in generating these externalities.

Assume the SMSA contains N individuals, N_1 in the central city and N_2 in the suburbs—with separate political jurisdictions.

(10) $$N = N_1 + N_2$$

In the present model we hold total SMSA population constant in order to isolate the effects of intrametropolitan locational distribution alone. The over-all character of the population remains unchanged, and we assume that every individual has the same per capita income. This makes plausible our assumption about the homogeneity and invariance of public sector output.

The public sector produces either a single type of output or—more realistically—a bundle of commodities with constant proportions among them. Only the scale of the bundle may change, not its internal composition. The population has an identical per capita effective demand for public output, and this is invariant over different locational distributions.[6] Each individual has an effective demand for public output—i.e., at the political deliberative, not the consumption, stage—only in the jurisdiction where he is a legal resident, regardless of where else he may actually consume public output. Thus:

(11) $$G^D = G^D(N),$$

where G is the size of the public output.

We assume that political decision making is such that whatever output is demanded is exactly supplied, so that actual budgeting is demand determined: government is "perfectly" responsive.

(12) $$G^S = G^D$$

An important aspect of the whole family of models being considered is that a distinction is made between the *output* of public goods and the productive *inputs* necessary to produce them. This distinction is rarely maintained elsewhere, partly because of the tradition of measuring value of public output by the total cost of the inputs used. This has stemmed largely from the difficulty in measuring output units and the absence of markets within which buying and selling transactions could provide market valuations for the several public commodities. Despite these conceptual and practical difficulties, we do distinguish here between the level of the ultimately wanted services and things that emerge from public production and the variety of productive resources that go to bring them about. We even distinguish between this "final" output and the intermediate input complexes that are proximate productive factors.

---

[6] The significance of this assumption, and a different interpretation, will be examined more closely after the nature of the interjurisdictional externalities is introduced.

As an example of this distinction, in police services we assume that individuals seek a particular level of security of property and person, of convenient traffic flows, rather than any particular number of policemen on the force, or numbers of detection laboratory chemicals, or even intermediate goods like number of patrolmen beat-hours, or suspects questioned, etc. Arrests or convictions, or crime rates, while they possess notable deficiencies, are closer indices of the output dimension. In the field of transportation, the citizenry seeks particular levels of convenience, speed, safety and accessibility—not tonnage of highway construction materials used, or man-hours worked, or even intermediate goods like numbers of rapid transit vehicles, width of streets, etc.

We now specify the resource cost functions corresponding to the production of public output. The central city and suburban jurisdictions have separate cost functions. We shall present two alternative functions, depending on whether or not there exist interjurisdictional externalities. Consider first the nonexternality case (Case I).

(13a) $$S_2 = S_2(N_2) = P_2 N_2$$

(14a) $$S_1 = S_1(N_1) = P_1 N_1 = P_2 N_1,$$

where P is constant; S_1 is the resource cost of the public sector in the central city; S_2 is the resource cost of the public sector in the suburbs; P_1 is the per capita cost (price) of the public output produced in the central city; and P_2 is the per capita cost (price) of the public output produced in the suburbs.

We assume that public output is produced at constant per capita cost in the suburbs, and this is equal to cost conditions in the city when no externalities occur.[7] The significant content of 13a and 14a is that resource costs for both jurisdictions depend solely on the resident population of each. The presence of either makes no difference to the other.

The presence of interjurisdictional externalities changes this.

(13b) $$S_2 = S_2(N_2) = P_2 N_2$$

(14b) $$S_1 = S_1(N_1, N_2) = P_2 N_1 + E(P_2, N_2) = P_1(N_1, N_2)N_1$$

$$= P_1 N_1 \geq P_2 N_1$$

$$E(P_2, 0) = 0 \qquad \frac{\partial E}{\partial N_2} > 0,$$

where $E(P_2, N_2)$ is the externality cost function.

---

[7] The externalities we shall adduce are a qualification to this linearity assumption, since they establish cost nonlinearity with respect to variables associated with average population density and spatial extensivity, which are related to population scale.

Externalities arise in the following way. When individuals move out of the city into the suburbs they do not thereby sever their relations with the central city. They are likely to continue many of their former city activities—employment, shopping, recreational, cultural. Thus, for a significant proportion of their time, they are still present in the city. They use many of the same public facilities as city dwellers—streets, police, museums, ball parks, etc. Their presence and use of city facilities mean that the municipal government must make larger resource expenditures per remaining resident in order to provide the same level of public output (with unchanged quality—e.g., congestion—level) as before the move: i.e., the denominator of the fraction expressing per resident expenses declines by one for every resident who moves away, while the numerator declines by less than the preceding per resident expenses because of his continued partial use of city public output. While it is true that many public services or facilities, once in existence, offer roughly similar benefits to a variable number of possible beneficiaries, the quality of those benefits does depend on the expected level of use, especially past some minimum congestion level. A municipality, having to plan for the expected total user population, will have to tailor its scale of output to the expected amount of suburban presence within the city. Thus, equation 14b shows the resource cost of public output in the central city influenced by the size of N_2 as well as N_1. The size and presence of the suburban population does make a difference. It is expressed in the externality cost function $E(P_2, N_2)$ where, broadly speaking, N_2 influences the real externality cost and P_2 normalizes this to dollar values in terms of the per capita cost of government output.

While reverse externalities may exist, where city residents use suburban public facilities (e.g., in connection with recreation or, increasingly, employment), we assume here that these are distinctly smaller in magnitude. The externality cost function represents in reality the *net* externality relationship between the two directions and can be tolerably used with its present arguments because of the postulated strong asymmetry between the two directions. As a result, P_1 no longer equals P_2 and exceeds it for any positive N_2.[8]

---

[8] We may interpret this less simply. The spatial distribution of business firms is exogenous in the present model. It is often believed that sizable business concentrations in a city decrease the residents' tax cost, since the taxes which firms pay or their activities induce others to pay exceed the expenses they add to the public budget. It is quite possible that so much of the SMSA business activity is located in the central city that the tax rate on residents there is *less* than that for suburbanites, despite the presence of substantial externalities. Since we shall be interested in following how an initial relationship between P_1 and P_2 is changed by migration, it does not change

This raises a problem. If suburbanites consume their "normal" amount of public output in the suburbs as well as additional amounts in the city, is not total G larger? Or, alternatively, if they consume only the same total public output regardless of where they reside, why do they not decrease the amount they demand in the suburbs to offset what they consume in the city? Given the assumption of homogeneous government output bundles, consumption in the city would seem to be a close substitute for consumption in the suburb.

Our model is oversimplified on this ground, but the simplification is convenient and the results not very sensitive to the issue. With respect to the constancy of G, G is taken to be the *effective* demand for government output. City residents continue to demand their same per capita public *output:* suburbanites' consumption of city public goods is not an *effective* demand by them for such goods, since they are disenfranchised in the city. Their consumption raises the *resource cost* of meeting the city dweller's effective demand, so it is as a cost rather than as a component of G that we treat it.

The second question is more important. Insofar as they are substitutes, suburbanites' consumption of public goods in the city should decrease their demand for public goods in the suburbs. This might be a significant effect with heterogeneous public goods. Then density or scale, or population heterogeneity requirements might lead to certain public goods being provided only by central cities and not by suburbs, while suburbanites continued to enjoy them by traveling to the central city. Locational specialization of this sort could be substantial.[9] In a homogeneous public goods world this is less important. Overhead and peak load considerations make it difficult for suburbanites to save much on streets, water and sanitation, police and fire, schools, and other standard functions of local government just because some members of the community—typically some member or members of some of the households—conduct some of their activities out of the jurisdiction. Something can be saved, but not much.

Our assumption of G invariant with spatial distribution thus has the effect of misclassifying part of the discrepancy between ideal and actual public cost as waste instead of as payment for productive input, thus overstating waste. But allowance for these substitutions increases the

the analysis to suppose that the initial ratio between them is 1 : 1.5 instead of 1 : 1. The initial distribution of population between N_1 and N_2 will of course be affected, since this is influenced by the distribution of business and the relative real cost of government in the two jurisdictions. But the succeeding analysis simply examines how this initial distribution will be changed by the presence of externalities.

[9] Consider the specialized provision of zoos, museums, major league ball parks, or opera houses in the real world of public good heterogeneity.

size of the discrepancy by making suburban location even more "artificially" attractive, thus understating waste. The net effect on measruement of waste is therefore uncertain. In any case, this issue does not affect the impact of externalities on location decisions.

Our discussion bears on our assumption of constant per capita costs, since this implies an absence of scale effects (for constant E). Yet the effect of the model's jurisdictional externalities is to establish a population density effect on cost (with thresholds): lower density through suburbanization increases total costs (partly in extra transportation).

We now specify how public costs are borne through taxes. We assume simply that tax liabilities are proportional to income. Since all individual incomes are equal, this is tantamount to a per capita tax. By suitable supporting assumptions relating real estate improvements to income, we may also interpret it as a tax on such improvements. Since the tax is associated with the individual and his income, when the individual shifts from one jurisdiction to another his tax liability moves with him. For a property tax interpretation we would have to assume that the assets upon which the tax is levied must also move with him. This is an appropriate long-run assumption for real estate improvements. What is precluded by this is a tax on land, since land remains in one place, along with its tax liability, regardless of the domicile of its owner.

We omit direct reference to business taxes, even though business firms exist and are presumably subject to taxation. The proper interpretation of this exclusion is that we assume that firms as a whole are subject to a total tax liability just equal to the portion of total costs for which they are responsible: they exactly pay their way. This means that the resource costs (S_1, S_2), per capita output prices (P_1, P_2), and tax rates (T_1, T_2) refer only to those for which services to households are responsible.[10] This is unsatisfactory for the interpretation of some real world phenomena, but does little analytic harm in the absence of a treatment of business location as endogenous.

The tax functions in the respective jurisdictions are:

$$(15) \qquad T_1 = P_2 + \frac{aE(P_2, N_2)}{N_1}$$

$$(16) \qquad T_2 = P_2 + \frac{(1 - a)E(P_2, N_2)}{N_2},$$

---

[10] This does not refer to any discrimination of public goods to different beneficiaries but only to the incremental effect on the size of total resource costs of the presence of a household population in addition to business firms. This treatment of business taxes bears on footnote 8 above. It implies that tax rates on households *are* similar in city and suburb except for externalities.

where T_1 is the central city tax rate on individuals (i.e., net of business influences); T_2 is the suburban tax rate on individuals (i.e., net of business influences); $(1 - a)$ is the percentage of expenses due to suburban-caused interjurisdictional externalities which is financed by suburbanites (a marginal tax rate); and a is the percentage of these expenses which, as a residual, is borne by city dwellers.

The tax rate for each jurisdiction is the sum of the per capita cost of the basic public output bundle P_2 and that portion of the total externality cost which is borne by inhabitants of that jurisdiction. We suppose that the decision is first made by the municipal government as to how much of the total externality cost can be placed on those on whose account it was incurred $(1 - a)$, and the residual (a) must be borne by the city population.

The last element in the model is the residential location function, expressing the factors which influence the decision of residents in selecting the jurisdiction in the metropolitan area within which they wish to reside.

(17) $$N_1 = L\left(N, A, C, \frac{T_2}{T_1}\right)$$

$$\frac{\partial L}{\partial \left(\dfrac{T_2}{T_1}\right)} > 0,$$

where L is the residential location function, showing determinants of jurisdictional mobility; A is the distribution of community amenities between city and suburb; and C is the city-suburb distribution of jobs and commerce (aggregate relative accessibility).

The decision to locate in one jurisdiction or another depends on the distribution of community amenities between jurisdictions (a composite index of tastes for city versus suburban way of life), the distribution of job and shopping locations (an aggregate relative accessibility variable), and the relative tax rates between the two jurisdictions. The presence of N is to normalize the size of N_1 to the given total SMSA population. The determination of N_1 automatically determines N_2. The relative price of land in city and suburb is included indirectly, because since it is assumed that the patterns of relative amenity and relative accessibility have determinable effects on location, this implies, given a set of transportation costs assumed to be unaffected by the changes of the present model (and therefore omitted as an explicit functional argument), that a land rent gradient can be inferred whose influence on location, along with the others mentioned, is consistent with observed choices.[11]

The Optimal Distribution of Population

Since total G is constant, but S varies, for different distributions of N between N_1 and N_2, we define the optimal population distribution as that which minimizes total resource cost. Thus, the goal is:

(18) $\min S = S_1 + S_2 = P_1 N_1 + P_2 N_2$

subject to the constraint that individuals choose their locations freely, i.e.,

$$N_1 = L\left(N, A, C, \frac{T_2}{T_1}\right)$$

We have two cases, one without externalities, the other with.

CASE I: EXTERNALITIES ABSENT. Form the Lagrangean expression

(19) $Y_I = P_2(N - N_2) + P_2 N_2 + \lambda(N - N_2 - L)$

from 13a and 14a. Then:

(20) a. $\dfrac{\partial Y}{\partial N_2} = \dfrac{\partial}{\partial N_2} [P_2(N - N_2) + P_2 N_2 + \lambda(N - N_2 - L)] = 0$

   b. $\dfrac{\partial Y}{\partial \lambda} = \dfrac{\partial Y}{\partial \lambda} = 0$

From a: $-P_2 + P_2 - \lambda - \lambda \left(\dfrac{\partial L}{\partial N_2}\right) = 0$ or $\lambda\left(1 + \dfrac{\partial L}{\partial N_2}\right) = 0$; but with no externalities $T_1 = P_2 = T_2$, so $\partial L/\partial N_2 = 0$, and therefore $\lambda = 0$, i.e., the social cost of a move by any individual is zero.

From b: $N - N_2 - L = 0$, or $N_1 = L$. Together this means that any distribution along L is optimal: redistributions do not affect total costs.

CASE II: EXTERNALITIES PRESENT.

(21) $Y_{II} = P_2(N - N_2) + E(P_2, N_2) + P_2 N_2 + \lambda(N - N_2 - L)$

Setting partial derivatives equal to zero for first order conditions:

---

[11] Our exclusion of land taxes means that tax changes do not necessarily become capitalized in land prices.

$$\text{(22a)} \quad \lambda = \frac{E_{N_2}}{1 + \dfrac{\partial L}{\partial N_2}} \quad \left(\frac{\partial L}{\partial N_2} \neq 0 \text{ generally, since } \frac{\partial \left(\dfrac{T_2}{T_1} \right)}{\partial N_2} \neq 0 \right)$$

Similarly, $N - N_2 - L = 0$, so

$$\text{(22b)} \qquad\qquad N_1 = L$$

Equation 22a is the crux. The right side represents the marginal social cost of an additional unit move to the suburbs, the left side the marginal social value. The marginal social cost comprises a direct and an indirect component. The numerator represents the marginal externality cost of a single unit's move to the suburbs; the denominator represents the number of units who make the move, both by direct initiation (i.e., 1) and as induced through the influence of such moves on $\dfrac{T_2}{T_1}$ $\left(\text{i.e., } \dfrac{\partial L}{\partial N_2} \right)$. $\dfrac{\partial L}{\partial N_2} = \dfrac{\partial L}{\partial (T_2/T_1)} \dfrac{\partial (T_2/T_1)}{\partial N_2} < 0$ (since $\dfrac{\partial L}{\partial (T_2/T_1)} > 0$ and $\dfrac{\partial (T_2/T_1)}{\partial N_2} < 0$); moreover, for stability purposes assume $-1 < \partial L / \partial N_2 < 0$. So

$$\text{(23)} \qquad\qquad \lambda > E_{N_2},$$

i.e., the social value of an additional move to the suburbs must exceed the mere marginal externality cost because the first move will induce others (interpreting "unit" as more than one person, so that $1 + L_{N_2}$ may represent at least one person), each of which incurs additional social costs.

An interpretation of marginal social value and of the equation as a whole in individualistic terms is that each move to the suburbs must be worth at least $E_{N_2}/(1 + L_{N_2})$ to the individual contemplating the move (and therefore, on the basis of individualistic value judgments, to the society) in order to be justified. Unjustified moves add more to social cost than to social benefits. A possible procedural rule for empirically determining the optimum distribution is for government to impose a charge equal to $E_{N_2}/(1 + L_{N_2})$ for the right to move to the suburbs, and then to allow anyone to move who is willing to pay the charge. We assume that individuals differ in their tastes in the matter of city versus suburb, so there will be an array of maximum charges that the members of N_1 will be willing to pay for the privilege of moving (some will be negative). The marginal mover will be the individual whose maximum charge just equals the official charge. Thus, $\lambda_j = E_{N_2}/(1 + L_{N_2}) = \lambda$, where individual j is this marginal mover.

Equilibrium Population Distribution

From here on, we consider only the situation with externalities present. In order to examine the discrepancy between optimal and realized population distributions we define the "neutral tax" case as one in which the relative tax rates of the two jurisdictions—the relative price facing each individual—just equals the marginal rate of substitution of a location move between them. Each individual would face market signals which gave the true marginal social cost of moving in either direction: the externalities would in an important sense be internalized.

(24) $\qquad$ Define $N_{1I} \equiv L_I \left(\dfrac{T_2}{T_1} = \dfrac{MSC_2}{MSC_1} \,\bigg|\, N, A, C \right),$

where N_{1I} is the "neutral tax" distribution (subscript I signifies "externalities internalized"), i.e., that N_1 population which comes about by free choice under given N, A, C, and T_2/T_1 equal to the marginal rate of substitution between city and suburb relocation—the ratio of the marginal social costs of a move in either direction $(MSC_2/MSC_1 = dN_1/dN_2 \,|\, S$ constant). In the present case $\dfrac{MSC_2}{MSC_1} =$

$\dfrac{P_2 + E_{N_2}/(1 + L_{N_2})}{P_2} = 1 + \dfrac{E_{N_2}}{P(1 + L_{N_2})}.$ So

(25) $\qquad N_{1I} = L_I \left(1 + \dfrac{E_N}{P(1 + L_{N_2})} \,\bigg|\, N, A, C \right)$

Now we shall express choice of city location (equation 17) as a function of N_{1I}, as follows:

(26) $\qquad N_1 = L \left(N, A, C, \dfrac{T_2}{T_1} \right) = N_{1I}[1 - M(d, A, C)],$

where $d = MSC_2/MSC_1 \div T_2/T_1$, i.e., the ratio of the marginal rate of substitution between location move and the relative tax rate. $M(d, A, C)$ is a function for which the following hold:

(1) $M(1, A, C) = 0;$

(2) $0 \leq M(d > 1, A, C) \leq 1;$

(3) $(1 - N/N_{1I}) \geq M(d < 1, A, C) \leq 0$;

(4) $0 \leq \partial M/\partial d \leq 1$.

Thus: (1) if externalities are completely internalized, $N_1 = N_{1I}$; (2) if the private cost of moving to the suburbs is less than the social cost, $N_1 < N_{1I}$; (3) if the private cost of moving to the suburbs is greater than the social cost, $N_{1I} \leq N_1 \leq N$; (4) an increase in the social cost relative to the private cost of moving to the suburbs decreases N_1, but with an upper limit on the magnitude of the effect.

Let us now bring in the tax system. Assume for simplification that E_{N_2} is constant over the domain of N_2 (i.e., $\partial E^2/\partial N_2{}^2 = 0$). Then $E_{N_2} = E/N_2$. We recall from equations 15 and 16 that $T_1 = P_2 + aE(P_2, N_2)/N_1$ and $T_2 = P_2 + (1 - a)E(P_2, N_2)/N_2$. If the tax system is to internalize the externalities, then each suburbanite must be faced with a charge that reflects the social cost which he incurs by his own use of city public output. Administratively, this may be approximated by imposing an appropriate charge on each and every occasion of use; or by imposing an annual charge on estimates of year-long costs incurred, based on certain characteristics of the individual's over-all situation. In either case the attempt is to pair each individual with the annual marginal cost of *his* being a suburbanite—i.e., a charge equal to E_{N_2}.

But the user-charges to approximate marginal costs are generally not available, not at least for many of the public goods involved. So charges on the suburbanites are likely to fall short of E_{N_2} for each, and fall short of E for all N_2. We assume $(1 - a)$ is the percentage of *total* external costs which falls on the suburbanites. Then a is the residual percentage which must be borne by the city dwellers, and the actual amount must be expressed as an *average* cost, because these are not met by user charges on city residents, since the residual depends on the amount of use by N_2, not N_1. Under our assumption of constant E_{N_2}, $E_{N_2} = E/N_2$, so we may rewrite equation 16 as $T_2 = P_2 + (1 - a)E_{N_2}$. (Any $1 - a$, $a(0 < 1 - a < 1)$ applied respectively to suburbanites on marginal or average cost basis, and to city dwellers on average cost basis, will exactly meet total E.[12])

We first examine two extreme tax cases and then the general case.

EXTREME CASE 1: $1 - a = 1$. Here the suburbanite pays the full private marginal externality cost. So no tax burden falls on the city dweller ($a = 0$). Then:

---

[12] This is not true for variable E_{N_2}, a matter which affects the complexity of the mathematics but not the basic issues examined here, exhaustion of E not being one of them.

$$(27) \qquad d = \left(1 + \frac{E_{N_2}}{P_2(1 + L_{N_2})}\right) \div \left(\frac{P_2 + E_{N_2}}{P_2}\right)$$

$$= \left(1 + \frac{E_{N_2}}{P_2(1 + L_{N_2})}\right) \div \left(1 + \frac{E_{N_2}}{P_2}\right)$$

But $L_{N_2} = 0$ in this case, because $\dfrac{\partial L}{\partial N_2} = \dfrac{\partial L}{\partial(T_2/T_1)} \cdot \dfrac{\partial(T_2/T_1)}{\partial N_2}$ and:

(1) $\partial T_2/\partial N_2 = 0$ because E_{N_2} is constant and therefore does not affect the user charge for the rest of N_2;

(2) $\partial T_1/\partial N_1 = 0$ because, under constant E_{N_2}, the full marginal cost tax on all members of N_2 totals exactly E, so the shift to N_2 does not change the size of the over-all residual of E (which is zero) to be financed by N_1.

Thus, $d = 1$, and so $\bar{N}_1 = N_{1I}$ (where $\bar{N}_1$ is equilibrium N_1). In a perfectly responsive system of user charges such that each suburbanite pays his full personal E_{N_2}, all externalities are internalized, and the distribution of population is optimal.

EXTREME CASE 2: $1 - a = 0$. Here the suburbanite pays no part of the externalities. The total is borne by an average cost tax on the city dweller ($a = 1$). Then:

$$(28) \qquad d = \left(1 + \frac{E_{N_2}}{P(1 + L_{N_2})}\right) \div \left(\frac{P_2}{P_2 + E/N_1}\right)$$

$$= \left(1 + \frac{E_{N_2}}{P(1 + L_{N_2})}\right)\left(1 + \frac{E/N_1}{P_2}\right) > 1$$

The inequality holds because both multiplier expressions >1 since E_{N_2}, P_2, E and N_1 are positive, while $-1 < L_{N_2} < 0$ (so that $0 < 1 + L_{N_2} < 1$). L_{N_2} here *is* affected by changes in N_2, since any increase in N_2 increases the tax burden on N_1 by E_{N_2}. So (1) $\partial T_2/\partial N_2 = 0$ (no part of E_{N_2} is borne by N_2), (2) $\dfrac{T_1}{N_2} > 0$, so together $\dfrac{\partial(T_2/T_1)}{\partial N_2} < 0$, and

therefore $\dfrac{\partial L}{\partial N_2} = \dfrac{\partial L}{\partial(T_2/T_1)} \dfrac{\partial(T_2/T_1)}{\partial N_2} < 0$.

The results are: (1) $d > 1$, (2) $\bar{N}_1 < N_{1I}$, (3) $\bar{N}_1$ is less the greater E_{N_2}, E/N_1 and $|L_{N_2}|$ are, and the smaller P_2, i.e., the larger are external costs relative to direct costs.

In this case there is a problem of the existence of equilibrium. Given an initial shift from the city to the suburb, this induces additional shifts through the relative tax rate effect which, in turn, induces further shifts via the same mechanism. Is there any convergence so that the shifting stops before $N_2 = N$? To answer this rigorously would require recasting the problem into dynamic terms. The scope of the paper precludes this. Instead we shall give an informal exposition of the issues involved.

Form the total differential of L.

(29) $$dL = \frac{\partial L}{\partial N} \, dN + \frac{\partial L}{\partial A} \, dA + \frac{\partial L}{\partial C} \, dC + \frac{\partial L}{\partial (T_2/T_1)} \, d\left(\frac{T_2}{T_1}\right)$$

The condition for equilibrium is that at N_2,

(30) $$\frac{\partial L}{\partial N_2} = \frac{\partial L}{\partial (T_2/T_1)} \, \frac{\partial (T_2/T_1)}{\partial N_2} = 0.$$

Our model essentially assumes $\dfrac{\partial (T_2/T_1)}{\partial N_2} =$ constant, so equation 30 requires $\dfrac{\partial L}{\partial (T_2/T_1)} = 0$. A reasonable specification for the partial relationship between T_2/T_1 and L is an exponential or growth curve, characterized critically for our purposes by increasing flatness at lower and lower values of L (i.e., N_1). This reflects the cost differentials that will induce different members of the population to shift from city to suburb. Since we assume a whole spectrum of tastes for city versus suburban living, at low values of L only intense city lovers are left as city dwellers and it takes larger and larger increments of the cost differential to induce more of these individuals to move.

In the continuous form specified there will be no convergence short of $N_2 = N$ so long as both partial derivatives are even slightly positive. An equilibrium is more reasonable if we recognize the discreteness of the population. Then the relationships of equation 30 become step functions. As N_2 increases, each new household shift causes a jump in T_2/T_1 (which we continue to assume is constant over the relevant range).[13] This jump induces a new jump in N_2. But these induced moves become smaller and smaller as N_2 gets larger. Finally, there comes a point where the constant jump in T_2/T_1 induced by the previous unit jump in N_2 is no longer as large as the T_2/T_1 jump that is necessary to induce the next least suburb-aversive person to make the shift (the growing cost differentials necessary to induce shifts are retained from the con-

[13] More realistically, this effect should vary over N_2. But this stems from a varying E_{N_2}.

tinuous case above). The shift process stops, and equilibrium is achieved, with an inequality rather than an equality in this discrete case. The equilibrium condition is:

$$
(31) \qquad \left| \dfrac{1}{\dfrac{\Delta L}{\Delta(T_2/T_1)}} \right|_{\bar{L}} > \left| \dfrac{\Delta(T_2/T_1)}{\Delta N_2} \right| > \left| \dfrac{1}{\dfrac{\Delta L}{\Delta(T_2/T_1)}} \right|_{\bar{L}+1}
$$

where $\bar{L}$ (or $\bar{N}_1$) is the equilibrium size of N_1.

Thus, equilibrium short of $N_2 = N$ exists only if these relative slope relationships exist in some range of N_2 short of $N_2 = N$—and this depends upon the empirical characteristics of the particular situation involved. Equilibrium is more likely to exist the wider the variety of tastes concerning city-suburban location among the population. If it exists, it will occur with smaller N_2 the larger the percentage of N that has intense tastes favoring city location.

Assume $0 < 1 - a < 1$. So both N_1 and N_2 must share in financing E. The general expression for d in this case is:

$$
(32) \qquad d = \left(1 + \frac{E_{N_2}}{P_2(1 + L_{N_2})}\right) \div \left(\frac{P_2 + (1 - a)E_{N_2}}{P_2 + aE/N_1}\right)
$$

$$
= \left(1 + \frac{E_{N_2}}{P_2(1 + L_{N_2})}\right)\left(\frac{P_2 + aE/N_1}{P_2 + (1 - a)E_{N_2}}\right).
$$

Without explicitly solving we can state sufficient conditions for $d > 1$. Since the first term exceeds 1, it is sufficient for $d > 1$ that:

$$
(33)
$$

$$
P_2 + \frac{aE}{N_1} \geq P_2 + (1 - a)E_{N_2}; \text{ or } \frac{aE}{N_1} > (1 - a)E_{N_2}; \text{ or } \frac{a}{1 - a} \geq \frac{N_1 E_{N_2}}{E}.
$$

Under our assumption of constant E_{N_2}, this can be interpreted as follows. $\bar{N}_1$ is less than optimal N_{1I} if the percentage of the marginal externality falling on N_1 (i.e., $a/(1 - a)$) exceeds the percentage of total E which N_1 would pay if *they* were subject to the marginal cost taxation imposed on N_2. With E_{N_2} constant this is a function of $a/(1 - a)$ and N_1 only: the larger is a or the smaller is N_1. If N_1 begins very large relative to N it takes a large relative a to oversuburbanize. If the appropriate L_{N_2} function is a growth curve, this is augmented by the smallness of L_{N_2} with large N_1, since the effect on T_2/T_1 of a small shift to N_2 is very small.[14]

---

[14] A growth curve implies that the absence of a critical mass of other people is a repelling force in location decisions. When population density is especially sparse in the suburbs, it takes a larger T_2/T_1 change to induce suburbanizing shifts.

Exact conditions for $d > 1$ bearing intuitive force are not easy to derive from equation 32. An intermediate form of manipulation helps some. The condition that $d > 1$ is:

(34)
$$1 > \frac{P_2^2(1 + L_{N_2}) + P_2(1 - a)(1 + L_{N_2})E_{N_2} - P_2 E_{N_2} - (aEE_{N_2}/N_1)}{[P_2 + (aE/N_1)][P_2(1 + L_{N_2})]}.$$

We may draw some presumptive inferences. $d > 1$ (and therefore oversuburbanization) is favored by: (1) high E, (2) high L_{N_2} (in absolute value), (3) low N_1, (4) high E_{N_2}, and (5) high a.

In the typical metropolitan area E_{N_2} is probably not much above zero. So the first term is probably not much above 1. But in some municipal tax systems a may exceed $1 - a$ considerably (especially since we deal only with the nonbusiness portion of taxes and expenses). For these systems, since $N_2 E_{N_2} = E$ by our assumption of constant E_{N_2}, so long as N_2 is at all comparable in size to N_1, d will considerably exceed 1. Thus, where tax systems fail to charge suburbanites a substantial part of their externality-generated costs, the distortion effect on allocation stemming from oversuburbanization will be noteworthy in those metropolitan areas where the suburban population is a sizable part of the total, the effect will be all the more the greater the influence of T_2/T_1 on the location decision.

The Character of Resource Misallocation

Suppose $N_1 < N_{1I}$. In what way is this suboptimal? Three aspects of resource misallocation are involved. First, suburbanization is carried inadvertently too far, because private incentives reflect social interests in a systematically distorted way. As a result, the whole pattern of consumption (e.g., transportation and housing combinations), and the pairing of individuals with jobs, differ systematically from what they would have been in the absence of uninternalized externalities, diverge from the best over-all accommodation of means to ends. So there are net productivity losses for households and businesses. Their magnitude depends on the specifics of the situation.

Second, excess suburbanization leads to excess resource costs of conducting local government in the metropolitan area. In our simple model the size of this excess is measured by the difference between actual externality costs at equilibrium $\bar{N}_2[E(P_2, \bar{N}_2)]$ and the optimal level of costs that compromises population tastes for city versus suburb with the social cost of buying different amounts of dispersed living

$[E(P_2, \hat{N}_2)]$. The public is willing to pay for this much enhanced resource cost for the privilege of $\hat{N}_2$ leading suburban lives.

It may be objected that $E(P_2, \bar{N}_2) - E(P_2, \hat{N}_2)$ overstates the true amount of wasted resources in the public sector because suburban consumption of city public goods does render social gain: part of the discrepancy is a resource payment for the production (and consumption) of extra public goods (G actually varies over different population distributions). This is controversial. Nonetheless, the public good decision is taken on the basis of monetary incentives that distort the true social costs of the decision. So some government waste *is* involved, and the differential $E(P_2, \bar{N}_2) - E(P_2, \hat{N}_2)$ is at least an *index*—if not a direct measure—of the extent of the distortion.

Third, distorting price effects, although so far omitted, will probably vary. If relative prices are admitted in the demand for public goods, excess suburbanization increases the real price of public goods for the city, thereby leading to a decreased combination of quality-quantity in their production. Introducing public output production as an argument in the location function may then show substantial locational impact. Some empirical results suggest that differences in tastes for city versus suburban living are much more sensitive to the public output dimension than to the public costs dimension. Thus locational resource misallocation may be more serious when the endogeneity of public goods output is considered. Even further types of effects may be approached, since this suggests an explicit treatment of heterogeneous public goods.

Addendum: Residential Location with Explicit Land Prices

In the model just presented equilibrium depended on the discreteness of certain relations ostensibly corresponding to the discreteness of the population. This is not satisfactory, since the relevant populations are large enough to be well approximated by continuous models. Additional mechanisms for equilibrating convergence are therefore desirable. An attractive candidate is the introduction of relative land prices into the residential location function, as follows:

$$(35) \qquad N_1 = L\left(N, A, C, \frac{r_2(N_2)}{r_1(N_1)}, \frac{T_2}{T_1}\right),$$

where r_1 and r_2 are the per acre price of land in the city and suburbs, respectively. This may be enriched further by making land values and developed acreage separately variable, as follows:

$$(36) \qquad N_1 = L\left[N, A, C, \frac{R_2(N_2)/M_2}{R_1(N_1)/M_1}, \frac{T_2}{T_1}\right],$$

where R_1 and R_2 are respective total land values, and M_1 and M_2 respective total developed acres, in city and suburb.

These steps permit introduction of an explicit property tax system, but we must distinguish between a tax on real estate improvements having the same interjurisdictional mobility in the long run as economic decision-making units, and which therefore influences location decisions; and a tax on land having no such mobility, regardless of its owner's residence, and so does not influence location decisions. We do this by recasting the definition of T_1 and T_2 thus:

$$(37) \qquad \text{a. } T_1 = P_2 + \frac{aE(P_2, N_2)}{N_1} - \frac{bR_1(N_1)}{N_1}$$

$$\text{b. } T_2 = P_2 + (1 - a)E_{N_2}(P_2, N_2) - \frac{bR_2(N_2)}{N_2},$$

where R_1 and R_2 are functions expressing total land values in city and suburb respectively and b is the land tax rate. (P_2 is now interpreted as a cost per unit of taxable real property.)

These modifications help build a self-balancing distributional mechanism. As persons move from city to·suburb they set in motion forces tending to augment further moves through a worsening tax rate situation in the city, but also tending some to *restrain* further moves. Their greater density in the suburbs tends to bid up land prices there, while the now-lower density in the city tends to make land prices fall there. These effects need not be linear over the domain of N_2, and their presence augments the increasing friction of inducing shifts through differences in tastes, thereby making stable equilibrium positions highly likely even in the continuous function case. Comparison of the effect of land prices and tax rates in influencing location decisions depends on relative values of land versus improvements (but the equilibrating power of land prices is lessened by inclusion of land tax revenues as a subtraction from the tax liabilities that influence location decisions).

Nonetheless inclusion of endogenous relative land prices does somewhat moderate, but not eliminate, the misallocative effects of externalities. To see the latter, suppose externalities did not exist, and population distribution was accomplished through equation 35. Now let externalities appear. The new effect on T_2/T_1 would change that distribution, and the endogenous change in land prices would then occur as an offset *only to the extent that some locational effect had already occurred.* Moreover, the braking effect could not logically reverse all traces of such an effect. It merely serves to moderate the net effect. Misallocation will continue to occur, but it will be smaller.

Sketch of a Model of Residential and Business Location

Space will not permit more than a brief look at how the location of business firms can be made endogenous in a model of the sort we have been developing. We present the basic equations:

(38) $$N = N_1 + N_2$$

(39) $$C = C_1 + C_2$$

(40) $$G = G(N, C)$$

(41) $$G_C = \alpha G_N \qquad\qquad 0 \le \alpha \le 1$$

(42a) $\quad S_2 = S_2(N_2, C_2) = N_2 \dfrac{\partial S_2}{\partial N_2} + C_2\alpha \dfrac{\partial S_2}{\partial N_2} = N_2 P_2 + \alpha C_2 P_2$

no externalities:

$$S_1 = S_1(N_1, C_1) = N_1 \frac{\partial S_1}{\partial N_1} + C_1\alpha \frac{\partial S_1}{\partial N_1} = N_1 P_2 + \alpha C_1 P_2 \quad (P_1 = P_2)$$

(42b) $\quad S_2 = S_2(N_2, C_2) = N_2 P_2 + \alpha C_2 P_2$

externalities:

$$S_1 = S_1(N_1, N_2, C_1, C_2) = P_1(N_1, N_2, C_1, C_2)N_1$$

$$= N_1 P_2 + \alpha C_1 P_2 + E(P_2, N_2, C_2)$$

$$E(P_2, 0, 0) = 0; \; E_{C_2} = \beta E_{N_2}$$

$$0 \le \beta \le 1 \qquad \alpha \gtrless \beta$$

(43) Residential location:

$$N_1 = L\!\left(N, A, C_1, C_2, \frac{T_2}{T_1}\right) = N_{1I}[1 - M(d, A, C_1, C_2)]$$

(44) Business location:

$$C_1 = K\left(N_1, N_2, A, \frac{T_2}{T_1}\right) = C_{1I}[1 - Q(f, A, N_1, N_2)]$$

$$(45) \quad T_1 = \frac{N_1 P_2 + \alpha C_1 P_2 + aE(P_2, N_2, C_2) - R_1(N_1, C_1)}{V_N(N_1 + \gamma C_1)}$$

$$(46) \quad T_2 = \frac{N_2 P_2 + \alpha C_2 P_2}{V_N(N_2 + \gamma C_2)} + (1 - a)E_{N_2}(P_2, N_2, C_2) - \frac{R_2(N_2, C_2)}{V_N(N_2 + \gamma C_2)}$$

where C, C_1, and C_2 are business units in total, city and suburb respectively (expressed in acres of occupancy); f is the ratio of marginal social cost of business in the suburb to that in the city divided by the ratio of the business tax rate in the suburb to that in the city; Q is a function with properties analogous to those of M in equations 26 and 43; γ is the coefficient showing a combination of lower per acre generation of public good cost and higher average taxable value of real improvements per acre than resident unit; N, N_1, N_2 have the usual meaning and are expressed in per person units, each bearing constant average taxable real improvements; V_N is assessable capital value per resident unit (person); and γV_N is assessable capital value per business unit (acre).

In this model a shift of one resident unit from city to suburb first affects relative tax rates in the usual fashion and induces further residential shifts in the usual fashion. But it also affects business location in two ways: first, through the same relative tax rate change and second, because businesses are attracted to residents for the same locational reasons (access to customers and labor supply) that attract residents to businesses (access to jobs and retail trade)—but with larger lags, larger thresholds and smaller impact. These induced business shifts then augment the second round resident shifts because of the new distribution of business in the SMSA, and thus the patterns of accessibility are changed. These in turn induce further business shifts and the interactive process continues.

Thus, locational interactions between households and businesses operate at every stage through both a direct (accessibility) and an indirect (relative tax rates) route. On the one hand the over-all locational shift for any given tax rate change will be much greater in the present model than in the first model with business location frozen. On the other hand, in this model E_{N_2} and E_{C_2} are not constant because they reflect the extent of residents' and businesses' continued dependency on the central city after moving to the suburbs. This dependency is based on the mix and scale of economic activities in the suburbs. As these become larger and larger with N_2 and C_2, the suburbs become increasingly independent of the central city. So each succeeding shift of resident or business generates a smaller and smaller externality. In the limit when suburb and city are equally self-dependent, further shifts cause no additional (asymmetric) externalities at all. Thus, the misallocative forces are greater for small to middling suburbs in this model than in our model of residential location, but they probably are weaker for large suburbs. Comparison of the over-all resultant misallocation in the two models is difficult in the abstract.[15] It rests on empirical particularities.

Epilogue: Intergovernmental Grants, Jurisdictional Consolidations and the Relevance of Local Government Scale Economies

Scale economies have relevance to the issues raised in these models. Home rule behavior tends to produce jurisdictions which are too small and homogeneous to be efficient. Two kinds of palliatives may be suggested: intergovernmental grants or consolidation. Scale economies concern the second. Intergovernmental grants to the central city or direct intervention from higher levels of government would mean for the redistributive function, either direct assumption of responsibility or transfers to permit the lower level city government to perform its continuing redistributive mission more effectively; for the externality issue, it would mean subsidization to effect partial or total offset to the adverse changes in relative tax rates, and thus to moderate the misallocative effects of externalities.

Jurisdictional consolidation (e.g., metropolitan government) would rectify the source of inefficiencies directly, but is not likely to be voluntarily accepted because the very incentives that led to jurisdictional fragmentation (the self-interest of small, homogeneous groups) would make it unattractive to the beneficiaries of that fragmentation. However, the benefits involved will be smaller if there are scale economies which prejudice small jurisdictions. Important scale economies often lead to creation of larger special districts. As suggested above (footnote

---

[15] The nonlinear impacts in this model make equilibria highly probable under reasonable circumstances with continuous functions.

2), these result in a different and undesirable form of fragmentation. Central city jurisdictions have bargaining wedges here that could lead toward partial or total jurisdictional coordination. They could offer to trade cooperative arrangements involving use of public goods they produce under substantial scale economies, cooperative arrangements involving functions where externalities, not scale factors, operate to *their* disadvantage. Such progressively extensive arrangements could be further enhanced if higher jurisdictions insisted on using them as agents for their intergovernmental transfers and other forms of local intervention.

We have argued in this paper that the efficiency of local collective decision making should not be taken for granted. Such efficiency is a subtly intertwined skein. We shall need more knowledge than we now possess to recognize the various forms of inefficiency that are likely to occur. We shall need much more knowledge—and patience and wisdom as well—to do something when we recognize that they do occur.

COMMENT

GORDON TULLOCK, *Virginia Polytechnic Institute*

I should like to begin by welcoming Rothenberg to the club. He is now the third person (Mancur Olson and I are the other two) who has been applying the particular type of reasoning he has presented today to the problem of the optimal size of government units. This approach is, I think, a natural outgrowth of recent work in both political science and economics. Clearly, the market does not work perfectly. In fact, it rather rarely works even close to perfectly. On the other hand, the political apparatus also does not work perfectly, and we must offset the defects of one apparatus against those of the other in order to choose which we will use in any particular application. This means, in general, that we should offset what are customarily called economic externalities with what Professor Rothenberg has referred to as political externalities. My choice of a necktie, for example, generates externalities and there is a finite chance that a citizen of Afghanistan would see my necktie and be annoyed by it. There is, therefore, an externality that extends all the way to Afghanistan. Clearly, however, no one would suggest that we have a world government for this particular activity.

On the other hand, national defense is (as we frequently hear these days) something which oppresses certain people in our society. There are certain people in our society who would purchase very much less national defense if the choice were theirs. Nevertheless, in this case we would all insist that the particular activity should be dealt with by the government even though it involves a political externality on certain of our citizens. In each of these cases we would anticipate that the costs would be lower with the particular mechanism we suggest.

Let me, however, turn to a technical appraisal of Professor Rothenberg's paper. Let me for the moment confine myself to allocational problems. Here Professor Rothenberg lists three goals: the minimization of political externalities, the internalization of the economic externalities, and capture of economies of scale. The third of these criteria is a mistake. As a general rule, we do not have to choose our political unit in terms of productive efficiency for any particular activity. There is no reason why political units cannot contract out services to either public or private organizations which are optimal in terms of production. In fact, we see a great deal of this in modern times. Police departments, education, fire department, etc., are quite frequently contracted out. In the area immediately surrounding Los Angeles this practice has been particularly well developed and some of the new small communities in that area have literally reduced their own government to a city council. Everything else, including collection of taxes, is contracted out.

Once we realize that government activities can be contracted out, we are of course free from any necessity of selecting governmental units in terms of an efficient producing unit. What we need is a unit in which the externalities are rather well internalized. If such a unit is much smaller than the optimal producing unit, it will buy rather than produce public goods. It should, of course, be kept in mind that we will never be able completely to eliminate the externalities. Political externalities grow steadily as the size of jurisdiction is increased and fall to zero only when we have complete individual choice. The economic externality, on the other hand, will always exist if we have more than one political unit because there will always be some effect at the border of a political unit. Thus, what we want to do is minimize the sum of these two types of externalities, realizing that this will characteristically not involve reducing either one of them to zero.

It should be noted that if we follow this simple rule for each activity, choosing an optimal size of governmental unit by minimizing the sum of the two types of externalities, we would end up with thousands and thousands of governmental units with each individual being a member and voter in each of these thousands. Clearly this in and of itself would be inefficient, and therefore we must combine these functions into larger units in order to simplify the decision problem of the individual. This is not entirely a negative factor, however. It permits logrolling, and logrolling makes it somewhat easier to obtain adjustment with individual preferences. In particular, it makes it possible for individuals with intense preferences in one field to exert a disproportionate influence in that field.

Continuing to talk only about allocational matters, I should say that in my opinion the general approach offered by Professor Rothenberg as to the problems of the cities is not well founded empirically. I have never been deeply impressed with the theory that the central city is exploited by the suburbs. When an individual moves to the suburbs, he automatically carries with him the largest single governmental expenditure which will be made for him, i.e., the education of his children. Further, if he continues to retain his place of business in the central city, he will continue paying taxes. It is by no means obvious to me that the reduction in the expenditures which he works on the city by moving to the suburb is less than the reduction in the taxes. Even if he moves his place of business also to the suburbs, and only visits the city occasionally (let us say, to go to the theater), it is by no means obvious that he is exploiting the city. Presumably, his custom in the theater means that there are more theaters and hence that the tax rolls of the city are somewhat higher. How can we be certain that his consumption of city services is more important than this increase in the taxes?

But here we have a matter for empirical research, not exchange of subjective opinions. It should be noted that Professor Rothenberg's equations would operate just as well if my belief as to what is true in the real world is true as they would if his belief is true. It is simply that some factors which are positive in his presentation might turn out to be negative, and the consequence would be that we could find the central city subsidizing the suburbs.

So far, I have said nothing at all about redistribution of income. Clearly, this is an activity of existing governments, and equally clearly there are some externalities here. Hence government activity can be justified. The problem that I see with Professor Rothenberg's approach, then, is not the justification of government activity but an arbitrary circle in his reasoning. Once we have determined the optimum amount of redistribution, we could (at least theoretically) design a governmental unit which will produce that particular amount of redistribution. I am by no means sure that we know enough about politics at the moment to do this, but let us for the time being grant Professor Rothenberg's view that we can so design government units. This requires, however, that we have some method of determining the appropriate amount of redistribution of income. Rothenberg's approach, somewhat concealed but nevertheless it is his approach, is to take an existing unit of government (which I think is the national state although he refers to it as "the system as a whole") and determine by some unspecified way what this particular political unit feels is the optimum amount of redistribution. He then uses this particular amount of redistribution to determine the amount of redistribution to be designed into governments.

This procedure obviously is circular. If we are trying to design political units so that they have some optimum amount of redistribution, we cannot obtain that amount of redistribution from the design of political units. Having said this much, however, I should go on to say that I do not know any other procedure for obtaining the "right" amount of redistribution. As a result I am inclined to the view that we should design government units without much concern for their redistributional characteristics. This is not because I think it would not be desirable to design units to give optimal redistribution, but because I can see no way of obtaining data as to the proper amount of redistribution. I should, of course, in this connection repeat my earlier skepticism as to whether we know how to design a government to get a certain amount of redistribution. To elaborate slightly, my recent research into redistribution in the United States would seem to indicate that American citizens do not want to give very much to the poor. If this is so, an optimal redistribution might be very small.

I should like to close by pointing out that most of my criticism of Professor Rothenberg's paper has been concerned with details. His general approach seems to me to be sound, and it seems to me also that a great many of the differences which now exist between the detailed results obtained by this approach by Olson, Rothenberg, and myself are the result of the simple fact that it is a new technique. If we have further discussions of this sort and further scholars become interested in the field, I suspect that many of these problems will fairly shortly be solved.

UNCOMPENSATED NONCONSTRUCTION COSTS WHICH URBAN HIGHWAYS AND URBAN RENEWAL IMPOSE UPON RESIDENTIAL HOUSEHOLDS

ANTHONY DOWNS

Real Estate Research Corporation

I. Introduction

Urban highways and urban renewal are public outputs which impose many nonconstruction costs upon households living in the metropolitan areas where they are located. Yet present public policies ignore most of these costs by failing to take them into account when planning the improvements concerned, and failing to compensate the citizens who are compelled to bear them. This dual failure results in very widespread injustice. Moreover, the heaviest burdens generated by such injustice tend to fall upon citizens least able to bear them because of their low incomes and generally restricted opportunities.

It may seem inappropriate to discuss the costs of two major government programs at a conference on the economics of public output. But one man's benefit is often another man's cost. So almost every public project produces some negative impacts on the output side as well as the negative impact of paying for its inputs. Yet too often public construction projects are evaluated by comparing only the benefits on the output side with the costs on the input side—or at least ignoring many significant costs generated by outputs.

NOTE. This paper is based upon a study conducted under the auspices of the Baltimore Urban Design Concept Team and financed by several federal agencies. The opinions expressed herein are solely those of the author and do not necessarily represent the views of the members of the Baltimore Urban Design Concept Team, the Maryland State Roads Commission, or any of the other local, state, and federal agencies connected with the Baltimore Highway Project.

This paper is aimed at remedying this imbalance concerning urban highways and urban renewal insofar as residential households are concerned.[1] It therefore seeks to (1) identify the nonconstruction costs which residential households are forced to bear by these two programs, (2) analyze which of these costs should be paid for by public authorities, (3) estimate the magnitude of certain key costs for which compensation should be paid but is not, and (4) indicate some policy implications of the analysis.

II. The Basic Principle of Compensation

People who are forced to move from their homes because of highways or urban renewal, or who suffer from environmental changes caused by these public outputs, thereby sustain certain financial and other losses. These losses are essentially personal sacrifices which they are compelled to bear for the good of the public in general, and of the beneficiaries of individual public projects in particular. It is therefore the duty of the public authorities concerned to compensate them for these sacrifices. Such compensation should place them in substantially the same status, in terms of economic and other well-being, that they occupied before being affected by the projects concerned.

Thus, the basic idea behind compensation consists of "making people whole" in relation to the injuries they sustain from public projects (other than paying their share of the input costs concerned, presumably through various taxes). Consequently, the losses imposed upon them should be identically offset by compensation provided to them, except to the extent that those losses are offset by the benefits provided by the project involved.

In some cases, this basic principle must be substantially modified in practice. Nevertheless, it is the fundamental concept on which the law concerning compensation is based (insofar as a nonlawyer like me can determine), and upon which my analysis will build.

---

[1] Other similar losses are imposed upon commercial, industrial, and institutional establishments by urban highways and urban renewal. Although many of the principles discussed in this paper also apply to losses sustained by these establishments, we have not considered any such losses or proper public policies regarding them in this paper.

III. The Kinds of Losses Imposed upon Residential Households by Urban Highways and Urban Renewal Other Than Construction Costs

The construction of major highways and urban renewal projects in urban areas imposes three basic types of losses upon residential households living in those areas, other than the losses resulting from paying for the costs of construction. These are (1) losses imposed upon households directly displaced by such projects, (2) losses imposed upon a variety of households because of uncertainty and delays connected with clearance and construction, and (3) losses imposed upon households not residing in the right-of-way or clearance area and so not displaced, but nevertheless affected by the projects concerned. These types of losses are listed on accompanying pages.

Some of the individual losses listed are relatively self-explanatory, but others require considerable clarification. Therefore, each is discussed briefly in the following paragraphs.

Losses Imposed upon Residential Households by Displacement Itself

DISRUPTION OF ESTABLISHED RELATIONSHIPS. Many households residing in any given neighborhood develop a number of well-established relationships with other persons, places, and firms in that area. These relationships include family ties and friendships with others living nearby, credit relationships with stores or banks, and habitual patterns of social and commercial intercourse. In some cases, particularly those of elderly households, these relationships represent the cumulative result of a large investment of time and energy in personal activity.

When these households are compelled to move, their relationships are often disrupted. The disruption can be either minor (as when the displaced household merely moves close by) or more serious or even fatal to the relationships concerned (as when the displaced household must relocate far away). The resulting losses are likely to cause the greatest hardship for elderly people, since many no longer have the energy or the financial means to make the new investments required to establish similar relationships elsewhere.

THE KINDS OF LOSSES IMPOSED UPON RESIDENTIAL
HOUSEHOLDS BY URBAN HIGHWAY AND URBAN
RENEWAL PROJECTS (OTHER THAN PAYING
FOR CONSTRUCTION COSTS)

A. LOSSES IMPOSED UPON RESIDENTIAL HOUSEHOLDS BY DISPLACEMENT ITSELF

1. Disruption of established personal and other relationships
2. Losses due to the taking of real property
3. Losses due to home financing arrangements, especially contract buying
4. Costs of seeking alternative housing elsewhere
5. Costs of paying for alternative housing elsewhere
6. Moving costs
7. Higher operating costs of residing elsewhere

B. LOSSES IMPOSED UPON RESIDENTIAL HOUSEHOLDS BY UNCERTAINTIES AND DELAYS

8. Deterioration in the quality of life during waiting periods
9. Inability of property owners to sell property at reasonable prices during waiting periods
10. Declines in the value of properties during waiting periods because of neighborhood and individual property deterioration
11. Losses of income suffered by owners of rental property because of the departure of tenants before actual taking occurs
12. Costs of maintaining property after its fair market value has been established for purposes of litigation

C. LOSSES IMPOSED UPON RESIDENTIAL HOUSEHOLDS
NOT DIRECTLY DISPLACED BUT LOCATED IN SURROUNDING AREAS

13. Higher taxes paid because of increased city costs to counteract vandalism and other deterioration in the area
14. Disruption of local communications through the blocking of streets
15. Reduction in the quantity and quality of commercial and other services available in the area because they have left or been displaced
16. Reduction in employment opportunities and increased costs of traveling to work because firms have been compelled to move elsewhere or have gone out of business
17. Spillover effects of deterioration in the clearance areas during the waiting periods
18. Higher rents or housing prices because of increased competition for housing among low-income households resulting from displacement
19. Reduction in the efficiency of community facilities through
    a. Loss of patronage if displacement has removed customers
    b. Overcrowding if displacement has removed alternative sources of supply (such as a local school)

(*continued*)

20. Losses in property values due to changes in the accessibility of various parts of the metropolitan area
21. Losses resulting from congestion, vibration, noise, street blockage, dust, and other negative factors involved in the process of constructing the new highway or urban renewal project
22. Losses in property values due to increased ugliness, noise, air pollution, or other adverse effects of the completed highway or urban renewal project

To a great extent, losses of this type are psychological rather than economic.[2] Moreover, they are often encountered in the normal process of urban living even when no displacement by public projects occurs. Therefore, moves caused by displacement resulting from public projects sometimes merely represent an acceleration in time of moves that would occur anyway. In such cases, the losses accurately attributable to the public improvements concerned are only those due to accelerating the time of movement by whatever period is concerned.

LOSSES DUE TO THE TAKING OF REAL PROPERTY. The creation of urban highways and renewal projects involves public acquisition of many parcels of land, both vacant and improved, for the loss of which the owners are compensated by the government. Normally, they are paid the "fair market value" of the real properties taken. Fair market value is defined as the money price which a willing buyer would pay a willing seller under current market conditions if neither was under any compulsion to complete a transaction, both were fully informed about the nature of the property and its environment, and the property was exposed to the market for a reasonable length of time. In essence, fair market value is determined by establishing what the property concerned would have brought if sold on the free market at the time the legal proceeding is brought against the owner.

LOSSES DUE TO HOME FINANCING ARRANGEMENTS. Urban highways and renewal projects are frequently located in relatively low-income neighborhoods. In such neighborhoods, households are often purchasing homes through the contract method of financing. When this occurs, the occupant normally purchases the property at a contract price far above its fair market value. The price he pays has been

[2] A discussion of such losses is presented by Marc Fried in "Grieving for a Lost Home: Psychological Costs of Relocation," in James Q. Wilson (ed.), *Urban Renewal: The Record and the Controversy,* Cambridge, Mass., 1966, pp. 359–379.

inflated in part as a compensation to the seller for accepting a very low down payment (if any), and for dealing with a buyer who has a credit standing inadequate for obtaining a normal mortgage loan.

In contract sales, the seller often retains legal title to the property until the buyer has made a great many payments. As a result, when public authorities purchase a property at its fair market value, they frequently pay the original seller, rather than the contract buyer. Since the buyer purchased the property at an inflated price, the fair market value paid by the government is almost always less than this purchase price.

In such cases, the seller receives less from the government than the buyer had agreed to pay him for the property. He may therefore hold the buyer liable for the difference. If so, the buyer may find himself still paying for the property—even after he has been ejected from it, and even though he himself did not receive any payment for it. This arrangement is clearly unjust; yet it is perfectly legal under present legislation in many states.

On the other hand, the buyer can rarely be forced to pay the difference between fair market value and the sales price under these circumstances. Either he does not have enough money for a court judgment against him to be meaningful, or else the court will refuse to compel him to pay under the circumstances. If the authorities are aware of a contract purchase and know the name of the buyer, they will often make both buyer and seller parties to the condemnation suit. This allows the court to wipe out all of the buyer's residual liability as part of the taking action. But the authorities do not always know contract sales are occurring, since there may be no legal record concerning the buyer until title actually passes.

When the government takes property obtained under a contract sale after the buyer has obtained title, the government's payment may be less than what he still owes on the property (which he has usually by then refinanced with a mortgage). However, this is less likely than the first occurrence described above.

In either circumstance, the government's taking causes an uncompensated loss to the contract buyer. He has been purchasing the property through monthly payments aimed at building up an equity in it. Yet when that property is taken by the government, the payment made for it is so small in comparison to his purchase price that all or nearly all of his equity is eliminated. This negates any efforts he has made in the well-established American tradition of saving money and investing it in the purchase of a home.

COSTS OF SEEKING ALTERNATIVE LOCATIONS. Persons displaced by highways must seek out alternative residential quarters. This requires the investment of time and sometimes money. Some persons are compelled to perform this search during working hours, and to take on expenses they would not otherwise incur (mainly travel costs).

COSTS OF PAYING FOR ALTERNATIVE LOCATIONS. Anyone forced to move his residence must immediately find another residence elsewhere. In theory, if he initially lived in a residence worth $5,000, he should be able to move to another worth $5,000 and thereby find himself in substantially the same position he was before displacement. But in reality, it is almost always impossible for residents in low-income neighborhoods to find alternative housing elsewhere at the same low cost they received from the government (if they were owner-occupants) or at the same rent they formerly paid (if they were renters).

The fair market value of low-cost homes condemned for highway projects is normally lower than the current cost of similar dwellings elsewhere for several reasons. First, the units condemned are often in run-down and dilapidated condition. Second, they were usually built many years ago. Therefore, they are obsolete in design, layout, and amenities. Third, they are often located in the most undesirable neighborhoods in the city (that is frequently why clearance is occurring there). Most housing units elsewhere are therefore worth more on the market. As a result, the owners of the units to be demolished cannot take the payments they receive from the government and buy comparable housing elsewhere without incurring additional cost. Or, persons formerly renting homes which are demolished cannot find other homes elsewhere available at equally low rents.

An example of this situation was recently revealed by a study made of 112 displaced owner-occupied households in Baltimore. On the average, each white household involved had to pay $2,500 more for comparable housing elsewhere than it received from the government for its original home, each nonwhite household, $3,900. Since the original payments involved were $5,700 per household on the average, the "excess relocation cost" of $3,000 represented an average 53 per cent extra burden upon the households concerned.[3]

The degree of hardship resulting from these circumstances is greatest among low-income households, especially those composed of older

---

[3] Unpublished letter describing the results of a survey conducted by the Baltimore Urban Renewal and Housing Agency.

people. Persons owning expensive homes which are taken by the government can find comparable housing elsewhere much more easily. New units of similar quality and price are being constructed each year. Moreover, such persons are generally more competent and experienced in seeking alternative housing. It is true that construction costs have been rising so fast recently that even families in high-priced homes cannot easily take the fair market value of their older homes and buy new ones of comparable size, quality, and location. But it is certainly easier for them to come close to this objective than it is for low-income households. Little new low-cost housing is ever built in the United States except in public housing programs. And those programs fall far short of meeting the demand or the need for low-cost units. Consequently, there is a perpetual shortage of low-cost housing in most large urban areas.

The supply of such housing becomes enlarged only through the gradual decline in the price of older existing units until they are economically accessible to very low-income households—the "filtering down process." But large-scale in-migration of low-income households into a given city, or a slowdown in new construction such as that caused in recent years by high interest rates, can keep the demand for existing older units, and therefore their prices and rents, high. Hence they remain beyond the economic reach of most low-income households. In such a situation, poor persons who have been given only the fair market value of their old homes find themselves unable to purchase comparable housing elsewhere—or any housing at all—for the same amount. For older persons no longer able to earn income, this can be a tragic hardship. Often they have worked hard to pay off all debt on the homes they were in so that those homes would provide them with shelter for life. Then the government forces them out of their homes, but pays them too little to buy any other housing elsewhere. They have neither the savings nor the earning capacity to pay the "excess relocation cost" necessary to find decent housing, and may be driven into destitution through no fault of their own.

By failing to pay residential households enough compensation so that they can move into comparable housing elsewhere without loss to themselves, the government is essentially passing some of the true cost of the public improvement onto those whom it displaces. Moreover, this practice tends to injure most severely precisely the persons least able to bear any injury at all.

To some extent, the higher cost of alternative housing accommodations results from the improved quality of those accommodations relative to the original units occupied by displaced households. Numerous surveys show that most such households relocate in dwelling units which would be classified as "standard" under criteria developed by the Department of Housing and Urban Development. Many of these households were displaced from dwelling units which would be considered "substandard" by the same criteria. To the extent that these displaced households live in better accommodations, it could be argued that the higher costs they pay do not constitute a loss imposed upon them by displacement.

On the other hand, this upgrading of housing quality is not necessarily the result of voluntary choice. Prior to displacement, they may have been living in substandard units which were relatively inexpensive because they chose to minimize the share of their incomes going to housing. After displacement, the share of their incomes devoted to housing almost always rises, whether they want it to or not. Insofar as improved housing quality is a result of involuntary restriction of their choice, it is not clear that this can be considered a pure benefit not requiring compensation. However, the improvement in housing quality which accompanies increased housing cost does constitute a complicating factor in any attempt to evaluate how much compensation should be provided in addition to fair market value.

This complicating factor is especially critical regarding renter households. Under present practices, displaced renters receive no compensation at all (except for moving costs in some states). A study of real property acquisition in federally assisted programs made for the Congressional Committee on Public Works in 1964 indicated that about 58.8 per cent of all displaced households and individuals were non-owner occupants.[4] A study of over 2,100 relocated households conducted by the Census Bureau showed that a majority of rent-paying households paid higher rents after displacement than before. Moreover, the fraction of their incomes devoted to rents rose, with the median shifting from 25.1 per cent to 27.7 per cent. The proportion of renter households paying over 20 per cent of their incomes for rent rose from 67 per cent to 76 per cent.[5] Thus, there is no doubt that

[4] Select Subcommittee on Real Property Acquisition, Committee on Public Works, U.S. House of Representatives, *Study of Compensation and Assistance for Persons Affected by Real Property Acquisition in Federal and Federally Assisted Programs,* Committee Print No. 31, 88th Congress, 2nd Session, Washington, D.C., 1965, p. 21. Henceforth this document will be referred to in both the text and footnotes as the Public Works Committee Report.

[5] U.S. Housing and Home Finance Agency, "The Housing of Relocated Families: Summary of a Census Bureau Survey," in Wilson, *op. cit.,* p. 344. Henceforth this document will be referred to as the Census Bureau Relocation Study.

displacement generally forces renting households to pay more for rent, even though many are paying very high fractions of their income for housing already. (In the Census Bureau sample, over 35 per cent of the nonwhites and over 24 per cent of the whites were paying *more than 35 per cent of their incomes for rent* both before and after displacement.)[6] Yet displacement also caused them to improve the quality of their housing, and even to occupy slightly larger units.[7] Deciding to what extent these households were compelled to bear "excess relocation costs" and to what extent they were merely upgrading their housing is certainly not easy. Yet there can hardly be any doubt that displacement forced these households to bear at least some uncompensated costs which they would have avoided if they had been able to do so.

MOVING COSTS. Clearly, transporting personal and other belongings from the dwelling acquired by highway authorities to the new dwelling costs resources. This fact is recognized by the law in most states. However, the Public Works Committee Report showed that only about 49.5 per cent of the households and individuals displaced per year by all federally related programs received payments for moving costs.[8] This study also estimated that only about 44 per cent of the families and individuals likely to be displaced by federally related programs after 1964 would be eligible for moving-cost payments under the laws in force at that time. Thus, about 54 per cent of the owners and 59 per cent of the nonowners forced to move would not be eligible for such payments, although they would certainly incur moving costs.[9]

The average size of payment made to displaced families or individuals for moving expenses was $119 under the highway program. This was larger than the average of $64 under the urban renewal program or $36 under the low-rent public housing program.[10]

HIGHER OPERATING COSTS AT ALTERNATIVE LOCATIONS. In many cases, living expenses (other than housing costs) at the location to which displaced persons move are higher than at their original location. This is particularly likely concerning commuting costs if they have had to move farther from their existing employment. The Census Bureau Relocation Study indicated that 37 per cent of the displaced workers surveyed who had fixed places of employment stated they had

---

[6] *Ibid.*
[7] *Ibid.,* pp. 340–341, 347–348.
[8] Public Works Committee Report, p. 24.

[9] *Ibid.,* p. 25.
[10] *Ibid.,* p. 37.

to spend "much more time" commuting to work than they did before relocation. Only 13 per cent reported having to spend much less time; the remaining 50 per cent spent about the same time commuting.[11] Moreover, households which have upgraded their housing involuntarily may encounter higher operating costs, such as greater heating bills and higher property taxes.

Losses Imposed upon Residential Households by Uncertainty and Delays

In many cities, considerable time elapses between the first designation of a specific location for a highway or an urban renewal project and the actual taking of property in that area. Moreover, even before official designation, a long period of discussion about where each project might go often takes place. During the entire time from initial discussion to actual taking, the area concerned is strongly affected by both the possibility and then the actuality of future clearance. Owners of property in the area are extremely reluctant to make costly improvements because they believe their property will soon be demolished. Moreover, people outside the area are unwilling to purchase property in it because they could only use it for a short period of time. Thus, *the mere possibility that a highway or an urban renewal project will be created in a certain neighborhood produces a severe disruption of the normal processes of property turnover and maintenance in that neighborhood.* Furthermore, once it has become relatively certain that a highway or project will be constructed in an area, both commercial and residential tenants begin moving out. Few others can be found to replace them. This causes a decline in rates of occupancy in both residential and commercial property, and depresses the incomes of persons owning that property.

In many cases, all these consequences result from the mere discussion of a given neighborhood as a potential right-of-way or project site. But such discussion may last for several years before any specific area is officially designated. So these consequences may seriously affect a neighborhood which is not ultimately selected as the official location. The owners who suffer such losses are not eligible for any compensation from the government, even though it caused their losses.

Specifically, property owners and residents in areas under discus-

[11] Census Bureau Relocation Study, p. 350.

sion or actually designated as potential rights-of-way or project sites normally suffer the following losses due to delay:

DETERIORATION OF THE QUALITY OF LIFE IN THEIR NEIGH-BORHOOD. This occurs because many store operators depart, reducing the variety of facilities available, and many residents depart, reducing the variety of persons living in the area. Furthermore, such departures create vacancies which encourage vandalism, crime, and physical dilapidation.

INABILITY OF PROPERTY OWNERS TO SELL THEIR PROPERTY AT REASONABLE PRICES. Under normal circumstances, when a family head is, say, transferred to another city, he sells his property on the market for its fair market value. But when a given neighborhood is under the cloud of impending demolition, few persons are willing to pay what was formerly the full fair market value for such property. Property owners are therefore confronted with a sharp depression in the prices they are able to receive for their homes. They are either forced to sell at these depressed prices because they must move, or forced to remain in the area because they are unable to get a price commensurate with their investment in the property. Persons who sell and move away also become ineligible for receiving any compensation when the highway authorities begin purchasing property. Thus, the financial losses they have been forced to endure by the highway are completely ignored under current legal processes.

DECLINES IN PROPERTY VALUE BECAUSE OF THE NEIGHBOR-HOOD DETERIORATION OCCURRING BETWEEN INITIAL DIS-CUSSION AND ACTUAL TAKING. For the reasons cited above, many properties decline in value once an area has been designated or even begins being discussed as a highway or urban renewal site. But in most states, the date at which fair market value is established is the date at which court action is taken by the government to purchase the property concerned. Many years may have elapsed from the time discussions of this site began to this legally established date. So the neighborhood may have sharply deteriorated through the mere "announcement effect" of the highway or project. Nevertheless, some sales probably have occurred in this area after such deterioration was far advanced. These sales then become the basis upon which appraisers establish fair market value, since appraisers use them to determine what willing buyers and willing sellers are actually paying for property in that area. Thus, property owners often receive from the government far less for their property than they paid for it, and certainly less than it was worth at the beginning of the process of discussion.

It is true that some owners of dilapidated and deteriorated residential property look forward to takings by the government. Such takings may "bail them out" of having to invest large sums in bringing their substandard properties up to conformance with local building and housing codes. For these owners, receiving even a relatively depressed price is a blessing in disguise. However, owners of code-violating properties are generally absentee landlords who are reasonably well-off economically, since owner-occupants generally maintain their property far better than absentee landlords. Thus, the small owner-occupants— particularly those possessing or buying single-family dwellings—suffer most from this.

LOSSES OF RENTAL INCOME. Owners of residential income property are compelled to receive lower incomes than normal because many of their tenants depart, and others are unwilling to replace them—unless rents are reduced drastically. Moreover, higher maintenance costs caused by vandalism induced by the resulting vacancies further reduce the net income from such properties during the waiting period.

COSTS OF MAINTAINING PROPERTY AFTER IT HAS BEEN APPRAISED. The appraised value of the property is based upon its state of repair at the time of appraisal. But in some cases several months may elapse between the appraisal and the legal action which finally takes the property. During this period, landlords may have to make certain vital repairs which do not appear in the appraised value and for which, therefore, they receive no compensation.

Losses Imposed upon Residential Households Not Directly Displaced But Located in Surrounding Areas

The impact of a major new expressway or urban renewal project is hardly confined to those persons displaced by its construction. Many other persons living or owning property nearby sustain losses because of the new improvement (and others gain benefits). The most significant of such losses can be described as follows:

HIGHER TAXES BECAUSE OF GREATER LOCAL GOVERNMENT COSTS. The local government may incur added costs to prevent vandalism, increase police protection, and pick up additional debris caused by the deterioration of the neighborhood during the waiting period. These costs eventually cause a rise in property taxes or a reduction in other local government expenditures. They may fall on some of the displaced households themselves before they move, but their primary impact is upon the remainder of the households in the city.

DISRUPTION OF LOCAL COMMUNICATIONS BY BLOCKING MOVE-MENT ON LOCAL STREETS. Unless a major highway is constructed on stilts, it normally blocks movement on a large number of the local streets formerly crossing its right-of-way. Urban renewal projects frequently involve the closing of local streets and the rerouting of traffic on more roundabout paths. Both these consequences decrease convenience of movement for local residents and others passing through.

REDUCTION IN THE QUANTITY AND QUALITY OF COMMERCIAL AND OTHER LOCAL SERVICES. Construction of a highway or an urban renewal project often adversely affects the quality of life in nearby neighborhoods by removing some of the facilities which served them. These can include commercial establishments (such as stores and restaurants), recreational areas, aesthetic attractions (such as trees), local transit service (disrupted by the blocking of local streets), cultural facilities (such as churches) and public education facilities. Not only may some of these facilities be removed through demolition, but also others lying outside the clearance area may abandon the neighborhood because of its reduced population, or may deteriorate in quality because of lower levels of patronage.

In many cases, the facilities removed were located in deteriorating or dilapidated structures. Therefore, an upgrading of the physical condition of the average commercial establishments may result. Nevertheless, a reduction in the number of such establishments and their variety always decreases the choice available to remaining residents.

When the facilities eliminated are in some way unique (such as an excellent school or a park), their removal may constitute an irreparable loss to the community, greatly reducing its over-all attractiveness. Under present legislation, no provisions are made for compensating the remaining community for losses of this kind.

REDUCTION IN EMPLOYMENT OPPORTUNITIES AND INCREASED COSTS OF COMMUTING. When industrial, commercial, governmental, or other employment-providing installations are displaced from an area, persons who formerly both lived and worked there are compelled to become unemployed or to travel farther for available jobs. Since most displaced establishments providing employment move somewhere else, loss of employment is usually not required. However, a relatively high proportion of small retail establishments in low-income areas forced to relocate are not reopened elsewhere. This proportion may run as high as 40 per cent, and usually exceeds 20 per cent.[12] The jobs formerly provided by these establishments are completely removed from the market. Since such establishments normally employ local residents, the negative employment effects are concentrated in the surrounding area. More significant in terms of number of persons affected is the increase in travel costs to work imposed upon persons who formerly both lived and worked in the neighborhood.

SPILLOVER IMPACT OF THE DETERIORATION IN THE CLEARANCE AREA. As noted above, significant deterioration often occurs in the area where a highway or an urban renewal project will be located during the interval between initial announcement of its location and its final construction. The adverse impacts of such deterioration may spill over into surrounding blocks. This may reduce property values there, at least until the new improvement is actually in being.

INCREASED COMPETITION FOR HOUSING AMONG LOW-INCOME HOUSEHOLDS. When major public projects are constructed in relatively high-density low-income neighborhoods, they may require the destruction of thousands of dwelling units within a given city. Such destruction causes a net decline in the number of housing units economically available to relatively low-income households. If this effect is not offset by increases in the inventory of housing available to low-income households elsewhere in the metropolitan area, the same number of such households as before will be competing for a reduced supply of housing units available in the price ranges they can afford. Theoretically, this will tend to raise the rents paid by *all* low-income households. The extent to which this theoretical effect is quantitatively significant in reality will depend upon the factors listed below.

a. *The number of housing units destroyed by the public project in comparison with the total number of units available to low-income households in that area.* Statistics concerning public projects in Baltimore illustrate the nature of this effect. In 1960, there were an esti-

[12] Public Works Committee Report, p. 30.

mated 95,000 housing units within the city limits of Baltimore occupied by low-income households (that is, those with incomes low enough to be eligible for public housing). About 64 per cent of these were renter-occupied and 36 per cent were owner-occupied.[13] In the period from 1951 to 1964, about 10,000 housing units in Baltimore were demolished because of various public programs, including highways and urban renewal.[14] Data concerning how many of the households displaced were low-income households are not available. An informed but arbitrary estimate is that 75 per cent had low incomes. In that case, about 7,500 low-income housing units were demolished in this thirteen-year period, or about 7.8 per cent of the entire low-income housing inventory as of 1960. This is slightly less than one per cent per year. Consequently, such demolition would not seem likely to exert a very large upward pressure on rents in the remaining inventory.

b. *The degree to which displaced households actually have access to low-income housing units elsewhere in the metropolitan area.* In most large cities, racial segregation effectively prevents many Negro households from having access to relatively low-rent or low-cost units located in all-white neighborhoods. Yet a high proportion of the households displaced by public programs are Negro. For example, the Census Relocation Survey selected a sample by getting the names of all families relocated by 163 local public agencies in the United States from June 1 through August 31, 1964. Of the 2,300 families finally interviewed from this sample, 52.6 per cent were nonwhite.[15] Since this sample includes local public agencies in many smaller communities, the proportion of nonwhites is probably much higher in larger cities. This conclusion is borne out by data from the particular larger city I have been citing. From 1951 through 1964, 89 per cent of all households displaced by public projects in Baltimore were Negro households.[16] In 1960, the total inventory of housing in Baltimore occupied by low-income Negro (nonwhite) households amounted to about 43,000 units.[17] In the period from 1951 to 1964, about 8,900 Negro households were displaced by public programs. Assuming one housing unit was demolished for each displaced household, this means that such demolition equalled about 20.6 per cent of the entire housing inventory occupied by low-income Negroes in 1960. The average of

[13] U.S. Census Bureau.

[14] Baltimore Urban Renewal and Housing Agency, *Displacement and Relocation—Past and Future* (for the period 1951 through 1964), March 1965. Henceforth this document will be referred to as the BURHA Report.

[15] Census Bureau Relocation Study, p. 337.

[16] BURHA Report.   [17] U.S. Census Bureau.

890 units demolished each year equaled about 35 percent of the additional number of nonwhite households entering the Baltimore housing market each year because of net nonwhite population growth in the decade from 1950 to 1960.[18] Thus, when data for the *key segments* of the housing market are examined in isolation, the possibility that demolition connected with public programs might cause upward pressure on rents and prices in the remaining *relevant sections* of the housing inventory seems much greater than if data for the housing market as a whole are used.

c. *The rate at which the supply of housing available to low-income households (and in particular, those being displaced) is being expanded through new construction or the "filtering down process."* The third factor in turn depends to a great extent upon whether the local housing market is in a relatively "loose" or "tight" condition. A "loose" housing market is one in which new units are being added to the total inventory faster than new households are entering or being formed in the area. As a result, the total available housing supply is increasing more rapidly than total demand, causing a downward pressure on both prices and occupancy rates. Under these circumstances, the "filtering down process" works relatively (but not absolutely) rapidly. Households in the middle- and upper-income ranges have many housing alternatives open to them. Therefore they more quickly upgrade their housing, thereby making a larger number of units available to lower-income families.

Conversely, a relatively "tight" housing market is one in which the demand for housing is rising faster than new supply is being created through construction (net of demolition). In such a market, increased competition for both the new housing units being created and the existing housing inventory creates an upward pressure on rents, prices and occupancy levels. Vacancies decline, and middle- and upper-income households find it more difficult to upgrade their housing. As a result, fewer existing units "filter down" to low-income households. Then demolition of some of the housing units already available to such households because of a highway or a renewal project will have a far more serious impact upon rents for low-income households than when the market is "loose."

Low-income households are particularly vulnerable to shifts in the relative "tightness" of the housing market. They occupy the residual part of the housing inventory not claimed for use by higher-income households. Since the latter have more money with which to bid for

[18] U.S. Census Bureau.

housing, their shelter needs are satisfied in the best part of the inventory. Moreover, new housing is almost always added to the upper-income end of the market, because cultural and other restrictions embodied in building codes and zoning regulations prevent the construction of new housing at low enough cost so that low-income households can afford it.[19] These two considerations emphasize the dependence of low-income households upon the "filtering down process" as a source of additional available housing supply.

The housing situation of low-income households has been worsened in the past two years by a sharp drop in the number of total new housing units started in the United States. In the period from 1962 through 1965, an average of 1.54 million new housing units were started each year. But in 1966 only 1.25 million units were started, and in 1967 only 1.29 million units. This reduction of about 18 per cent in new housing starts occurred because of higher interest rates in the economy, rather than any reduction in the demand for new housing. In fact, the demand for housing has been stimulated by high-level prosperity. The resulting combination of rising demand and restricted additions to supply has created a very "tight" housing market in most metropolitan areas. This has caused a decline in vacancies and an upward pressure on rents at all levels of the market. *Consequently, the "filtering down process" has recently become a less efficient method of making new housing units available to low-income households.*

The impact of a significant demolition of low-income housing units in a given neighborhood is magnified by the relatively restricted mobility of low-income households. Numerous studies have shown that members of many low-income households typically spend much of that part of their lives lived in the city within areas circumscribed by a very few blocks. As a result, they are relatively unfamiliar with

---

[19] The only exception is public housing. It is just as expensive as private housing to build, but is subsidized sufficiently so that low-income households can afford it. But the supply of public housing in the United States is very small in comparison with the number of low-income households. Since 1937, about 780,000 low-rent dwelling units had been created by public housing programs through 1966. However, in 1966 there were over 11 million households classified as having incomes below the "poverty level" as defined by the Social Security Administration. Thus there were approximately fourteen times as many poor households (including both families and individuals) as there were public housing units in 1966. The ratio of poor households to public housing units is considerably lower within certain central cities. Nevertheless, it still is fair to say that the number of public housing units in any major city in the United States is far below the number of households either eligible for such units, or desirous of living in them. This is confirmed by the long waiting lists for entry into public housing in most cities.

housing alternatives available in distant parts of the metropolitan area. This is particularly true of Negroes because racial discrimination excludes them from many portions of the housing market. When such low-mobility households are displaced from their homes, they restrict their search for new housing to other areas nearby. Thus, *the increased competition for low-cost housing created by demolition for public projects does not spread itself out evenly across the entire housing market. Rather it becomes focused most sharply on other relatively low-income neighborhoods in the immediate vicinity of the clearance areas.* Consequently, demolition of what seems to be a relatively small number of housing units in comparison with the total number in the metropolitan area may still have a significant impact upon rents and occupancy in low-income neighborhoods surrounding the demolished houses.

However, it is extremely difficult to measure this impact accurately. The effects of the pressure on rents and prices from this source cannot be separated from similar pressures from other sources (such as a general rise in the price level).

REDUCTION OF THE EFFICIENCY OF COMMUNITY FACIL-ITIES SERVING SURROUNDING AREAS. Schools, churches, stores, and other facilities near the clearance areas may be forced into less efficient operation by both the demolition of residences and the creation of the new projects. This can occur for either one of two opposite reasons. First, the reduction in their clientele or patronage may cause them to operate at an inefficiently low scale. This can adversely affect not only commercial establishments like retail stores, but also churches, social organizations, public schools, and medical facilities. This occurs when a significant proportion of the clientele of an organization is removed from the area, but the organization itself remains because it lies outside the clearance area, or the organization is cut off from convenient accessibility by its patrons. In contrast, if a public facility lies within the clearance area and is demolished, the diversion of its former load onto some nearby facility may overload that facility. An example would be removal of a public school and the diversion of its pupils to another already crowded school nearby. In either case, the reduced efficiency of the facilities concerned imposes a cost upon residents who live near but not within the clearance area.

CHANGES IN RELATIVE ACCESSIBILITY. The purpose of a major highway is to improve the mobility of a large number of persons residing within the metropolitan area concerned. By altering the relative accessibility of different parts of the metropolitan area, such a highway has a dramatic impact on land values. The values of certain sites rise sharply (such as sites lying near major interchanges and easily accessible to them). The values of other sites fall just as sharply (such as sites lying along former main arteries which lose traffic once the new highway is opened). These losses occur in all parts of the metropolitan area, not just in neighborhoods through which the highway itself passes. This impact is unique to highways, and does not result from urban renewal projects.

LOSSES RESULTING FROM THE PROCESS OF CONSTRUCTION. Building a major public improvement often has a very disruptive effect upon the immediate vicinity. Local traffic is impeded both by added congestion and by the blocking of movement due to construction. The local government has to pay increased costs for traffic control and for the creation of alternative access paths. Businesses on surrounding streets lose sales because access to their property is diminished and heavy traffic congestion discourages patronage. Noise and vibration associated with construction may disrupt productive processes in nearby industries and generally lower the quality of the environment. Under present laws, no compensation is paid for all of these losses, even when they are substantial.

LOSSES RESULTING FROM INCREASED UGLINESS, NOISE, AIR POLLUTION, OR OTHER ADVERSE ENVIRONMENTAL CHANGES. Public projects—particularly highways—often produce certain adverse changes in their immediate environment which reduce property values of adjacent parcels. For example, major expressways generate constant noise, higher levels of localized air pollution from exhaust fumes, the glare of lights at night, and increased congestion on some local streets near interchanges (but reduced congestion on others). Urban renewal projects may cause greater traffic congestion because of a higher proportion of car use among the new residents than the original ones and diversion of traffic. Even the sheer aesthetic effect of a major public improvement may influence nearby property values—usually downward in the case of major highways, and upward in the case of completed renewal projects (though perhaps downward during the waiting period before such projects are finished).

Distinguishing Between Real Resource Losses and Redistributional Effects

Some of the 22 nonconstruction costs cited above represent real absorptions of resources caused by highway and urban renewal projects. Examples are moving costs, losses caused by the process of construction, and costs generated by increased vandalism during periods of delay. But certain other costs cited previously do not involve resource absorption. Rather, they are redistributions of wealth from some households to others. Examples are higher rents or housing prices because of increased competition for housing among low-income households resulting from displacement, and losses in property values due to changes in the accessibility of various parts of the metropolitan area. For each household which suffers from these costs, other households gain corresponding (though not necessarily identical) benefits. Thus, when rents for low-income households rise, tenants suffer but landlords benefit. And when property values fall in some area that has reduced relative accessibility, they rise in another area where such accessibility has been improved by the project concerned.

Welfare economists have long argued that these two kinds of costs must be distinguished from each other in making public decisions. Actions that absorb resources represent *real costs* that must be taken into account in deciding the allocative *efficiency* of undertaking some project. But actions that merely redistribute resources from one household or group to others represent *distributional effects* that are irrelevant to efficiency, as that term is used by welfare economists. Rather, such distributional effects are relevant to the *equity* of the project concerned.

All welfare economists agree that efficiency should be a key factor in determining public (and private) investment decisions. But whether such decisions should be based solely upon efficiency grounds, or upon both efficiency and equity grounds, is a matter of some dispute. In my opinion, equity effects are just as important as efficiency effects in deciding whether to undertake a project. However, exactly how these two types of effects should enter into particular decisions is an extremely complex subject which cannot be fully discussed in this paper.

In fact, this paper focuses exclusively upon the questions of equity and justice relevant to residential households which arise from the nonconstruction costs generated by highway and urban renewal projects. But the redistribution effects relevant to equity can result from *both* actions that absorb resources and those which merely shuffle them around among different households. Therefore, I have had to discuss both kinds of costs or losses here. However, I have not distinguished between them insofar as their relationship to resource-allocation efficiency is concerned. I am not concerned here with the allocative efficiency of highway or urban renewal projects at all, and will not discuss or refer to that important and complex subject any further.

IV. Application and Modification of the Basic Principle of Compensation

Why Compensation Should Not Be Paid for All Losses

In reality, it is neither desirable nor possible to provide direct public compensation for all of the costs and losses discussed in the preceding section. In some cases, the positive impacts of the highway or urban renewal project tend to offset these negative losses insofar as individual households are concerned. Therefore, the public improvement inherently tends to "make people whole" even if no specific public compensation is paid to them. In other cases, there is no practical way of "making people whole" for the losses they suffer. Finally, there are a variety of losses which it is proper for the public to disregard for several different reasons. All these factors are discussed briefly below.

THE POSSIBILITY THAT SOME LOSSES WILL BE OFFSET BY BENEFITS FROM THE PUBLIC IMPROVEMENTS. As mentioned above, many land parcels gain greatly in value because of the increased accessibility provided by each new highway, or the local environmental improvement provided by most new urban renewal projects. This effect may offset some of the losses caused by the public improvement concerned. For example, increased ease of access to distant shopping centers may compensate automobile-driving local residents for the loss of some local community facilities. (Since most low-income residents do not own automobiles, this benefit has a relatively restricted distribution, however.) Similarly, if a completed urban renewal project greatly increases the number of high-income households in the neighborhood, it may attract new and more diverse shops and improve the quality of services available in the area. Also, the elimination of low-cost residences and commercial facilities through clearance tends to reduce competition among those remaining, and may thereby enhance their value.

It is certainly true that the exact distribution of these benefits is not likely to be the same as the exact distribution of the costs and losses described earlier, even for a limited set of specific parcels (such as those near the project itself). Nevertheless, public authorities are legitimately entitled to take these benefits into account when trying to decide which types of losses should be directly compensated for.

WHY SOME LOSSES MUST BE CONSIDERED INESCAPABLE RISKS OF PROPERTY OWNERSHIP. Dynamic change is one of the fundamental characteristics of a free enterprise economy. It inevitably produces unexpected and unforeseeable increases in the value of some properties, and equally unexpected and unforeseeable declines in the values of others. To some extent, such changes must be regarded as inherent in a successful free enterprise system. Hence there is no reason why the government or anyone else should guarantee continuance of existing property values as of any given moment.

It is true that governments adopt many policies specifically aimed at stabilizing values for whole classes of property, or entire areas. For example, zoning laws have this function. Yet even zoning laws do not protect the owners of every individual parcel from possible variations in value due to dynamic factors which influence the relative desirability of his neighborhood, or even of his parcel (such as the creation of a weird modern-design house by the man across the street).

In reality, major public improvements constitute only one of the many factors which change property values. Others include purely private developments (such as new housing or industrial plants), natural events (such as hurricanes and earthquakes), changes in technology and over-all economic demand (such as replacement of coal by petroleum for many uses, and the subsequent replacement of petroleum by nuclear energy) and social and cultural trends (such as the increased popularity of skiing).

Insofar as major urban highways and urban renewal projects are concerned, their impacts upon property values can be arbitrarily divided into *diffused* impacts upon properties in all parts of the metropolitan area, and *locally concentrated* impacts upon properties immediately adjacent to the improvements concerned, or almost that close. The diffused impacts can properly be considered as another of the many dynamic effects influencing property values which are inherent in a growing and changing economy. Therefore, the government need not compensate the myriad individual property owners who lose from this process, any more than it imposes special taxes upon those who gain. The losers can expect to pay lower property taxes if their property actually declines in value and this is reflected in assessments, just as the gainers can expect to pay higher property taxes for the opposite reason.

But the locally concentrated impacts are far more likely to be both larger in proportion to total property value, and more easily traced to the specific public improvements concerned, as opposed to all other factors. Hence a reasonable case could be made, for example, for compensating property owners along a highway right-of-way for losses in value due to increased noise, ugliness, air pollution, and night glare.

However, if such compensation is paid to locally concentrated losers, then it would be equally just for locally concentrated gainers to pay special taxes to offset their windfall capital gains. The absence of both these devices can be considered indirect evidence that the public affected prefers to risk suffering uncompensated losses in order to have a chance to benefit from unrecaptured gains. This is especially likely since total gains presumably outweigh total losses, or the improvements would not be made. Moreover, the difficulties and costs of computing precisely who gains and who loses from such property-value shifts, and by how much, are another strong argument for ignoring either positive or negative compensatory action, as is discussed below.

A dynamic economy similarly imposes certain psychological costs upon those living in it. Stable relationships are continually being disrupted or affected by the changes inherent in such an economy. A private apartment house developer is not expected to pay for the psychological costs he imposes on previous tenants at a site where he buys some old tenements which he demolishes, replacing them by a new apartment project. Private developers are expected to pay the fair market price for the properties concerned, but not all of the other costs associated with change in any situation. Consequently, it would be unreasonable to expect the government to compensate every person who experiences a psychological loss because of the creation of a new public project, since it is part of the dynamic process of change inherent in social progress.

THE DIFFICULTIES OF MEASURING LOSSES OF CERTAIN TYPES. Some of the losses which have been described earlier cannot be accurately measured in such a way as to make compensation of the individual households concerned truly practical. Three specific difficulties connected with measurement are delineated below.

a. *Nonmeasurability.* There are no accurate methods of quantifying certain costs (or benefits), particularly psychological ones associated with the disruption of existing relationships. It is not possible, therefore, for the state accurately to assess the degree of such loss and compensate those concerned. This is particularly true because the only persons capable of assessing the loss—the persons affected—have a natural motive for exaggerating that loss if compensation is offered.

b. *Nonseparability.* Certain kinds of costs (and benefits) can be measured, but they embody composite effects of the public project and other forces at work in the economy. It is often not possible to discover how much of these effects can be accurately attributed to the project, and how much must be attributed to other forces. For example, increases in the value of any given land site can be caused by the impact of a project, by increases in population, by general inflation in the price level and by a host of other factors. Hence, it is extremely difficult even to estimate to what extent the public project is responsible for the increase (or decrease) of land values which occurs in a given period.

c. *Nonaccountability and wide individual variation.* Certain types of costs are measurable and separable but difficult for public authorities to account for accurately, particularly because they are subject to wide individual variation. For example, the amount of time spent looking for alternative quarters can vary tremendously from individual to individual. It would be quite possible for each person to keep track of that time, and for authorities to place a value on each time unit. But excessive individual variations, plus a tendency toward overreporting flowing from the natural interest of each person to maximize his compensation, would make complete compensation for every individual impractical and undesirable.

There are three basic methods of coping with the difficulties of measurement described above. The first is overlooking the costs concerned altogether. This is especially appropriate when the losses involved are probably not large for each individual concerned on the average. Second, standard estimates can be used as proxies for losses which are either nonaccountable or nonmeasurable. Third, public authorities can undertake actions aimed at providing benefits which tend to offset certain costs generated by the highway. For example, if public authorities created one new housing unit accessible to low-income households for every demolished unit occupied by a low-income household, and the new units were similar to the old in size and style and ownership, then no upward pressure on rents or occupancy levels would be generated by the reduction in the supply of housing available to such households. Rather than attempting to measure the highly diffused losses caused by the highway, the authorities would nullify them by creating offsetting benefits. Such compensatory action is probably the only way to counteract costs which are diffused and probably small in each individual case, but occur over a great many cases.

The Tests Which Losses Must Pass to Be Directly Compensable

Any practical policies of compensation must take into account both the basic principle described in the first part of this report and the modifications set forth above. The result should be a set of practical policies designed to pay people direct compensation whenever the losses they sustain meet certain key tests. These tests can be summarized as follows:

1. *Attributability:* the loss concerned is in fact caused by the public project or the relocation generated by it, rather than by other economic or social forces.
2. *Significance:* the loss is relatively large both absolutely and in relation to the economic capabilities of those persons who suffer it.
3. *Noninherent Riskiness:* the loss cannot be considered an inescapable risk of property ownership, or an inevitable price of progress in a dynamic society.
4. *Identifiability:* the individuals or class of persons who suffer the loss can be personally identified.
5. *Measurability:* the magnitude of the loss can be measured or estimated with reasonable accuracy, at least sufficient to design roughly offsetting beneficial actions.
6. *Deliverability:* compensation made for the loss by public authorities can be accurately directed at those who suffered that loss, whether they are individuals or an entire class of persons, and will not be received by others who did not suffer any such loss.
7. *Net Negative Impact:* the loss is not likely to be offset by benefits resulting from the public improvement and likely to be distributed in the same way as the loss itself.

It is clear that these tests represent value judgments rather than the application of purely scientific, economic or legal principles. Hence they are inescapably arbitrary. Yet, in my opinion, a compensation policy based upon both justice and practical feasibility will include compensation for all losses which pass the above tests. Regarding all losses which do not pass these tests, I believe they are either not deserving of compensation, or else no practical means of providing it can be arrived at. However, my judgments are certainly open to argument and modification.

The Types of Losses Which Pass These Tests, and Therefore Should be Compensable

The table set forth on an accompanying page shows all of the specific types of losses due to highways or urban renewal described earlier in this paper. It indicates which of these losses pass the seven tests mentioned above. The table also shows which tests are failed by those losses which do not pass all seven tests, and whether or not those which do pass are compensable under existing laws and regulations.

It should be emphasized that the judgments expressed in this table are partly subjective in nature. Therefore, they are open to dispute on nonscientific grounds. Moreover, these judgments are not based upon the professional expertise of lawyers, but rather the inferences of economists. So they are certainly subject to further modification. However, they have been set forth here as a tentative start toward a more systematic development of public compensation policies than is embodied in present laws and regulations.

Based upon the findings set forth in this table, six of the twenty-two specific types of losses described earlier in this report are subject to full compensation, and four others to partial compensation. Eight of these ten losses are not now considered compensable under existing laws and regulations. Hence the analysis we have presented has led to conclusions quite divergent from existing compensation practices, as will be further explored below. The ten fully or partly compensable losses can be divided into four basic types.

1. Compensation paid directly to individuals displaced for non-waiting costs, including: (a) Payment of the fair market value of real property taken as of the time of the taking; (b) Payment for some of the losses of investment resulting from specific financing arrangements not accounted for in the computation of fair market value; (c) Payment for the "excess relocation costs" of acquiring or renting alternative property; that is, the costs of such acquisition or renting in excess of fair market value or previous rentals paid; and (d) Payment for the costs of moving.

TABLE 1

The Kinds of Losses Imposed Upon Residential Households	Does It Pass All Seven Tests?	If Not Which Test Does It Fail?	If Yes, Is Compensation Now Payable?
A. Losses imposed upon residential households by displacement itself			
1. Disruption of established relationships	no	measurability	
2. Losses due to the taking of real property	yes		yes
3. Losses due to home financing arrangements	yes (part)		no
4. Costs of seeking alternative housing elsewhere	no	measurability, significance	
5. Costs of paying for alternative housing elsewhere	yes		no
6. Moving costs	yes		yes
7. Higher operating costs at new location	no	attributability	
B. Losses imposed upon residential households by uncertainties and delays			
8. Deterioration in the quality of life	no	noninherent riskiness, measurability, attributability, identifiability	
9. Inability of property owners to sell property at reasonable prices during waiting periods	no	noninherent riskiness, measurability, attributability	
10. Decline in the value of properties during the waiting period because of neighborhood and individual property deterioration	yes		no
11. Loss of income suffered by owners of rental property because of the departure of tenants	no	noninherent riskiness, attributability	
12. Costs of maintaining property after its fair market value has been established for purposes of litigation	yes		no

C. Losses imposed upon residential households not directly displaced by the highway but located in surrounding areas

13. Increased city costs to counteract vandalism and other deterioration, which eventually raise local taxes	no	attributability, deliverability
14. Disruption of local communications through the blocking of streets	no	measurability, noninherent riskiness
15. Reduction in the quantity and quality of commercial and other services available in the area	no	measurability, deliverability
16. Reduction in employment opportunities, and increased costs of traveling to work	no	measurability, attributability, noninherent riskiness
17. Spillover of deterioration in the right-of-way during the waiting period	no	attributability, noninherent riskiness, measurability
18. Increased competition for housing among low-income households	yes	no
19. Reduction in the efficiency of community facilities through loss of patronage or overloading	yes (part)	no
20. Losses due to changes in the accessibility of various parts of the metropolitan area	no	attributability, noninherent riskiness, net negative impact
21. Losses resulting from the process of construction	yes (part)	no
22. Losses due to increased noise, ugliness, air pollution, and other adverse environmental changes	yes (part)	no

2. Compensation to owners of property for costs created by delays in the project, including: (a) Estimated losses of fair market value occurring between the time a site is officially adopted and the time the legal proceedings are made against individual property owners; and (b) Estimated costs of maintenance and repairs made between the time of final appraisal and actual taking procedures.

3. Compensation to the housing market in general to offset the impact upon rents and prices of a reduced inventory of dwellings available to low-income households. This would consist of the provision of additional dwelling units by public authorities (whether built by them or paid for by them and built by private interests) so as to counteract the increasing "tightness" of the low-income household market caused by demolition of housing units formerly available in that market. The number, size and type of units which would be made available by public authorities in comparison to the number demolished would depend on particular housing conditions in the area concerned, including the degree to which racial segregation restricted the accessibility of the existing inventory to members of racial minority groups displaced.

4. Compensation to the neighborhood in general and the property owners in areas lying outside the clearance area, including: (a) Payments for disruptions connected with the construction of the highway itself; (b) Provision of additional public facilities and services to offset facilities demolished in order to create the highway (such as public schools); and (c) Payments to adjacent or nearby owners to offset losses in value due to increased noise, ugliness, air pollution, or other adverse environmental effects.

V. The Seriousness of the Injustice Resulting from Failure to Pay Such Compensation

The fact that governments fail to pay compensation for losses they inflict upon certain residential households does not in itself indicate that present compensation policies should be changed. No social institution perfectly conforms in practice to what it should do theoretically. In many cases, society endures such behavioral imperfections because their consequences are not serious. Those consequences neither constitute a great injustice for any sizable group, nor waste significant amounts of resources that could be more effectively used, nor threaten the rest of society with dire consequences. Correcting such imperfections is often not worth the cost in terms of legislative, administrative and general public attention, even if it might produce some net economic benefits or greater justice.

Therefore, in order to assess the policy implications of government's failure to pay compensation for the losses that I have indicated are properly compensable, it is necessary to estimate roughly the nature and magnitude of that failure's consequences.

The Concentration of These Losses Among Low-Income
Minority-Group Households

The losses caused by urban highways and urban renewal for which no compensation is now paid are not spread evenly throughout the nation's population. By their very nature, they are concentrated upon the households which these public programs displace, and other households living close to the clearance areas involved. But these public programs tend to select locations where a high proportion of low-income, minority-group households reside.

This is true for four reasons. Three result from the fact that such households have a high proclivity for living in the oldest and most dilapidated housing in each metropolitan area, particularly within central cities. They do so because such housing is the least expensive available, and they are poor. Also, their choice of alternative locations —particularly in the suburbs—is restricted by ethnic discrimination in housing markets.

Urban highways and urban renewal projects are concentrated in areas where such housing is found because:

1. City planners often use these programs as a means of getting rid of the oldest and least desirable housing in the existing inventory. This is one of the explicit functions of urban renewal, which can only be done in relatively deteriorated areas.
2. The oldest housing is usually found in close proximity to central business districts, since U.S. cities (like most others) developed outward from the center. But major highways also focus on the area peripheral to central business districts because that is the optimal location for certain traffic arteries skirting or serving the downtown area.

3. Property in these areas is less expensive than elsewhere, since it is older and more dilapidated. Therefore, routing highways through such neighborhoods reduces total acquisition costs—especially since so many of the true costs of displacement are not borne by the government but by the households displaced.

4. Members of low-income ethnic minorities have not in the past been organized enough politically to oppose the routing of highways through their neighborhoods, or the location of urban renewal projects there. In contrast, higher-income residents and owners of industrial and commercial property generally have the organizational and financial capability, and the political connections, to offer strenuous opposition to the location of these public improvements in their neighborhoods. This has happened in dozens of cities across the country, from Beverly Hills to Cambridge. To at least some extent, highway and urban renewal officials responsible for selecting routes and sites are naturally motivated to follow the geographic path of least political resistance. Until recently, that path has often run directly through the lowest-income neighborhoods.

As a result of these factors, almost all urban renewal projects, and a great many inner-city segments of federally assisted highway systems, either have been constructed, or are planned for, sites and routes in low-income, minority-group neighborhoods, particularly Negro areas.

As the recent report of the National Advisory Commission on Civil Disorders clearly established, the residents of these neighborhoods include many of the poorest and most deprived citizens in the nation.[20] To concentrate the uncompensated losses resulting from urban highways and urban renewal upon them is triply unjust, as well as socially dangerous. It is triply unjust because these households are the least able to pay such costs, derive the least benefits from the projects concerned, and are already unfairly compelled by society to bear heavy burdens resulting from racial discrimination and segregation. It is socially dangerous because the residents of these areas have recently begun to react violently to their conditions of life, and may be stimulated to further violence by the injustices of society's failure to pay proper compensation for the losses described earlier

In most cities, government officials are not likely to ameliorate the loading of these uncompensated losses upon low-income minority

[20] See especially Chapters 7 and 8 in the *Report of the National Advisory Commission on Civil Disorders,* Washington, D.C., March 1968.

households by rerouting highways into wealthier areas. The "political heat" from such rerouting would be too great. Nor are they likely to shift urban renewal projects out of low-income neighborhoods, because the legal requirements for eligibility require concentrating them in such neighborhoods. Therefore, this kind of unjust concentration of losses can be avoided only by ceasing to construct such public projects altogether, or providing adequate compensation for the losses involved.

Rough Estimates of the Magnitude of Certain Key
Uncompensated Losses

But how large are these uncompensated losses? If they are relatively small, then perhaps they will not stimulate disorder. Nor will they create any more injustice than a thousand of the other essentially irremediable frictions that are inescapable in a large modern society. Thus, at least a rough quantitative analysis is crucial in assessing the policy implications of these losses.

The number of households likely to be displaced by all urban highways and urban renewal projects has been estimated by the Public Works Committee Report. About 96,400 households (including both families and individuals) will be displaced each year from 1964 through 1972. This includes all urban renewal displacement, and 82 per cent of all highway displacement (since 18 per cent of highway displacement in the past few years has been in rural areas).[21]

In past urban renewal displacement, about 27 per cent of all displaced households were individuals, and 73 per cent were families. The median-size displaced family contained 3.0 persons.[22] If these figures are applied to future urban displacement for both highways and urban renewal, then about 237,200 persons per year would be displaced by these programs. Moreover, it is reasonable to assume that at least an equal number of persons in surrounding areas are likely to be affected by some of the costs described earlier. Thus, in the eight years from 1964 to 1972, a total of about 3.8 million persons would be unfairly compelled to pay costs associated with displacement resulting from these two programs—including 1.9 million who would be directly displaced. Although this total constitutes less than 2 per cent of the entire U.S. population, it is clearly a significant number.

[21] Public Works Committee Report, pp. 260–261.
[22] William L. Slayton, "The Operations and Achievements of the Urban Renewal Program," in Wilson, *op. cit.,* p. 212, and the Census Bureau Relocation Study, p. 339.

Estimating the magnitude of uncompensated costs imposed upon these persons is much more difficult than estimating the number of persons involved. However, a few rough calculations can be made.

1. About 61,300 renter households will be displaced each year in urban areas by highways and urban renewal.[23] Displacement will compel most of these households to pay higher rents. The Census Bureau Relocation Study estimated that median rents for families (excluding individuals) were raised by relocation from $65 per month to $67 among nonwhites, and from $68 per month to $83 among whites.[24] The federal government has proposed compensating such renter families by granting a lump sum equivalent to a monthly rent subsidy over a two-year period. The monthly subsidy would equal the difference between the family's rent after relocation in standard housing and 20 per cent of its monthly income.[25] I am not familiar with the logical justification for this particular compensation formula. Perhaps a better one could be conceived. But for purposes of initial estimation, I have used it. Employing the median incomes of relocated families for 1964 reported in the Census Bureau Relocation Study, and assuming that 53 per cent of all relocated families would be nonwhite, I calculated a weighted average total compensation of $221 for each renter family displaced. I further assumed that individuals should receive the same compensation as families. (Even though individuals pay lower rents, they also have lower incomes.) Under these assumptions, the annual cost of compensating all displaced renter households for being compelled to pay higher rents would be $13.5 million.

2. About 35,100 owner-occupant households will be displaced each year in urban areas by highways and urban renewal.[26] In order to buy housing of quality comparable to that from which they were displaced (or somewhat superior), these households will have to pay a premium over the fair market values of their original homes. The Public Works Committee Report indicates the fair market values of a sample of 26,900 homes purchased by various government authorities in clearance operations were as follows: [27]

---

[23] Public Works Committee Report, pp. 260–261.
[24] Census Bureau Relocation Study, p. 345.
[25] Public Works Committee Report, pp. 141–142.
[26] *Ibid.*, pp. 260–261. [27] *Ibid.*, p. 22.

Under $6,000   29.0%
$6,000–15,000   51.5%
Over $15,000   19.5%

I assumed that the average value of all homes under $6,000 was $4,000; the average value of those from $6,000 to $15,000 was $10,500; and the average value of those over $15,000 was $20,000. These assumptions yielded a weighted average fair market value of about $10,500. The relocation study in Baltimore cited earlier indicated that the average premium paid by home owners with relatively low-valued homes was about 53 per cent.[28] But the premium for higher-value homes is likely to be a lower percentage. Therefore, I arbitrarily calculated the average premium for all future home-owner relocations at both 30 per cent and 50 per cent. The total compensation required to offset such premiums per year would thus be $110.6 million at 30 per cent, or $184.3 million at 50 per cent.

3. The destruction of 96,400 housing units per year in urban areas by highways and urban renewal will reduce the supply of housing available there, especially for low-income households. This will tend to drive up the cost of housing (either owned or rented) for thousands of households who are not displaced, as well as for those who are displaced. Owners will gain from this effect, since the values of their properties will rise. But renters will suffer, since they will have to pay more. However, it is impossible to measure accurately the increase in rents which each individual nondisplaced household will have to pay because of this supply-reduction effect. Therefore, I believe the only practical way to compensate them is to offset the drop in supply caused by displacement by building new housing available to low-income households. In "tight" housing markets, such an offset might require building one new unit for every one demolished. In "loose" housing markets, very little new construction might be required. It is extremely difficult to estimate accurately the requirements for such an offset for the nation as a whole. A crude estimate is that one new unit should be constructed for every two units demolished. If the average unit so constructed cost $15,000, then the total capital cost of building 48,200 units would be $723.0 million per year.

However, it would be possible to provide incentives for private

[28] See footnote 4.

investors to put up all of this capital. The government would have to furnish subsidies that would virtually guarantee a successful market for such housing at a reasonable rate of return. Use of a below market interest rate subsidy would not enable the very lowest-income households to afford such housing. But it would make it available to most displaced households. I have assumed the government would underwrite 6 per cent interest by borrowing money with 6.0 per cent bonds and lending it at zero per cent interest. If 40-year financing is used, this form of subsidy would involve a cash outlay of $623 per unit per year. Therefore, creation of 48,200 units per year would require an annual subsidy of $30.0 million.

It is not certain, and may even be unlikely, that the cost of thus preventing nondisplaced renters from suffering injuries from a reduction in housing supply would equal the size of the injuries they would sustain if no prevention occurred. Yet there is no simple way to estimate the size of these injuries; so I will arbitrarily assume they equal the cost of preventing them.

4. The Public Works Committee Report estimates that about 20,520 households per year to be displaced by highways will not be covered by programs providing compensation for moving costs.[29] (All households displaced by urban renewal will be covered by such programs.) The average payment for moving expenses made to those households displaced by highways who actually received such payments was about $119.[30] If this same average payment is extended to an additional 20,520 households per year, the annual cost will be $2.4 million.

The above calculations do not cover all of the uncompensated costs likely to be imposed upon residential households in urban areas by highways and urban renewal. However, I believe they encompass the largest of those uncompensated costs. The total amount required to provide compensation for those discussed above would range from $156.5 to $230.2 million per year, depending upon the size of the premium which displaced owners would have to pay to obtain comparable housing elsewhere.

Thus, *present practices in urban areas regarding residential households displaced by highways and urban renewal projects will unfairly impose uncompensated costs of at least $156.5 to $230.2 million per*

[29] Public Works Committee Report, p. 26.
[30] *Ibid.*, p. 37.

year upon approximately 237,200 displaced persons and at least another 237,200 nondisplaced persons. In my opinion, this represents injustice on a massive scale. It amounts to an uncompensated loss averaging from $812 to $1,194 per household for each of the estimated 192,800 households involved. The median income of these households is probably around $4,000 per year.[31] Therefore, the average uncompensated loss which each is compelled to suffer amounts to confiscation of from 20 to 30 per cent of one year's income. Admittedly, the calculations upon which these conclusions have been based are extremely crude. Yet I believe they are more likely to be too low than too high. How much proportionally would paying proper compensation for these costs add to the present nonconstruction costs of urban highways and urban renewal? Expected compensation for all real property—residential and nonresidential—to be acquired in urban areas under these two programs is estimated at $1.084 billion per year from 1964 to 1972 by the Public Works Committee Report.[32] This does not include moving and other relocation costs. But those costs are undoubtedly smaller than the costs of acquiring nonresidential property. So this figure is a high estimate of all costs which will be paid to displaced residential households under current compensation practices. Adding the estimated costs of paying compensation for the specific losses quantified above would increase this total by from 14 to 21 per cent per year.

VI. Conclusion

It is clear that present compensation practices related to residential households displaced by highways and urban renewal are grossly unfair. Those practices in effect shift a substantial part of the true costs of acquiring property for these improvements onto the residential households they displace and others nearby. These households are forced to bear from 14 to 21 per cent of the real costs of acquiring urban residential land for such improvements. This injustice results in forcing relatively low-income families and individuals to bear heavy financial burdens which really ought to be paid by society as a whole or by the specific beneficiaries from the improvements concerned.

Public policies which clearly cause massive injustice should be

[31] Census Bureau Relocation Study, p. 338.
[32] Public Works Committee Report, pp. 252–253.

changed as soon as possible. Therefore, I believe the authorities responsible for urban highways and urban renewal projects should immediately begin detailed exploration of practical methods for correcting these undesirable results of their past and present behavior. These methods should include finding means of calculating the magnitude of each presently uncompensated loss suffered by each household concerned, and means of either paying proper compensation for such losses, or taking actions which will offset their effects.

Some suggestions for achieving these objectives have been made in various parts of this paper. Yet the real purpose of this paper has been to indicate the nature of the problem, and to prove that it is large enough to demand immediate remedial action. If it has succeeded in this purpose, then the complex and difficult work of devising such action should soon begin.

COMMENT

by BURTON A. WEISBROD, *University of Wisconsin*

Within the last decade or so, economists concerned with government investment expenditures have focused increasing attention on the distributive effects, as well as the allocative efficiency, of projects. Anthony Downs has made a useful contribution to this continued development. We cannot concern ourselves with efficiency alone if we expect to address real-world problems and decisions. Equity considerations are also relevant to government decision making.

It is in this context that I see Downs' paper; indeed, in his opening paragraph we read that "widespread injustice" results from the failure of public policy to take nonconstruction costs of urban highways and urban renewal into account, and from the failure to compensate those who bear such costs—particularly when the costs fall upon low-income, disadvantaged persons. "Injustice" is the name of the Downs' story, and "compensation" is its hero.

Now the plot. Downs sets forth twenty-two kinds of losses imposed upon residential households that are affected either directly or indirectly by the construction activities or the accompanying displacement and relocation. He does not consider the losses imposed on non-residential units—business firms—and this strikes me as a notable omission. I suppose, however, that Downs is less concerned about effects on business on the grounds that they are less needy of assistance. I am not so certain, especially when small retail establishments are concerned.

My opening remark suggested that I am more than sympathetic to the increased emphasis on distributional equity in the evaluation of public expenditure programs. Economists' now-traditional emphasis on efficiency—Pareto optimality—and disregard of equity on the grounds of the controversiality of value judgments cannot endure if we are to address ourselves to the real world. But neither should we go too far in the opposite direction, disregarding efficiency. It is in connection with the relationship between equity and efficiency that Downs' paper is not sufficiently clear, and, in some respects, is misleading.

Throughout this truly instructive paper Downs repeatedly emphasizes his concern about justice and equity—which, he states, require the compensation of losers for a number of forms of losses resulting from urban renewal and highway construction. Although his concern in this paper is with equity alone, he implies that the interests of equity and efficiency do not conflict.

My concern is this: in providing his catalog of losses associated with these urban construction projects, Downs has tended to take a particular and partial point of view—primarily that of the low-income households affected. A general-equilibrium analysis would disclose, however, that while some of the losses are real social costs, others are income transfers. From the standpoint of the individual being hurt, this distinction is irrelevant. But not so from the standpoint of a government decision maker who is concerned with allocative efficiency as well as equity. The point, which I shall illustrate below, is that we may wish—on equity grounds—to compensate persons who are adversely affected by income-redistributional side effects of public actions, but we should recognize that redistributions are not real-resource costs and, thus, the amount of redistributions should *not* normally be counted among the project costs when the project's efficiency is being considered. If compensation for socially unwanted redistributions is to be made—and Downs argues that such redistributions can frequently be made—then a highway or renewal project should be evaluated solely in terms of its allocative efficiency (inclusive of costs of administering the compensation). Even if compensation payments are not made, it would be an error to include the "losses" from redistributional side effects among program costs without also considering the redistributional "benefits" to those who gain.[1]

[1] In the revision of his paper, subsequent to the conference, Downs recognizes the difference between allocative efficiency and distributional equity, and he acknowledges the relevance of the distinction for policy purposes. He now states explicitly that his concern in this paper is exclusively with "equity and justice,"— not with allocative efficiency—and this clarification is helpful.

The point that Downs does not make quite clear, however, is that there are two senses in which distributional equity consequences should be considered: (1) *After* a decision has been made to undertake a project; in this situation a strong case can be made (on equity grounds) for compensating the losers, especially when the losers are, to begin with, largely among the disadvantaged. But (2) *before* a decision has been made as to whether a project will be undertaken, the nature of the redistributions it would cause should be understood so that a decision can be made either to compensate the losers or to regard the absence of compensation as a disadvantage (cost) of undertaking the project. In the latter case the problem remains of devising a metric for making these distributional effects commensurable with real resource costs, in order that the over-all "grand efficiency" of the project can be assessed. [For further discussion see my "Income-Redistribution Effects and Benefit-Cost Analysis," in S. B. Chase, Jr. (ed.), *Problems in Public Expenditure Analysis,* Washington, D.C., 1968, pp. 177–209.]

There are a number of illustrations of Downs' failure to distinguish real losses from redistributions. Four of them pass all of his seven tests for determining whether compensation should be paid. These are numbered 3, 5, 18, and 19 (see Downs' Table 1). Each of these—to be analyzed shortly—is indeed a source of loss to certain individuals; but the losses to these people constitute only one side of the income-redistribution effects. Perhaps the bearers of these losses should be compensated; this is a value judgment issue, of course, though, for what it is worth, I share Downs' concern about adverse side effects upon low-income persons and especially upon low-income Negroes. Regardless of whether compensation is paid, however, the "losses" (or amount of the compensation) should not be added to real resource costs to determine total project costs. (To be sure, they should be added to determine total project *expenditures.*) For if this addition were carried out, and if decisions on whether or not to undertake a particular project were based on a comparison of such "total" expenditures with expected benefits, some investments which were actually socially efficient would fail to be undertaken. I have argued elsewhere that if compensation cannot be made, then the net welfare loss resulting from the undesired income redistribution should be taken into account by government decision makers.[2] But this net welfare loss is overstated by the dollar amount of the gross income transfer, as long as the benefits to beneficiaries count at all.

Since some of the losses discussed by Downs are real external diseconomies of urban renewal and highway projects, while others are income redistributions, further analysis of the various losses is required. I shall examine four.

"Losses Due to Home Financing Arrangements" (Downs' Loss #3). The loss identified here is the consequence of a high-risk home buyer paying a risk premium for a house (what Downs refers to as "contract method of financing"). When public authorities pay the "fair market value" for a home, Downs tells us, they often pay less than the contract purchase obligation, since the latter reflects the risk premium; hence, a loss is imposed on the purchaser.

This "loss," however, does not reflect a resource cost; it is, in effect, a lump sum tax or transfer of wealth *away* from the house occupant and *to* the seller of the contract, assuming that the occupant must eventually pay the seller the difference. Or it is a transfer in the opposite direction if the seller is unable to collect the difference. Regardless of our value judgments regarding the equity of either type

[2] *Ibid.,* pp. 178–184.

of transfer, the amount of the transfer is not properly additive to the resource costs for the purpose of assessing the economic efficiency of the project.

"Costs of Paying for Alternative Locations" (Loss #5). This loss to displaced persons results insofar as "the fair market value of low-cost homes condemned for highway projects is . . . lower than the current cost of similiar dwellings elsewhere. . . ." As I understand the point, such a difference results when there occurs a nonmarginal decrease in the housing stock of "low-cost" housing. For then the price of remaining housing can be expected to rise. Thus, if displaced home owners were paid a "fair market value" based on housing prices prior to the destruction of part of the supply, the owners would be paid less than the cost of replacement. This change in housing prices, it seems to me, is also the source of Loss #18, "Increased Competition for Housing Among Low-Income Households," for the increase in prices of low-cost housing presumably is felt by all low-income persons, not only by those being displaced.

There is no doubt that whenever urban renewal and highway construction do destroy nonmarginal portions of the low-cost housing stock, prices of the remaining stock can be expected to rise. If "fair market value" disregards this, then all occupants of low-cost housing, and all persons displaced from it, suffer a loss. Moreover, although Downs does not say so, the losses are not restricted to the low-cost housing segment; the initial increase in housing prices at the low-cost end of the spectrum will filter upward in response to the altered relative prices among housing of various quality.

These losses to low-income persons renting housing or to low-income home owners displaced by the renewal or highway project are "pecuniary" losses—transfer payments; they have their precise counterparts in pecuniary gains to owners of the remaining housing stock. We may deplore such a redistribution of income or wealth, but it should be recognized as a redistribution. We may wish to compensate the losers (and, perhaps, tax the gainers), but the allocative efficiency of the project is not affected by a decision to pay compensation. The amount of the compensation should not be added to the resource costs of construction and land acquisition for the purpose of assessing the benefit-cost relationship, although the administrative cost of making the compensation payments and collecting the taxes is relevant.

It seems clear that Downs sees the change in prices of low-cost housing as the principal concern, for nearly half of his discussion of the 22 forms of losses is devoted to this point (Losses #5 and

#18). Thus, it is quite important that the transfer payment nature of these "losses" be recognized.

A brief comment is also in order regarding Loss #19, the "Reduction in the Efficiency of Community Facilities Through Loss of Patronage or Overloading." There are really two points here—one involving the loss of patronage, the other involving overloading.

Downs illustrates the "loss of patronage" point by reference to the adverse effects on "schools, churches, stores, and other facilities near the clearance areas [that] may be forced . . . to operate at an inefficiently low scale." These losses, however, are not real costs; they represent sunk costs, which, as such, ought to be irrelevant to current investment decisions, though not to the compensation issue.

Downs illustrates "overloading" costs by the crowding in schools that may result as displaced people relocate. Such crowding or congestion—to the extent that it occurs—is a *real* external cost of urban renewal and highway construction. These costs should be counted when the efficiency of the particular project is being considered.

The real external costs of urban construction programs presumably are disregarded by public decision makers—and it is clear that such disregard is inconsistent with efficient decision making. At the same time, external real effects of urban construction are not limited to public programs. Private construction programs have similar effects, which are ignored no less by private decision makers than by government officials. When an old building is torn down to make way for a new private office or apartment building, these displaced residents also incur losses because of disruption of personal relationships (Downs' Loss #1), the need to search for substitute housing (Loss #4), moving costs (Loss #6), and many of the other forms of loss identified by Downs. Income-redistributive side effects also result from private programs, just as from their public counterparts.[3] As a result, caution is required lest constraints be placed unwittingly on public decision makers that would bias the allocation of resources away from the public sector and toward the private. In a world of second best, allocative neutrality between public and private sectors can be an elusive goal.

Finally, I would like to comment on some of Downs' empirical

---

[3] Because eminent domain proceedings cannot be used for private projects, we can assume that adverse effects on *owners* of property required for private projects will be reflected in sale prices. Nevertheless, third-party effects—of which Downs discusses quite a few—presumably are not taken into account by private decision makers any more than by government planners.

estimates and accompanying suggestions for methods of making compensation payments. He points out, helpfully, that even when compensation seems desirable, we should also investigate the cost of deciding which specific persons should be compensated, and in what amounts. In the end, the benefits of compensation—whether in terms of efficiency or justice—might be smaller than the costs.

When we come to the matter of how much compensation to pay, I cannot agree with Downs that the increased housing expenditures made by displaced persons after relocation are an adequate measure of their welfare loss and, hence, of the compensation required to offset the loss. One reason—though not the most important—is that the government's purchase of owner-occupied residences eliminates the home owner's costs of search for a buyer. I assume that at any point in time there are some home owners who would prefer larger, more expensive housing but who fail to act because of the burdens of finding a suitable buyer for their present home and searching for a new home. When such home owners sell to the government they may be expected to seek more costly housing. This represents no welfare loss at all—quite the contrary.

But there is a more serious objection to measuring the welfare loss by the increased expenditures for housing. Downs argues that urban construction activities destroy low-income housing, thereby causing its price to rise. This is another way of saying that a shift in relative prices occurs—with housing becoming more expensive. A rational consumer would adjust to the new relative prices, possibly by increasing or decreasing the amount he spends on housing. In either event he would suffer a welfare loss. The point, then, is that the welfare loss—which presumably serves as the justification for compensation payments—may be badly estimated by changes in expenditure levels.

As noted already, Downs is also concerned about the effects of a reduced low-cost housing supply or nondisplaced households, who can expect to pay increased rents. Finding it "impossible to measure accurately" the size of increases, Downs proposes that compensation take the form of a government financial stimulus to construct low-cost housing to replace the housing destroyed. I am not persuaded. It would seem better to determine the cost of implementing this proposal, and then to use this sum to make cash payments to low-income households—thus providing them with the choice of whether to use the money for housing or for something else.

Notwithstanding my lack of agreement with some of Downs' efforts at estimating the size and form of compensation payments, I wholeheartedly applaud his effort. There is a need for much more research effort to develop generalizations about which groups of people are hurt by public expenditure programs, which are benefitted, and in what amounts. Downs has made a fine start with respect to urban renewal and highway projects.

Identifying the losers from public projects would not only facilitate realization of equity objectives, but could also contribute to more efficient decisions. The failure to compensate losers can produce a vocal opposition group; in a one-man, one-vote political context this can spell long delay, if not defeat, even for highly efficient projects. For this reason the interests of equity and efficiency will sometimes be served simultaneously. Nevertheless it is important that those compensation payments that offset redistributional side effects of public programs not be viewed in the same way as those that reflect real external costs—even though their impact on the government budget is indistinguishable.

ADMINISTRATIVE DECISION MAKING AND PRICING: EXTERNALITY AND COMPENSATION ANALYSIS APPLIED

OLIVER E. WILLIAMSON

University of Pennsylvania

This paper deals with an administrative decision-making and pricing problem which, by itself, is so special as almost to be unique. It involves the prospective interference in the reception of television signals that will result from the construction of the World Trade Center in New York City. Despite its uniqueness, the issues which it poses are common to a much wider class of administrative decision-making and pricing problems. Certain of these are issues which, in the past, have been incompletely analyzed.

The theoretical area into which this prospective television interference problem falls is that of externality analysis. Three general issues are posed: First, how does the stipulation that spillover costs be explicitly recognized influence project design? Although the answer to this is straightforward, that to the next question is somewhat more subtle. Given any project design, what are the allocative efficiency implications of paying compensation for damages? Determination of the optimal policy here requires an extension of the existing theory of externalities to allow for a comparison between what Frank Michelman has referred to as "demoralization costs"[1] on the one hand and the administrative costs of paying compensation on the other. Once the relevant model has been devised, the final question becomes: Under what circumstances are demoralization costs apt to be especially great? A fourth issue, but one which is discussed only very briefly, concerns the "necessity" for centralized review of administrative decision making so as to assure sensitivity to spillover conditions.

NOTE. Research on this paper was supported by a grant from the National Science Foundation. I would like to express my appreciation for comments received from R. M. Cyert and others when I presented an earlier version of this paper at seminars at M.I.T. and the University of Wisconsin.

[1] F. I. Michelman, "Property, Utility, and Fairness: Comments on the Ethical Foundations of 'Just Compensation' Law," *Harvard Law Review*, April 1967, Vol. 80, pp. 1165–1258, especially pp. 1208–1218.

The paper is divided into four parts. First, the nature of the problem and the prevailing institutional realities are briefly summarized. The analytical framework within which to examine spillover conditions of the sort described is then developed in the second section. This framework is applied to the television interference problem in Section III. The conclusions follow in the last section.

I. The World Trade Center Problem and an Administrative Solution

On January 8, 1968, Mayor Lindsay's Advisory Task Force on CATV and Telecommunications (henceforth referred to as the Task Force)[2] submitted an interim report to the Mayor dealing with the problem of television interference posed by the construction of the World Trade Center.[3] The essence of this report, as it bears on the spillover and compensation question, is as follows:[4]

> The World Trade Center, now under construction by the Port of New York Authority, will include twin towers 1,350 feet high. The towers will be erected separately, at an interval of eight months. During part of their construction, the towers will reflect the television signals now transmitted from the Empire State Building. The reflection will . . . cause objectionable interference with television reception in parts of Manhattan and the Bronx. There are conflicting estimates on the number of television homes that will be affected—ranging between 100,000 to 600,000 homes. The interference will commence early in 1970 and will last for at least a year, and perhaps for as much as two years.
>
> When the north tower of the Center is near completion, the broadcasters will make it their regular television transmitting site, with new facilities embodying the latest developments in the state of the art. Once actual transmission from the north tower begins, the objectionable interference is expected to disappear, and the Task Force assumes that thereafter there will be improved television reception in the City.
>
> The Task Force has examined a variety of proposals for the solution

[2] The author served as an economic consultant to the Task Force. Except for references to the Task Force report, the views expressed here are my own and do not necessarily reflect those of the Task Force.

[3] A summary appears in the *New York Times* of January 13, 1968.

[4] The Mayor's Advisory Task Force on CATV and Telecommunications, *A Report on the World Trade Center and Television Reception in New York City,* January 8, 1968, pp. i–ii.

of the problem of objectionable interference. One proposal was that the height of the towers be restricted, but because the City Government can legally neither impose nor enforce such a restriction, it was not considered a solution. In the end, the Task Force found that the only possible solutions are (1) the use of directional transmitters and/or translators and (2) cable television. Neither offers a complete solution.

In particular, as the report goes on to point out, the capability to serve all of the affected areas by cable television does not presently exist and may not by the time the interference develops. In addition, subscription to cable television at prevailing New York City rates costs $60 per year. This is not a negligible expense in any case— especially for the low-income families in Harlem and the Bronx, who are among those expected to be affected. Both by reason of non-availability and cost, therefore, cable was not felt to be an adequate solution to the interference.[5]

The course of action favored by the Task Force, consistent with the legal restrictions facing the city, was that UHF directional transmitters and/or translators be used to bring a "focused" television signal into the affected areas. "The frequencies at which . . . [these] would operate would have to be in the UHF band because there are not enough unused VHF channels [the broadcasting stations already on VHF will continue to transmit at these frequencies, since most of the City and surrounding areas will not experience the objectionable interferences in question] and because directional transmitting equipment for the VHF band is too heavy and too large to mount on the Empire State Building." [6] What is involved, therefore, insofar as the affected areas are concerned, is a shift of frequencies into unused portions of the UHF band, with directional transmitting used to focus the signal and thereby avoid interference.

Unfortunately, however, there are real costs to the public entailed by this solution. For one thing, sets must be able to receive UHF. It is estimated that at the time the objectionable interference first begins 25 per cent of all the television sets in the city will lack an all-channel capability.[7] In addition, the Task Force was advised that an outdoor UHF antenna will be required to receive the directional signal, and "relatively few . . . now have one or are expected to have one by 1970."[8] The estimated cost of the antenna is $10, and for those unable to install their own an additional charge of $12.50

[5] *Ibid.*, pp. ii, 19.   [7] *Ibid.*, p. 17.
[6] *Ibid.*, p. 14.   [8] *Loc. cit.*

will be involved.[9] Thus, even assuming that set replacement is imminent for those lacking an all-channel capability, aggregate costs of from $2 million to $13 million are involved (depending on which estimate of the interference cone is used) if families living in the affected areas are to receive an acceptable directionally transmitted signal.[10]

A constitutional bar prohibits compensation in this instance,[11] which may go far to explain the neglect of these spillover costs in the initial design. As the Task Force Chairman, Fred W. Friendly, observed, the responsibility for considering these spillovers appears to have "fallen between stools." Lest this situation recur in subsequent administrative decision-making situations, he offered the following suggestions in his transmittal letter to the Mayor:[12]

> At the risk of reciting the obvious, I offer a personal observation as one new to the problems of City planning. It seems to me that those who plan a project of large scope, such as the World Trade Center, must always ask themselves how the project will affect the total City—how it will infringe upon the urban environment in which so many millions of us live and work. They must probe the implications of the project for such things as the shape of contiguous parts of the City, traffic and the movement of persons, aviation safety, and the construction of similar projects in other parts of the City—as well as for television reception throughout the City.
>
> Moreover, in a City such as ours, where the activities of its inhabitants are so complex and interdependent, there must be within

[9] *Ibid.,* p. 18.

[10] This is not an exhaustive treatment of the spillovers involved, but is sufficient at least to establish that these are nontrivial in magnitude. Omitted from the estimate are: (1) prorated set replacements costs; (2) interference that extends beyond New York City to affect reception in Connecticut; (3) the opportunity costs of time expended to arrange for the installation of an outdoor antenna (the implicit installation cost assigned to those who install their own is the commercial charge of $12.50, which is obviously an upper bound); (4) the possibility that the outdoor antenna will have usefulness that extends beyond the period of interference. Also neglected is the possibility that, once the antennas are transferred from the Empire State Building to the World Trade Center, improved reception in much of the city is expected. But perhaps 400,000 homes will find it necessary to reorient outdoor receiving antennas (at a cost of $7.50 each) at that time also (*ibid.,* p. 11). Ideally, all of these factors are taken account of in the building design; but for our purposes here only the transitional signal interference problem will be considered.

[11] This was the interpretation of counsel to the Task Force of terms in the New York State Constitution.

[12] Letter from Fred W. Friendly to the Honorable John V. Lindsay, January 8, 1968, p. 3.

our system of public administration a single focus empowered to look at and to weigh, one against the other, all the implications of a large project. It may well be that the sum total of the adverse implications will require that a project be shaped differently, or perhaps even abandoned, whereas no single negative, looked at in isolation, would have this weight. In the case of the World Trade Center, authority has fallen between so many stools—the City, the States of New York and New Jersey, and two separate agencies of the Federal Government—that no single body has been able to assume aggregate responsibility for this task.

II. Efficiency and Demoralization Costs

An efficiency framework for deciding whether to compensate spillovers is developed in Part 1 of this section. Distributional considerations are introduced in Part 2.

1. Demoralization Costs

As indicated previously, the concept of demoralization costs introduced here is attributable to Frank Michelman. It refers to secondary or adaptive responses taken by those who are made subject to what they regard as capricious redistributions. Secondary adjustments of two types are distinguished: protective and aggressive responses. Protective responses involve asset reallocations by members of society (not necessarily or exclusively the victims) who, observing the circumstances of capricious redistribution, are anxious to forestall a similar fate. These reallocations are induced solely by the failure of compensation to be paid on spillover costs experienced in a nonmarket transaction, and force owners of human or nonhuman assets to accept lower returns than they could otherwise obtain. Aggressive adaptations take the form of disruptive acts against society. In response to what is regarded as a willful destruction of asset values, the victims and their sympathizers respond in kind.[13] Although adaptive responses

---

[13] A third type of adaptive response not mentioned by Michelman might be characterized as "despondency." This is demoralization of an extreme sort: productive activity on the part of losers and their sympathizers is substantially reduced, and the responsibility for their care may be turned over to the state. For our purposes here, only adaptive responses of the protective or aggressive varieties will be treated in the text.

of both types have been noted previously,[14] they appear not to have received the systematic treatment that Michelman supplies.

Our purpose in the remainder of this part will be (1) to generalize the Michelman model and develop the allocative efficiency criteria for determining when compensation should be paid; and (2) *to make evident the reasons why, even when a project is "optimally" designed, failure to pay compensation can give rise to an allocatively inefficient result.*[15] The analysis proceeds on the assumption that allocative efficiency and income distribution objectives can be meaningfully separated, an aspect of the argument that is examined more thoroughly in Part 2 below.

Let the scale of a project be given by X; let $G(X)$ be the benefits accruing from the project less the direct costs, $S(X)$ be the assessed value of the spillover costs if compensation for the full amount of the losses is paid, $D(X)$ be the demoralization costs (which, as indicated above, are the secondary responses induced in "uncompensated losers, their sympathizers, and other observers disturbed by the thought that they themselves may be subjected to similar treatment on some other occasion")[16] that are incurred if compensation is not paid, and $A(X)$

---

[14] With regard to protective adaptive responses to uncompensated spillovers, see O. E. Williamson, D. G. Olson, and August Ralston, "Externalities, Insurance, and Disability Analysis," *Economica,* August 1967, Vol. 34, pp. 240–41, 243. In some respects, the model appearing in this paper is merely a simple extension of that developed in the paper just cited. But the present version is more complete in its statement of motivational assumptions, has greater generality, and develops the rule-making implications of the analysis in a way that was not apparent to us at the time the *Economica* paper was written. The possibility of aggressive adaptive response is referred to in a footnote by Jerome Rothenberg, *The Measurement of Social Welfare,* Englewood Cliffs, N.J., 1963, pp. 74–75, fn. 25.

[15] I neglect the potential misallocative effects which obtain in small numbers situations when spillover costs are assessed on the agent responsible for the externality but compensation is not paid. An opportunity to arrange a bargain between the parties which shifts the solution away from the social optimum (judged in allocative efficiency terms) exists in principle in these circumstances. (See J. M. Buchanan and W. C. Stubblebine, "Externality," *Economica,* November 1962, Vol. 29, pp. 381–83.) I would not judge this to be a significant factor in practice.

[16] Michelman, *op. cit.,* p. 1214. Note that what I treat as demoralization costs is different from Michelman. He also includes what might be characterized as the immediate experience of disutility borne by losers from the realization that no compensation will be paid. This is the spillover cost term in my model. Absent secondary effects (or effects of the sort mentioned in footnote 15, *supra*), there would be no necessity for compensation in order to reach an allocatively efficient result—although, of course, design size should reflect all costs, including spillovers.

FIGURE 1

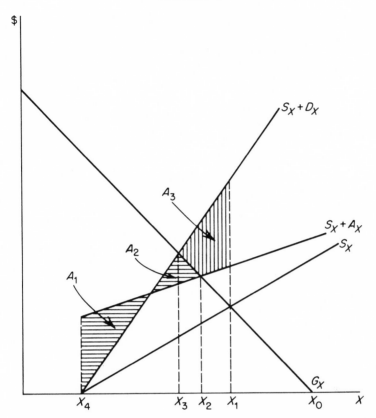

be the administrative costs of determining who is adversely affected and to what extent. Assume that if compensation is paid at all that it is paid in the exact amount of the loss experienced. Then the welfare function can be expressed as:

(1) $$V = G(X) - S(X) - \min \{D(X), A(X)\},$$

and the objective is to choose the optimum project scale so as to maximize V.[17] This can be shown graphically in Figure 1. Assuming

[17] For simplicity of exposition, and so as to focus better on the demoralization cost issue of principal concern to us here, the argument has been simplified by omitting two essential aspects of the problem. Thus, whereas we optimize only with respect to the scale of operations and the decision as to whether or not to compensate, we should also be sensitive to (1) the mode as well as the scale of operations and (2) the possibility that spillover can be efficiently mitigated by taking adaptive action. Implicit in the above formulation is an assumption that

that all costs manifest themselves as marginal rather than lump sum values, and treating $S_X + D_X$ and $S_X + A_X$ as vertical summations of the corresponding marginal terms, this can be interpreted as follows: The optimum facility size in the absence of external effects is X_0. Given the spillover costs shown by S_X, however, externalities begin to take effect at output X_4, the marginal value of which costs increase monotonically with project size. In the absence of demoralization costs, or if the administrative costs of paying compensation were negligible (and compensation were actually paid), the optimum facility size would be X_1. Given positive demoralization costs and administrative expense, however, the size must be reduced to X_2 or X_3 for the facility to be optimally designed. Whether X_2 is to be preferred over X_3 depends on the comparison of over-all net gain, which can be judged by the reference to the areas designated A_1 and A_2.[18] If A_1

the system has been optimized in both of these latter two respects. Although the decision of whether or not to compensate sets up incentives such that adjustment with respect to one of these dimensions will be induced, intervention is necessary to secure simultaneous satisfaction with respect to both (assuming that bilateral bargaining is not feasible).

Thus, if compensation is not to be paid, those who sustain the spillover will have the incentive to adapt against it. Expressing adaptation expense as Z, their objective, for any given value of X, is to choose Z so as to minimize $S'(X, Z) + Z$, where $\partial S'/\partial Z < 0$. If compensation is to be paid, and if spillover varies with the mode as well as the scale of operations, those who are responsible for the project will naturally be sensitive to both mode and scale in its design. In the absence of instructions to the contrary, however (or unless social welfare considerations reliably prevail), this incentive to select the optimal mode vanishes if compensation is not required. Those who are responsible for the spillover may be expected to choose instead the mode that maximized direct net benefits alone: "excessive" spillover costs are thus apt to be generated. Likewise, the decision to pay compensation attenuates the incentive of those who experience the spillover to adapt efficiently against it. A potential breakdown of incentives thus exists whichever way the compensation decision is made. It should therefore be stipulated that (1) if compensation is to be paid, damages will be assessed in the amount necessary to restore wealth to a *status quo ex ante* condition "as if" adaptation against spillover has been made, and (2) if compensation is not to be paid, those who are imposing the externality will be required to select the optimal mode anyway.

For a discussion of these issues in the context of compensation for accidents, see Williamson, Olson, and Ralston, *op. cit.*, pp. 237–39. Also see Ronald Coase, "The Problem of Social Cost," *Journal of Law and Economics,* October 1960, Vol. 3, pp. 41–42.

[18] The total net benefit of operating at X_2 and paying compensation is given by the area between G_X and $S_X + A_X$ from the origin to X_2. The total net benefit of operating at X_3 and not paying compensation is given by the area between G_X and $S_X + D_X$ from the origin to X_3.

To see that A_1 and A_2 are the relevant areas, let A_2' be that part of the shaded area A_2 to the left of X_3 and A_2'' be that part of A_2 to the right of X_3. Now if exceeds A_2, compensation should not (on allocative-efficiency grounds) be paid and project size should be limited to X_3. If instead A_1 is less than A_2, compensation should be paid and the facility should be extended to size X_2. (Obviously if the curve $S_X + D_X$ and the curve $S_X + A_X$ are nonintersecting over the relevant region, one always selects the lower of the curves as the appropriate one for determining optimum facility size, and compensates or not accordingly.)

Note that if the facility is mistakenly designed to size X_1 (or larger), the area A_3 (or its counterpart if X exceeds X_1) also needs to be considered in making the decision on whether or not to compensate. The criterion here is compensate if $A_2 + A_3$ is greater than A_1, otherwise not. More generally, the following proposition is advanced: whatever the facility size, if the redistributive consequences of an activity can be expected to induce secondary responses, failure to allow for such adaptations can lead to an allocatively inefficient compensation policy. Contrast this with the more common proposition that once facility size is fixed and its immediate spillover consequences established, the question of whether or not to compensate involves only equity but not allocative considerations. But clearly more than a simple transfer payment is involved if nontrivial administrative costs will be incurred in paying compensation, and/or if protective or aggressive adaptive responses to noncompensation are reasonably probable.[19]

It might be protested that this is all well and good, but that it is equity, not efficiency, that really matters. The vital issue is "what

the facility were built to size X_3, the region A_1 would represent costs which could be avoided by not paying compensation, while the area A_2' would be avoidable costs if compensation were paid. All other costs are the same, whatever the compensation decision. Since the benefits, given by the area under G_X from the origin to X_3, are identical in both cases, the choice rests on the relation of A_1 to A_2': if A_2' is greater than A_1 compensate, otherwise not.

The analysis is incomplete, however, because if the decision is made to compensate, the optimal size is X_2 not X_3. If the size of the facility is extended from X_3 to X_2 under the stipulation that compensation will be paid, the additional net benefit A_2'' will be realized. Thus the complete criterion is: if $A_2(= A_2' + A_2'')$ is greater than A_1 operate at X_2 and compensate; otherwise operate at X_3 and do not compensate.

[19] Uncompensated pecuniary spillovers might also give rise to secondary adaptive responses which have allocative effects. Relevant in this connection is Burton Weisbrod's comment on Anthony Downs' paper. Weisbrod points out that many of the spillovers identified by Downs are pecuniary but not real. This may be correct in terms of immediate consequences. But despite his principal emphasis on fairness rather than efficiency, Downs is expressly concerned that noncompensation may induce aggressive adaptive responses—which is an efficiency aspect of the problem.

ought to be done?"; the above is merely a digression. But this misses the point. What ought to be done cannot be judged without considering the cost implications. Otherwise, presumably, we would always compensate—a rule which, manifestly, society has rejected. An analytical framework is evidently needed to explain this condition. The above analysis organizes the issues in a way which, if it does not fully dispose of the compensation question, at least reveals the trade-offs.

The model can be extended to allow for the possibility of "imperfect" compensation. Thus, let Y be the degree of precision in compensation attempted (where, say, Y is the coefficient of variation in compensation paid, and a value of $Y = 0$ reflects exact compensation in the precise amount of the damage inflicted).[20] Obviously, the administrative cost of ascertaining compensation increases as Y decreases. It also seems plausible to assume that demoralization costs are an increasing function of Y—either because of risk aversion or because, when precise compensation is paid, it is evident that society is earnestly concerned over redressing damages imposed. Both protective secondary investments and aggressive secondary responses are therefore apt to be an increasing function of Y. Thus the model becomes

$$(2) \qquad V = G(X) - S(X) - [D(X, Y) + A(X, Y)],$$

and the purpose now is to select X and Y optimally so as to obtain an allocatively efficient solution. The maximization is again straightforward, the difference being that X and Y are now determined simultaneously, whereas previously Y was arbitrarily set equal to zero. In the absence of relatively large fixed administrative expenses (expressed in relation to the extent of demoralization anticipated if no compensation is paid), compensation (however imperfect) would become usual on every occasion of spillover. Also note that only if D and A are additively separable in X and Y will the optimum design size always be independent of the degree of precision in compensation attempted.

Consider now the circumstances under which the demoralization costs resulting from the noncompensation of losses occasioned by deliberate social action are apt to be especially great. Assuming that individuals or groups are wealth maximizers, the general proposition

---

[20] Note that a value of Y greater than zero does not imply an undercompensation bias. It merely reflects a willingness to accept greater variance in the estimate of losses.

is this: individuals or groups who (a) either bear or observe the conditions of spillover and (b) can reasonably expect that they will be similarly disadvantaged in the future have an incentive to adapt in ways that are calculated to discourage the repetition or attenuate the effects of similar administrative decisions made subsequently. Within this framework, the following criteria are advanced as a basis by which to judge when to compensate. *Ceteris paribus,* demoralization costs increase, and thus the case for compensation becomes stronger, as any of the following happen.[21]

1. THE PURPOSIVENESS OF THE ACT AND THE FORESEEABIL-
ITY OF ITS CONSEQUENCES INCREASES. The criterion is based on the assumption that disadvantaged individuals are apt to feel especially aggrieved, and hence most apt to adapt against the possibility of being made to bear such spillover costs at some future date, if it can reasonably be inferred that they are being deliberately exploited. The calculated choice to impose spillover costs thus has special counterproductive potency. Unanticipated spillovers, by contrast, are regarded as essentially random occurrences. The individuals experiencing such spillovers have less cause for believing that they are being discriminated against, and hence have less incentive to forestall subsequent spillovers by adapting against such contingencies.

2. THE MORE EVIDENT IT IS THAT THE ADMINISTRATIVE
COSTS OF SECURING SETTLEMENT ARE LOW. The assumption here is that disadvantaged individuals have an appreciation for the real costs that would be imposed on the state by the stipulation that all spillovers, however trifling, be compensated. When it is evident, however, that the administrative costs of securing settlement are low, failure to pay compensation encourages those who bear the spillover

---

[21] The first five criteria are substantially those proposed by Michelman (*op. cit.,* pp. 1217–18, 1223). The rationale supplied in each case is mine.

Note that Peter Steiner, in his comment on this paper, contends that "These criteria are not derived from the theory of demoralization costs." This is true. But demoralization cost theory is merely intended as a means by which to organize the issues and relate this important concept to conventional externality theory. The criteria for judging when demoralization costs are apt to be especially great are all derivable from the simple (wealth maximizing) proposition that people are more prone to adapt when the subjective probability of otherwise being exploited is perceived to be high. This is, I assume, at least reasonable if not obvious.

to believe that their property rights have little standing. Hence they are inclined to adapt (protectively or aggressively) accordingly.[22]

3. THE GREATER THE HARM EXPERIENCED. When, either individually or collectively, the harm experienced is large, individuals and groups who bear the spillover are apt to regard the case for compensation to be especially great. The assumption of decreasing marginal utility of money would tend to support claims of compensation whenever any individual experiences substantial harm. Spillovers that are individually small but collectively great, especially if they fall disproportionately on a well-defined minority group in the population, tend to encourage the view that the group's interests are being subordinated under the prevailing administrative decision-making process. Hence the inclination to adapt.

4. THE LOWER THE "SIMPLE" NET GAINS [G(X)] THAT THE PROJECT PRODUCES. The approval of projects for which the "simple" net gain is small suggests that either special interests or extra-economic considerations have been accorded great weight. Had the relevant spillover costs been included, the project might well have failed to pass the usual economic tests. Again, the apparent subordination of the interests of disadvantaged parties is what stimulates the adaptive responses.[23]

5. THE LESS EXTENSIVE IS THE PARTICIPATION IN THE BENEFITS OF THE PROJECT BY THOSE WHO EXPERIENCE THE EXTERNALITY. Circumstances for which evident reciprocities between burden and benefit are lacking are ones which, in the absence of compensation, suggest exploitation of the disadvantaged parties. Adaptive

---

[22] Even if adaptive responses by individuals were independent of the administrative costs of settling claims, the case for compensation becomes stronger as administrative costs decline. This follows directly from an examination of equation 1 and Figure 1 above.

[23] Kenneth Arrow raised a question at the conference over this criterion. He suggested that disadvantaged parties might feel especially aggrieved if, for a project that had enormous net gains (and hence, presumably, the capacity easily to pay existed), compensation was refused. The point has merit and deserves to be investigated. Possibly the relationship between compensation and "simple" net gains is U-shaped.

An additional justification for requiring compensation for marginal projects is that such a rule would serve to discourage the uneconomic expenditure of society's resources. Whatever the merits of this judgment, it does not bear directly on the demoralization question per se.

responses calculated to avoid such results in the future are thus encouraged.

6. THE GREATER THE EXTENT TO WHICH THE DISADVAN-
TAGED GROUP HAS PRE-EXISTING GRIEVANCES (BY REASON
OF HAVING BEEN MADE TO BEAR SPILLOVER COSTS IN THE
PAST) AGAINST THE STATE.[24] This criterion moves beyond the
consideration of the project taken by itself to consider expected net
consequences over a series of programs. A group that is disadvantaged
in one case, favored in another, unaffected in a third instance, etc.,
may regard the administrative decision-making calculus as one which,
in a composite sense, is "fair." Groups, however, who find themselves systematically disadvantaged have a strong incentive to reduce
their exposure to exploitation.

Since it is costly to apply the above analysis in individual cases to
determine whether, on *every* occasion of spillover, demoralization costs
are greater than or less than settlement costs, it may be efficient to
develop some crude organizing principles ("rules of thumb"). One
that is commonly recognized by the law is that whenever there is
physical invasion, however small the cost, compensation shall be
paid.[25] The reasoning here, presumably, is that the physical taking of
property represents a general threat to secure expectations. Hence,
however trifling the infringement, compensation is paid. A second
rule to deal with situations (such as the case examined above) where
physical invasion is absent might involve a threshold specification.
Whenever the expected aggregate loss or whenever any individual loss
exceeds some specified set of values, the spillover will have its demoralization and administrative costs evaluated. A third would be to
give special consideration to compensation in cases involving previously disadvantaged and aggrieved parties. (Note, however, that it is
probably easier for administrators than for the courts to put such a
rule into effect. For continuing programs involving high exposure to

---

[24] With respect to each criterion, but perhaps especially criterion 6, one would
expect, *ceteris paribus,* that the probability of aggressive reaction would vary
directly with the degree to which the affected group perceives that the community
is sympathetic to its grievances; grievances that have "legitimacy" in this sense
will, if acted upon, be less vigorously repressed by the exercise of police powers
by the state. Such grievances, eventually, may lead to a legislative correction if
the violation of rights persists.

[25] As Michelman points out, the courts "*never* deny compensation for a
physical takeover. . . . This may be true although the invasion is practically
trifling from the owner's point of view: a marginally encroaching sidewalk, for
example" (*op. cit.,* pp. 1184–85).

loss of previously disadvantaged parties, legislative action to provide explicitly for compensation may be warranted.[26]) Doubtlessly other "efficient" rules would emerge as experience in implementing the model proposed is accumulated.

2. *Distributional Considerations*

Objections to analyses of the above type can and have been made on grounds that it is inappropriate to separate allocative efficiency from income distribution.[27] This is fundamentally correct. In every allocative efficiency judgment for which a redistribution is involved there exists an implicit distributional weighting: usually, that the benefits and costs are weighted equally "to whomsoever they may accrue." This might seem to be an insufficiently refined assumption, especially if one is inclined to the view that "The determination of prevailing values for a given community . . . is a proper and necessary task for the economist."[28] Unfortunately, however, the procedures by which the economist is expected to respond to this injunction and operate upon it are not provided.[29] It is, perhaps, instructive to note that, immediately following the statement quoted above, Bergson goes on to state that the necessary value-determination process "is a project which I shall not undertake here."[30]

Lacking a specification of community values, can a case for the above analysis, with its emphasis on allocative efficiency, nevertheless be made? At least three arguments suggest themselves. First, for

[26] Michelman also recognizes the difficulties that the courts experience with such cases, and suggests that legislative remedies may be appropriate where the conditions of such spillover occur repeatedly (*op. cit.,* pp. 1254–56).

[27] See, for example, Rothenberg, *op. cit.,* pp. 100–103, and references cited therein.

[28] Abram Bergson, "A Reformulation of Certain Aspects of Welfare Economics," *Quarterly Journal of Economics,* February 1938, Vol. 52, p. 323.

[29] An approach that has recently been proposed that has promise is the treatment of distributional questions at a rule-making (constitutional) level. On this see J. M. Buchanan and Gordon Tullock, *The Calculus of Consent,* Ann Arbor, Michigan, 1963, Ch. 6; Harvey Leibenstein, "Long-run Welfare Criteria," in Julius Margolis (ed.), *The Public Economy of Urban Communities,* Baltimore, Maryland, 1965, pp. 39–51; Michelman, *op. cit.,* 1218–24. Conceivably the law can evolve appropriate rules by framing the distributional issue in a repeated play context of this sort, but for this one would expect that the allocative efficiency framework developed above can be used as input to such a process. Indeed, as Michelman points out, "we shall find ourselves asking much the same questions to determine whether a compensability decision is fair as were suggested by the [allocative efficiency] approach" (*op. cit.,* p. 1223).

[30] Bergson, *op. cit.,* p. 323.

purposes of illustrating the *general* properties of the model, any distributional assumption will do. (For example, the functions and curves could be interpreted as ones which already embed the appropriate distributional weights.) The same types of implications with respect to a treatment of externalities will obtain.[31] Second, if one assumes that the political process has already "solved" the distributional problem, one might take the position that, subject to the condition that the movements involved are small, neutrality at the margin is appropriate.

Third, whether distribution is "correct" or not, it may be impolitic to employ any valuation scheme other than one which, in the first instance at least, weights benefits and losses equally. It should be noted, however, that to proceed in this way does not, if demoralization costs are introduced in the way suggested above, suppress distributional considerations entirely. Thus whether a program or set of rules is apt to have serious secondary consequences is a function of *who* the affected parties are. Hence, even within what is conceived of as an allocative efficiency framework, distributional considerations can manifest themselves in at least a limited way.

If, as seems plausible, the very rich are the ones most apt to make asset reallocations in response to uncompensated spillovers, while the poor will be most ready to engage in aggressive behavior, the broad middle class may be the group least compensated under these rules. This may appear inequitable, and a remedy therefore indicated. Such, however, moves outside the allocative efficiency framework herein developed. Constitutional questions of fairness are involved.

III. Application to the World Trade Center

My first purpose will be to indicate what appear to be the properties of the World Trade Center design under the prevailing institutional arrangements. Given this design (and assuming away for the moment the constitutional bar to compensation), the proposed criteria by which to judge when demoralization costs are apt to be especially great are successively applied to the television interference problem. Finally, the centralized versus decentralized decision-making problem is briefly considered.

---

[31] An exception might be noted. If, under the prevailing social value system, no uncompensated spillovers are admissible, the demoralization cost expression vanishes. Here, optimality always occurs at X_2 (where $S_X + A_X$ intersects G_X), and compensation is always paid.

1. The World Trade Center Design

Inasmuch as the television interference effects (and possible other height-related spillovers—e.g., air traffic interference) apparently were not considered when the Center was designed, the value of X_0 on Figure 1 presumably reflects the design height selected of 1,350 feet. The value of X_4 represents the height at which interference first becomes significant, namely 900 feet, and X_2 or X_3 is the optimal facility size.[32] Which of these two values is allocatively the most efficient depends on a comparison of administrative and demoralization costs. Are there genuine secondary effects to be concerned over, and are the administrative costs of paying compensation too great as to justify bearing them?[33]

2. The Criteria Applied

Consider criterion 1: the purposiveness of the act and the foreseeability of its consequences. There is no question that the World Trade

[32] "There is general agreement that if the towers were to rise no higher [than 900 feet] there would be no objectionable interference with television reception in New York City" (Task Force, op. cit., p. 12). There is at least a possibility that were the Port Authority even now presented with the requirement that compensation be paid for interference created, redesign might still occur—although this is perhaps doubtful. Inasmuch as the estimated cost of the World Wide Trade Center is $575 million (ibid., p. 4), redesign might be prohibitively expensive.

[33] Peter Steiner, in his comment on this paper, poses the question: Is the concept of demoralization costs operational? My numerous references to Michelman's fundamental examination of this question (op. cit.) did not, apparently, satisfy him. The answer that emerges from my reading of Michelman is that demoralization costs have long played an implicit role in the development of compensation law, but that the law has suffered from the lack of an explication of this concept. Michelman's purpose and mine is to correct this condition by providing the relevant organizing framework.

That demoralization costs can be interpreted as an extension to conventional externality analysis must be regarded as a distinct gain. Although the economics profession long questioned the operationality and empirical significance of the externalities concept, I would judge that this has been resolved affirmatively in both respects. Recent refinements and applications of the theory have contributed to this result. Subsequent refinement and experience with the demoralization cost concept should improve its power also.

Even without these, and confining attention to the papers reported in this volume, the concept has relevance that extends beyond the World Trade Center situation. It can also be brought to bear on the uncompensated urban highway and urban renewal spillovers examined by Downs.

Center construction is deliberate, and even if only at a late stage the extent of its spillover effects became apparent, design changes might still have been made—albeit that the city could not itself require these. Thus criterion 1 is satisfied in large measure.

Criterion 2 is concerned with the administrative costs of securing settlement. Is it realistic to expect in this instance that the identity of and effect on disadvantaged parties can be determined at low cost? With respect to the identity question, it must be conceded that genuine differences exist. Two engineering studies sponsored by the Port Authority indicate that the cone of objectionable interference will be 3 to 5 degrees wide, while a third study places the cone at 30 degrees. Which of these is more nearly correct will obviously affect the optimal design. But it should nevertheless be possible to establish objectively— e.g., with a test set brought into each neighborhood—the extent of interference experienced *ex post*. Such an approach would be consistent with the objective observer standard proposed by Michelman.[34] Also, it should be noted, *precise* satisfaction of every claim is not necessary for compensation to be effective. A combination of an objective test of interference with an "average" compensation payment would seem in this instance sufficient to drive administrative costs to relatively low levels.[35]

With respect to criterion 3, the extent of harm experienced, there is ample reason for regarding a spillover of from $2 million to $13 million as serious. As the Task Force puts it "there is no doubt that the television set is a constant source of professional entertainment and a constant window on the significant events that occur in the nation and throughout the world. This is particularly true for those who live in the deprived sections of northern Manhattan and the Bronx, which will lie directly in the path of the cone of objectionable interference caused by the construction of the twin towers of the World

[34] Michelman's objective observer loss-estimation standard is that which we would "impute to ordinarily cognizant and sensitive members of society" (*op. cit.*, pp. 1215–16). Otherwise estimation is apt to degenerate into a gaming relationship.

[35] As the extended version of the model makes clear, compensation is better regarded as a matter of precision than in either-or terms. As indicated in the text, if the administrative expense of paying compensation is subject to a large fixed cost, optimal compensation may be to pay nothing; but generally, where significant secondary responses can be anticipated, compensation to victims in an amount equal to the expected value of the loss would appear indicated. The degree of precision attempted turns not on the mean compensation paid, but on the deviation in the value of actual loss from estimated.

Trade Center."[36] Those who experience the interference will therefore make the expenditures necessary to receive the directional UHF signals or, lacking resources, will be denied an important source of satisfaction.[37]

Criterion 4 deals with the intrinsic merit of the project. There are those who insist that the World Trade Center is even lacking in this respect. I will assume for our purposes here, however, that it qualifies as a project having positive net gains at design size X_0—at least if spillover costs are neglected.

The primary objectives specified by the Port Authority for the design of the Trade Center are relevant in considering criterion 5. These are: "that the Center serve as a symbol and focus for the interest and involvement of the Port of New York in international trade and commerce; that the Center meet the highest aesthetic standards and be a pleasure to eye and spirit; and that the Center provide ten million square feet of rentable exhibition and office space."[38] Families living in Harlem and the Bronx are not obviously the principal beneficiaries of such an undertaking. Such indirect employment benefits as result would probably obtain for any building providing ten million square feet of useful space. One must conclude that evident reciprocities between burden and benefit are missing.

Finally consider criterion 6—whether substantial numbers of those required to bear the spillover costs have what they regard as pre-existing grievances against society, where these have a recognized legitimacy. Families living in the deprived neighborhoods of Harlem and the Bronx almost certainly fulfill the conditions of this criterion.

With the single exception of criterion 4, and possibly even here as well, a consistent reading is obtained on each of the criteria: positive demoralization costs, possibly nontrivial in magnitude, are to be expected if compensation is not paid. Against this must be weighed the administrative costs of paying compensation—which, in this instance, are evidently low. The crude quantitative estimate that

---

[36] Task Force Report, *op. cit.*, p. 25.

[37] Conceivably the cost of bearing the spillover will be shifted back on the landlords, who will either install the necessary antenna or experience reduced rentals. This, however, I find doubtful. Landlords must be anxious to forestall relocation by their tenants for this to transpire. For one thing, rent controls in New York City may cause landlords to welcome rather than resist decisions to relocate. Furthermore, even in the absence of this issue, threats to relocate may not be viable. The interference is a transitory phenomenon; relocation is an expensive response to it.

[38] Task Force Report, *op. cit.*, p. 3.

emerges, given the apparent order of magnitude difference that separates these two factors, is that compensation is clearly indicated—at least at the design size of 1,350 feet.[39] Whether compensation would continue to be necessary were the building redesigned to take explicit account of the interference costs is unclear. But compensation here involves more than a simple transfer: allocative efficiency considerations reinforce equity arguments in its favor.

Thus, although secondary responses of the protective variety are probably not to be expected in this instance (coaxial cable service may not be available or sufficiently attractive, and this may substantially exhaust the range of "long-term," anticipatory, defensive investment responses to TV signal interference of the type described), the expressed social discontent (aggressive secondary response) is less easy to dismiss. The evidently low administrative expenses that would be incurred in paying compensation would appear to be well below the expected value of the demoralization costs of this reactive type.

3. Centralization versus Decentralization

The inability of the Task Force to require either redesign of the World Trade Center or compensation for damages caused its chairman to propose an alternative administrative decision-making procedure: "there must be within our system of public administration a single focus empowered to look at and to weigh, one against the other, all the implications of a large project." Conceivably the prevailing political and legal realities make this the only feasible solution. The relatively high costs of moving to a centralized decision-making system of this sort should, however, be appreciated.[40]

It could be argued, of course, that the situation described above is not typical. It might be claimed, for example, that ordinarily, when-

[39] Although Steiner agrees with my evaluation that compensation should be paid under the criteria proposed, he indicates that "for some other list, compensation should not be paid." Agreed. Suppose, for example, each of the criteria were replaced by its opposite. The judgment on compensation would then be reversed. But unless Steiner proposes such a change, which I find doubtful, or is explicit on other criteria he has in mind, his observation lacks operational significance.

[40] Some of these are discussed in my "Hierarchical Control and Optimum Firm Size," *Journal of Political Economy,* April 1967, Vol. 75, pp. 123–38. See also Gerald Sirkin, *The Visible Hand: The Fundamentals of Economic Planning,* New York, 1968, Chap. 4.

ever social goals and bureaucratic goals are in conflict, differences are resolved in favor of social goals. But this requires stewardship behavior of an unusual sort. I suggest that it is more realistic instead to recognize that there exists a "bureaucratic cost" counterpart for the term private cost in the usual social cost versus private cost distinction. To proceed on the supposition that spillover costs for which no compensation is required will, nevertheless, be fully reflected in the decision making of public or quasi-public agencies appears, at the very least, to be unnecessarily hazardous.

The preferred economic solution to this (and similar) administrative decision-making problems is to supply the agency with the relevant set of pricing signals. The stipulation that compensation must be paid if demoralization costs can reasonably be expected to exceed the administrative costs of paying compensation should tend to induce *both* superior designs *and* a preferred mix of programs. The above analysis is thus but another example of how, under the appropriate institutional rules, the use of prices can be made to help solve complex economic issues in a decentralized way.[41]

IV. Conclusions

Four principal conclusions emerge. First, with respect to the particular spillover condition examined above, allocative efficiency considerations would appear to support the payment of compensation for the prospective television interference that will result from the World Trade Center construction. This judgment is reinforced by appeals to equity. The failure of compensation to be required in circumstances of this sort strongly suggests that the social decision-making apparatus is defective.

Second, evaluating the efficiency implications of spillovers of the sort considered above requires that the concept of externalities be expanded to include costs which take the form of secondary adaptive responses (demoralization costs). These need to be weighed against the administrative costs of paying compensation. The latter costs are apt to be great, and hence compensation may be prohibitively expensive, if it is stipulated that, whenever compensation is made, damages

---

[41] The tax implications of this compensation argument would presumably require that it be qualified. An examination of this question is beyond the scope of the present paper.

shall be ascertained exactly. However allowing as we have for "imperfect" compensation restores the likelihood that, absent large fixed administrative expenses, allocative efficiency will support compensation whenever nontrivial secondary responses to spillover conditions are reasonably probable.

Third, although the emphasis throughout has been on allocative efficiency, one should not suppose that an essential conflict with equity exists. As Michelman has observed, the same general criteria as are invoked under an allocative efficiency standard will ordinarily be operative in reaching an equity judgment. This applies not merely to the question of whether to compensate but also to the matter of precision: one would expect that the conditions under which demoralization costs are especially sensitive to the exactitude of compensation would also be ones for which equity demands precision.

Finally, an issue that has been exposed but incompletely examined in the above discussion warrants acknowledgement. This concerns the long-run rule-making implications of the theory, which is the principal interest of the law. To evaluate each case separately would clearly have serious administrative cost implications and would subject decision makers to excessive uncertainty. The law is therefore concerned with the design of policies to deal effectively with general classes of damage exposure in the long-run. If, as appears to be the case, allocative efficiency analysis has reached a higher stage of development than has the evaluation of equity, and if, in addition, the conflict between these two criteria in individual cases is rarely substantial, demoralization cost analysis would appear to have special relevance for the rule-making process. But note in this connection that if interdependencies between rules are significant, effective rule making may require a pre-ordering or simultaneous determination of issues. Development of this aspect of the argument, however, is beyond the scope of this paper.

COMMENT

by PETER O. STEINER, *University of Michigan*

I am flattered by the fact that Williamson, apparently in response to my discussion, has both shortened his paper and revised it in such a way that my major criticisms of his original paper are no longer relevant. I am embarrassed only by the fact that what remains of my discussion paper is so short as to suggest either sloth or acquiescence on my part. The five numbered paragraphs immediately below are what is left of my original comment. Since Williamson chooses to discuss my comments (in his footnotes 33 and 39), I will respond briefly in the last two paragraphs.

(1) I have contemplated the phenomenon known as Oliver Williamson for some time and offer the hypothesis that he is not an individual at all, but rather a committee. This is consistent with his enormous productivity over the last several years, most of which is superb, and also, less flatteringly, with this paper. Here he brings, again with enormous energy and diligence, a large body of theory to bear on the interference caused to the reception of television signals by the construction of the World Trade Center. My complaint is that his appetite has run somewhat ahead of his digestion—that the real data about the policy questions does not support as much apparatus as he brings to bear on them, nor (conversely) is the theory sufficiently original or powerful to be a major contribution in its own right.

(2) The central fact reported by Mayor Lindsay's task force appears to be that the Port of New York Authority is designing and building two towers which will cause massive TV interference to several hundred thousand homes for two years. It is clear that the Authority made its decision without contemplating this adverse effect. Williamson suggests that it is possible (and perhaps likely) that had the Authority been obliged either to avoid the damage or compensate those damaged, it would have redesigned its facility.

(3) The example is interesting in several ways. It provides illustration of the well-known theorem that if a producer does not pay the marginal cost of a resource (in this case, altitude), he is likely to overuse it. Second, it reminds us that the mere fact that the producer

is a public agency provides no protection against a divergence between "private" (i.e., producer's) and social costs. Third, it does so with particular force since the damaged parties are mainly members of relatively underprivileged groups in our society, groups whom we are particularly reluctant to disadvantage further.

(4) All of this is both useful and suggestive. Williamson's interest in the case is twofold. First, as a vehicle for insightful application of Michelman's concept of demoralization cost—a particular form of externality-induced response that may be socially costly. I found the concept of substantial interest in and of itself, but not especially helpful in discussing the World Trade Center. The reason is evident in the maximizing equation. In equation 1 the objective function is given as $V = G(X) - S(X) - \min \{D(X), A(X)\}$. But the essence of the criticism of the Port of New York Authority is not its neglect of the relative sizes of demoralization costs, $D(X)$, compared to the administrative costs of compensation, $A(X)$, but rather its neglect of $S(X)$, the spillover cost. Nothing in the case, as developed, measures or identifies the demoralization costs or gives a clue as to whether this is an operational concept.

(5) Williamson's second major interest is in suggesting rules for when compensation *should* be paid. To the five criteria suggested by Michelman, he adds a sixth. My objection here is not to this list of normative judgments, but to Williamson's apparent failure to realize that it is wholly self-contained. Given this, it follows that compensation ought to be paid in the World Trade Center situation. For some other list, compensation should not be paid. These criteria are not derived from the theory, nor do they enrich it. Williamson has neglected to integrate them into his analysis.

My query in paragraph 4 is not whether demoralization cost is an operational concept, but whether the analysis of the World Trade Center case sheds any light on the operationality of the concept. I believe Williamson has made a contribution in extending and refining Michelman's rather loose concept. Granting this, does his review of the World Trade Center case attempt to measure the size of the demoralization cost, or merely illustrate anecdotally the concept? I continue to believe it is the latter.

My query in paragraph 5 seems so clearly stated that I am astounded that Williamson misses the point in his footnote 39. Suppose I were to say that compensation should be paid whenever (a) those damaged had legally enforceable claims, or (b) had incomes that were below the national average. These are value judgments that are not without support in our society, but they do not derive from the Michelman-Williamson analysis. Thus they provide an answer to the compensation question that is independent of that analysis. The same is true of Williamson's six criteria.

AN EFFICIENCY BASIS
FOR FEDERAL FISCAL EQUALIZATION

JAMES M. BUCHANAN
Virginia Polytechnic Institute

AND

RICHARD E. WAGNER
Tulane University

Discussions of the "financial crisis" faced by state and local governments in the United States are continuing, and pressures mount for some form of remedial action. Various bloc-grant and revenue-sharing proposals began to command increasing attention in the mid-1960's. Almost all of the suggested bloc-grant schemes involve the transfer of tax revenues from the federal to the state-local governments with some provision made for equalizing adjustments in state shares.[1]

Strong arguments can be mustered to support tax sharing in a federalist system. In its basic form, however, tax sharing is explicitly nonequalizing as among separate states. We shall neglect this here; our paper is limited to an examination of possible efficiency bases for the introduction of *equalizing* elements into a program of bloc or unconditional grants. Several economists, including one of the authors, have advanced equity arguments to support fiscal equalization. But we propose also to leave this set of issues out of this discussion. Our

NOTE. Wagner's research was supported by a grant from the Relm Foundation.

[1] The "Heller-Pechman scheme" is the most familiar of the various plans, especially among economists, although the Pechman Task Force Report in which it was initially outlined was never officially released. Specific proposals are contained in Walter H. Heller, "Strengthening the Fiscal Base of our Federalism," in his *New Dimensions of Political Economy*, New York, 1966, pp. 117–72; and Joseph A. Pechman, "Financing State and Local Government," *Proceedings of a Symposium on Federal Taxation*, New York, 1965, pp. 71–85. Other proposals, all of which are similar in essential respects, are associated with the names of Congressman William Brock, Secretary of Defense Melvin Laird, and Senators Charles Goodell and Jacob Javits. The Republican Coordinating Committee has also proposed a broadly similar policy scheme.

analysis is confined solely to efficiency considerations relative to equalization.

In Section I, the previous discussion on efficiency and equalization is selectively and briefly reviewed. Section II analyzes fiscal equalization under the assumption that state and local governments provide purely public or collective goods, and that they do so efficiently. Section III drops the assumption of purely public nature of government-provided goods and introduces impure public goods. This change is demonstrated to have significant implications for the analysis and the ultimate set of policy conclusions. Section IV specifically examines some of the more relevant policy suggestions that emerge from the analysis.

I. Some Previous Discussion

Early analyses of federal finance were all grounded in neoclassical orthodoxy. The overriding efficiency norm was summarized in the term "least-price distortion," and there was little or no integration between the tax and the expenditure sides of the fiscal account. In his early work, Buchanan reduced the analysis to interindividual comparisons that allowed both sides of the account to be considered. His predominant concern was, however, the satisfaction of horizontal equity norms, and efficiency considerations were treated as secondary. Buchanan did argue, nonetheless, that the set of interarea fiscal transfers designed to achieve horizontal equity over geographic space in a national economy was defensible on efficiency grounds. If resources are to yield the maximum gross product, defined in price values of privately produced goods and services, differential fiscal treatment of the like resource units must be eliminated.[2]

A. D. Scott independently came to the opposing conclusion about the efficiency effects of equalizing transfers, and several of the fundamental issues here were treated in the Buchanan-Scott exchange that followed.[3] Scott argued that transfers from richer to poorer areas

[2] James M. Buchanan, "Federalism and Fiscal Equity," *American Economic Review,* Vol. 40, September 1950, pp. 583–99.

[3] Anthony D. Scott, "A Note on Grants in Federal Countries," *Economica,* Vol. 17, November 1950, pp. 416–22; James M. Buchanan, "Federal Grants and Resource Allocation," *Journal of Political Economy,* Vol. 60, June 1952, pp. 208–17; Scott, "Federal Grants and Resource Allocation," *ibid.,* December 1952, pp. 534–36; Buchanan, "A Reply," *ibid.,* pp. 536–38.

slow down resource reallocation, thereby reducing national income and its rate of growth. Transfers were alleged to provide amenities to persons living in states with poor resource endowments, amenities that reduce incentives to migrate to wealthier, more productive areas. Buchanan argued that no generalized conclusions of this sort were possible, and that different types of transfers exert different effects on resource shifts. Some grants were alleged to affect potential migration decisions for high productivity families while others affected low productivity families. Hence, grants for unemployment compensation seemed likely to be more resource distorting than grants for education. Buchanan's argument here may be interpreted as a negative basis for equalization; it was held that a properly designed grant program need not distort the regional allocation of resources. Buchanan did not, however, emphasize the positive arguments, implicit in his earlier paper, in demonstrating that some equalization is necessary to prevent regional allocation distortion. In retrospect, the whole Buchanan-Scott discussion was not so pointed as it might have been because each participant employed a different analytical framework. Scott assumed an economy out of long-run equilibrium whereas Buchanan's implicit model was one of comparative statics.

Until the mid-1950's, despite some recognition of the inadequacy of existing models, the discussion of federal finance remained strictly neoclassical in the sense that efficiency in allocation was defined in terms of GNP measured by market prices of private goods and services. The general inadequacy of the private-goods, neoclassical orthodoxy was revealed in Paul A. Samuelson's two fundamental papers on public-goods theory.[4] For the first time, at least in the English language tradition, efficiency norms were extended to the world that included public as well as private goods. The whole notion of allocative efficiency in public finance was modified, and subsequent discussions of federal finance reflected this change in the underlying analytical framework.

The 1959 Universities-NBER Committee Conference provided the occasion for papers on federal finance by Tiebout and Musgrave.[5]

---

[4] Paul A. Samuelson, "The Pure Theory of Public Expenditure," *Review of Economics and Statistics,* Vol. 36, November 1954, pp. 387–89; "Diagrammatic Exposition of a Theory of Public Expenditure," *ibid.,* November 1955, pp. 350–56.

[5] Charles M. Tiebout, "An Economic Theory of Fiscal Decentralization," *Public Finances: Needs, Sources, and Utilization,* New York, NBER, 1961, pp. 79–96; Richard A. Musgrave, "Approaches to a Fiscal Theory of Political Federalism," *ibid.,* pp. 97–122.

Tiebout incorporated modern public-goods logic in his efficiency examination of multilevel fiscal structures, and his paper contains the seeds of many subsequent and more detailed analyses. The second part of Musgrave's paper contains the material relevant to the question we are trying to analyze here. Musgrave noted that if all states provide public goods efficiently, in terms of the standard public-goods efficiency conditions, net fiscal differentials among separately-located equals will be eliminated, and, consequently, Buchanan's earlier joint equity-efficiency argument for the making of equalizing interarea transfers would vanish. In his criticism of the Musgrave paper, Buchanan noted that net fiscal differentials would continue to exist even when all states provide public goods efficiently because of the relevance of total as well as marginal fiscal effects in locational decisions.[6] Richer communities can provide a higher taxpayer's surplus than poorer communities, so movement will take place in response even if the necessary marginal conditions for public-goods efficiency are fully satisfied. To this argument, Musgrave replied that he did not think that

. . . such influences on the location of X should be classified as "distorting" the regional allocation of resources. Rather it appears that they constitute a given datum for location, just as does the geographical location of natural resource deposits. The fact that the benefit incidence of public services is spatially limited, and that this has a bearing on how people wish to group themselves, is part of the economic map which determines resource allocation. Efficiency is not served by erasing this feature of the map. Indeed, a central policy aimed at nullifying resulting differentials (such as remain with universal benefit taxation) in state finance will interfere with efficiency in the regional structure of public finances.[7]

In terms of the models presented prior to his contribution, Musgrave's reply seems essentially correct. Within that context, there appeared to be no efficiency basis for fiscal equalization so long as the several states provided public goods efficiently. State-local governments rely, of course, on the traditional tax instruments to finance their outlays; hence, the conditions for allocative efficiency are necessarily violated. This raises the interesting question as to whether

---

[6] James M. Buchanan, "Comment," *ibid.*, pp. 122–29; along with Musgrave's "Reply," *ibid.*, pp. 132–33. Much of the literature has been surveyed recently in Anthony D. Scott, "The Economic Goals of Federal Finance," *Public Finance,* Vol. 19, 1964, pp. 241–88.

[7] Musgrave, *op. cit.*, p. 133.

efficiency norms can be invoked in support of fiscal equalization when state-local systems are inefficiently organized.[8] But this question is not our primary concern here. Instead, we shall assume in our basic models that state-local governments provide public goods efficiently, and we shall reexamine the efficiency basis for fiscal equalization.

II. Purely Public Goods under State Provision in a Federalism

A Constant Cost, Full Mobility Model

Initially we shall postulate the existence of a wholly closed economy extending over a defined geographic space. All goods and services are fully divisible as among persons; that is, all goods and services are purely private. The economy is perfectly competitive and *all* resources are fully mobile over space. In this initial model, "land," as such, or space itself, is not a productive resource. There are no natural advantages in particular locations.

Under these conditions, resource equilibrium is attained when identical units of resource earn like returns at the several margins of employment.[9] National product will be maximized by the allocation dictated by this equilibrium. Resource units in the broad functional classifications need not be fully homogeneous, of course, and there may exist many different resource categories or classes. Therefore, earnings will vary widely among separate resource classes even though returns are equal for all units within each particular class. In this equilibrium allocation, we should expect to find that different areas of the geographic space would be characterized by differing mixes among resource classes. Some such pattern may be generated by assuming random locational shifts, or we may think of spatial clustering in response to differential limits of market specialization. In any case, equilibrium will be characterized by variations in per capita incomes among different areas of the national economy. Some regions will contain relatively more high income earners than others.

---

[8] See Albert Breton, "A Theory of Government Grants," *Canadian Journal of Economics and Political Science,* Vol. 31, May 1965, pp. 175–87. In this paper, Breton supported a system of grants partially on these grounds, but he did not develop the analysis fully.

[9] We neglect the possibility of equalizing differences in monetary returns since this is not directly relevant for our analysis.

The income structure of the surface will be similar to its central place structure; in both cases a hierarchical ranking in terms of income and order of central place can be formed.[10] The basic idea of central place theory is that there exists a hierarchy of cities and types of goods. A city of order $n + 1$ provides the same activities as cities of order n, plus additional activities, not found in lower order places, that service both the higher order place and its tributary area of lower order places. Likewise, a city of order $n + 2$ provides the same activities as cities of order $n + 1$, plus additional activities not found in the lower order places. A hierarchical order of cities and goods is thus formed. Christaller described a system of central places in terms of the now-familiar geometrical pattern of interlocking regular hexagons. In terms of the strict geometry, the hexagonal-shaped areas and the regular spacing of central places are clearly not accurate descriptions of empirical reality. Central place theory can be viewed much more favorably, however, as a perceptive way of looking at the spatial structure of an economy rather than as an attempted theoretical explanation of reality. In this manner, the notion of higher and lower order goods and places is maintained, but the rigid geometrical patterns are considered only as a way of looking at the spatial structure.[11] Under the postulated conditions of competitive equilibrium, perfect resource mobility, and a uniform distribution of resource endowments over the area, regional variation in per capita income will reflect the variation in the central place structure of the area.

We now impose a federalized political structure on this all-private-goods economy. Initially, we assume that the central government, which is coincident in area with the national economy, exists but that it provides no goods and services. Subordinate units of government—states—contain equal populations, and each state provides a single purely public good under ideally neutral conditions. Each citizen pays a marginal tax-price equal to his own marginal evaluation for the

[10] The seminal contribution to central place theory, which attempts to explain the size and geographical distribution of and the functional variation among cities and their tributary areas, is Walter Christaller, *Die zentralen Orte in Süddeutschland*, Jena, 1933, a large part of which has been recently translated by Carlisle W. Baskin, *Central Places in Southern Germany*, Englewood Cliffs, N.J., 1966. For a comprehensive bibliography, see Brian J. L. Berry and Alen Pred, *Central Place Studies: A Bibliography of Theory and Applications*, Philadelphia, 1965.

[11] For an excellent criticism of Christaller's geometry along these lines, see Rutledge Vining, "A Description of Certain Spatial Aspects of an Economic System," *Economic Development and Cultural Change*, Vol. 3, January 1955, pp. 147–95 (especially pp. 164–66).

good, and the summed marginal evaluations equal marginal cost. The required total conditions are also assumed to be met.[12] Furthermore, we assume that the range of publicness extends only to state boundaries; there are no spillovers beyond these limits.

If this public-goods provision by the separate state governments is suddenly imposed on the pre-existing private-goods equilibrium, the latter no longer holds even when the public goods are, in themselves, supplied efficiently. The higher income states are able to provide the same quantity of the public good at lower tax rates, or a larger quantity at the same tax rates. The tax-price per unit of public good will, in any case, be lower in the wealthier areas. This provides a strictly fiscal incentive for individuals to migrate to the wealthier regions of the economy.

Under the starkly simple conditions of this model, this resource flow will continue until all persons are located in the single highest income state. Under the constant-cost assumption, private resources are equally productive in all areas; hence no private goods are sacrificed by resource shifts as among areas. And, since one production unit of a purely public good embodies an unlimited number of potential consumption units within the appropriate geographic limits, residents who move from one area to another secure the full value of this consumption without reducing the public-goods consumption of prior residents. Consequently, resources initially required for public-goods production in the areas of out-migration can be released once resources have shifted. Under such conditions as these, total value of output is maximized only when the entire population is located in a single state.[13]

---

[12] The significance of the individual and total marginal conditions for the tax-pricing of publicly provided goods is discussed in James M. Buchanan, *The Demand and Supply of Public Goods,* Chicago, 1968.

[13] Some problems of national product accounting might fruitfully be raised here to indicate some of the issues introduced by public goods. The existing convention is to measure private goods at market prices and public goods at cost outlays. Under these circumstances, it is quite conceivable that current measures for national product would exhibit no change after the movement of all resources to one region. Before movement the national product of *AB* is the sum of the market values of private goods and the cost-outlays on public goods in the two areas. After all resources shift to *B*, the only difference is in accounting for the resources that were formerly used for public-goods production in *A*. It seems entirely possible that the cost-outlay of this former production in *A* would not differ from the market value of private goods now produced in *B* by the released resources. If so, no change in national product would be reported. Some of the issues raised by public goods for national accounting are examined in Richard A. Musgrave, *The Theory of Public Finance,* New York, 1959, pp. 184–201, and by Francesco Forte and James M. Buchanan, "The Evaluation of Public Services," *Journal of Political Economy,* Vol. 69, April 1961, pp. 107–21.

FIGURE 1

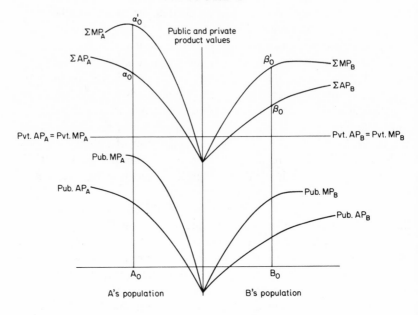

Although the argument here is straightforward, geometrical illustration will prove helpful in providing a framework for later discussion of more complex models. Figure 1 presents a model of population allocation between states *A* and *B* in a two-state federalism. The abscissa measures total population in each state; we assume that the total population in the federalism is fixed. Along the ordinate, we measure the values for both private and public product, as these are related to population, for a single person. Under the assumptions of this model, movement from one region to the other does not affect private product values. This is reflected in the constant value for the curves of marginal and average private product over-all sizes of population.[14]

The curves for public-product value must be more carefully examined. Once each state commences to provide the single public good, efficiently under our assumption, there will arise recognizable differences between the two regions for the individual. The greater per capita

[14] Since the product curves are those experienced by a single person, these have a common point on the ordinate. The individual is equally productive in the market economy regardless of his location. The fact that relatively more high income earners reside in state *A* does not affect the private productivity of any single person in this model.

income in A insures either that the same quantity of the public good can be provided at a lower tax-price than in B or that some greater quantity can be provided at the same tax-price. In any event, the individual faces a potential fiscal gain in migrating from B to A over reasonable patterns of population distribution. As drawn in Figure 1, the public product value curves originate along the ordinate at negative values. This indicates that, over some initial ranges of population concentration in either state, the individual may secure a negative "taxpayer's surplus" because of the relatively small number of taxpayers available to share in the cost of the public facility. As population increases in each state, we assume that the "mix" among income-earning types is representative of that which characterizes the equilibrium pattern. This means that the curve for public-product value in A, the state with the relatively higher per capita income, diverges from that in B as soon as we depart from the one-person level in each state.

It should be emphasized that the curves for public-product value faced by the individual embody both tax-price and benefit components. In this model, where the goods provided by the two states are, by definition, purely public in the Samuelsonian sense, the individual's evaluation of the service flow received is not directly influenced by the number of persons with whom he shares the benefits. On the tax-price side, however, the individual's net fiscal position is affected. As more persons enter the sharing group, the tax-price to any resident member declines so long as new entrants pay any taxes at all.

If we take the simplest case of equal per capita sharing in costs of the public good, average tax-price declines with in-migration along a rectangular hyperbola, assuming a fixed-sized public facility. For almost any other reasonable sharing assumption, and with variability allowed in the size of the public facility, the hyperbolic decline in tax-price remains characteristic, although no particular shapes can be assigned. It is this decline in average tax-price for the individual resident in the state which experiences in-migration that generates the curves of rising average and marginal public-product values as population increases. As the construction indicates, the curves tend asymptotically toward some maximum value equal to the individual's marginal evaluation of the public good. Tax-price to the individual approaches zero as population tends to infinity, leaving only the benefit component.[15]

---

[15] It should be noted that our analysis does not assume a fixed size facility. As the tax-price of the public good falls, more will be demanded so long as the price elasticity of demand exceeds zero. Likewise, less will be demanded in the state where the tax-price increases.

We can now sum the private and public product value curves to show the fiscal pressures that will induce migration away from the purely private-goods population equilibrium, which we can arbitrarily designate as $A_0 = B_0$. As Figure 1 shows, at this initial population allocation the summed product values, either in average or marginal terms, are greater in A than in B.[16] This will induce the individual, whose calculus the figure depicts, to migrate to A. As this sort of movement continues, the differential in product values between the two states for remaining persons will increase. In such a model as this, resource equilibrium is never attained because this requires an infinite migration. The final position reached is that which is imposed by the constraint of the fixed total population in the economy.[17]

An Increasing Cost, Ricardian Model

"Realism" can be added to the analysis by introducing locational fixity in at least one productive factor, say, "land." The fiscal surplus or public-product value curves are unchanged from those drawn in Figure 1. But curves for private-product values are modified; these no longer are unaffected by population shifts. As the population of a state increases, the marginal productivity of a resource unit, measured in terms of derived private-product valuations, declines. This is indicated by the configuration of the marginal private-product value curves in Figure 2.[18] The purely private goods equilibrium population allocation is A_0 in A and B_0 in B, where the total population is A_0B_0.

In this Ricardian model, there is a determinate amount of fiscally induced migration, given the initial assumption about the private goods equilibrium population distribution. This is indicated in the construction of Figure 2 where $A_1 - A_0 = B_0 - B_1$ people have shifted from

[16] In marginal terms $A_0\alpha_0' > B_0\beta_0'$; in average terms $A_0\alpha_0 > B_0\beta_0$.

[17] This conclusion is not independent of the initial population distribution assumption. If population differences are sufficiently wide, the fiscally-induced migration flows may be reversed. If the initial population in A is sufficiently small relative to that in B, the larger per capita income in A will be more than offset by the larger number of sharers in B, and migration from A to B will occur. The possibility of multiple equilibrium in this and in subsequent models should be acknowledged. We suggest however, that the assumptions generating migration to the wealthier state are more reasonable than those generating migration to the poorer state.

[18] The possibility of increasing returns over the initial ranges of population growth cannot be excluded, but our abstraction from this possibility does not affect the analysis so long as actual population levels lie beyond any possible range of increasing returns.

FIGURE 2

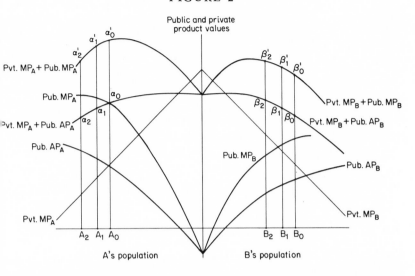

B to A. This equilibrium is attained when the marginal private-product value plus the *average* public-product value is the same in the two states. The position reached by individuals making their own migration decisions will not be Pareto optimal. Optimality would require that resources shift to the point where marginal private-product value plus *marginal* public-product value are identical in the two states. Individuals "should" migrate from B to A so long as the marginal loss in private-product value is less than the marginal gain in public-product value. In the construction of Figure 2, Pareto optimality or efficiency would require a total population shift from B to A of $A_2 - A_0 = B_0 - B_2$. This position could be attained only if property rights could somehow be assigned in public-product values. The establishment of a set of property rights would permit states to set prices upon and require the purchase of the right to migrate to that state. In terms of our illustration, state A could offer subsidies to individuals to migrate from B which B could not match until the A_2, B_2 population distribution is reached. Since such property rights do not exist, and probably would not be desirable if they could be established, individual choices must be analyzed in terms of responses to differentials in average public-product values.[19]

[19] This model is only one among many conceptually interesting and often policy-relevant institutional settings that require an analysis of individual response to differentials in average rather than marginal values. For a closely

In this Ricardian model in which states provide purely public goods, there will be too little migration from the poorer state *B* to the richer state *A*. There is no efficiency argument for fiscal equalization here. In fact, an efficiency case can be made out for disequalizing transfers *from* the poorer state to the richer state so as to induce additional migration sufficient to attain full Pareto optimality in resource location in space. This policy would be based on an acknowledgement that people are allowed to choose on the basis of average rather than marginal public-product values, with the change in the results generated by a modification in the levels of these average values themselves.

III. Impurely Public Goods under State Provision in a Federalism

Initially, we assumed full resource mobility along with state provision of purely public goods. In the last part of Section II, we dropped the mobility assumption of the model. In this section, we relax the other restrictive assumption, that of purity in the public good. When we introduce impurely public goods, one production unit no longer embodies an unlimited quantity of consumption units in an area. Each production unit does, however, embody more than one consumption unit, so long as we are not all the way to the other pole, the purely private good. For the impurely public good, given any fixed-size public facility, the addition of one person to a beneficiary group reduces the quantity of consumption units available to other members, although the correspondence is not normally one-to-one. This amounts to saying that as population increases in any given region or area, congestion in the usage of the publicly supplied good sets in ultimately and, as a result, individual evaluations of the commonly shared facilities fall.[20]

related discussion, even if on a different problem, see Leland B. Yeager, "Immigration, Trade, and Factor Price Equalization," *Current Economic Comment,* Vol. 20, August 1958, pp. 3–8. In this paper, Yeager shows that despite the analytical similarities between trade and immigration, they differ precisely because immigration normally allows sharing in socially-created values that are not directly related to the marginal productivities of the in-migrants. Trade, of course, does not involve this sort of sharing.

[20] Complex problems of measurement arise in the model with impurely public goods. Conceptually, it is possible to measure the benefit flows to individuals in physical units, but it is relatively easy to confuse changes in physical service flows with changes in individuals' evaluations of fixed quantity flows.

The introduction of impurely public goods significantly modifies our previous analysis. The private-product value curves of Figure 2 remain unchanged, so long as we remain in the Ricardian model, but the fiscal surplus or public-product value curves take on quite different configurations. The tax component is unchanged; the tax-price confronted by the individual declines as the size of the sharing group is increased. The change here comes from the benefit side of the account. Individual evaluation curves for the state-supplied good take on different shapes. With purely public goods, these evaluations remained unaffected by the size of the group.[21] When impurity is introduced, individual evaluations of the public good decline with the size of the group once the point of initial congestion is passed. Under the most reasonable assumptions, it seems likely that this decline will be at an increasing rate; successive doublings in the size of the sharing group will tend to yield successively increasing reductions in individual evaluations. In terms of our geometry, this implies that the fiscal surplus or public-product curves no longer rise continually over group size. They will now decline from the point where the negative effects from congestion of the facilities offset the positive effects of the tax-price reductions. The optimality of individual migration decisions under these modified conditions can now be examined.

Social Consequences of Individual Migration Adjustment

Individual choice behavior will generate nonoptimal results in this model under the most plausible set of assumptions. In making their private decisions concerning migration, individuals will not take into account the effects of their behavior on others. In this sense, the model is similar to the one previously analyzed; individuals adjust to average rather than marginal fiscal product. The direction or pattern in which the private-equilibrium adjustment equilibrium departs from Pareto optimality may, however, be different in this model. With purely public goods in the Ricardian model, migration to the richer region tends to be less than optimal because individuals do not incorporate the tax-price reductions that their migration generates for other members of the

---

[21] Indirectly, through changes in the quantity supplied, the individual marginal evaluations may be affected by changes in group size, even in the purely public goods case. For any given quantity, defined in production units, however, the size of the sharing group does not influence the individual's marginal evaluation.

FIGURE 3

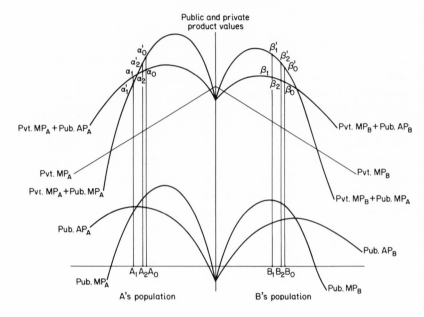

wealthy-state sharing group. With impurely public goods, this effect remains, but it may well be dominated by a second. Individuals will fail to take into account in their decisions the effects that their actions exert on others due to congestion of the publicly supplied facilities. With purely public goods, the individual in-migrant to the richer state exerts an external economy on residents of that state and an external diseconomy on residents of the state which he leaves. With impurely public goods, these tax-side externalities may be swamped and reversed by benefit-side externalities.

Figure 3 incorporates the changes that are required by the introduction of impurity in the public good. As drawn, the socially optimal amount of migration is $A_2 - A_0 = B_0 - B_2$, where the summed marginal values of private and public goods are equal in the two states and both are in the declining range. Individual adjustments will, however, lead to an excessive migration, indicated by $A_1 - A_0 = B_0 - B_1$.[22]

[22] In this Ricardian model, even with the impure public goods, it is possible that private adjustment will generate a position in the range of increasing marginal public-product value curves. If over-all population levels were sufficiently small to permit this, marginal public-product values would exceed average public-product values, and the analysis of Figure 2 would hold. If population

The situation here is generally equivalent to that discussed by Pigou and Knight in terms of the now-classical crowded good road-uncrowded bad road illustration.[23] Knight showed that individual choice behavior leads to too much traffic on the good road and too little on the bad road only in the absence of established property rights in the good road. Knight's emphasis was that of demonstrating the social function of property rights in allocating scarce resources. The problem that we examine in this paper is fully equivalent to the road illustration. The excessive migration generated by private choice can be mitigated by the granting of property rights to residents of subordinate units of government in the federalism. Practically, this would amount to allowing such political communities the right of excluding in-migrants. Individuals then wishing to migrate would be forced to purchase these rights. Conceptually, this set of institutions would be possible, but, even should the competition among the several states be sufficiently intense, the implied limitations on individuals' freedom of movement seem inimical to the functional values of Western civilization. For this reason, we simply rule out any further consideration of schemes designed to allow states directly to exclude immigrants as a means of correcting spatial resource inefficiencies.

levels are sufficient to allow the declining range of public-product values to be reached, however, the privately-determined equilibrium involves an excessive shift of resources into the richer areas. Detailed discussion is limited to this case, which seems the more meaningful in the modern federal setting, especially in the United States.

For completeness, the analysis which assumes full mobility but which incorporates the impurely public good can be briefly discussed with the construction of Figure 3. In this case, curves for marginal private-product value are unaffected by population shifts, and would assume the shape of those in Figure 1. Optimal migration levels are indicated by the points where marginal public-product values are equal in both states. But individual adjustment would generate migration to the points where average public-product values are equal, which would imply, of course, excessive migration to the wealthier state, *A*.

[23] The issues are most clearly defined in Frank H. Knight, "Some Fallacies in the Interpretation of Social Cost," *Quarterly Journal of Economics,* Vol. 38, 1924, pp. 582–606, originally written as a comment on A. C. Pigou's, *The Economics of Welfare,* London, 1918.

In an important recent paper that, unfortunately, is not known to English-language readers, Francesco Forte discussed the problem of internal migration, with especial reference to the south-north Italian population shifts, in the Pigovian framework. Forte specifically relates his analysis to the Pigou-Knight good road-bad road discussion. See Francesco Forte, "Le migrazioni interne come problema di economia del benessere," *Studi Economici,* Vol. 17, March–June 1962, pp. 97–124.

Fiscal Equalization as a Substitute for Exclusion Rights

Under the conditions discussed, too many people will migrate to the wealthier political subdivisions of the federalism. National income, appropriately measured to include valuations on public goods, would be higher if the excessive resource shifts could somehow be prevented. Since property-exclusion rights are ruled out as a relevant policy alternative, optimality requires some other institutional means of eliminating the sources for the excessive population flows. This suggests that some means should be found for reducing the fiscal surplus differentials so that individuals in their responses to average differentials will be induced to promote the same outcome that would emerge under their conceptual response to marginal surplus differentials. With reference to Figure 3, this might be achieved if the curve for average public-product value in state A is shifted downward while the curve for average public-product value in state B is shifted upward, such that the sum of private marginal product and public average product becomes equal between A and B at population levels A_2 and B_2. Under these modified conditions, rational individual choice of locations would generate collectively efficient allocations of population.

The institutional embodiment of the process described here is, of course, a transfer of funds from state A to state B, an equalizing grant. After a grant of the appropriate magnitude, state B will be able, at identical rates of tax, to provide a larger quantity of the public good than before, and state A will be able to provide a smaller quantity than before. A partial equalization of fiscal capacities will have taken place.[24]

As our analysis demonstrates, the transfer suggested will be Pareto optimal. Fiscal equalization of the sort described will be to the advantage of citizens of *all* regions. The analysis also indicates that the formula for making the interarea transfers should be based on some appropriate measurement of optimal-sized sharing units. This suggests, in turn, that the size of the required transfers should be directly related to the goods, services, facilities, and "atmosphere" generally that are to

---

[24] Full equalization of fiscal capacities, defined in terms of fiscal surplus differentials, would eliminate resource flows entirely, and would be clearly nonoptimal. In Pareto-optimal conditions, the individual who remains in state B, the poorer of the two in our model, earns a somewhat higher private income and enjoys the benefits of somewhat less congested public facilities than his equal in state A. These two advantages are, however, offset by the fact that he must pay a somewhat higher tax-price for the units of public good that he does receive.

be commonly shared. If state-local units provide many goods and services that are quantitatively important, the efficiency distortions generated by uncorrected private choice behavior will be greater than in the case where state-local units are less active fiscally. Increasing collectivization at the state-local level in a federalism enhances the efficiency basis for making equalizing fiscal transfers.[25]

There are two characteristics of an optimal equalization program that warrant mention. First, the type of transfer indicated is not, even conceptually, one among individuals but instead is among *collectivities* of individuals. The source of the excessive migration lies in the provision of public goods, which are not fully divisible among persons; corrective measures must work through a similar process.[26] Second, the system of optimal equalizing transfers would be zero sum or purely redistributive as among separate states. No net budgetary activity by the central government would be required.[27]

Inefficiency in State Provision of Public Goods

To this point we have deliberately ignored those problems that might be raised by distributional differences among the fiscal structures of the state governments. In one sense this introduces a secondary set of issues, and these should not be allowed to distract attention from the central analysis presented above. In the latter, differential fiscal surpluses generate population movement even when all states provide public goods efficiently; that is, when all persons in each state pay marginal tax-

[25] We have wholly neglected central government provision of public goods and services in our analysis. If the central government provides goods and services directly over the whole national economy, whether these be pure or impure, some divorce of the central government tax structure from a measured money income base is indicated in any Ricardian model. Since one of the necessary equilibrating adjustments is in the levels of money earnings for like resource units that are differently located, central government tax adjustments should take this into account. If this proves to be impracticable, as seems to be the case, an additional, if limited, argument for equalizing transfers to the poorer states is provided.

[26] This represents a different formulation for equalizing transfers from Buchanan's early proposals which, ideally, called for transfers among individual citizens differently located. See "Federalism and Fiscal Equity," *op. cit.*

[27] This is similar to the West German system for fiscal equalization. This is one of zero-sum transfers, but the effects are secured through variations in the amount of tax collections that each state returns to the federal government. For a recent description, see Emilio Gerelli, "Intergovernmental Financial Relations: The Case of the German Federal Republic," *Weltwirtschaftliches Archiv*, Vol. 97, 1966, pp. 273–302.

prices equal to their marginal evaluations of the public goods provided. States probably come much closer to satisfying these extreme efficiency norms than central governments; income-wealth redistribution as an objective explicitly divorced from allocative goals cannot readily be sought by states in a federal system. Nevertheless, states may embody departures from neutrality in their fiscal structures, and it will be useful to examine the effects on the results of our earlier analysis.

Initially, we assume that, even if state-local fiscal systems embody net redistribution at the margins of public-goods provision, the aggregative marginal conditions for efficiency remain satisfied for each state. That is, the summation of marginal tax-prices equals the summation of individual marginal evaluations, but the "rich" pay marginal tax-prices in excess of their own marginal evaluations while the "poor" pay marginal tax-prices offsettingly lower than their marginal evaluations. In this setting, insofar as the separate states attempt roughly the same degree of marginal redistribution, the previous analysis is not significantly modified. All resource owners in states of below-average incomes will have a fiscal incentive to migrate.

The introduction of marginal redistribution becomes important for our purposes only when the separate states differ substantially one from another concerning the amount and direction. Assume, for example, that an above-average-income state tries to accomplish more net income redistribution than its below-average-income counterpart. For a convenient illustration, suppose that California increases its rate of income tax progression to finance an increase in welfare payments. This change will increase the fiscal pressures felt by high-income groups and reduce the fiscal pressures felt by lower-income groups. The effect will be to alter the structure of migration from lower-income states to California in the direction of increasing the proportion of lower-income migrants.

By contrast, if a below-average state attempts to accomplish greater net redistribution than its higher-income counterparts, the initial disparity in income levels will be aggravated by the patterns of migration that this change will produce. A greater proportion of higher-income groups will migrate out, and the remaining population will be changed in the direction of more lower-income earners.

When departures from optimality in the over-all quantity of public goods are introduced (when the aggregative marginal conditions are no longer satisfied), the results depend critically on the effects of the attempted redistribution at the margin on the position of the taxpayer-beneficiaries in the median income ranges. Spending programs may be above or below optimal levels, depending on the coalition structure that is decisive in collective choices and upon the tax institutions that are utilized. If spending programs are reduced below optimal levels, the effects on migration discussed in our general models tend to be less significant; if spending programs are increased above optimal levels, the effects on migration tend to be more significant.

IV. Some Policy Implications

Policy implications have been implicit in the preceding analysis, but it will be useful to discuss these more directly. To the extent that the conditions of the central model are at all descriptive of real-world institutions, an efficiency basis exists for making equalizing fiscal transfers in a federalism. The potential real-world relevance is clear from the simple logic of the analysis; individuals make migrational choices on the basis of marginal private values and *average* public values because of the absence of enforceable property rights in the latter. Only if this essential fact can somehow be denied would the analysis lose its potential relevance. The actual relevance, of course, is an empirical matter that depends upon current congestion levels and interstate population levels. Empirical relevance requires that the largest populations not reside in the poorer states; this requirement is clearly fulfilled. Furthermore, the observed congestion of existing public facilities in areas of population concentration also supports the applicability of the central model in the United States of the late 1960's and 1970's. The argument strongly suggests the desirability of initiating equalizing fiscal transfers aimed at offsetting to some degree the differentials in fiscal surplus that privately motivate excessive resource concentration in space.[28] At current margins of decision, there is likely to be a greater return per dollar invested in keeping a family in Arkansas than in helping Chicago finance a part of the external costs that this family's migration might impose on current Illinois residents.

[28] Although our analysis has been posed in terms of the efficiency of equalizing *interstate* transfers, it is equally applicable to the efficiency of equalizing *intrastate* transfers.

The general problem that we have examined has also been examined recently by Koichi Mera. He, however, failed to escape the shackles of the purely private goods orthodoxy, so his analysis was irrelevant for the major issues. See "Trade-off Between Aggregate Efficiency and Inter-regional Equity: A Static Analysis," *Quarterly Journal of Economics,* Vol. 81, November 1967, pp. 658–74.

Perhaps the most significant policy implications currently are negative. The central argument provides a warning against relying too heavily upon the use of massive central government grants to urbanized areas in attempting to improve the urban environment. Such a policy of grants can aggravate existing allocative distortions by providing still further fiscal incentives for individual migration to the high-income, urbanized sectors.[29] The spatial pattern of population distribution that satisfies Pareto-efficiency requirements, including efficiency in the utilization of public goods (including "atmosphere"), surely dictates some slowing down of the continuing flow of population into the areas where public facilities seem currently to be congested. This seems clearly to be an important, and much neglected, problem where individual or private responses to market forces generate socially inefficient outcomes.[30]

[29] Any detailed discussion would, of course, have to take into account the different migration patterns for different income groups. But the potential relevance of our analysis can be sufficiently demonstrated by imagining that, through some political "miracle," the cities of the United States were to be suddenly transformed into the crime-free, pollution-free, amenities-bountiful "paradises" envisaged in some of the current discussion. Unless this policy would be accompanied by some limitation on migration, congestion would soon reemerge with little net improvement over the existing situation.

The whole problem here is, of course, identical to the attempt to relieve traffic congestion by the continual construction of larger and better superhighways. Private decisions will insure that traffic flows will ultimately increase to the level of the improved highway capacity and beyond. Economists make vigorous policy proposals in the highway-street case, and they have normally suggested that efficient outcomes can be secured by pricing scarce space in accordance with standard marginal-cost criteria. The full efficiency of this pricing mechanism may be questioned, even in the highway model, and, with the movement of population over space, direct pricing solutions seem to be neither feasible nor desirable.

[30] Another policy implication is that attempts to redistribute income in kind through an increased provision of various social services are likely to be significantly dissipated through the additional in-migration induced by their provision.

COMMENT

by MARTIN S. FELDSTEIN, *Harvard University*

The paper by Buchanan and Wagner is both stimulating and provocative. It presents an analytic discussion of an important policy issue—the role of federal grants to state and local governments. While previous treatments of this subject have dealt with it in terms of equity, fiscal capacity, and tax competitiveness, Buchanan and Wagner concentrate on the efficiency aspect of the problem. Although I now believe that its primary conclusions are wrong and that the analysis is incorrect in several places, I would nevertheless defend the usefulness of the paper in focusing our attention on the implications of population migration for the efficiency of public goods provision and intergovernmental grants.

The authors consider two basic models: pure public goods and impure public goods. Although they briefly consider a fixed cost model, attention is primarily on the Ricardian model in which land is a fixed factor and increased population lowers the marginal product of labor. Their basic conclusion is that in a world of pure public goods there would be too little migration while, in a world of impure public goods, migration would be excessive. I shall show that the first conclusion comes from an incorrect treatment of a pecuniary benefit as if it were a real benefit. The second conclusion depends on the very special case which the authors treat. In general, neither conclusion is correct.

Let me first summarize their discussion of the pure public goods case. In the model which they consider, two states are providing public goods of the same fixed size. Land is a fixed factor while labor is mobile; increasing the labor-land ratio decreases the marginal product of labor. In State A, per capita income is higher, the population is larger, and the individual's tax payments are "therefore" lower than in State B.[1]

---

[1] The reason for lower per capita taxes in the richer state is not clear from the paper. At one point the authors use a model in which: (1) each citizen pays a tax-price equal to his own marginal evaluation of the public good; (2) the size of the good is determined by the requirement that the sum of the marginal evaluations equals the marginal cost of the good; (3) neutral taxes and transfers correct any deficit or surplus; and (4) the income elasticity of demand for public goods is positive. These assumptions imply that an individual with a given income will pay a lower tax *per unit of the public good* if he lives in the richer state. However, the total tax paid by the individual might be higher

When an individual migrates from *B* to *A,* he "benefits" the individuals in State *A* by lowering the tax rate which they pay. Because there are only pure public goods, there is no congestion effect lowering the benefit of the public good to the previous residents of State *A*. But the potential migrant does not consider his effect on the tax level in State *A*; his decision is based on his private marginal benefits and costs. Individuals therefore continue to migrate from *B* to *A* until the difference between the tax rate in the two areas balances the higher private productivity of labor in Area *B*. At this equilibrium point, the residents of State A would still like more inward migration because this lowers their taxes. Because the potential migrant cannot internalize this, he does not move. Buchanan and Wagner therefore conclude that the amount of migration is *less* than Paretian-optimal.

I don't find this analysis convincing. In fact, I come to the opposite conclusion: under the Buchanan-Wagner assumption about tax sharing there will be too much migration in the pure public goods case. I reason that since the quantity of public goods to be produced in the two states is fixed and the goods are pure public goods, the requirement for Paretian optimality is that the population be divided between the two states in such a way that the marginal product of labor is the same in both states. If the land area is the same in both states, this calls for an even division of the population; i.e., no migration. I see no rationale for taking into account the transfer mechanisms by which the provision of public goods in the two states is financed. The "benefit" conferred by the migrants is purely a pecuniary benefit while the cost they confer is real. If I am right in concluding that Paretian optimality requires no migration in the pure public goods case, and if Buchanan and Wagner are right in saying that a positive determinate amount of migration would be induced, then even in this pure public goods case there is reason for federal grants to the areas from which migrants are coming.

The issues raised by "impure" public goods are of greater policy significance. The primary conclusion reached by Buchanan and Wagner

if he lived in the richer state. In the context of this model, the reason for migration to richer states is not that the taxes are lower but that consumer surplus is higher.

A few paragraphs later, the basic model is changed. Now the public good is assumed to be of fixed size and there is equal per capita sharing of the costs of the public goods. But while it is obviously true that the per capita tax cost falls under this scheme as more people enter an area, it is no longer clear that more individuals will be attracted to the richer area under the equal cost-sharing arrangement.

is that the presence of impure public goods induces more migration from poorer states to richer states than would be economically efficient. A person entering the richer state reduces the benefits that the previous residents obtained from the impure public goods. In more concrete terms, he adds to the congestion in their use. The social marginal cost of his migration is greater than his private marginal cost, or, as Buchanan and Wagner prefer to state it, than the social average cost which the migrant pays. It is this divergence between social and private marginal costs that causes the "excess" migration. Although there is some validity in this analysis, the conclusion is wrong. While the divergence between social and private marginal cost does imply that the final distribution of population will probably not be socially optimal, the conclusion that there is *excess* migration from poor to rich areas is based on a number of very special assumptions in the Buchanan-Wagner analysis. For example, if we drop the obviously artificial assumption that the two states are originally of equal size and with equal population, it is quite possible that there is too little migration. One need only think of migration from a small, poor area to a rich large area; the external decongestion benefits of leaving the former may outweigh the congestion costs imposed in the larger. The Buchanan-Wagner conclusion can also be reversed by relaxing the assumption that the public goods are of the same size in both states and recognizing that there may be economies of scale in producing the public good. Perhaps most important, we must recognize that people who live in cities have different *preferences* with respect to congestion than those who live in rural areas. This implies that the relative welfare significance of migration between the two places cannot be evaluated by a simple head-count measure of congestion. In short, one cannot say in general that the presence of impure public goods causes excess migration from poor to rich areas.[2]

Let me now return to the policy recommendations that Buchanan and Wagner derive from their analysis of the impure public goods case. They conclude that, on grounds of efficiency, federal equalizing grants should be paid to poorer areas but that "massive central government grants to urbanized areas . . . can [only] aggravate existing allocative distortions" (p. 158). In addition to the problems in their analysis which I have already discussed, their implied advice not to give federal

---

[2] The authors also introduce the false benefits of per capita tax reduction in their analysis of the Paretian efficiency of migration in the presence of impure public goods. Just as in the pure public goods case, a correct treatment would ignore these pecuniary benefits.

grants to the cities ignores three primary aspects of the fiscal problem facing urban areas. First, there is the obvious fact that it is to very poor areas and to those with predominantly Negro populations, that much of the proposed aid would be directed. Although these are areas of high population density, this is clearly not because of the lavish provision of public goods! Considerations of equity, and perhaps of long-run efficiency, imply public programs far in excess of the financial capacity of the local urban areas. Second, intercity tax competition keeps the level of spending in urban areas below the level that would be chosen collectively. Federal action is necessary to achieve a Paretian optimal level of expenditure and taxation by the cities. Finally, the cities are part of larger metropolitan areas to which they provide public good services but from which it is difficult to obtain revenues. Without support to the cities, the level of public good provision to the entire metropolitan area will be too low. A combination of high tax rates in the central city and the opportunity for residents of neighboring suburbs to enjoy the goods provided by the city would only accelerate migration to the suburbs and exacerbate the fiscal difficulties that the cities face today.

CHANGING ROLES OF
DIFFERENT LEVELS OF GOVERNMENT

GEORGE F. BREAK

University of California, Berkeley

A time of fiscal stress and of great uncertainty about the future seems an appropriate moment in which to assess once again the changing roles of different levels of government in this country during the past sixty years or so. Those years were hardly tranquil ones, and whatever certainties shaped them have become evident only in retrospect. Such clues, therefore, as analyses of past trends can provide to the mysteries of our own time should be carefully weighed even though the fiscal problems confronting us seem to be of unprecedented proportions. By looking backward the present paper attempts to determine where we are and where we appear to be going with the U.S. federal system of government. Section I discusses the broad picture as it is revealed by a selected group of expenditure measures computed from Bureau of the Census (BOC) and National Income Accounts (NIA) data for four past periods—1902 to 1966, 1927–29 to 1966, 1940 to 1966, and 1948 to 1966. Section II analyzes the major factors that appear to have accounted for the changes observed in the first section, and Section III concentrates on those more current developments that seem to be making for change in the near future. Section IV summarizes the conclusions reached.

I. The Broad Picture

Between 1902 and 1966, when the expenditures of all levels of government were growing at average annual rates of between 7 and 8½ per cent, depending on the specific concept used in measuring them, both federal and state shares expanded at the expense of local governments. In Table 1 six alternative expenditure measures, based on published Bureau of the Census data, have been arranged in descending order of scope, and for each series the percentage shares of the three levels of

TABLE 1

FEDERAL, STATE, AND LOCAL EXPENDITURE SHARES[a]
SHOWN BY SIX ALTERNATIVE BUREAU OF THE CENSUS
MEASURES OF AGGREGATE GOVERNMENTAL
EXPENDITURES, 1902, 1927, 1940, 1948, AND 1965–66

Aggregate Expenditure Measure[b]		Years				
		1902	1927	1940	1948	1965–66
1. Own-financed total expenditures (OFTE)	F[c]	34	31	49	65	64
	S	11	17	22	17	17
	L	55	52	29	18	19
2. Own-financed general expenditures (OFGE)	F	36	33	54	69	63
	S	11	17	20	15	18
	L	52	50	25	16	19
3. Direct general expenditures (DGE)	F	36	32	49	65	56
	S	8	13	15	12	15
	L	56	55	36	23	28
4. Own-financed general expenditures for civil purposes, Series I (OFGE:C-I)	F	29	29	50	54	46
	S	13	18	22	23	26
	L	58	53	28	24	28
5. Direct general expenditures for civil purposes, Series I (DGE:C-I)	F	28	28	44	48	36
	S	9	14	17	18	23
	L	62	58	39	34	42
6. Direct general expenditures for civil purposes, Series II (DGE:C-II)	F	18	16	39	34	28
	S	11	16	18	22	25
	L	71	68	43	45	47

SOURCES: Series 1: 1902–48 from Tax Foundation, *Facts and Figures on Government Finance, 1967,* New York, 1967, p. 20. 1965–66 computed from data given in U.S. Bureau of the Census, *Governmental Finances in 1965–66,* Washington, D.C., 1967. Series 2–6: Appendix Table A.

[a] Percentages of total expenditures made by each of the three levels of government.

[b] For definitions of the alternative measures see text.

[c] F = federal; S = state; L = local.

government are shown for the five years selected for discussion in this section. These six series do not, of course, represent all of the possible choices, but they do illustrate the problems involved in choosing a few broad measures to show past trends in expenditure shares, and these problems will be discussed in the process of deriving the 1902–66 picture.

Total governmental expenditures, as defined by the Bureau of the Census, include the costs of water, electric, gas and transit systems that are owned and operated by local governments (utility expenditures), the costs of liquor stores operated by state and local governments, and the benefit payments of governmental insurance trust systems.[1] The first two of these inclusions raise fundamental questions concerning the proper definition of governmental activities which are too complex to be discussed here at length,[2] and the last one involves tax-transfer operations, which shift command over resources among different groups in the private sector rather than between that sector and the government. This last distinction is an important one and easily warrants separate treatment of resource-using and transfer expenditures in the measurement of federal-state-local expenditure shares. In addition, the dividing line between government owned and operated public utilities and liquor stores and similar enterprises that are privately owned and operated under close governmental supervision seems an especially thin one. For these reasons the Census Bureau total expenditure series (series 1 in Table 1) is rated here as too broad to serve as a basic measure of the changing roles of different levels of government. It is worth noting, nevertheless, that of all the Table 1 measures, series 1 shows the greatest 1902–66 increase in the importance of the federal expenditure share (a rise of nearly 90 per cent), though it does not usually show the highest federal share in any given year. It should also be noted that intergovernmental expenditures[3] are included in the share of the grantor, but that intergovernmental revenues, as in all of our own-financed series, are deducted from the expenditures of the recipient in order to

[1] Insurance trust activities include both contributory retirement systems for public employees and governmental social insurance and life insurance programs. Social insurance provides protection against economic hazards arising from disability, death, accident, illness, and unemployment. The administrative costs of these programs are defined as general, rather than as insurance trust, expenditures. See, for example, U.S. Bureau of the Census, *Census of Governments: 1962*, Vol. VI, No. 4, *Historical Statistics on Governmental Finances and Employment*, Washington, D. C., 1964, p. 3. Hereafter cited as *Historical Statistics: COG, 1962.*

[2] For a useful survey of the issues involved see C. Lowell Harriss, "Government Expenditures: Significant Issues of Definition," *Journal of Finance*, Vol. IX, December 1954, pp. 351–64.

[3] Intergovernmental expenditure is defined as "amounts paid to other governments as fiscal aid in the form of shared revenues and grants-in-aid, as reimbursements for performance of general government activities and for specific services for the paying government, . . . or in lieu of taxes. Excludes amounts paid to other governments for purchase of commodities, property, or utility services, any tax imposed or paid as such, and employer contributions for social insurance." U.S. Bureau of the Census, *Compendium of State Government Finances in 1965*, Washington, D.C., 1966, p. 55.

show the spending of each level that is financed from its own sources. The second series in Table 1, own-financed general expenditures, excludes utility, liquor store, and insurance trust operations, but includes other commercial-type public enterprises, such as airports, housing projects, toll highways and the U.S. Postal Service. The latter group does appear to include enterprises whose public purposes are relatively more pronounced, but they are still a diverse lot, and it is not easy to define a simple, uniform measure that will accurately show the importance of their public activities. Whereas the Census Bureau treats them on a gross basis, including total costs on the expenditure side of the accounts and total revenues on the receipts side, the national income accounts use the net basis, subtracting revenues from costs and showing only net expenditures (positive or negative) on the output side of the accounts.[4] Neither procedure is entirely satisfactory. A public housing project, for example, exists to raise the real living standards of the poor, but gross government expenditures overestimate the extent of the government's intervention in private economic affairs, and NIA net expenditures will typically underestimate it.[5] The difficulties are both conceptual and statistical, and it is by no means clear that their resolution would be worth the effort. In the meantime, it is advantageous to have alternative expenditure series that treat public enterprises on both a net and a gross basis, and the governmental roles shown by NIA and BOC data should be interpreted with these differences in mind.

The second and third series in Table 1 differ only in their treatment of intergovernmental expenditures and revenues. Whereas own-financed general expenditures, as already noted, assign the expenditure weights to the level of government that does the financing rather than

[4] In the NIA framework the operating surplus or deficit (sales receipts minus all current operating costs other than interest payments and depreciation charges) of government enterprises is consolidated with direct business subsidies on the output side of the government sector, and the capital expenditures of public enterprises are combined with other government purchases of goods and services. See U.S. Department of Commerce, Office of Business Economics, *National Income: 1954 Edition,* Washington, D.C., 1954, pp. 49 and 148. A list of federal enterprises and of the major types of state and local enterprises is given on p. 66 of the same publication.

[5] Over the lifetime of the project, NIA expenditures will equal the amount of the original capital investment plus the sum of the annual operating deficits. Since the latter exclude both interest payments on borrowed capital and an imputed rate of return on owned capital, the total NIA expenditure figure will underestimate the subsidy given to the housing occupants, though in any given year fluctuations in government investment and in private rates of return to landlords might produce the opposite result.

to the level that actually provides the benefits to the private sector of the economy, direct general expenditures do the reverse.[6] Comparing the two measures, therefore, one may note the fairly stable importance of state-to-local intergovernmental financing (reflected in the larger state share of own-financed general expenditures) and the rapidly increasing importance of federal grants-in-aid. Further analysis of these developments is given in Section II.

The final three measures shown in Table 1 all focus on the civil functions of U.S. governments. Here again one encounters conceptual and statistical difficulties that cannot be satisfactorily resolved. As a result two alternative measures are provided. The two series marked C-I (numbers 4 and 5 in Table 1) incorporate a relatively broad conception of federal civil activities by excluding only the BOC measure of federal expenditures for national defense and international affairs.[7] Many would feel, however, that some account should be taken of the indirect costs of past wars, and one way of doing this, used by James A. Maxwell and others,[8] is used in series C-II (number 6 in Table 1). In it federal civil expenditures are defined to exclude not only defense and international expenditures but also interest payments on general debt and the costs of veterans' services not allocated by the Census Bureau to other functional categories.[9] Clearly, not all federal debt can be attributed to past and current wars, nor can it be determined what share of veterans' expenditures represents payments

[6] In the direct general measure, in other words, intergovernmental expenditures are excluded from the expenditures of the grantor, and intergovernmental revenues are not deducted from the expenditures of the grantee.

[7] A still broader concept could, of course, be provided by excluding military expenditures alone.

[8] See, for example, Maxwell, *Financing State and Local Governments,* Washington, D.C., 1965, p. 14.

[9] In 1965–66 total federal expenditures on veterans' services of $6,711 million were allocated as follows:

Category	Amounts (millions of dollars)	
Intergovernmental expenditures		16
Insurance trust expenditures		572
Direct general expenditures: total		6,123
education	336	
public welfare	38	
health and hospitals	1,239	
not elsewhere classified	4,510	

It is the last figure shown that is excluded in the derivation of series C-II.

for past services rendered or injuries incurred rather than benefits that the federal government would have provided in any case.

Our civil expenditure series, therefore, are necessarily based on some arbitrary distinctions, and while these are no better than a number of other alternatives, they do have the virtue of being subject to statistical measurement over long periods of time. As expected, the federal shares shown by the three civil expenditure measures are significantly below that level's share of total expenditures. Moreover, these differences were notably wider at the end of the period than they were at the beginning. This may be seen in the following tabulation of expenditure share differentials, computed by subtracting federal civil shares from federal shares of the corresponding total expenditure series.

Expenditure Measure	Federal Share Differentials: Excess of Total Over Civil				
	1902	1927	1940	1948	1965–66
Own-financed general, Series C-I	7	4	4	15	17
Direct general, Series C-I	8	4	5	17	20
Direct general, Series C-II	18	16	10	31	28

Developments during the other periods shown in Table 1 can be summarized briefly. The 1927–66 period shows the same picture of rising shares for both federal and state governments as occurred from 1902 to 1966. Between 1940 and 1966, on the other hand, federal shares of civil expenditures fell while federal shares of total expenditures rose.

Absolute Changes in Expenditure Shares, 1940–66

Higher Federal Share			Lower Federal Share		
OFTE	F	+15	OFGE: C-I	F	−4
	S	−5		S	+4
	L	−10		L	0
OFGE	F	+9	DGE: C-I	F	−8
	S	−2		S	+5
	L	−6		L	+3
DGE	F	+7	DGE: C-II	F	−11
	S	0		S	+7
	L	−8		L	+4

Finally, from 1948 to 1966 the federal share of all six Table 1 series fell, the greatest relative declines occurring in the three civil expenditure measures, but with direct general expenditures showing a nine-point reduction that almost matched them. In each case both state and local shares rose, the largest being in direct general civil expenditures, series I, and the smallest in own-financed total expenditures.[10]

TABLE 2

FEDERAL AND STATE-LOCAL SHARES[a] OF SIX
NATIONAL-INCOME-ACCOUNTS MEASURES
OF AGGREGATE GOVERNMENTAL ACTIVITY,
1902, 1929, 1940, 1948, AND 1966

Measure[b]		Years				
		1902	1929	1940	1948	1966
1. Own-financed expenditures	F[c]	—	26	54	69	68
(OFE)	SL	—	74	46	31	32
2. Purchases of goods and services	F	23	15	43	52	50
(P)	SL	77	85	57	48	50
3. Own-financed expenditures for	F	—	—	48	61	55
civil purposes—I (OFE:C-I)	SL	—	—	52	39	45
4. Civil purchases—I (P:C-I)	F	19[d]	—	32	28	18
	SL	81	—	68	72	82
5. Wages and salaries of govern-	F-M[e]	—	6	7	21	19
ment employees (WSGE)	F-C	—	22	41	33	26
	SL	—	72	52	46	55
6. Number of full-time equivalent	F-M	—	8	9	21	24
government employees (FTEGE)	F-C	—	18	45	29	20
	SL	—	74	46	50	56

SOURCE: Appendix Table B. Civil purchase shares for 1903 were computed from data on nonwar federal, and total state-local, payrolls and purchases given in Solomon Fabricant, *The Trend of Government Activity in the United States Since 1900,* New York, NBER, 1952, pp. 225–34.

[a] Percentages of total activity accounted for by each level of government.

[b] For definitions of the alternative measures see text.

[c] F = federal; SL = state-local.

[d] Figures are for 1903.

[e] F-M = federal, military; F-C = federal, civilian; SL = state-local.

[10] Before rounding, the state share of own-financed total expenditures rose from 17.3 per cent in 1948 to 17.4 in 1965-66.

Much the same broad picture is shown by the six NIA series presented in Table 2. Note, for example, the consistent increase in state-local shares between 1948 and 1966 as well as the substantial fall in those shares between either 1902 or 1929 and each of the following three years shown. The one notable exception is the series for civil purchases of goods and services (item 4 in Table 2). From 1939 on, this measure was derived by excluding official estimates of national defense purchases from total federal purchases of goods and services, and for 1903 Fabricant's estimates of nonwar payrolls and purchases were used.[11] Though the two figures are not strictly comparable, it seems unlikely that the required adjustment would convert the slight increase in the state-local share shown between 1903 and 1966 into a substantial decline. Also impressive is the large 1948–66 decline in the federal share of civil purchases.

A final point of interest concerns the behavior during the 1929–66 period of the major types of governmental expenditure distinguished in the national income accounts. It will be noted in Table 2 that whereas in 1966 own-financed total expenditures were divided approximately two-to-one between the federal and state-local levels respectively, purchases of goods and services were split exactly 50-50. Two main factors account for this gap. The first is federal aid which keeps the own-financed expenditures of state and local governments below their direct expenditures. The allocation of the latter is shown in Table 3, and it will be noted that though in 1929 the impact of federal aid on spending shares was minor, by 1940 it had shifted a 54-46 division of own-financed expenditures to one of 49-51 for direct expenditures, and by 1966 the gap between these two series had increased to 7 points.

The second explanatory factor is the division between the two levels of government of net interest paid and of transfer payments to persons. As Table 3 shows, these two series have in recent years been dominated by the federal government, and in each of the benchmark years selected for discussion in this section federal use of resources, reflected in the Table 2 series on government purchases, has been considerably lower, relative to state and local governments, than its participation in programs designed to shift command over resources from one private group to another. Further aspects of this important difference are discussed in the next two sections.

[11] Solomon Fabricant, *The Trend of Government Activity in the United States Since 1900,* New York, NBER, 1952, pp. 214–35.

TABLE 3

FEDERAL AND STATE-LOCAL NIA EXPENDITURE
SHARES, BY MAJOR TYPE,[a] 1929, 1940, 1948, AND 1966

Type of Expenditure		Years			
		1929	1940	1948	1966
1. Direct expenditures[b]	F[c]	24	49	65	61
	SL	76	51	35	39
2. Direct nonresource-using expenditures[d]	F	70	70	87	92
	SL	30	30	13	8
3. Transfer payments to persons	F	76	53	72	82
	SL	24	47	28	18
4. Net interest paid	F	45	56	94	97
	SL	55	44	6	3

SOURCES: U.S. Department of Commerce, Office of Business Economics, *The National Income and Product Accounts of the United States, 1929–1965*, Washington, D.C., 1966, and *Survey of Current Business*, July 1967.

[a] Omitted are purchases of goods and services which are shown in Table 2.

[b] All expenditures except federal grants-in-aid to state and local governments.

[c] F = federal share; SL = state-local share.

[d] All expenditures except grants-in-aid and purchases of goods and services.

II. Changing Functional Shares

In this section our discussion of the changing roles of different levels of government shifts from broad aggregates to specific functions of particular significance. These have been divided into three categories: (1) those functions which by their nature are suited only to the federal government, (2) those functions whose cost appears to be especially sensitive to the urbanization process, and (3) public expenditures for the maintenance and development of human capital which have reacted in important ways to the technological, communications, and transportation revolutions of the last quarter century.

Federal and Nonfederal Functions

For purposes of discussion here a relatively conservative definition of federal functions has been adopted. Included in that category are only five program areas whose assignment to the national government seems beyond dispute: national defense, international relations, space research and technology, veterans' services and benefits, and postal services. No implication that these should be the only federal functions is intended—indeed, far from it—but it seems useful to treat this group separately and to compare its rate of growth over specific periods with that of all other governmental expenditures. The relevant data are given in Tables 4, 5, and 6.

TABLE 4

AVERAGE ANNUAL GROWTH RATES[a] OF FEDERAL AND NONFEDERAL EXPENDITURES DURING SELECTED PERIODS, 1902–66

BUREAU OF THE CENSUS DATA (PER CENT)

Period	National Defense and International Relations	Veterans' Services Not Elsewhere Classified	Postal Service	Federal Functions	Nonfederal Functions
1902–13	3¾	2	7¼	4½	6½
1913–27	6¾	8¾	7¼	7½	10
1927–36	4¾	13	½	6½	4
1936–40	14	−26	1¾	−3¾	5¼
1940–48	33	26	10	28	8½
1948–56	13	−¾	6¾	11	8
1956–62	3¾	5	6	4¼[b]	8¼
1962–66	3½	2¼	8½	5[b]	6¾
1965–66	9	7½	8½	9½[b]	9
1902–66	9¾[c]	5½	6	8½[b]	7½

Source: Computed from data given in Appendix Table D.

[a] Rates are compound annual rates of growth expressed to the nearest ¼ per cent for rates under 10 per cent and to the nearest 1 per cent for all others.

[b] Includes expenditures on space research and technology which began in 1958 at $89 million, increased to $1,242 in 1962 and to $5,869 million in 1966. These increases represent average annual growth rates of over 90 per cent and 47 per cent respectively.

[c] Military functions alone, which are shown separately by the Bureau of the Census, increased at 9½ per cent per annum between 1902 and 1966 while the remaining national defense and international functions rose at an average rate of 14 per cent a year.

TABLE 5

AVERAGE ANNUAL GROWTH RATES[a] OF FEDERAL AND NONFEDERAL EXPENDITURES 1956–62 AND 1962–66

NATIONAL INCOME ACCOUNTS DATA (PER CENT)

Period	National Defense	Space Research and Technology	International Affairs and Finance	Veterans' Benefits and Services	Postal Services	Federal Expenditures	Nonfederal Expenditures
1956–62	4¼	—	3	2½	5¼	4½	10
1962–66	4¼	35	2½	1¾	5¾	5¼	8

SOURCES: Computed from data given in *The National Income and Product Accounts of the United States, 1929–1965* and the *Survey of Current Business,* July 1967, Table 3.10.

[a] Rates are compound annual rates of growth expressed to the nearest ¼ per cent for rates under 10 per cent and to the nearest 1 per cent for all others.

TABLE 6

AVERAGE ANNUAL GROWTH RATES[a] OF DEFENSE AND
NONDEFENSE GOVERNMENT PURCHASES OF GOODS
AND SERVICES, SELECTED PERIODS, 1939–67
(PER CENT)

Period	Defense Purchases	Nondefense Purchases	Total Purchases
1939–48	27	6¼	10
1948–56	18	8	12
1956–62	4¼	9½	7
1962–66	4	9½	7
1964IV–1967IV[b]	15	10	12
1966–67	20	11	14
1939–67	16	8	9¾

SOURCES: Computed from data given in *The National Income and Product Accounts of the United States, 1929–1965* and the *Survey of Current Business,* July 1967 and February 1968, Table 1.1.

[a] Rates are compound annual rates of growth expressed to the nearest ¼ per cent for rates under 10 per cent and to the nearest 1 per cent for all others.

[b] Fourth quarter seasonally adjusted data at annual rates.

For the entire period under study, as shown in the last line of Table 4, national defense and international expenditures grew more rapidly than nonfederal spending, while veterans' benefits and postal services grew less rapidly. The defense and international functions were sufficiently important, however, to hold the growth rate of federal expenditures well above that of nonfederal spending. The result was strong upward pressure on federal expenditure shares for the period as a whole and for the three subperiods 1927–36, 1940–56, and 1965–66. However, during the early part of the century, in the later years of the Great Depression, and between the Korean and Vietnamese Wars the growth of federal functions tended to lag behind the expansion of other governmental expenditures. Much the same picture of the last decade is given by the NIA data in Table 5. Two of the components of federal expenditures, however, are measured differently, and it will be noted that the NIA series for veterans' benefits increased less rapidly than the BOC measure and that the NIA postal deficit also grew less rapidly than did BOC gross postal expenditures.

Finally, it is interesting to see what changes occur when the focus is narrowed from total expenditures to government purchases of goods and services and from federal functions to national defense programs only.[12] As Table 6 shows, all of the same features remain. The period 1939–56 exhibits a very rapid, and 1956–66 a relatively slow, growth in defense purchases, but after late 1965 defense purchases again outpaced other resource-using government programs.

The High-Cost Urban Functions

With the increasing urbanization of the country during this century— the proportion of the population living in metropolitan areas rose from 42 per cent in 1900 to 50 per cent in 1920, to 60 per cent in 1950, and to nearly 65 per cent in 1965—one might expect those governmental functions that are especially costly to perform in urban areas to grow at above-average rates, and by doing so to help sustain local government expenditure shares. Such has not been the case, how- ever. Five important local functions involved much higher per capita expenditures in 1962 in metropolitan than in nonmetropolitan areas, as Table 7 shows, but taken as a group they grew at barely 6½ per cent

TABLE 7

LOCAL DIRECT GENERAL EXPENDITURES PER CAPITA: RATIOS OF METROPOLITAN TO NONMETROPOLITAN AREAS, 1962

High-Cost Functions		Other Major Functions	
Housing and urban renewal	5.52	Libraries	1.86
Parks and recreation	3.73	Health	1.73
Fire protection	2.75	Public welfare	1.70
Sewerage and sanitation	2.51	Hospitals	1.32
Police protection	2.46	Education	1.05
		Highways	0.83
		Natural resources	0.83
Direct general expenditures		1.34	

Source: Alan K. Campbell and Seymour Sacks, *Metropolitan America: Fiscal Patterns and Governmental Systems,* New York, 1967, p. 74.

[12] Another advantage is that the relevant NIA data are available over a longer period of time, 1939–67 for the purchase series rather than only 1952–66 for the federal-nonfederal total expenditure comparison.

per annum, on the average, between 1902 and 1966. Though not a low absolute rate, 6½ per cent is below the growth rate of other local expenditures. As a result the five urban functions began the century at 20 per cent of total local spending, receded to 15 per cent in the 1930's, and were not far above that level in 1966.

Expenditures on High-Cost Urban Functions as a Per Cent of
Local General Expenditures

Year	Per Cent	Year	Per Cent
1902	19.4	1948	17.9
1913	18.0	1957	17.2
1927	16.0	1962	17.4
1934	14.8	1966	16.5
1938	14.8		

SOURCES: *Historical Statistics: COG, 1962*, p. 47 and *Governmental Finances in 1965–66*, pp. 22–23.

It is not in these functional areas, it would appear, that one is likely to find much support for local expenditure shares in the future.

Human Capital Expenditures

Expenditures for the maintenance and development of human capital, on the other hand, are a predominately local function that has rather consistently outpaced other nonfederal public programs, as Table 8 shows. At the same time, in an increasingly mobile and interrelated communicative society there are compelling reasons for moving both the financing and at least some of the control of human capital programs to higher levels of government. In such a society the benefits of those programs are no longer highly localized, and the quality of their services consequently becomes a matter of considerable federal and state concern.[13] The extent to which this concern has already affected the relative roles of the three levels of government, and the potential impact of further developments along the same lines is the subject of this section.

If we look first at the provision of services, as shown by BOC direct general expenditure shares in Table 9, we note that in general the expected upward shift has occurred, but with some important excep-

[13] For a discussion of the intergovernmental aspects of these developments see George F. Break, *Intergovernmental Fiscal Relations in the United States,* Washington, D.C., 1967, Chapter 3.

TABLE 8

AVERAGE ANNUAL GROWTH RATES[a] OF EDUCATION,
WELFARE, HEALTH, AND NONFEDERAL DIRECT
GENERAL EXPENDITURES, SELECTED PERIODS,
1902–66

(PER CENT)

Period	Education	Public Welfare	Health and Hospitals	Nonfederal Direct General Expenditures
1902–13	7¾	3	5½	6½
1913–27	10	7¾	10	10
1927–36	½	22	3½	4
1936–40	4½	7	5½	5¼
1940–48	13	6¼	13	8½
1948–56	8	5	8½	8
1956–62	8¼	8¼	8½	8¼
1962–66	11	8	8	6¾
1902–66	8	8½	8	7½
1927–66	7¼	10	8	6¾
1948–66	8¾	6¾	8½	7¾

SOURCE: Computed from data given in Appendix Table **D**.

[a] Rates are compound annual rates of growth expressed to the nearest ¼ per cent for rates under 10 per cent and to the nearest 1 per cent for all others.

tions. In education the state share has risen, and the local share declined, fairly steadily during the present century, but the federal share has fluctuated widely, being currently below the 7 per cent level that prevailed just prior to World War II and again in 1956, and well below the 25–30 per cent levels during the late nineteen-forties.[14] Public welfare programs have also shifted upward from local to state governments, but the federal share has declined both from its Great Depression peaks and from the levels prevailing in the first three decades of the century. Health and hospital operation, in contrast, has

---

[14] Within the education category the operation of local schools, of course, has remained in the local sector—BOC direct general expenditure shares moving only from 0-0-100 in 1902 to 0-1-99 in 1966—while the operation of public institutions of higher learning has shifted from state to local governments. In 1952, for example, the state-local shares of direct expenditures on higher education were 93-7, and by 1965–66 they had become 88-12.

The Analysis of Public Output

TABLE 9

FEDERAL, STATE, AND LOCAL SHARES OF DIRECT
GENERAL EXPENDITURES FOR EDUCATION, WELFARE
AND HEALTH AND HOSPITALS,
1902, 1927, 1940, 1948, AND 1966

(PERCENTAGE DISTRIBUTIONS)

Functions		Years				
		1902	1927	1940	1948	1966
Education	F[a]	1	0[b]	7	30	4
	S	7	10	13	14	22
	L	92	90	80	56	74
Public welfare	F	10	6	12	2	3
	S	24	25	40	45	45
	L	66	69	48	53	52
Health and hospitals	F	5	18	17	36	29
	S	51	39	41	43	35
	L	44	43	42	29	35
Education, welfare, and health	F	3	3	10	26	8
	S	16	15	25	23	27
	L	81	82	66	51	65

SOURCE: Appendix Table C.
[a] F = federal; S = state; L = local.
[b] Less than ½ per cent.

become much more of a federal responsibility, with the state and local shares declining correspondingly but remaining about equal to each other.

The upward shift in the financing, as distinct from the operation, of human capital public programs has been both more pronounced and more sustained. When federal and state intergovernmental expenditures in these areas are related to state-local and local human capital expenditures respectively, the picture that emerges is one that intersperses periods of increasing centralization of financing with periods of relative stability. Federal aid to education, for example, rose from a level of barely ½ per cent of state-local expenditures during the first quarter of this century to nearly 8 per cent in 1948, remained close to 5 per cent from 1952 to 1962 and then rose again to 9 per cent in 1965–66 (Table 10). Federal aid for public health and welfare was

TABLE 10

RELATION OF FEDERAL AND STATE INTERGOVERNMENTAL EXPENDITURES TO STATE AND LOCAL EXPENDITURES FOR EDUCATION, HEALTH, AND WELFARE, SELECTED YEARS, 1902–66

Function	1902	1913	1927	1938	1944	1948	1952	1957	1960	1962	1966
PER CENT OF FEDERAL INTERGOVERNMENTAL EXPENDITURES TO STATE-LOCAL EXPENDITURES											
Education	0.4	0.5	0.4	4.5	6.9	7.8	5.2	4.3	5.1	5.3	9.0
Public welfare, health and hospitals	n.a.	n.a.	n.a.	14.3	26.8	23.4	26.4	25.3	26.9	27.8	30.8
PER CENT OF STATE INTERGOVERNMENTAL EXPENDITURES TO LOCAL EXPENDITURES											
Education	18.9	15.7	14.5	30.6	37.4	36.2	37.0	35.7	35.6	36.1	39.5
Public welfare	—	—	5.4	56.2	66.2	57.0	70.8	68.5	67.9	69.0	79.6
Health and hospitals	n.a.	n.a.	n.a.	n.a.	4.9	6.5	11.9	9.2	9.3	8.8	9.3

n.a. = not available.
SOURCES: *Historical Statistics, COG 1962*, pp. 48–49, and *Governmental Finances in 1965–66*.

about 25 per cent of state-local expenditures on those functions in all of the years shown in Table 10 between 1944 and 1960 but rose modestly thereafter to 31 per cent by 1966.

Similar alternating intervals of expansion and stability characterized the role of state assistance in local human capital programs. Note in Table 10 the rapid rise in state educational grants between 1932 and 1944 and again between 1962 and 1966; the substantial expansion in the financing role of state welfare grants from 1927 to 1938, 1948 to 1952, and 1962 to 1966; and finally, the 1944–57 increase in health and hospital assistance that tended to be sustained through 1966.

TABLE 11

FEDERAL AND STATE-LOCAL SHARES OF OWN-
FINANCED AND DIRECT GENERAL EXPENDITURES
ON SELECTED FUNCTIONS, 1902 AND 1965–66
(PER CENT)

Function		Own-Financed Expenditures		Direct Expenditures	
		1902	1965–66	1902	1965–66
Education	Fa	2	13	1	4
	SL	98	87	99	96
Public welfare	F	12	54	10	3
	SL	88	46	90	97
Health and hospitalsb	F	n.a.	33	5	29
	SL	n.a.	67	95	71
Highways	F	0	32	0	1
	SL	100	68	100	99
Housing and urban renewal	F	—	67	—	42
	SL	—	33	—	58
Natural resources	F	n.a.	82	47	80
	SL	n.a.	18	53	20
Natural resources excluding farm	F	n.a.	70	47	67
price support programs	SL	n.a.	30	53	33

n.a. = not available.

SOURCES: Computed from data given in *Historical Statistics, COG 1962,* and *Governmental Finances in 1965–66.*

a F = federal share; SL = state-local share.

b In the earliest available year, 1934, the F-SL shares of own-financed and direct general expenditures were 24–76 and 22–78 respectively.

The result of these relative increases in the importance of inter-governmental assistance was the creation of substantial gaps between own-financed and direct general expenditure shares in the health, education and welfare area. Perhaps the most dramatic contrast shown in Table 11 is the virtual cutting in half of the state-local share of own-financed welfare expenditures (from 88 per cent to 46 per cent) between 1902 and 1966 while the operation of welfare programs remained almost completely in state-local hands. Federal financing of health and hospitals presumably also increased materially, though full data are available only since 1934, but neither that area nor education matched the shift in highway financing from complete state-local responsibility in 1902 (and 1913) to a $\frac{1}{3}$–$\frac{2}{3}$ federal-state/local division in 1966.

Finally, it is of interest to compute the hypothetical impact on expenditure shares of a rather radical change in the financing of the nation's 1965–66 human capital programs. If, for example, welfare expenditures were to be financed, as some have suggested, entirely by the federal government, if the division of health and hospital costs were to be exactly reversed from its present one-third federal and two-thirds state and local allocation, if education expenditures were to be financed equally by the two levels of government, and if all this were to be done without changing the current levels of expenditure on the three program areas, the impact on government roles could be summarized as follows:

	Expenditure Shares			
Series	Actual 1965–66		Hypothetical 1965–66	
	F	SL	F	SL
Own-financed expenditures on health, education and welfare	22	78	60	40
Own-financed general expenditures	63	37	73	27
Own-financed general expenditures for civil purposes, I	46	54	60	40

While future increases in the financing role of the federal government can be forecast with some confidence, it seems most unlikely that they would occur in the manner just described. Some more probable possibilities are discussed in the next section.

III. Current and Prospective Developments

Like the country as a whole, intergovernmental fiscal relations appear to be in the midst of a period of accelerating change. As a result of incentives from above and pressure from below, new levels of local government are in the offing, promising to add further complexities to the intergovernmental picture. Pointing in the same direction is a strong, and probably increasing, interest in the use of tax, rather than expenditure, incentives to accomplish public purposes, and most uncertain of all are the roles that the different levels of government would play in a post-Vietnamese world that would permit a major functional reallocation of fiscal resources. These three current and prospective developments will be discussed in that order.

New Levels of Local Government

Among the major challenges to the U.S. federal system in the next few years, it now seems clear, will be the formation of more rational and effective systems of local government. While the solution of some of the most important urban problems requires integrated, areawide policy action, groups with special tastes and needs for public services are primarily concerned with local autonomy. What seems to be needed is some magic blend of centralizing and decentralizing changes that will create simultaneously both larger and smaller units of local government than any that now exist.

The federal government, through its grant-in-aid programs, is already providing a strong stimulus to the first line of development. Financial support is now available for the formation of comprehensive metropolitan planning agencies, bonus grants can be obtained for projects that are carried out by regional (interstate or interlocal) agencies, and the trend in urban development grants is to require the aided project either to be part of a comprehensive, areawide plan or to be reviewed by such a planning agency. Mainly enacted by the 88th and 89th Congresses (1963–66), these incentives were incorporated in federal grant programs with fiscal 1967 expenditures of nearly $2.8 billion and a projected two-year growth rate of over 50 per cent (Table 12).

Whether federal financial assistance, together with local recognition of the gains to be realized by dealing with regional problems on a

TABLE 12

EXPENDITURES OF FEDERAL GRANT PROGRAMS
PROVIDING INCENTIVES FOR COMPREHENSIVE
REGIONAL PLANNING, FISCAL YEARS 1967 AND 1969
(MILLIONS OF DOLLARS)

Agency and Program	Type of Incentive[a]	Amount of Expenditure	
		Actual 1967	Estimated 1969
Department of Agriculture:			
rural water and waste disposal facilities	c,f	11	34
Department of Transportation:			
federal-aid highways in urban areas with over 50,000 population	c	2,154	3,336
Department of Commerce:			
economic development assistance	c,f,i	20	151
Department of Health, Education, and Welfare:			
regional medical programs	f	3	35
comprehensive health planning and services	c,f	—	110
air pollution control	i	31	80
urban and industrial health	c,f	17	33
Department of the Interior:			
water pollution control	c,i	99	191
Water Resources Council:			
comprehensive regional planning	f	2	3
Department of Housing and Urban Development:			
urban renewal	c	370	700
urban transportation assistance	c,f	42	150
urban planning grants	f,i	22	46
basic water and sewer facilities	c	6	130
open space land and urban beautification	c	19	60
model city grants	c,f,i	—	242
neighborhood facilities	c	1	32
metropolitan development incentive grants	f,i	—	3
Total		2,797	5,336

SOURCES: *The Budget of the United States Government, Fiscal Year 1969* and *Special Analyses, Budget of the United States, Fiscal Year 1969*, Special Analysis K.

[a] c = compatibility required with comprehensive plan.

f = financial assistance to comprehensive planning authorities.

i = incentive grants for projects carried out by comprehensive regional or metropolitan agencies.

regional basis, will result in the creation of a new level of metropolitan governments, with their own revenue-raising powers and jurisdiction over an appropriate set of areawide public programs, is far from clear. Prominent among the possible harbingers of such a development is the growing group of metropolitan councils of governments which began in 1954 in Detroit with that area's Supervisors' Inter-County Committee. Formation of these voluntary regional councils of elected local officials was subsequently stimulated by the provision of federal financial assistance in 1965 and by the requirement after mid-1967 that applications for federal aid for specified urban development projects be accompanied by the review and comments of an areawide body authorized to carry out comprehensive planning for the metropolitan area in question.[15] Though over thirty councils of governments were operating in late 1967, their powers and sources of funds were strictly limited, and in evaluating their future prospects the Advisory Commission on Intergovernmental Relations (ACIR) stated:

> There is no real prospect that the associations of local governments are destined to become "super governments" or metropolitan governments in the classic sense. Rather they appear to be developing, first into the planning phase of cooperative decision-making, and second into a limited, step-by-step realization that it is better for local governments cooperatively to program and implement decisions than to turn regional affairs over to a series of legally and financially autonomous special districts over which elected officials in a region have little, or no, control.[16]

Another form of regional government that has received a good deal of attention from the experts is the areawide financing district. This might be restricted to a single function, such as schools, for which it might levy and collect an areawide property tax,[17] or it might be a general-purpose agency that imposed, say, a supplement on the state sales tax or levied a surcharge on the state income tax returns of all metropolitan residents and then distributed the proceeds to the different urban governments according to some agreed-upon formula. It is

[15] Section 701(g) grants authorized by the Housing and Development Act of 1965 (PL 89-117) and Section 204 of the Demonstration Cities and Metropolitan Development Act of 1966 (PL 89-754), respectively.

[16] ACIR, *Metropolitan Councils of Governments,* Report M-32, August 1966, p. 30.

[17] As a result of its 1966–67 study of fiscal balance in the American federal system the ACIR recommended that states authorize such regional school property taxing districts. See their *Ninth Annual Report,* Washington, D.C., 1968, p. 21.

not easy to obtain such agreement in normal times, but that may not be much of a barrier in future years.

At the opposite end of the local government spectrum is another phenomenon of great current interest—neighborhood subunits of existing public agencies. In order to bring its public services more in line with the tastes of its different citizens groups, San Francisco, for example, has recently been discussing both miniboards of education for individual schools within its large consolidated school district and mini police stations to improve people-to-government relations in the poorer areas of the city. Perhaps the boldest move in the decentralization direction is that proposed for New York City by the Bundy Report, which would establish sixty or so largely autonomous school districts within the metropolitan region.[18] The development of neighborhood service centers, supported by federal grants that are expected, as Table 12 shows, to grow rapidly between 1967 and 1969, is another manifestation of the same pressures for more responsive and more responsible local government.

The local government sector, in short, is in a state of flux, the duration and outcome of which cannot now be foreseen. On the one hand, only a relatively minor restructuring of the system may result, in which case it seems reasonable to predict that state and federal expenditure shares will tend to expand at the expense of local, at least for programs that have significant benefit spillouts to regional and national levels. On the other hand, autonomous metropolitan and regional governments may be formed either to help finance traditional units of government or to deal with problems that transcend their boundaries, and the traditional entities may also establish sets of subunits with some independent powers to deal with programs generating benefits that are highly localized and servicing groups with distinct and diverse tastes.[19] Should this be the case, one would expect to observe a more vigorous, and relatively more important, local public sector, though one whose structure might differ sufficiently from that of the past to require future analysts of governmental roles to recognize more than one distinct level within the local sector.[20]

[18] See *Reconnection for Learning—A Community School System for New York City,* Report of the Mayor's Advisory Panel on Decentralization of the New York City Schools, 1967.

[19] On this point see the highly suggestive, theoretical model developed by Charles M. Tiebout in "A Pure Theory of Local Expenditures," *Journal of Political Economy,* Vol. 64, October 1956, pp. 416–24.

[20] The mere establishment of intergovernmental regional authorities or neighborhood subunits does not, of course, mean that a new level of government has come into being. The crucial questions concern the amounts of independent

Tax Credits and Subsidies

When a government wishes to stimulate private activities that generate important social benefits, it normally can choose between expenditure and tax subsidies for its purposes. Each alternative has its own distinctive merits, but what concerns us here is the impact of the choice on the measurement of the expenditure shares of different levels of government. In principle, there should be none, but in practice there may be effects that are difficult to eradicate. For some measures of governmental activity, and this is one of their advantages, there would be no problem. Federal and state-local shares of NIA purchases of goods and services, for example, would not be affected by the choice, on the part of either level of government, of tax, rather than expenditure, subsidies. Total expenditure shares, on the other hand, would change unless an explicit adjustment were made. Suppose, to take a hypothetical example, that total expenditures are 200, divided equally between the federal and state-local sectors, and that the federal government wishes to inaugurate a new incentive program for private enterprise that is expected to cost 10. If it does this by means of expenditure transfers financed, say, by new taxes of equal amount, total government expenditures will rise to 210, assuming no fiscal interactions between the new program and other federal expenditures or state and local spending, and the shares of the two levels will change from 50-50 to 52-48. Alternatively, the federal government might establish tax credits of 10 for the relevant private groups and finance them by additional taxes of 10 on other groups. Assuming again the absence of fiscal interactions, we note that in this case the initial expenditure share pattern of 50-50 would remain unchanged unless we transferred the new tax credits to the other side of the budget and included them with other expenditures.[21]

The problem with making adjustments of that sort, of course, would

power accorded the new entities and the extent to which they are responsible to their electorates. If these distinctive qualities of government are lacking, the new units may simply be parts of a more decentralized, higher level of government, or they may be separate authorities with mixed public and private characteristics.

[21] A similar problem arises in the choice between measuring government enterprise activities on a gross, or on a net, basis. If the former is selected, additional subsidies generated by lowering an enterprise's selling prices would not affect governmental shares of total expenditures, whereas subsidies resulting from spending more money in order to raise the quality of the enterprise's services would. An advantage of the net basis of measurement is that the two policies would have the same effects as long as their net costs to the enterprise were equal.

be to identify the tax subsidies that should qualify for special treatment. If the purpose of a specific tax favor were purely and simply to stimulate some private activity with social benefits, the answer would be clear, but governmental actions are seldom that uncomplicated. The point may be illustrated by considering a few of the relevant features of the current federal tax system. The investment tax credit, which was established to increase the growth, productivity and international competitiveness of the U.S. economy, seems an obvious candidate for inclusion in the measurement in total expenditure shares, but if this is done, should not some portion of existing depreciation allowances be treated in the same way on the grounds that Congress has made them more generous than "true" depreciation for the same reason that it established the investment credit? On the other hand, one cannot be certain that the real purpose of the investment credit was not to reduce effective corporate tax rates in a politically palatable manner, or that accelerated depreciation is not intended mainly to offset the effects of inflation on conventional measures of business taxable income. Similarly, percentage depletion deductions may be regarded either as means of stimulating activities that are important for the national defense or as necessary adjustments to make the income tax neutral among activities involving different degrees of risk, and charitable contribution deductions may be viewed either as stimulants of socially desirable enterprises or as necessary expenses of earning income.[22]

The necessary distinctions being unclear, it might be argued that the best course of action is to ignore tax incentives in the measurement of expenditure shares and to hope that they never become important enough to matter. Unfortunately, it may already be too late to rest very easy with such a solution, and the prospects seem to be that the situation is likely to become worse, rather than better. In 1965–66 the investment tax credit reached an annual level of over $2 billion, Pechman places the tax cost of excess depletion allowances above $1.5 billion a year,[23] and charitable contribution deductions probably reduced individual tax burdens by about $2.5 billion in 1966.[24] To-

[22] For further discussion of these purposes see, for example, Joseph A. Pechman, *Federal Tax Policy,* Washington, D.C., 1966, pp. 124–25, and C. Harry Kahn, *Personal Deductions in the Federal Income Tax,* Princeton for NBER, 1960, pp. 13 and 46–48.

[23] *Op. cit.,* p. 124.

[24] Taussig estimated that the cost of charitable deductions to the government was over $2 billion in 1962, and in recent years total deductions have been growing at about 5¼ per cent a year. See Michael K. Taussig, "Economic Aspects of

gether these tax incentives were slightly over 3 per cent of the direct general expenditures of all levels of government in 1965–66, about 2.7 per cent of total NIA expenditures in 1966, and over 10 per cent of the 1966 sum of NIA transfers, subsidies and the net current deficits of government enterprises. As for future prospects, Senator Robert F. Kennedy sponsored bills (S. 2088 and S. 2100) to encourage private investment in industry and housing in urban poverty areas which rely heavily on tax incentives to achieve their purposes, and the National Advisory Commission on Civil Disorders has recently adopted a similar approach. The time may be fast approaching when more meaningful measures of government subsidies than we now have will be required.[25]

Post-Vietnam Governmental Roles

The single event with the greatest potential of changing the roles of the different levels of government in a short period of time would undoubtedly be the end of the Vietnam War, or at least of any major U.S. role in it. Special Vietnam expenditures are currently projected at $26.3 billion in fiscal 1969.[26] Though this whole sum would not be available for reallocation during the first postwar year, full-employment federal tax revenues are currently rising automatically by $10 billion a year or more,[27] and the federal government would clearly be in a position to make major changes in nondefense expenditures and tax revenues. What concerns us here are the potential effects on federal and state-local expenditure shares. Ideally one would like to compute these, for a limited number of policy alternatives that Congress could be expected to consider seriously, from a comprehensive econometric model that took full account of fiscal interactions, feedbacks and differential time paths. Specification of that limited set of alternatives, however, is not possible at this stage of the war, and that being the case, it seems unnecessary to attempt more here than a few

the Personal Income Tax Treatment of Charitable Contributions," *National Tax Journal,* Vol. XX, March 1967, p. 1, and U.S. Treasury Department, Internal Revenue Service, *Statistics of Income, 1965: Individual Income Tax Returns,* Washington, D.C., 1967, p. 210.

[25] For a recent discussion of the conceptual issues see Warren C. Robinson, "What Is a Government Subsidy?" *National Tax Journal,* Vol. XX, March 1967, pp. 86–92.

[26] *The Budget of the United States Government, Fiscal Year 1969,* Washington, D.C., 1968, p. 83.

[27] *Economic Report of the President,* Transmitted to the Congress, February 1968, Washington, D.C., 1968, p. 67.

rough approximations of the impact effects of the major policy alternatives.

Official projections of federal NIA expenditures for fiscal 1969 have been selected as the reference base for our calculations.[28] If to these are added projections of state and local expenditures from fiscal 1967 to 1969 at the same rate as those expenditures actually increased between fiscal 1965 and 1967, the expenditure amounts and shares shown in the first two columns of Table 13 are the result. Comparison of these

TABLE 13

PROJECTED AND HYPOTHETICAL FISCAL 1969 FEDERAL
AND STATE-LOCAL EXPENDITURE SHARES UNDER
ALTERNATIVE POST-VIETNAM FEDERAL
FISCAL POLICIES

Measure		Projected Shares		Hypothetical Shares Under Policies:[a]				
		Amounts (billions of dollars)	Per Cent	#1	#2a	#2b	#3	#4
						(per cent)		
Own-financed	F[b]	185.0	68	68	68	75	64	68
expenditures	SL	86.5	32	32	32	25	36	32
Own-financed expenditures:	F	106.2	55	60	60	68	54	60
civil-I	SL	86.5	45	40	40	32	46	40
Purchases of goods	F	99.4	51	51	31	43	42	43
and services	SL	97.0	49	49	69	57	58	57
Civil purchases: I	F	20.6	18	32	15	18	17	18
	SL	97.0	82	68	85	82	83	82

SOURCE: See text for description of methods of derivation.

a Policy 1: nondefense purchases substituted for $25 billion of defense purchases.

Policy 2: grants-in-aid to state and local governments substituted for $25 billion of defense purchases.

      2a: state-local marginal propensity to spend = 1.
      2b: state-local marginal propensity to spend = 0.

Policy 3: defense purchases and federal taxes reduced by $25 billion.
Policy 4: transfer payments substituted for $25 billion of defense purchases.
b F = federal share; SL = state-local share.

[28] *Special Analyses of the United States Budget, Fiscal Year 1969,* Washington, D.C., 1968, Special Analysis B, p. 22.

with the 1966 shares given earlier in Table 2 shows that three of the four series are unchanged and that the federal share of total purchases of goods and services is projected to rise from 50 to 51 per cent during the period.

While the precise content of the preferred post-Vietnam policy package cannot now be foreseen, it seems highly likely that it will be a blend both of federal tax reduction, particularly since the special "wartime" surtax has been enacted, and of expenditure increases for nondefense purchases, grants-in-aid to state and local governments, and transfer payments. The potential impacts of these four types of postwar fiscal policy on federal and state-local expenditure shares will accordingly be discussed in turn. For convenience it is assumed that the change made in each case amounts to $25 billion a year, and only the impact effects are shown in Table 13.

Suppose, first, that nondefense federal purchases of goods and services were simply substituted for defense (i.e., Vietnam) purchases.[29] Because of the lower import content of the former, this substitution would probably have a net expansionary effect on aggregate demand, and unless private demands were suitably sluggish, which seems unlikely, would need to be supplemented with restrictive tax and/or monetary policies. If the effects of the latter on state and local expenditures are ignored, the shift from military to nondefense purchases would affect only our two civil expenditure measures, increasing the federal share of own-financed civil expenditures from 55 to 60 per cent and the federal share of civil purchases from 18 to 32 per cent (Table 13).[30]

Our second policy alternative is a more complicated one. Federal grants-in-aid have been growing rapidly in recent years, as Table 14 shows, and this behavior alone implies a preferred role for them in any post-Vietnam federal policy package. In addition, there has been considerable interest in new types of federal aid, including unconditional Heller-Pechman grants and source-oriented income tax sharing, and this interest can be expected to intensify whenever defense pressures on the federal budget moderate to any significant degree. Policy alternative 2 in Table 13 is intended to cover both an increase in the projected growth rate of existing functional grant programs and the

---

[29] While some military expenditures fall in the transfer payment category, their relative importance is slight. In 1966, for example, military purchases were 98 per cent of total military expenditures (*Survey of Current Business,* July 1967, p. 29).

[30] In each case these changes result from a $25 billion increase in federal expenditures above the amounts shown in the first column of Table 13. Note that this assumes more than a doubling of projected 1969 civil federal purchases.

TABLE 14

AVERAGE ANNUAL GROWTH RATES[a] OF FEDERAL
GRANTS-IN-AID TO STATE AND LOCAL
GOVERNMENTS, SELECTED PERIODS, 1902–67
(PER CENT)

Period	Average Annual Growth Rate[b]
1902–13	5½
1913–22	26
1922–27	¾
1927–36	25
1929–37	26
1937–47	8½
1947–57	9¼
1957–67	14¼
1957–62	13¾
1962–67	14¾
Fiscal Years	
1964–67	14½
1964–69	14¾

SOURCES: Computed from data given in *Historical Statistics: COG 1962, The National Income and Product Accounts of the United States, 1929–1965, Survey of Current Business,* February 1968, and *Special Analyses, Budget of the United States, Fiscal Year 1969.*

[a] Rates are compound annual rates of growth expressed to the nearest ¼ per cent for rates below 15 per cent and to the nearest 1 per cent for higher rates.

[b] Bureau of the Census data used for 1902–13, 1913–22, 1922–27, and 1927–36; National Income Accounts data used for all other periods.

inauguration of some new kind of federal aid. In each case the impact effect on the federal budget would be a $25 billion increase in own-financed civil expenditures and a $25 billion decrease in total purchases, but no change in either total expenditures or in civil purchases.[31]

[31] The only problem arises in the case of source-oriented income tax sharing. If the amounts returned to the states of origin are treated as federal aid, and hence included on the expenditure side of the federal budget, the impact effects would be those described in the text. Alternatively, the whole policy might be treated as a combination of federal tax reduction and an agreement by the federal government to collect an equal amount of income tax revenue for each of the states. In that case, total federal own-financed expenditures and purchases of goods and services would each fall by $25 billion, and civil expenditures and purchases would remain unchanged. The budgetary treatment assumed in the text seems the preferable one.

The impact on state and local expenditures is more difficult to specify, depending as it does on such things as the matching requirements in the functional grant programs that are expanded and the average spending propensities of the states that happen to receive the major share of any new unconditional grant or tax sharing program that is initiated. In the face of these uncertainties, only two simple alternatives are presented in Table 13: the first (Policy 2a) assuming that state-local expenditures increase by the exact amount of the additional federal aid,[32] and the second (Policy 2b) making the admittedly unrealistic assumption that state-local expenditures are unaffected by the increment in federal aid and that state-local taxing and borrowing operations are reduced accordingly. The second alternative, therefore, consistently shows a higher federal expenditure share than the first.

In general, the potential impact on federal expenditure shares of a substitution of federal aid for defense purchases may be summarized as follows:

Federal Share Measure	Predicted Impact on Federal Share (F)
Own-financed expenditures	$\Delta F \gtreqless 0$ as state-local mps[a] $\lesseqgtr 1$.
Own-financed civil expenditures	F rises unless grants are strongly stimulatory of state-local expenditures.
Purchases of goods and services	F falls.
Civil purchases	$\Delta F \lesseqgtr 0$ as state-local mps $\gtreqless 0$.

[a]mps = marginal propensity to spend.

The third policy shown in Table 13 combines $25 billion reductions in defense purchases and federal tax revenues. Since it is assumed, as a first approximation, that the impact of this policy on aggregate demand is the same as those of the alternative policies being considered, the only effect on state and local expenditures will come from a propensity on their part to raise their own tax rates as federal rates fall. Here again it is difficult to be precise, and Table 13 simply uses

---

[32] This means, of course, that state-local, own-financed expenditures would remain unchanged. The increase in state-local purchases used for Policy 2a in Table 13 ($23.5 billion) is based on the 1967 ratio of state-local purchases to total expenditures (0.94).

an arbitrarily small induced state-local expenditure increment of $5 billion to illustrate the point. It is clear, in any case, that state-local shares would tend to rise at the expense of federal, though probably not by large amounts for the two civil expenditure measures. An interesting variant of a general tax reduction policy would be the adoption by the federal government of a fractional credit for state and local individual income taxes.[33] Since each dollar of federal tax revenue lost in this way would be expected to stimulate more state-local expenditures than one lost through straight tax reduction, incorporation of the credit in Policy 3 would tend to raise state-local expenditure shares above the levels shown in Table 13.

Our final post-Vietnam fiscal policy involves the substitution of federal transfer payments for $25 billion of defense purchases. No change would occur in the interlevel division of either own-financed total expenditures or civil purchases, but the federal share of own-financed civil expenditures would rise by 5 points and the federal share of total purchases would fall by 8 points. One way of implementing Policy 4 would be to enact a negative income tax, and in that eventuality some of the most interesting effects would be the fiscal interactions between the tax and both federal and state-local expenditures on income-maintenance programs. Suppose, to take one possibility, that the negative income tax simply replaced all public welfare expenditures. Projected to fiscal 1969 at their 1962–66 growth rate of 8 per cent per annum, these would amount to almost $9 billion, and if fiscal 1966 financing arrangements remained unchanged, own-financed welfare expenditures would be about $5 billion for the federal government and $4 billion for the state-local sector. A negative tax plan with a gross cost of $30 billion to the federal government could consequently be enacted,[34] and it would replace state-local spending of $4 billion. The impact on expenditure shares, however, would not be great. In both of the own-financed series shown in Table 13 the federal share would rise, and the state-local share fall, by one point only, and the impact on the other two series would be still less since state-local welfare expenditures are currently about one-third purchases and two-thirds transfers.

[33] For a discussion of one such proposal see John Shannon, "A Partial Federal Tax Credit for State Income Tax Payments," *Proceedings of the Fifty-Ninth (1966) Annual Conference on Taxation*, Columbus, 1967, pp. 382–94.

[34] For an analysis of alternative plans, together with rough estimates of their costs, see James Tobin, Joseph A. Pechman, and Peter M. Mieszkowski, "Is a Negative Income Tax Practical?" *Yale Law Journal*, Vol. 77, November 1967, pp. 1–27.

If one were to predict, on the basis of the preceding discussion, the direction in which post-Vietnam expenditure shares are likely to move, it would be that the federal share of own-financed expenditures, and also of civil purchases to a lesser extent, would rise, while the relative federal use of the nation's resources, as reflected in its share of total governmental purchases of goods and services, would decline.

IV. Conclusions

From the many factors accounting for the changing roles of different levels of government in this country during the present century this paper has selected three sets for emphasis: (1) differential growth rates among functions whose nature requires that their performance be concentrated in the hands of one specific level of government, (2) the increasingly wider geographical spread of the benefits of certain programs that have traditionally been operated at state or local levels, and (3) an upward shift of the financing function that has been only partially a response to (2) and partly a result of greater revenue-raising efficiency at higher levels of government together with man-made restrictive barriers of one kind or another at the lower levels. The main conclusions reached may be summarized as follows:

1. Though at the present time the federal government is clearly the dominant partner in the U.S. federal system, its superiority shows up mainly in the financing and other redistributive functions rather than in the use of resources. Own-financed government expenditures in 1966 were divided ⅔-⅓ between the federal and state-local sectors, with the state and local levels being about equal in importance. If expenditures are allocated to the level of operation, rather than of financing, however, the federal share drops to 55–60 per cent, and the local level becomes twice as important as the state. The greatest contrast of all is between resource-using and redistributive expenditures (transfers and subsidies), the former being shared equally between the federal and state-local levels and the latter being over 90 per cent federal.

2. Those functions which by nature must be performed by the federal government—defense, international relations, space research and technology, veterans' benefits and postal services—have as a group grown more rapidly during the present century than have the remain-

ing nonfederal expenditure programs, though there have, of course, been subperiods, such as 1902–27 and 1956–65, when the reverse was true.

3. Expenditures for the maintenance and development of human capital have also tended to have above-average growth rates. It is in this area that the modern communications and transportation revolution has done most to spread the incidence of program benefits outward from local to regional and national levels, and the changing roles of government have reflected these forces to some extent, though not as much as many experts would regard as desirable. Whereas in both 1902 and 1927 the federal and state governments made less than 20 per cent of the nation's direct expenditures on health, education and welfare, by 1966 their share had risen to 35 per cent, of which state governments contributed more than three-quarters.

4. Though urbanization has been a prominent feature of the present century, those government functions whose per capita costs are especially high in metropolitan areas—police, fire, sanitation, parks and recreation, housing and urban renewal—have not grown as fast as other local general expenditure programs. Large and growing needs in the housing, recreation and waste disposal areas, however, may alter this pattern in the future.

5. The upward movement of the governmental financing function has tended to proceed in a series of fairly broad steps whose impact, over the total period of time considered here, has been most impressive. Whereas at the beginning of the century, for example, direct expenditures were almost entirely financed by the governmental level that made them, by 1966 the federal share of total own-financed governmental expenditures was seven percentage points above its share of total direct expenditures. During the same period federal aid rose from ½ per cent to nearly 17 per cent of state-local revenues, and state aid increased from 6 per cent of local general revenues in 1902 and 1913 to 31 per cent in 1966.

6. Within the local level of government there are strong forces making for the centralization of some functions and the decentralization of others. One possible outcome, and one that should help maintain the vitality of the local sector, would be the development of several distinct levels of local government, ranging from regional, urban and rural, authorities down to autonomous neighborhood subunits of existing governments. In the absence of these structural changes it seems likely that state and federal roles will increase at the expense of local, at least for programs with significant benefit spillouts.

7. A lively current interest in the use of tax credits to stimulate private activities that have significant social benefits raises important questions about the proper treatment of fiscal incentives in the measurement of the roles of different levels of government. Unless the tax-transfer system is treated as a unit, with the negative components (taxes) being netted against the positive components (transfer payments), tax incentives, it is argued, should be explicitly added to the expenditure side of the budget whenever quantitative comparisons, over time or between levels of government in a given period, are to be made.

8. Some of the sharpest changes in the roles of different levels of government have occurred during and after wars. Though the Vietnam War has not as yet caused a major break in past trends, it has had an important impact on both the level and the intergovernmental distribution of civil expenditures. Its termination, consequently, is likely to be followed by some significant changes in the U.S. federal system. Though these are difficult to foresee in detail, the general prospect seems to be for a greater federal role in financing and redistributive functions and for more state participation in both the financing and operation of public programs.

Appendix

TABLE A: FEDERAL, STATE, AND LOCAL
GOVERNMENTAL EXPENDITURES BASED ON
MEASURES, SELECTED

Aggregate Expenditure Measure	Level of Government[a]	1902	1913	1922	1927	1932	1936
Own-financed general ex-	F	36.4	32.2	42.5	33.2	36.0	57.7
penditures (OFGE)	S	11.3	12.4	13.8	17.2	21.4	18.3
	L	52.3	55.4	43.7	49.5	42.6	24.0
Direct general expenditures	F	35.8	31.7	41.1	31.9	33.9	51.7
(DGE)	S	8.5	9.8	11.6	13.0	16.7	14.0
	L	55.7	58.5	47.3	55.1	49.4	34.2
Own-financed general ex-	F	28.9	26.1	36.2	29.1	31.8	55.1
penditures for civil pur-	S	12.6	13.5	15.3	18.3	22.8	19.4
poses: series I[c]	L	58.5	60.5	48.5	52.6	45.4	25.5
(OFGE: C-I)							
Direct general expenditures	F	28.3	25.5	34.6	27.7	29.6	48.7
for civil purposes: series	S	9.5	10.7	12.9	13.8	17.8	14.9
I[c] (DGE: C-I)	L	62.2	63.7	52.5	58.5	52.6	36.4
Direct general expenditures	F	18.5	19.8	20.8	16.5	18.4	38.8
for civil purposes: series	S	10.8	11.5	14.7	16.0	20.7	17.8
II[c] (DGE: C-II)	L	70.7	68.7	64.5	67.5	60.9	43.4
Direct general expenditures	F	11.6	11.2	25.5	17.0	16.6	38.6
for nonfederal pur-	S	11.7	12.8	14.7	16.0	21.1	17.9
poses[c]	L	76.7	76.0	59.8	67.1	62.3	43.5

SOURCES: U.S. Bureau of the Census, *Census of Governments: 1962*, Vol. VI, No. 4, *Historical Statistics on Governmental Finances and Employment,* and *Governmental Finances in 1964–65 and 1965–66.*

[a] F = federal; S = state; L = local.

[b] For 1902 through 1962 local government expenditures were grouped by fiscal

PERCENTAGE SHARES OF AGGREGATE
SIX ALTERNATIVE BUREAU OF THE CENSUS
YEARS, 1902–66[b]

1938	1940	1944	1948	1950	1952	1956	1961	1962	1964–65	1965–66
51.1	54.3	92.7	68.5	66.7	74.2	67.4	64.8	64.9	63.4	63.1
21.1	20.3	3.3	15.5	16.3	12.2	15.2	16.1	16.0	17.3	17.8
27.8	25.4	4.0	16.0	17.1	13.5	17.4	19.1	19.1	19.3	19.1
46.2	49.1	91.8	64.7	62.5	71.4	64.1	59.6	59.6	57.1	56.3
15.8	15.1	2.5	12.3	13.2	9.5	12.1	13.7	13.7	15.1	15.4
38.0	35.9	5.7	23.0	24.3	19.1	23.9	26.7	26.7	27.9	28.3
47.8	49.9	64.9	53.5	52.1	45.4	43.9	45.4	45.4	46.1	45.7
22.5	22.3	15.8	22.9	23.4	26.0	26.2	25.0	24.9	25.5	26.2
29.7	27.8	19.3	23.6	24.5	28.6	29.9	29.6	29.7	28.4	28.1
42.5	44.2	60.3	48.0	46.2	39.4	38.3	37.4	37.2	35.6	36.7
16.9	16.5	11.9	18.2	19.0	20.1	20.7	21.2	21.2	22.7	22.2
40.6	39.3	27.8	33.8	34.8	40.5	41.0	41.4	41.5	41.7	41.1
36.5	39.0	54.9	33.8	35.6	28.4	28.2	28.3	28.9	28.8	27.6
18.7	18.0	13.6	21.6	21.8	23.5	24.0	24.2	24.0	25.0	25.5
44.8	42.9	31.5	44.6	42.5	48.1	47.8	47.5	47.1	46.2	46.9
36.8	39.4	57.2	39.0	38.9	31.4	31.4	30.7	30.4	27.8	26.4
18.6	17.9	12.9	21.3	21.5	22.7	23.0	23.4	23.6	25.3	25.9
44.6	42.7	29.9	39.6	39.6	45.8	45.6	45.9	46.1	46.9	47.7

years ending within the calendar year specified. In 1963 a shift was made to a fiscal-year basis, so that 1964–65, for example, refers to the expenditures of local governments with fiscal years ending between July 1, 1964 and June 30, 1965. No change was made in 1963 in the recording of either federal or state expenditures, which have consistently been reported on a fiscal-year basis.

c For definitions of these series, see text.

TABLE B: FEDERAL AND STATE-LOCAL PERCENTAGE
MEASURES OF GOVERNMENTAL ACTIVITY,

Aggregate Expenditure Measure	Level of Government[a]	1902	1913	1922	1927	1929	1932
Own-financed expenditures	F					25.6	29.9
(OFE)	SL					74.4	70.1
Purchases of goods and	F	22.9	19.5	16.7	14.5	15.5	18.0
services (P)	SL	77.1	80.5	83.3	85.5	84.5	82.0
Own-financed expenditures for civil purposes: series I[b] (OFE:C-I)	F SL						
Civil purchases, series I[b]	F						
(P:C-I)	SL						
Transfer payments to per-	F					76.0	65.0
sons (TPP)	SL					24.0	35.0
Wages and salaries of gov-	F-M					6.2	5.9
ernment employees	F-C					22.0	21.3
(WSGE)	SL					71.8	72.8
Number of full-time equiv-	F-M					8.2	7.5
alent government em-	F-C					17.8	17.4
ployees (FTEGE)	SL					74.0	75.1

Sources: U.S. Department of Commerce, Office of Business Economics, *The National Income and Product Accounts of the United States, 1929–1965; Survey of Current Business,* July 1967. Purchases of goods and services in 1902, 1913, 1922 and 1927 are unpublished special tabulations prepared for John W. Ken-

SHARES OF SEVEN NATIONAL-INCOME-ACCOUNTS
SELECTED CALENDAR YEARS, 1902–66

1936	1938	1940	1944	1948	1950	1952	1956	1961	1962	1965	1966
53.9	51.3	54.1	92.7	69.3	67.1	75.9	69.0	68.5	68.9	66.4	68.1
46.1	48.7	45.9	7.3	30.7	32.9	24.1	31.0	31.5	31.1	33.6	31.9
41.2	41.7	43.0	92.2	52.3	48.6	69.3	58.0	53.3	54.1	49.1	49.9
58.8	58.3	57.0	7.8	47.7	51.4	30.7	42.0	46.7	45.9	50.9	50.1
		47.8	51.8	61.0	57.2	52.6	49.5	53.6	54.2	54.0	55.2
		52.2	48.2	39.0	42.8	47.4	50.5	46.4	45.8	46.0	44.8
		32.2	17.2	27.8	18.1	20.4	13.7	16.0	18.0	19.4	17.6
		67.8	82.8	72.2	81.9	79.6	86.3	84.0	82.0	80.6	82.4
70.5	49.7	53.0	59.7	72.3	75.7	73.2	78.0	82.0	81.8	81.5	81.8
29.5	50.3	47.0	40.3	27.7	24.3	26.8	22.0	18.0	18.2	18.5	18.2
4.3	4.4	6.7	60.8	21.1	22.3	31.6	25.2	19.5	19.2	17.5	18.8
48.3	45.1	41.6	23.9	32.3	31.3	30.5	28.8	27.9	27.6	26.9	26.3
47.4	50.5	51.7	15.3	46.6	46.4	37.9	46.0	52.6	53.2	55.9	54.9
4.7	5.3	8.8	66.3	21.5	22.8	36.0	29.0	24.2	25.0	22.5	24.0
52.0	48.8	45.0	17.5	28.4	27.0	24.9	23.6	22.4	22.1	20.8	20.5
43.3	45.9	46.2	16.2	50.1	50.2	39.1	47.4	53.4	52.9	56.7	55.5

drick, *Productivity Trends in the United States,* Princeton for NBER, 1961,
Table A-IIb.
[a] F = federal; SL = state-local; F-M = federal military; F-C = federal civilian.
[b] For definitions of these series, see text.

TABLE C: PERCENTAGE SHARES, BY LEVEL OF
MAINTENANCE AND DEVELOPMENT OF
1902–

Expenditure Series	Level of Government[a]	1902	1913	1922	1927	1932
Direct general expenditures:						
Education	F	1.2	0.9	0.5	0.4	0.6
	S	6.6	9.4	9.6	9.7	12.0
	L	92.2	89.7	90.0	89.9	87.4
Public welfare	F	9.8	8.8	7.0	6.2	0.2
	S	24.4	28.1	29.7	24.8	16.6
	L	65.8	63.2	63.3	68.9	83.2
Health and hospitals	F	4.8	4.4	26.7	17.6	21.8
	S	50.8	46.9	35.5	39.4	36.9
	L	44.4	48.7	37.8	42.9	41.3
Total	F	2.8	2.0	5.1	3.3	4.2
	S	16.3	16.5	14.9	15.1	16.9
	L	80.9	81.5	80.0	81.6	78.9
Own-financed expenditures:						
Education	F	1.6	1.4	0.9	0.8	1.1
	SL	98.4	98.6	99.1	99.2	98.9
Public welfare	F	12.2	12.3	7.8	6.8	0.5
	SL	87.8	87.7	92.2	93.2	99.5
Health and hospitals	F					
	SL					

Sources: U.S. Bureau of the Census, Census of Governments: 1962, Vol. VI, No. 4, *Historical Statistics on Governmental Finances and Employment,* and

GOVERNMENT, OF EXPENDITURES FOR THE
HUMAN CAPITAL, SELECTED YEARS,
1966

1936	1938	1940	1948	1950	1952	1956	1961	1962	1965–66
7.9	6.1	6.7	30.3	25.6	13.3	6.6	3.0	2.6	4.5
12.6	13.1	13.3	14.0	14.1	15.6	15.1	17.9	18.7	21.7
79.5	80.8	80.0	55.7	60.3	71.1	78.3	79.1	78.7	73.8
17.1	13.3	12.0	2.1	0.8	1.5	1.4	1.2	1.2	3.0
42.3	36.7	40.1	44.9	52.8	49.8	50.4	48.4	48.8	45.0
40.6	50.0	47.9	53.0	46.4	48.7	48.2	50.4	50.0	52.0
21.1	18.7	16.8	36.4	35.5	31.7	25.9	28.1	29.2	29.3
37.3	39.5	41.0	43.3	34.9	35.4	39.3	36.2	35.2	35.5
41.6	41.7	42.2	29.3	29.6	32.9	34.8	35.7	35.6	35.2
12.2	9.9	9.6	26.2	22.6	15.0	9.3	7.2	7.2	8.4
23.8	23.4	24.7	22.9	25.3	25.8	24.7	25.8	26.2	27.3
64.0	66.7	65.7	50.9	52.2	59.2	66.0	67.0	66.6	64.3
14.2	10.3	12.7	35.7	29.4	17.9	10.4	7.9	8.1	13.1
85.8	89.7	87.3	64.3	70.6	82.1	89.6	92.1	91.9	86.9
46.1	31.0	31.8	35.9	39.0	43.2	47.2	46.8	48.8	54.4
53.9	69.0	68.2	64.1	61.0	56.8	52.8	53.2	51.2	45.6
	20.8		39.3		35.9		30.8	32.0	33.2
	79.2		60.7		64.1		69.2	68.0	66.8

Governmental Finances in 1965-66.
a F = federal; S = state; L = local; SL = state-local.

TABLE D: AMOUNTS OF DIRECT GENERA
GOVERNMENT ON SELECTEI
(MILLION

Functions	1902	1913	1922	1927	1932	1936	193℮
1. National defense and international affairs	165	250	875	616	721	932	1,04
2. Veterans' services not elsewhere classified	141	177	425	579	928	1,699	59
3. Postal service	126	270	553	711	794	751	77
4. Space research and technology	—	—	—	—	—	—	—
5. Federal functions (total 1, 2, 3 and 4)	432	697	1,853	1,906	2,443	3,382	2,40
6. Nonfederal functions	1,146	2,325	7,001	8,684	9,305	12,455	13,86
7. Education	258	582	1,713	2,243	2,325	2,365	2,65
8. Public welfare	41	57	128	161	445	997	1,23
9. Health and hospitals	63	113	352	431	583	592	67
10. Human capital functions (total 7, 8, and 9)	362	752	2,193	2,835	3,353	3,954	4,56

SOURCES: U.S. Bureau of the Census, Census of Governments: 1962, Vol. VI, Nc
4, *Historical Statistics on Governmental Finances and Employment,* and *Goverr*
mental Finances in 1964–65 and 1965–66.

XPENDITURES OF ALL THREE LEVELS OF
UNCTIONS, 1902–66
F DOLLARS)

1940	1944	1948	1950	1952	1956	1961	1962	1964–65	1965–66
1,590	85,530	16,075	18,355	48,187	42,680	49,387	53,225	55,810	60,832
501	529	3,293	2,796	2,428	3,097	3,965	4,129	4,190	4,510
808	1,085	1,715	2,270	2,612	2,899	4,025	4,101	5,261	5,706
—	—	—	—	—	—	735	1,242	5,058	5,869
2,899	87,144	21,083	23,421	53,227	48,676	58,112	62,697	70,319	76,917
5,226	20,706	29,005	37,280	38,063	53,480	81,049	86,462	103,312	112,489
2,827	2,805	7,721	9,647	9,598	14,160	21,214	22,814	30,021	34,837
1,314	1,150	2,144	2,964	2,830	3,184	4,779	5,147	6,420	6,966
732	857	1,934	2,711	3,199	3,739	5,681	6,135	7,671	8,363
4,873	4,812	11,799	15,322	15,627	21,083	31,674	34,096	44,112	50,166

TABLE E: AMOUNTS OF EXPENDITURES BY ALL
ALTERNATIVE MEASURES,
(BILLIONS

Measure	1902	1913	1922	1927 1929[b]	1932	1936
General expenditures:						
BOC[c]	1.6	3.0	8.8	10.5	11.3	15.8
NIA[c]				10.3	10.6	16.1
Purchases of goods and services (NIA)	1.2	2.5	6.0	8.5	8.1	12.0
Direct general expenditures (BOC), civil, series I	1.4	2.8	8.0	10.0	11.0	14.9
Nonfederal (BOC)	1.1	2.3	7.0	8.7	9.3	12.5

SOURCES: U.S. Bureau of the Census, *Census of Governments: 1962,* Vol. VI, No. 4, *Historical Statistics on Governmental Finances and Employment* and *Governmental Finances in 1964–65 and 1965–66;* U.S. Department of Commerce, Office of Business Economics, *The National Income and Product Accounts of the United States, 1929–1965; Survey of Current Business,* July 1967; and John W. Kendrick, *Productivity Trends in the United States,* Princeton for NBER, 1961,

THREE LEVELS OF GOVERNMENT: FIVE
SELECTED YEARS, 1902–66[a]
OF DOLLARS)

1938	1940	1944	1948	1950	1952	1956	1961	1962	1965	1966
16.2	18.0	107.9	49.9	60.4	91.3	102.1	138.8	148.9	173.6	189.6
16.8	18.4	103.0	50.3	60.8	93.7	104.1	149.0	159.9	185.8	209.8
13.0	14.0	96.5	31.6	37.9	74.7	78.6	107.6	117.1	136.4	154.3
15.2	16.5	22.3	34.0	42.3	43.1	59.5	89.8	95.9	117.8	128.6
13.9	15.2	20.7	29.0	37.3	38.1	53.5	81.0	86.5	103.3	112.5

Table A-IIb, Column 10, for purchases of goods and services, 1902, 1913, and 1922.

a Fiscal years for BOC series (see footnote b, Table A); calendar years for NIA series.

b 1927 for BOC series; 1929 for NIA series.

c Own-financed and direct general expenditures.

TABLE F: GOVERNMENT EXPENDITURES AS A PER CENT
EXPENDITURE MEASURES,

Measure	1902	1913	1922	1927 1929c	1932	1936
General expenditures:						
BOC	7.3	7.7	11.9	11.0	19.5	19.1
NIA				10.0	18.3	19.5
Purchases of goods and services (NIA)	5.7	6.3	8.0	8.2	13.9	14.5
Direct general expenditures (BOC): civil, series I	6.6	7.0	10.8	10.5	19.0	18.1
Nonfederal (BOC)	5.3	6.0	9.5	9.0	16.0	15.1

SOURCES: Table E and U.S. Bureau of the Census, *Long Term Economic Growth, 1960–1965,* pp. 166–167, and *Survey of Current Business,* July 1967.
a NBER (Kendrick) estimates for 1902; NIA estimates for other years.

OF GROSS NATIONAL PRODUCT,[a] FIVE ALTERNATIVE
SELECTED YEARS, 1902–66[b]

1938	1940	1944	1948	1950	1952	1956	1961	1962	1965	1966
19.1	18.1	51.3	19.4	21.2	26.4	24.4	26.7	26.6	26.5	26.5
19.8	18.5	49.0	19.5	21.4	27.1	24.8	28.6	28.5	27.2	28.2
15.3	14.0	46.0	12.3	13.3	21.6	18.7	20.7	20.9	19.9	20.8
18.0	16.6	10.6	13.2	14.9	12.5	14.2	17.3	17.1	18.0	18.0
16.4	15.3	9.9	11.3	13.1	11.0	12.8	15.6	15.4	15.8	15.7

[b] Fiscal years for BOC series (see footnote b, Table A); calendar years for NIA series.

[c] 1927 for BOC series; 1929 for NIA series.

COMMENT

by MANCUR OLSON, *University of Maryland*

Professor Break has left us all in his debt with his interesting calculations, detailed breakdowns, and judicious recommendations about the relative roles of different levels of governments. What else could we ask for? Only a model or theory that could explain his interesting, and on occasion even somewhat paradoxical, conclusions. But Break had no obligation to provide a logically complete explanation of his findings and recommendations, especially as he has done quite enough for a single paper. Yet, what he says does invite an attempt to provide an explanatory model, so I will accordingly try to set out the broad and rough outlines of such a model here. There is perhaps some evidence of the need for an explanatory model in this area in the fact that two of the other participants in this conference, Jerome Rothenberg[1] and Gordon Tullock,[2] have independently attempted to provide explanations of some of the same phenomena. In addition, a Canadian economist with a particular interest in the process of federalism in Canada has previously offered a model with partly similar purposes.[3]

What particularly needs systematic explanation in Break's paper is the seemingly conflicting evidence about whether centralization or decentralization is on the rise, and his own somewhat paradoxical recommendation that there is a need not only for more centralization but at the same time also more decentralization. Break shows that the federal government's share of all government expenditures has increased markedly in this century, to the point where the federal government is now "clearly the dominant partner in the federal system." Where "redistributive" monies are at issue, Break finds that they are "over 90 per cent federal." Nonetheless, Break's computations and breakdowns also show that since 1948, by any one of a number of

NOTE. Some of the author's work on this topic has been supported by the National Science Foundation under NSF Grant No. GS2588.

1 Jerome Rothenberg, "Local Decentralization and the Theory of Optimal Government," in this volume.

2 See Tullock's "Comment" on Rothenberg's paper in this volume, and his article on "Problems of Scale," in *Public Choice*, Vol. VI, Spring 1969, pp. 19–29.

3 Albert Breton, "A Theory of Government Grants," *Canadian Journal of Economics and Political Science*, Vol. XXXI, May 1965, pp. 175–87.

reasonable measures, both state and local expenditures have been increasing *more* rapidly than federal expenditures. When the growth in federal government spending on defense and international purposes is excluded, this increase in the state-local share of total public expenditures is particularly striking. Within the local level, says Break, "there are strong forces making for the centralization of some functions and the decentralization of others."

To add to the ambiguity, that most two-sided variable in any analysis of changes in the relative importance of different levels of government, grants-in-aid from higher to lower levels of government, has increased disproportionately in the present century. At the turn of the century, federal subsidies accounted for only ½ of one per cent of state and local revenues, but by 1966 they accounted for nearly 17 per cent. Over the same period state aid increased from 6 per cent to 31 per cent of local general revenues. In recent years, there has been a particularly notable growth of state and local spending of federal money; from 1957 to 1967, federal grants-in-aid to state and local governments have increased at a compound rate of more than 14 per cent per annum.

There is both centralization and decentralization in Break's predictions and recommendations as well. He says that "new levels of local government are in the offing, promising to add further complexity to the intergovernmental picture." One important possibility is that "autonomous metropolitan and regional governments may be formed either to help finance traditional units of government or to deal with problems that transcend their boundaries, and the traditional entities may also establish sets of subunits with some independent powers to deal with programs generating benefits that are highly localized and servicing groups with distinct and diverse tastes" (such as miniboards of education and mini police stations in poorer areas of the big cities). Some such amalgam of centralization and decentralization is not only a probability, but desirable as well: "What seems to be needed," he says, "is some magic blend of centralizing and decentralizing changes that will create simultaneously both larger and smaller units of local government. . . ."

The key to explaining Break's seemingly ambiguous findings and somewhat paradoxical recommendations can be found in the relationship between the boundaries of a government or jurisdiction and the distribution of the benefits of its activities. We shall assume that governments provide only collective or public goods, which in this particular argument are defined to be goods such that at least some non-purchasers of these goods cannot be denied their benefits without prohibitive costs. The phrase "at least some" is included in the definition because it is here necessary to take account of one important complication which many discussions of public goods ignore: the fact that, in practice, a great many collective goods do not benefit *all* of the people in the nation, or for that matter *only* people within a nation. A program that lessens air pollution or water pollution, for example, will benefit people in a particular metropolitan area or a particular watershed, but not everyone in the country. Similarly, a particular television station provides a collective good to the people within the range of its broadcasting tower, but not to others. The benefits of pure or basic research, by contrast, spill beyond the boundaries of the government that pays for the research to the entire world. Accordingly, the assumption here is that each collective good has determinate beneficiaries, who may be a small group of citizens in a single community or the citizens of the entire world. This determinate client group may exactly coincide with those who live within the boundaries of a given nation-state, but need not and usually will not do so.

There are four logically possible relationships between the scope of the benefits of a collective good and the boundaries of the jurisdiction that provides it:

1. Some (or in rare cases even all) of the beneficiaries of a collective good live outside the boundaries of the jurisdiction that provides it;
2. All of the beneficiaries of a collective good are within the boundaries of the jurisdiction that provides it, but they comprise only a subset (and often only a small subset) of those within the jurisdiction;
3. Some of the beneficiaries of a collective good are outside the boundaries of the jurisdiction, and those inside the jurisdiction who enjoy its benefits are but a subset of those inside the jurisdiction;
4. The scope of benefits of a collective good exactly matches the boundaries of the jurisdiction that provides it.

We must now consider each of the logical possibilities in turn.

The case in which some (or even all) of the benefits of a collective good reach beyond the boundaries of the jurisdiction that provides it is simple and familiar. There is in this case an "externality" for the jurisdiction that provides the collective good, and it ignores the benefits that spill out beyond its borders, with the result that, from the point of view of the society as a whole, only a less than Pareto-optimal quantity (and conceivably none) of the collective good is supplied. In addition, there is a tendency for the "exploitation of the great by the small,"[4] that is, a tendency for those jurisdictions that put the largest absolute value on any collective good shared by several jurisdictions to bear a disproportional share of the burden of providing whatever amount is provided.[5] This case is typified in the metropolitan area enjoying many metropolis-wide collective goods, but containing both a relatively large center city government and many relatively small suburban jurisdictions. And the outcomes that at least many observers find in such situations are exactly what the model predicts: a less than optimal supply of public services for the metropolis, with the center city government bearing a disproportionate share of those metropolitan services that are provided.

The case in which the beneficiaries of a collective good all live within the confines of the relevant jurisdiction, but comprise only a subset (and often only a small subset) of the citizens of that jurisdiction, is unfortunately not so familar. There is in this case an "internality" that parallels the "externality" in the preceding case. Unless the subset of the citizens of the jurisdiction happen to be a majority of those in the jurisdiction,[6] it will follow (assuming majority rule) that even a collective good that *must* be provided to attain Pareto-optimality for the jurisdiction (and the larger society) will often *not* be provided at all, or if it is, may not be provided in Pareto-optimal quantities. Though the gains from a Pareto-optimal public project by definition exceed its costs, the number of *losers* from the project exceeds the number of *gainers,* because the benefits reach only the subset and the tax costs are borne by the population of the jurisdiction as a whole.[7] Here there is what might perhaps be called the "exploitation of the few by the many."

The collective goods for a metropolitan area (such as air pollution

---

[4] See my *Logic of Collective Action,* Cambridge, Mass., 1965, Chapter I.

[5] See Mancur Olson, Jr., and Richard Zeckhouser, "An Economic Theory of Alliances," *Review of Economics and Statistics,* Vol. 48, August 1966, pp. 266–79.

[6] In this case there is no tendency for less than Pareto-optimal provision.

[7] If there is an institutional arrangement that imposes a special tax only on the subset that benefits from the collective good, that arrangement constitutes a jurisdiction and it fits under case four below.

control, or an educational television station) will again provide an instructive example. Why doesn't the *federal* government provide such goods whenever it is Pareto-optimal to provide them? Because the people in a metropolitan area will be the only gainers, and the constituents of the congressmen and senators representing the rest of the nation will be losers. It is commonly observed that bills need to be written in such a way that the constituents of a great many congressmen benefit before they are likely to pass. Legislation for poor or depressed areas, for example, sometimes must be amended to qualify so much of the nation's area for the benefits the bill provides that the legislation's capacity to serve its initial purpose is lost or impaired.

To be sure, it is not *always* the case that a small subset of the people in a jurisdiction must fail to obtain a Pareto-optimal good. Logrolling or bargaining among enough small groups with needs for separate collective goods can, in principle, make it possible for them to put together a package of individual projects which in the aggregate commands a majority. But logrolling or bargaining is costly, and also chancy because it can pay each party to the bargaining to "bluff" or in other ways hold out for a better bargain. Thus bargaining is not ordinarily feasible unless there are only a small number of groups who need collective goods, and each of them is organized to bargain, and together they constitute a majority. The "pork barrel" process that gives "logrolling" its unfortunate and undeserved popular reputation usually involves the special case of projects that have a "monumental" quality that helps the congressmen who promoted them, and *that are all in the province of a single committee in each house, which decisively lowers the cost of the needed bargaining.*[8] Thus the logical possibility of bargaining cannot refute the conclusion that "internalities" normally lead to a less than Pareto-optimal provision of collective goods.[9]

In the third possible case, where there is both an externality and an internality, it is obvious there is again a tendency to provision of a less than Pareto-optimal quantity or collective good.

The only case in which there is no such tendency is that in which

---

[8] I am thankful to my colleague Charles Schultze for calling this point to my attention. He has told me of cases in which measures that could have left all parties at issue better off were unable to pass because it was not feasible to logroll across committee lines.

[9] This point is justified with additional argument in my "Principle of 'Fiscal Equivalence,'" *American Economic Review, Papers and Proceedings*, Vol. LIX, May 1969, pp. 479–87.

there is "fiscal equivalence," or matching boundaries of the collective good and the jurisdiction that provides it. This case is the only one consistent with the necessary conditions for Pareto-optimal resource allocation.[10]

The advantages of fiscal equivalence, and the total lack of a needed public service that usually arises when the jurisdictional structure of a society departs *too far* from this principle, may help explain why Break felt that "new levels of local government are in the offing," even though there are already tens of thousands (according to the Committee for Economic Development, 80,000)[11] of local governments in the United States, and most expert observers think there should be far fewer. The foregoing argument shows that there is a case (albeit a case that is much qualified when all the detail and diversity of the real world are taken into account) for a separate jurisdiction for every collective good with a unique boundary, and thus a need for a great number and variety of governments. Since some collective goods cover the whole world, there is a case for a comprehensive international organization, and since many cover only small communities, there is also a case for a large number of local governments, not to mention the governments in between. The fact that even the different local or subnational collective goods a single individual enjoys have different boundaries (e.g., the airshed which gives the boundaries of the air pollution he wants controlled are usually not the same as those of the watershed or other area that bounds his water pollution problem) means that it is a necessary condition of efficient resource allocation that at least many individuals should each be subject to several different "local" jurisdictions with varying boundaries, offensive as such a state of affairs has been to those who accept the conventional wisdom in these matters.

There is, to be sure, no need for each and every jurisdiction to have a host of elected officials—in many cases the appropriate "jurisdiction" is simply legal machinery whereby a higher level of government can make it convenient for a group of citizens to tax themselves in order to meet some local need. A federation of local governments, whose

---

[10] Governments are obviously concerned with stabilization and redistribution as well as resource allocation. The rule of fiscal equivalence would give the federal government responsibility for stabilization policy, since a stable economy is a collective good to the whole nation. The federal government should also have responsibility for redistribution, since rich persons tend to move out of (and poor people tend to move into) localities which redistribute income to the poor.

[11] *Modernizing Local Government*, New York, 1966, p. 17.

boundaries together match those of a collective good, but which has no direct elections of its own, can also satisfy the need for "fiscal equivalence" without the costs of unnecessary officials and elections.

If the argument here is correct, there is a need not only for a larger number of governments than expert opinion has thought fitting (though perhaps not as many as the United States now has), but also for new local and regional jurisdictions as metropolitan areas grow, the population shifts, and technology changes. Even a new sense of ethnic identity, if combined with demands for particular types of collective goods not desired by others, can create a need for new jurisdictions.

This latter need will exist when historical patterns of segregation or other factors have created ghettos, or enclaves inhabited exclusively by one race or ethnic group. If the race or ethnic group in the ghetto has a distinct cultural background and demands special collective goods[12] (such as more black policemen or courses in Afro-American history) the situation will then be analytically identical to a situation in which the people of a given area have some localized physical problem, such as air pollution, which is a collective good for them but not for those living outside the given area. The boundaries of the ghetto, in other words, mark the boundaries of some potential or actual collective goods, and the principle of fiscal equivalence then demands a separate jurisdiction for the ghetto. This may help explain Break's sympathy for mini police districts and school boards, as well as many of the current demands for black power separatism, the new left focus on decentralization, and the ideology of "power to the neighborhoods."[13] Of course, when long-run considerations are taken into account, a solution which neglects the whole notion of "consumer sovereignty," but rather tries to impose common public policies on diverse social groups in the hopes that this will ultimately produce a more cohesive and integrated society, may in some moral sense be thought superior to fiscal equivalence for the inner city. But whatever policy is in practice preferred, it is important to remember that separate jurisdictions with boundaries matching those of the ghetto will sometimes be a necessary condition for Pareto-optimal efficiency in the provision of public services in the short run.

Nothing that has been said so far explains Break's point about the extraordinary growth in subsidies from higher to lower levels of gov-

[12] See Nathan Glazer, "For White and Black, Community Control Is the Issue," *New York Times Magazine,* April 27, 1969.
[13] See Norman Mailer, "Why Are We in New York?" *New York Times Magazine,* May 18, 1969.

ernment. To obtain a proper understanding of this problem we need to look not only at the "catchment areas" of collective goods, but also at how the cost of production of these goods varies with the size of the jurisdiction that provides them.

It is necessary, first, to be clear that economies of scale (as opposed to diseconomies of scale) cannot lead to any modification of the principle of fiscal equivalence. This is because, when all of those who would benefit from a collective good are in the relevant jurisdiction, as fiscal equivalence demands, there could be no point in expanding the government still farther. Several jurisdictions might obtain savings from purchasing needed goods or services from large contractors, perhaps, but there could be no case for making a jurisdiction larger than fiscal equivalence would suggest. This can best be seen by considering the example of a dam built for flood control purposes. Fiscal equivalence would require that all of the people in the flood plain be in the relevant jurisdiction. There would be no point in adding others to the jurisdiction, even if big dams should involve lower unit costs than small ones.

Where there are diseconomies of scale, on the other hand, the situation is more complicated. Suppose that, when the jurisdiction has been expanded to the point that all the externalities have been internalized, it is so large and bureaucratic that it has higher unit costs of production than a smaller government would have had. Education and police services *may* be of this nature. In this case, maximum economic efficiency requires a higher level jurisdiction encompassing all of the externalities, and a lower level jurisdiction of whatever size minimizes unit costs of production of the collective good. The lower level jurisdiction should then produce the collective good, and the higher level jurisdiction should give it a subsidy that lowers its marginal costs (not a block grant) by the amount of the social value of the benefits that spill out beyond the boundaries of the lower level jurisdiction. In this way fiscal equivalence is preserved and costs of production are also at a minimum.

In view of the improvements of transportation and communication, and the increasing mobility (including longer commuting) of the population, the domains over which spillouts occur are probably increasing over time. At the same time there may be a growing uneasiness about the insensitivity and ineptness of bureaucracy, growing demands for "democratic participation" via decentralization, and other misgivings about the efficiency of large bureaucracies.[14] Thus the

---

[14] See Glazer, *op. cit.*

extraordinary growth in subsidies from higher to lower levels of government, which Break emphasizes, should not be either surprising or alarming. A considerable number of such subsidies may be a necessary condition of the Pareto-optimal provision of collective services, even when jurisdictional boundaries are perfectly drawn. And as Albert Breton's pioneering paper[15] has shown, if the boundaries of local and provincial governments are drawn in such a way that there are more spillouts than would be the case with more rational boundaries, there is a further need for subsidies from higher to lower levels of government.

The real world is vastly more complicated than the unusually simple model adumbrated here, so it is not appropriate to go directly from the model to definite and specific policy recommendations. A complete policy analysis would, for example, have to take account of the fact that many governments provide quasi-private goods whose benefit boundaries are ill defined or subject to change by policymakers, or of the possible savings in certain cases of multifunctional governments.[16]

Yet what has been said here does strongly suggest that Break's most basic recommendation deserves the most sympathetic consideration. "What is needed," he says, "is some magic blend of centralizing and decentralizing changes that will create both larger and smaller units of local government." It is difficult indeed to see how a Pareto-optimal provision of public services could be achieved without such a blend of changes, or without the intragovernmental subsidies he rightly emphasizes.

[15] See Breton, *op. cit.*

[16] These and other complications and qualifications are discussed in Olson, " 'Fiscal Equivalence.' "

ASSESSING THE ROLE OF SYSTEMATIC DECISION MAKING IN THE PUBLIC SECTOR

HENRY S. ROWEN

The RAND Corporation

Two principal theories of the nature of decision making in the public sector have been articulated in recent years. These approaches have such prominent strengths and weaknesses and they differ so sharply in character that it seems useful to explore how fundamentally incompatible they are and to explore to what extent they can be reconciled. This paper undertakes such an explanation.

The Two Theories

One view, associated principally with C. E. Lindblom and A. Wildavsky, is that decision making in the public sector is, and should be, a disjointed, partisan, incremental, consensus seeking activity.[1] This view holds that only such a process satisfies the needs of a democratic society with its diverse values, that decisions are made on matters of complexity that are beyond the competency of decision makers to deal with comprehensively, that there are no generally accepted criteria for policy decisions in the public sector, that ends and means interact strongly, and that consistency among policies is unattainable. It is also argued that such a process facilitates the reaching of agreement by those having differing objectives, that it reflects the breadth and intensity with which values are held within society, and that, in stress-

NOTE. In the course of preparing this paper I had the opportunity of hearing a talk by Charles Schultze on this general subject. A number of the ideas in the paper were stimulated by his talk, but he should not be blamed for the bad ones.

[1] D. Braybrooke and C. E. Lindblom, *A Strategy of Decision*, New York, 1963; C. E. Lindblom, *The Intelligence of Democracy*, New York, 1965; A. Wildavsky, *The Politics of the Budgetary Process*, Boston, 1964, and "The Political Economy of Efficiency," *The Public Interest*, Summer 1967.

ing agreement based on the expression of interest, it helps to meet an essential political requirement of democratic government.

The other view, which is associated with a longer list of names, including Tinbergen, Hitch, McKean, and McNamara, among many others, has been concerned with causing public sector decision making to be a more systematic, analytical, scientific, efficiency oriented process. This approach, strongly influenced by economic theory, stresses the importance of systematically examining objectives, identifying various ways of achieving them, and estimating—often in quantitative terms—the benefits and the costs of each possibility. Much of this interest in recent years has centered on the evolution within the federal government and a growing number of local governments of a planning, programing, budgeting system (PPBS). That this development has generated a good deal of attention is evidenced by several Congressional hearings during the past two years. At present, the attitude among congressmen seems to be either that PPBS is an oversold, primitive, misused technique of little or negative merit or that it is such a useful innovation in decision making that the Congress should apply it to its own activities.

There is no important disagreement between these two views on the "normal" workings of the public sector decision making process. It is quite evidently a disjointed, fragmented, partisan, consensus seeking one. What is at issue is the adequacy of the "normal state" and the results to be expected from the introduction of more systematic decision making methods. The main questions in my view are the following:

1. Does a partisan, incremental decision process seem to produce satisfactory results or is there good reason for believing that it could be improved upon?
2. Are there some classes of activities or particular kinds of decisions which should be left to the traditional method and others for which the systematic approach should be emphasized?

With regard to the adequacy of partisan incrementalism there are several tests that might be applied. First, in the spirit of this approach, there may be growing a sense in this country that much of the public sector is not performing as well as it should, that agreement simply on having programs isn't enough and that better results are needed. One might also forecast that the growing number of people trained in analytic skills motivated towards more systematic decision making will help to bring about a change in decision making styles. This development might be accepted with good grace by those whose primary concern is reaching a consensus but not necessarily by those oriented towards systematic decision making. They should look to the results.

A second test might be to introduce more systematic decision making methods and see what happens—in short, to experiment. Something like this has been happening, for example, in recent years in the tax collection activities of a number of Latin American countries; the decision making innovations of Robert McNamara in the Defense Department provide another example; a third is the PPBS effort underway in New York City. However, one should not expect unambiguous results, for there is no ultimate test of the "correctness" of public policies. Values differ and history runs past only once. But the investigation of such experiments may yield useful insights as to what seems to work well and what does not.

Third, objective measures of program performance are available. The efficiency with which mail is moved, pounds of payload put into orbit, tuberculosis rates reduced, crime reduced, children taught to read, or incomes increased can be examined, experimented upon, and subjected to regional and international comparisons. The results sometimes yield evidence of large inefficiencies. (For example, the Presidential Commission on the Post Office is expected to report soon that about 20% of the Post Office's $7 billion budget is wasted.) These indicators do not measure ultimate values, but they should not be despised. They have political significance. And to the extent that they are accepted, they provide a basis for judging the efficiency of government programs. They, of course, need not be accepted, and the investigation of such measures of performance is one of the principal aims of systematic decision making.

In sum, my impression is that there is a growing sense of dissatisfaction with the adequacy of the performance of many activities in the public sector, that some of the recent changes in decision making will meet the market test of usefulness and be incorporated into decision making routines, and that in a large number of specific program areas there is strong evidence of inefficiency. However, this does not constitute an indictment of partisan incrementalism. Far from it. For to my view the objective should be a strengthening of this system with its built-in adversary features, a strengthening of the ability of different groups and centers of power to compete in the political market place.

The Effect of Policy and Program Characteristics on the Scope for Systematic Decision Making

The variety of activities to be found in the public sector is so great that one should expect to find substantial differences in the scope for change in decision making styles. The following factors seem to be among the more important ones in influencing this scope.

THE NATURE OF THE DEMAND. First, there is the demand for *specific services* by consumers. It is useful to distinguish two kinds of consumption services: (a) those where the consumer knowledge of the service is generally good (mail delivery, library services, garbage collection, housing services); (b) those services with generally poorly understood characteristics (health care and education services). In the latter case consumers generate a demand for these services in input terms, such as physician visits and accessibility of classrooms with a given teacher-pupil ratio and a given ethnic mix but, on the whole, they do not generate a demand for health care and education with well defined outputs. They do not largely because of consumer ignorance. Where consumer ignorance is large the consumer is in a poor position to judge the adequacy of government performance. In such cases the pressures for effective results and for efficiency are likely to be especially weak. It is especially in such cases that the pay-off from systematic analysis aimed at informing consumers as to the quality of the service they are receiving may be high. Second, there are those activities for which the demand is for *money transfer* (crop support programs, welfare payments). These demands for income transfer are oriented geographically or by socioeconomic group. In either case the issue is one of income distribution. This does not rule out questions of efficiency but it sharply reduces the intensity of interest in them. Third, there are *public goods* often involving issues remote from the consumer's ken. Fourth, there are *intermediate* products usually involving well defined outputs (timber from national forests, oil from off shore lands). Fifth, there is the demand for public works as *monuments* (courthouses, Post Office buildings).

THE NATURE OF THE PRODUCTION FUNCTION. A well defined production function with its known relationship between inputs and outputs permits predictable outputs and makes estimates of efficiency relatively straightforward. A production function might be poorly defined for several reasons: it might involve fundamental uncertainty (basic science research activities), it might involve outputs strongly dominated by subjective elements (aspects of health care), it might be dominated by behavioral uncertainties (response of recipient countries to foreign aid programs), or it might be a relatively unexplored activity (the relationship between welfare programs and population migration or the effects of different teaching techniques on pupil performance). Examples of activities with relatively well defined production functions are those of the Internal Revenue Service, space programs, Forest Service logging operations, the air traffic control system and our old age insurance system. (I am not, of course, asserting that there is necessarily a high degree of agreement on the value of the outputs produced by these activities.)

Where the production function is poorly understood, programs are judged mainly in input terms: the money spent, the people employed, the cases handled. Professional standards get developed which sanctify these inputs in the absence of output measures in which there is much confidence (e.g., the now abandoned "demographic" argument for increasing basic science budgets at 15 per cent a year, hospital bed requirements per unit of population). Where the production function is unclear, the payoffs from more systematic decision methods are likely to be high. In the well defined cases, decisions are likely to be made fairly efficiently, or, if they are not being so made, the reason is probably fragmented authority or overriding political constraint (as in the case of the Post Office).

THE AVAILABILITY OF DATA. The production function might be known to some but not necessarily to those making important decisions. For example, if programs are run by local governments and the federal role is primarily one of providing funds, the likelihood is fairly high that decision makers at the federal level (including members of Congress) will not have much relevant program data available. It may not be in the perceived interests of the grantors of funds or the recipients to collect and disseminate program data. The former may not demand it, for they are not held responsible for program performance; the latter may not readily volunteer it because they are.

PUBLIC VS. PRIVATE GOODS. In the production of public goods partisan pressures are weaker than in nonpublic goods production. There may remain intense partisanship over inputs (e.g., the location of facilities) but there is less about outputs.

FRAGMENTATION OF RESPONSIBILITIES. There must be a division of labor in the management of complex activities. But many problems to which public programs are addressed often cut sharply across jurisdictional lines and do so in ways that seem to prevent effective performance. For example, there is good reason to believe that educational performance, family environment, housing, jobs, and the incidence of crime are strongly interactive. Yet these are typically the responsibility of different bureaucracies with different motivations and professional outlooks. Partisan adjustment among the bureaucracies and professional groups concerned with these areas may fail to take anywhere near adequate account of these interactions.

THE EFFECT ON INCOME DISTRIBUTION. Income distribution is always relevant and it is often dominant. With many ongoing programs the recipients have virtually established rights to support from government programs. In any case, where income distribution is the objective, there are two kinds of efficiency issues: One is the efficiency with which funds are put in the hands of the preferred recipients. The other is the economic efficiency of the activity which is used as the vehicle for transferring the funds (the water project, crops produced or not produced, jobs subsidized). The main point with those income distribution dominated programs and strongly vested interests is that they have usually been developed over time through a process of a bargaining and negotiation and consensus building that makes them relatively impervious to change in decision making methods. They are often Congressionally dominated program areas. (Even so, it appears that cost-benefit analyses have resulted in some of the worst programs being cut out.)

The case for the more intensive application of systematic decision methods would seem to be strongest for those activities that involve public goods, strong externalities, fragmentation of responsibilities, a poorly understood but potentially understandable production function, poor consumer knowledge of the quality of services provided, Presidential more than Congressional power to decide, and are not a traditional income transfer vehicle. The unreconstructed partisan, incremental approach either is relatively acceptable in terms of the results produced or is nevertheless likely to prevail where the opposite conditions hold.

The Need for a Strengthened Adversary System

The issue of the nature of decision making in the public sector, as frequently posed, is the wrong one. The alternative to a partisan, incremental system is not necessarily a centralized, synoptic, hierarchical one. It is necessary to accept—not only as a fact but as a positive good—the existence of a multiplicity of sources of political power and influence frequently operating as adversaries; and it is necessary to accept the impossibility of comprehensive, consistent decision making, and nevertheless seek to improve upon the workings of this system. This means changing the rules of the game somewhat, but accepting that it is basically the same game.

Decision makers (congressmen, governors, mayors, executive branch officials, city councilmen, lobbyists, newspaper editors, trade associations, members of public commissions) should be encouraged to adopt the practice of demanding and producing more systematic, quantitative data on objectives and costs and benefits of alternative programs and policies in areas for which they have a responsibility or interest. One should expect that these data and analyses will frequently be biased. It is for the partisans of differing views to supply countervailing data and analyses. To some extent this style of decision making is practiced in our society today, for a partisan often feels motivated to have his case buttressed with an analysis. But it is far from as common as it might be.

It will be objected that it frequently will not be in the interest of partisans to behave in this fashion—especially if they have an already vested interest in ongoing programs. What could compel them to behavior possibly contrary to their perceived interests? Several things could: one is the strength of the ethos of rational behavior in our society. It is difficult, although far from impossible, even for strong partisans to reject totally the legitimacy of the demand for data and analysis on public issues. They may provide false or distorted material but complete stonewalling is fairly rare. (More common is the inability of the partisans to provide coherent data because they don't have it. An especially interesting case is that of the bureaucrats who don't collect data even for themselves so that they can't be called on to provide it to others.)

It may also be argued that analysis may be too costly. This may be, and clearly much decision making must be done routinely. But it is also true that much of what is needed by way of analysis is pretty elementary. And, with the substantial increase taking place in the number of analytically trained people in our society, this argument is losing force.

The beginnings of a system of adversary analytic groups exists within the federal government. It is understood that the analytic output of the Agriculture Department or the Office of Economic Opportunity or the Defense Department will reflect not only the responsibilities but what to some might be regarded as the partisan bias of these agencies. But, even so, the gains can be substantial—at best, explicitness of analysis, data on estimated costs and benefits, statements of uncertainties, the citation of experimental evidence. It is possible for those of differing persuasion to meet the argument in detail. The best may be rare but even distant approximations to it can be useful. It may be possible to get second order agreement and clarify differences. These are not hypothetical possibilities. They can happen when contending analyses meet head-to-head.

Among the multiplicity of decision making groups there should be some prepared to take a synoptic view—for example, in budget bureaus of cities, states and national governments—but *not* with the expectation that comprehensive, consistent choice of optional policies will result. Rather it is to provide better data, theories, insights of partisans of the "big picture." And analyses at a "high" level can usefully interact with those at lower levels.[2]

In conclusion, this paper emphasizes the values to be obtained from an interactive analytic process rather than the substantive correctness of a particular problem solving approach. This way of viewing the role of systematic decision making is relevant to a number of issues that have been raised recently. One is the interest in parts of the Congress in having access to modern analytic resources. A second is the interest in strengthening the PPBS system in the foreign affairs area.[3] A third is the interest on the part of a number of governors

[2] Much of the discussion about suboptimization fails to stress the influence of bureaucratic motivation on the behavior of subordinate units and the value of having countervailing views available at higher decision levels. The strong degree of independence and the parochial character of the criteria frequently found in subordinate units makes consistency between the objectives of these units and higher levels far from certain or even probable. This increases the importance to higher levels of having multiple sources of data and advice.

[3] T. C. Schelling, in a Memorandum prepared for the Government Operations Committee of the Senate in January, 1968, states the view that the main effect of such a change would not be directly improved budgetary allocations in foreign programs but the enhancement of the authority of the Secretary of State in relation to other departments of the government.

and mayors in improving their decision systems. What these examples have in common is a recognition that power and influence flow not only from traditional sources but also from the ability to command data and analyses. Much of the work that will be done in the future, as in the past, under the heading of systematic decision making will be unscientific, unsystematic and partisan. But much of it will be socially useful nonetheless.

COMMENT

by WERNER Z. HIRSCH, *University of California, Los Angeles*

Rowen asks in an interesting way, "Are the results of present-day public decisions adequate? Or, could they be improved by more systematic decision making? And if so, for which classes of activities could decision making be improved?" The paper contains little new insight, either analytical or empirical, into the first question and, therefore, I turn to that part of the paper that deals with six characteristics of activities that are likely to lend themselves to improved results through systematic decision-making methods. As I interpret his conclusions, the six criteria are: if there is poor knowledge of service demand; if production relations are poorly understood; if there is a paucity of program data; if the good is a public good; if operational responsibilities are fragmented; and if major income transfers are attempted. I would like to review some of these characteristics, and attempt to add a few.

I like the approach of first looking at some of the demand characteristics. However, the phenomenon of poorly understood services is not identical with the phenomenon of consumer ignorance. In economic terms the issue is whether there are detectable demand functions, and if so, how well do we estimate them. A rather reliable demand function emerges if the service is priced, if its various characteristics lend themselves to quantification, and if it has few merit good characteristics. The absence of these conditions, and therefore of a demand function, leads to poor knowledge or to lack of knowledge by decision makers about service demand. But even though decision makers do have good knowledge about consumer demand, consumers still might be ill-informed or ignorant (and vice versa). The question of whether consumers have enough knowledge to want the "right" quantity and quality of public service is only in part an economic question. Under certain conditions, "right" in an equilibrium sense exists if the service is priced with the aid of user charges. More often "right" involves ethical issues and is related to the merit good characteristics of public services.

As to the production function, there can be no doubt that program budgeting can improve decisions when outputs are reasonably definable but so far have not been estimated. However, in this connection attention must be paid to the degree of uncertainty associated with production. Thus, while in a narrow sense I can see the output of the Internal Revenue Service being defined and estimated with relatively high degrees of certainty, the output of space programs appears much more difficult to define and empirically project into the future.

Absence of relevant high-quality data is not unique to circumstances in which intergovernmental fiscal instruments are prevalent. Since most officials detest situations in which their performance can be evaluated, they are reluctant to see appropriate data generated. In some instances, however, their resistance to providing data is justified. In an administration that seeks to base decisions on "hard facts," programs which produce mainly intangible benefits are likely to be starved for funds compared to programs whose output can be measured more readily. The ensuing underinvestment in the former programs can be harmful from the viewpoint of both the agency and society.

I am less sure about the conclusion that systematic decision-making methods are more applicable to public than to private goods. The reason given is that in the production of public goods partisan pressures are weaker than in the production of private goods. This conclusion appears to be somewhat inconsistent with the discussion and conclusion about the nature of demand. For example, public programs can be financed through user charges if joint consumption, externalities in consumption, costs of exclusion, and distribution or welfare considerations do not dominate. These conditions, which are more often met by private than by public goods, permit the estimation of demand functions, which in turn facilitates systematic decision making through program budgeting. Decisions about public goods also can be improved by program budgeting if important cost and benefit spillovers associated with these public goods can, in fact, be made to accrue to those who produce them.

To the fifth criterion, fragmentation of operational responsibility, should be added fragmentation of fiscal responsibilities. In the presence of complicated intergovernmental fiscal relations it might become extremely difficult, even though extremely important, to apply program budgeting techniques as a means of improving decisions.

This leads me to the last criterion, the income distribution characteristics of an activity. It appears important not to give up on these issues merely because the program areas are often dominated by Congress. Admittedly, congressmen often do not want revealed who benefits and who loses. However, some important features of program budgeting are that it permits an identification of preferred solutions and indicates the effects of a program's activity on specific income, racial, geographic and other groups in terms of their gains and losses. This brings me directly to my next point. After reading Harry Rowen's suggestive paper I am left with the impression, and possibly without good reason, that his main concern is with the application of systematic decisions as a means of increasing economic efficiency. While this might be the single most important purpose, it seems desirable to explore also the relevance of systematic decision making to economic growth, income distribution, and other objectives.

Finally, if the question posed in this paper constitutes the most crucial criterion for the application of PPBS, a significant policy implication emerges. Since apparently very few government activities are of a nature that PPBS assures success in improving decision making about them and yet many trade-off decisions are possible among subprograms of different programs, select analytic studies of high quality, where appropriate, should take precedence to a governmentwide program budget. In many respects, this would have turned back the clock to the days before the Presidential directive of August 1965, in whose writing Harry Rowen played such a key role. It would lead us to seek better select analytic studies. Perhaps there are other criteria that support efforts at constructing department- and even governmentwide program budgets to be used in conjunction with analytic studies.

COST FUNCTIONS AND BUDGETS
(COST CONSIDERATIONS IN SYSTEMS ANALYSIS)

G. H. FISHER
The RAND Corporation

Introduction

The President of the United States held a news conference on August 25, 1965. One of the most significant things he said was the following:

> This morning I have just concluded a breakfast meeting with the Cabinet and with the heads of Federal agencies and I am asking each of them to immediately begin to introduce a very new and very revolutionary system of planning and programming and budgeting throughout the vast Federal Government, so that through the tools of modern management the full promise of a finer life can be brought to every American at the lowest possible cost.[1]

The era of program budgeting had begun for the entire federal government. In effect what the President said was: "I want all department and agency heads to try to do what McNamara and Hitch have been attempting in Defense since 1961."

Even in 1961 the basic concept of program budgeting was not new. It had been proposed for the Department of Defense as early as 1953,[2] and something akin to it had been used by the War Production Board in World War II.[3] Its use in industry apparently dates back to at least 1924.[4]

But in spite of this history, the President's announcement in the

NOTE. Any views expressed in this paper are those of the author. They should not be interpreted as reflecting the views of The RAND Corporation or the official opinion or policy of any of its governmental or private research sponsors.

[1] *New York Times*, August 26, 1965.

[2] David Novick, *Efficiency and Economy in Government Through New Budgeting and Accounting Procedures*, R-254, Santa Monica, Cal., 1953.

[3] David Novick (ed.), *Program Budgeting: Program Analysis and the Federal Budget*, Cambridge, Mass., 2nd ed., 1967, pp. xvi–xix.

[4] *Ibid.*, pp. xxi–xxii.

summer of 1965 did pose something of a "revolution" for many departments and agencies in the federal government. In terms of the ultimate
goal, planning, programming and budgeting would have to become an
integrated process—something which (surprisingly) was not generally
true at that time. The "pure requirements" approach to planning would
have to be modified. Staunch advocates of new programs could no
longer argue effectively in terms of: "We need new program X
because there is a requirement for it; there is a requirement because
we need it"; and so on.

In the planning process, alternatives would have to be examined
systematically, subject to realistic resource constraints. And alternative
programs under consideration would have to be "costed out" to reflect
their complete incremental resource impact for the long-term future—
not merely the "down payment" as portrayed by next fiscal year's conventional budget.

All of this sounds commonsensical enough. It is basically very
similar to what economic planners have been talking about for years.
In its simplest terms, program budgeting is primarily the identification
and systematic examination of objectives and the alternative ways of
achieving them. The main focus is on *output*-oriented programs or
"packages of public product," not the input orientation of the conventional budget, which stresses personnel, equipment, facilities, transportation, travel, contractual services, and the like.

In terms of the current jargon, the very heart of program budgeting
is contained in the expression "systems analysis." While systems analysis cannot be defined with precision, the following would probably be
accepted as a reasonably adequate description by most of the practi-
tioners today:

> Systems analysis may be defined as inquiry to assist decision-makers
> in choosing preferred future courses of action by (1) systematically
> examining and re-examining the relevant objectives and the alternative
> policies or strategies for achieving them; and (2) comparing quanti-
> tatively where possible the economic costs, effectiveness (benefits),
> and risks of the alternatives. It is more a research strategy than a
> method or technique, and in its present state of development it is more
> an art than a science. In sum, systems analysis may be viewed as an
> approach to, or way of looking at, complex problems of choice under
> conditions of uncertainty.[5]

[5] For a further discussion of systems analysis, see E. S. Quade and W. I.
Boucher, *Systems Analysis and Policy Planning: Applications in Defense,* New
York, 1968, Chapter I.

The foregoing provides the necessary frame of reference for the discussion of the main subject of this paper: "Cost Functions and Budgets." Perhaps in view of such a framework a more descriptive title would be "Cost Considerations in Systems Analysis." In any event, the latter is the perspective we shall stress.

The Key Issues

In discussing cost analysis as a part of systems analysis, it appears that we can segregate the main issues into two categories:

1. The conceptual problems.
2. The practical problems involved in establishing cost analysis capabilities in the federal government and elsewhere.

Both of these are important. But at the present time there appears to be a special interest and sense of urgency regarding the second category. We shall therefore stress practical problems in this paper. Before turning to such a discussion, however, let us outline briefly some of the characteristics of the necessary conceptual framework for a cost analysis capability to support systems analysis studies.

The Conceptual Framework

In large measure the basic concepts underlying systems (program) cost analysis draw very heavily on concepts taken from economic theory and analysis.

A representative, but far from complete, listing of these basic concepts is as follows:[6]

1. An explicit relationship between inputs and outputs, with a strong emphasis on output-oriented identifications.
2. A strong emphasis on economic (not accounting) costs. Fundamentally this means the concept of opportunity cost.

[6] The ordering in no way reflects relative importance. Also, many of the items are interrelated. Finally, in some instances it is not clear that the particular point being made is conceptual or methodological—a distinction that is very often difficult to make.

3. As a further elaboration of (2) is the requirement to deal with such concepts as:
   a. Marginal or incremental (and hence "sunk") costs.
   b. Fixed and variable costs.
   c. Recurring and nonrecurring costs.
   d. Joint costs.
4. Explicit treatment of uncertainty. Simple "expected value" models very often will not suffice.
5. An awareness of scaling considerations. As in economic theory, many problems dealt with in systems cost analyses do not scale up or down in a simple fashion.
6. Explicit treatment of problems associated with time—e.g., the problem of time preference.
7. A strong emphasis on comparative analyses of alternatives— e.g., fixed cost (budget) comparisons and/or fixed utility (effectiveness) comparisons.
8. A recognition of the importance of sensitivity analysis, contingency analysis, *a fortiori* argument, and the identification of new alternatives as ways of assisting in the all important search for dominances.[7]

These eight points represent some of the most important characteristics of the conceptual framework for cost analysis in support of systems analysis studies. From a purely conceptual point of view, there would seem to be little room for argument about the relevance of these concepts. The main issues arise when the cost analysts try to implement the basic ideas. Let us consider two examples briefly.

Most analysts agree that in principle the matter of time preference should be treated explicitly. The disagreement arises over how this should be done—for example, what discount rate seems most appropriate for equalizing cost streams over time. Numerous seminars and conferences have been held on the subject of discounting, and the issue is still unresolved.[8] Many analysts feel that it cannot be completely

---

[7] Perhaps this point is more methodological than it is conceptual. We include it in the list anyway, because of its central importance in systems analysis. (Also, it is strongly related to (4)—explicit treatment of uncertainty.)

[8] Recently a survey was made of 23 federal agencies to obtain information on discounting techniques used in making evaluations of future government programs. One of the results is that the rates used vary from about 3 to 12 per cent. See statement by Elmer B. Staats, Comptroller General of the United States, before the Subcommittee on Economy in the Government, *Congressional Record—Senate,* January 30, 1968, pp. S632–S634.

resolved and that in most instances the matter is less consequential than many of the other cost analysis problems.

In fact, the analyst can do a great deal to sharpen the intuition and judgment of the decision makers[9] without resolving the rate issue. For one thing, the analyst can point out to the decision makers that an "undiscounted" situation usually does not exist. A case in point occurs in the Department of Defense where cost streams are projected 10 or 15 years into the future "without equalizing them for time preference." Here, the analyst can make the time preference assumption explicit: namely, a zero per cent discount rate for 10 or 15 years and a very high rate thereafter. He can also calculate cases built on a reasonable range of time preference assumptions and show the impact on final results (the ranking of the alternatives being considered). Finally, he can compute the "break-even point"—i.e., the case containing that discount rate which would have to be used to make the present value of two alternatives equal.

As a second illustration, let us consider the concept of opportunity cost. Again, there would seem to be little argument about the concept itself. Opportunity costs are generally recognized as being relevant in the examination and evaluation of alternative future courses of action. They are certainly much more relevant than, say, accounting-type costs generated for fiduciary financial management purposes.

Problems arise, however, when the analysts attempt to apply the concept of opportunity cost in systems analysis studies. For example, the cost analysts often generate estimates of the dollar costs of various program or system alternatives being considered in long-range planning deliberations.[10] Such estimates may be expressed in terms of time-phased expenditures and/or obligational authority, or in terms of "static" indexes of total system or program cost.[11] The specific issue is: Do these dollar cost estimates adequately reflect the opportunity costs (benefits foregone) of the alternatives being examined—at least for the purposes of the types of comparisons made in systems analyses?

They probably are not in all cases. However, most of the experts seem to think that for the purposes of comparing distant future alternatives, dollar costs *do* provide a reasonably appropriate index of

[9] To sharpen the intuition and judgment of the decision makers is the primary role of systems analysis. Generally speaking, an analysis cannot *make* the decision (e.g., see A. C. Enthoven's statement contained in an article in *Business Week,* November 13, 1965, p. 189).

[10] Other measures of cost are also calculated—e.g., manpower.

[11] That is, the sum of development (if any) and investment costs plus a number of years operating cost.

opportunity costs in many applications. This point of view is argued vigorously, and rather convincingly, in the context of Department of Defense planning by Hitch and McKean:

> If we examine the problem of planning future programs from the standpoint of the Defense Department, it seems fairly obvious that money costs are pertinent. The Department faces a budgetary constraint. For the most part it does not face a limitation on particular weapons or supplies but can buy more of them by paying their prices. What does the Department give up in order to implement one course of action? The answer is money—or, to go one step further, the alternative weapons or supplies that could otherwise be purchased. The Department could substitute one item for another by paying the price of the one instead of paying the price of the other. Dollar costs do reflect what must be given up in order to adopt a particular policy. They reflect real sacrifices by the Department because the prices of different items show the rates at which they can be substituted for each other.
>
> This is not to say that money costs perfectly represent resources sacrificed by the Defense Department. The prices of goods to be bought in the future are uncertain. One course of action may itself drive up the price of particular weapons or materials, and it is not possible to predict these effects with complete accuracy. The characteristics and cost of some items will change as technology advances. The quantity of some exceptional items may literally be fixed, or nearly fixed, even if we are looking several years ahead. Nonetheless, imperfect as it is, the money cost of a future program usually shows the sacrifice that would be required of the Department better than other measures of cost. While dollars do not precisely measure the real sacrifices, costs in terms of metals and manpower would be grossly misleading. Saying that airplanes cost so much aluminum and ships so much steel plate does not tell us how one may be exchanged for the other. Saying that each costs so many dollars adheres more closely to the facts, namely, that the services can, in making future plans, trade one for the other.[12]

[12] Charles J. Hitch and Roland N. McKean, *The Economics of Defense in the Nuclear Age,* Cambridge, Mass., 1960, p. 26.

The above quotation is concerned with dollars as a proximate measure of economic cost from the viewpoint of the Department of Defense. What about from the standpoint of the nation? Hitch and McKean consider this question, and argue the case by means of an illustrative example (see *ibid.*, pp. 27–28). Their general conclusion is:

> As a consequence, money costs of *future* defense activities approximate the real alternatives that are foregone—the real sacrifices that are entailed— when one activity or weapon system is selected. This will be true for those problems in which a general monetary constraint is proper, that is, for

Our concern in this paper is not so much with whether Hitch and McKean are correct. Rather the point is that the issue under consideration pertains more to the matter of *implementation* of a concept rather than to the relevance of the concept itself. It is generally recognized that economic cost is one of the relevant considerations to be taken into account in systems analysis studies. The question is how to do it in practice.

This leads to our next subject: cost analysis in support of systems analysis in practice. How is it done? What are some of the problems?

Cost Analysis in Practice

In general terms the central problem facing cost analysts is to develop methods and techniques which will permit assessment of the resource impact of proposed alternative output-oriented programs and/or alternative combinations (mixes) of future programs.

The basic characteristics of such a cost analysis capability stem directly from the conceptual framework discussed in the preceding section. A few of the more important of these characteristics are as follows:

1. While most of the basic estimating work must be done on the input side in terms of manpower, equipment, facilities, supplies, etc., the results of a cost analysis must be packaged in the form of output-oriented entities which are of prime concern to the long-range planning decision makers.
2. Cost analysis procedures (models) must be "open-ended" with respect to key performance and other variables which characterize the class of output-oriented entities under consideration. This facilitates doing parametric-type analyses which are of prime importance in extending the range of alternatives that can be examined, in making *a fortiori* arguments, in making sensitivity tests, in exploring scaling factors, and the like.
3. Related to (2) is the requirement to deal explicitly with the problem of uncertainty. Parametric cost models help by facilitating the computation of a range of cost estimates (rather than "point" estimates alone),[13] and by permitting determination of

problems pertaining to dates sufficiently in the future to permit the production and procurement of varying quantities of weapons and materiel (*ibid.*, p. 28).

[13] For example, "high," "medium" and "low" cases.

the sensitivity of total system or program cost to variations in the values of key parameters about which we are uncertain.

4. Both (2) and (3) imply the need for cost analysis models which are in part automated. If a large number of cases are to be computed within a reasonable amount of time and effort, manual calculation alone is usually out of the question.[14]

5. A strong emphasis must be placed on developing cost analysis procedures which will permit assessment of *incremental* costs— i.e., the additional costs implied by the proposed future course of action under consideration. The costs of past actions ("sunk" costs) and the costs of firmly committed ("locked-in") future actions must be excluded.

6. Finally—and perhaps most important of all—a substantial amount of time and effort must be devoted to the continuous development and maintenance of an appropriate data base: i.e., information on past, current and near future programs to serve as a basis for the derivation of estimating relationships to be used in projecting to the distant future.

We have stressed the prime importance of "output-oriented entities" or "program packages." What does this mean in areas of specific application? In the case of the Department of Defense these entities are by now rather widely recognized as being weapon and support systems and force mixes of such systems. What about the nonmilitary realm? The following are a few examples.

In the transportation area output-oriented entities may be various future modes of transportation—rail systems (surface and subsurface), "automated" freeway systems, airlift systems, etc., and mixes of these modes. In the mental health area the planners may be interested in such things as alternative systems for dispensing mental health services (e.g., community mental health centers), alternative programs for narcotic and drug abuse, etc. In the National Aeronautics and Space Administration the prime concern is with alternative ways of attaining certain goals in space—e.g., alternative space systems for performing future missions in the lunar, earth-orbital, and planetary areas.

In any event, the cost analyst must be able to conduct his studies in terms of the types of identifications or "planning units" that are of

---

[14] In some instances a tremendous number of individual calculations are required for a single case. For example, the total force structure cost model developed by The RAND Corporation to assess the resource impact of a projected total Air Force plan over a 10-year period makes about 500,000 computations for the typical single case.

FIGURE 1

SYSTEM COST VERSUS PROGRAM SIZE

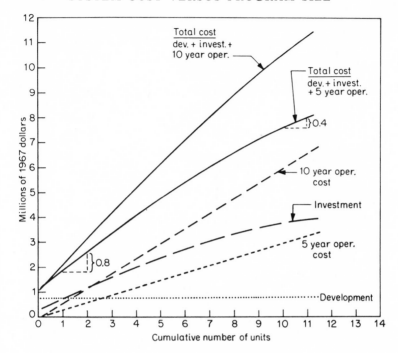

primary interest to the long-range planners. This is just as true in nonnational security problem areas as it is in defense, and the basic problems are very similar.

Let us now consider a few hypothetical examples to illustrate some of the types of output from the cost analysis process which are useful in systems analysis. In these illustrations the "output-oriented entities" are assumed to be alternative system or program package proposals being considered in the long-range planning process.

A very useful output of the cost analysis process (an input to systems analysis) is a cost function relating projected total system (program) cost[15] to the size (cumulative number of units) of a proposed future course of action. An example is shown in Figure 1. Here, total

[15] Here, total system (program) cost is defined as development (if any) plus initial investment plus a fixed number of future years' operating cost. Oftentimes the number of years' operation is treated parametrically to see whether the assumption about this factor affects significantly final results (the ranking of the alternatives being considered).

FIGURE 2

MARGINAL COST CURVE

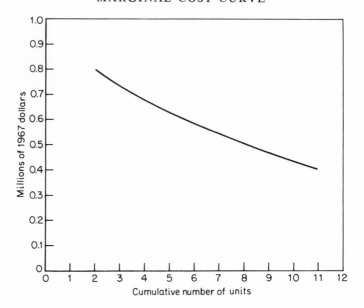

NOTE: Based on total development, investment, and five-year operation curve contained in Figure 1.

system cost is increasing at a decreasing rate, and hence marginal cost (the cost of an additional unit) is a decreasing function of the cumulative number of units. This is portrayed in Figure 2.

Cost functions expressing total system cost as a function of cumulative number of units are particularly useful in a fixed budget comparative framework of analysis. Here, the systems analyst often wants to know: "How many units of the various alternatives under consideration can I get out of certain stipulated future budget levels?"[16]

An example is presented in Figure 3 for alternatives *A* and *B*. If

[16] This is one example of why cost functions relating cost to the scale of proposed future programs are useful in systems analysis work.

Many of the cost functions emphasized in conventional economic theory relate cost to rate of output. Rate-of-output cost functions are also useful in certain types of problems in systems analysis. For example, in studying alternative configurations of proposed community mental health centers, we might want to examine how unit costs change as daily out-patient capacity rate is varied over a relevant range. In the case of military aircraft systems the analyst often examines how system cost (for a fixed force size) changes as the activity rate (e.g., flying hours per aircraft per month) is varied over a certain range.

FIGURE 3

TOTAL SYSTEM COST VERSUS PROGRAM SIZE
FOR ALTERNATIVES *A* AND *B*

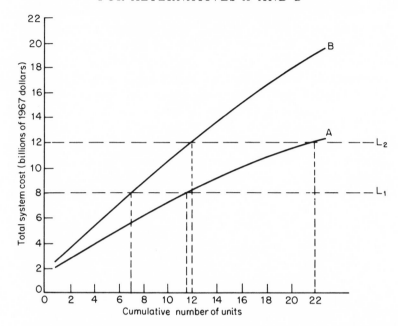

the specified cost level to be used in the comparative analysis is $8 billion, 11.5 units of alternative *A* or 7 units of alternative *B* are obtainable. This is a key output of the cost analysis, which then becomes a major input to the effectiveness (utility) analysis.

Notice that in this illustration the results do not scale linearly with respect to changes in the stipulated cost level. For example, if L_1 is increased by 50 per cent to $L_2 = \$12$ billion, the outcome is 22 units of *A* or 12 units of *B*. The increase in the number of units is greater than the increase in L_2 over L_1:

$$L_2/L_1 = 12/8 = 150\%$$

$$A_2/A_1 = 22/11.5 = 191\%$$

$$B_2/B_1 = 12/7 = 171\%$$

In a simple way this demonstrates that in the context of a fixed budget framework of analysis, scaling considerations suggest the desirability of conducting the comparisons for more than one cost level. For example, three cases might be examined: high, medium, and low.

To illustrate a somewhat different point, let us now consider a fixed effectiveness framework of analysis for comparing alternative proposed future courses of action. Here, the analysis attempts to determine that possibility (or feasible combination of possibilities) which is likely to achieve some specified level of effectiveness at the lowest economic cost. The cost analysis in effect produces the final results after the effectiveness analysis has determined how much of each alternative is required to attain the stipulated level of effectiveness.

As one simple illustration of this approach, suppose that alternatives *C* and *D* are under consideration, and that the results of the effectiveness analysis indicate the following ranges of quantities (number of units) of *C* and *D* required to attain some specified level of effectiveness E_0:

	C	D
Low	20	4
Expected value	22	6
High	24	12

Notice that in this case the range for *D* is considerably greater than for *C* because of uncertainty.

Suppose now that the estimated total system costs as a function of cumulative number of units for *C* and *D* are as shown in Figure 4. Taking the expected value outputs from the effectiveness analysis, we see from Figure 4 that *D* is the least cost alternative for attaining effectiveness level E_0: $7.5 billion for *D* vs. $15.3 billion for *C,* or a factor-of-two difference in favor of *D*. If the uncertainties in the effectiveness analysis are taken into account, alternative *D* still holds up well, even in the situation where the worst case (highest cost) for *D* and the best case (lowest cost) for *C* are paired up. Thus, at least with respect to the uncertainties taken into account in the problem, alternative *D* appears to be a dominant solution—something which the systems analyst is always seeking, but rarely finds.

So far, our examples have been essentially "static," i.e., projected costs have not been treated explicitly as a function of time. In many decision contexts, however, the alternatives have to be examined in terms of time-phased cost streams projected a number of years into the future.

For example, suppose there are two new proposed alternatives,

FIGURE 4

TOTAL SYSTEM COST VERSUS PROGRAM SIZE

FOR ALTERNATIVES *C* AND *D*

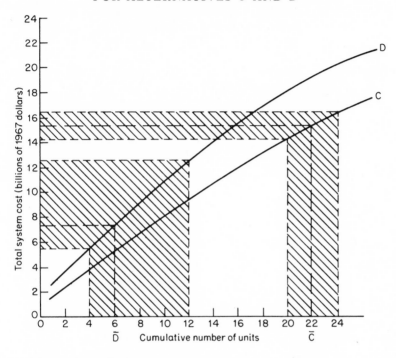

NOTE: Fixed effectiveness = E_0.

programs *E* and *F*, which are estimated to be capable of accomplishing the same objective in the future with essentially the same degree of effectiveness for the time period of interest (a "fixed-effectiveness-over-time" framework of analysis). Suppose further that the time-phased total program costs over a 15-year period in the future are as portrayed in Figure 5. Here, the time preference assumption is a *zero* discount rate for the first 15 years, and a very high rate (over 100 per cent) thereafter. Notice that in each case when the yearly costs are summed over the 15-year period, the totals are the same ($9 billion each for *E* and *F*).

On the basis of the data presented so far, we have an equal-effectiveness, equal-cost situation; so presumably the decision makers would be indifferent regarding the choice of *E* or *F*—at least on the basis of the quantitative information available at this point.

FIGURE 5

TIME-PHASED PROGRAM COSTS FOR ALTERNATIVES
E AND *F*

(DISCOUNTED FOR TIME PREFERENCE AT 0.0 PER CENT FOR THE
FIRST FIFTEEN YEARS, 100+ PER CENT THEREAFTER),

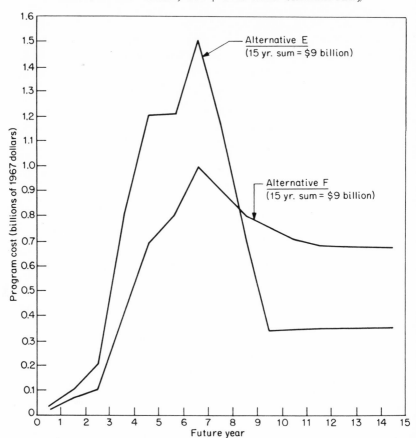

Notice, however, that the time impacts of the costs for *E* and *F* are considerably different. The basic reason for the difference is that alternative *E* requires higher cost outlays (relative to *F*) early in the period because of greater development and investment costs. These outlays pay off·in terms of an efficient operational program having relatively low operating costs later in the period. Alternative *F*, on the other hand, has lower development and investment costs than *E*. This, however, implies a less efficient operational program than *E*, with the result that larger operating costs are required to accomplish the specified task with the same degree of effectiveness as E. Therefore, the costs for F during the latter years of the 15-year period are about two times those of E.

In view of these differences in the time impact of the costs of E and F, the question arises as to whether the planners would still be indifferent regarding the choice of E or F if the time preference assumptions are varied. Suppose the base case (Figure 5) is modified to reflect the following time preference specifications: a discount rate of 6 per cent for 15 years, and a very high rate (over 100 per cent) thereafter. The results are as follows:

Present Value in Billions of Dollars

	Base Case (0; 100+%)	First Modification (6; 100+%)[a]
Alternative E	$9	$5.8
Alternative F	9	5.3
Difference	0	0.5

[a] The time-phased cost profiles for this case are presented in Figure 6.

Thus, the first modification (6 per cent for the first 15 years) results in a rather sharp reduction in the present value of the 15-year costs for *both* E and F. However, the difference between them can hardly be regarded as significant in view of the many uncertainties involved in the total analysis. The decision makers are likely to continue to be indifferent regarding the choice of E or F on the basis of the present values of the two cost streams.

Would this still be the case for a discount rate considerably higher than 6 per cent? Let us try a 10 per cent rate for 15 years, and a very high rate (over 100 per cent) thereafter. The results are:

Present Value in Billions of Dollars

	Base Case (0; 100+%)	First Mod. (6; 100+%)	Second Mod. (10; 100+%)
Alternative E	$9	$5.8	$4.5
Alternative F	9	5.3	3.9
Difference	0	0.5	0.6

The second modification results in a further reduction in the present values of the fifteen-year costs for both E and F. Here again it is very

FIGURE 6

TIME-PHASED PROGRAM COST FOR ALTERNATIVES *E* AND *F*

(DISCOUNTED FOR TIME PREFERENCE AT 6 PER CENT FOR THE
FIRST FIFTEEN YEARS, 100+ PER CENT THEREAFTER)

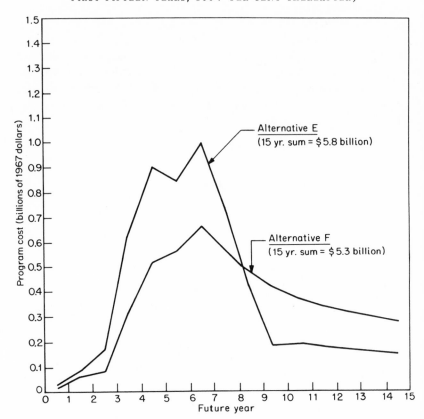

doubtful that the difference in present values between *E* and *F* is significant. The uncertainties in the basic problem are such that a 15 per cent difference in cost is no doubt well within the "noise level" of the analysis. Also, it should be pointed out that in most contexts a 10 per cent discount rate for time preference is fairly high,[17] which makes the second modification a rather extreme case.

[17] Recall that in this exercise we have been discounting for time preference only—not for time preference *plus* a supplemental rate for risk. When analysts apply rates like 10 to 15 per cent, they usually have in mind a combined rate to allow for time preference and risk or uncertainty.

In sum, in this particular example, the conclusion would seem to be that the decision regarding the choice of alternative *E* or *F* is likely to be independent of the assumptions made with respect to the treatment of time preference.[18]

As a final example, let us consider the examination of variations in total system (program) cost as the characteristics of the system (program) are varied, assuming a fixed number of years of operation. This is an important technique of analysis in systems analysis.

For an illustration, we shall use the context of the national security area and consider the case of a proposed future aircraft system where the mission requires that a fleet of aircraft be continuously airborne on a series of stations which cover a large geographical area. A Navy antisubmarine warfare (ASW) mission in the future is a possible example.

Continuously airborne alert aircraft systems typically involve a host of significant variables: endurance hours of the aircraft to be employed in the system, extent of the area coverage, nature of the payload requirements, aircraft maintenance policy (one, two, or three shifts), and the like. Intrasystem cost analysis must usually explore the consequences of variations in these variables.

Figure 7 shows an example for a future ASW system to patrol and destroy ballistic missile carrying enemy submarines, where aircraft endurance hours and area coverage (nautical miles out to sea from U.S. coastlines) are varied. Here total system cost is defined to be research and development + investment + five years of operation. Notice that as the area coverage is extended, the requirement for longer endurance becomes increasingly more severe.

Figure 8 contains another ASW system cost example. Here total system cost (defined as in Figure 7) for each pound of payload (elec-

[18] Examples of other cases are the following:

Case	Present Value in Billions of Dollars		
	Alt. *E*	Alt. *F*	Difference
6% for 25 yrs.	$6.9	$7.4	$0.5
10% for 25 yrs.	5.0	4.9	0.1
15% for 25 yrs.	3.5	3.1	0.4
5% for first 10 yrs. 10% for next 5 yrs. 20% for next 5 yrs. 50% for next 5 yrs.	6.6	6.5	0.1
10% for first 15 yrs. 50% for yrs. 16–25	4.6	4.2	0.4

FIGURE 7

ASW SYSTEM COST VERSUS AIRCRAFT ENDURANCE FOR
SEVERAL AREA COVERAGES

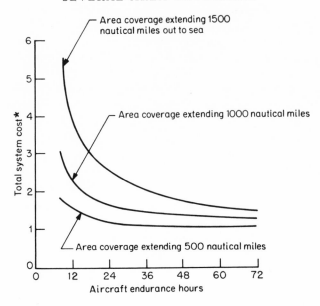

* Synthetic number scale.

tronics, ASW missiles, etc.) on station is expressed as a function of the pounds of payload carried per aircraft.[19] Curves are shown for three types of aircraft that might be candidates for use in the proposed ASW system.

Notice that the use of conventional jets in this mission application results in a considerably higher minimum cost point than for long-endurance aircraft, and that system cost per pound of payload on station is very sensitive to individual aircraft payload weight. Note also that as we move to the large, long-endurance aircraft, the costs become much less sensitive to a particular loading or payload weight. This might suggest that if the size of the payload to perform the future mission is clouded by uncertainties, then flexibility may be achieved by going to the large, long-endurance aircraft.

[19] Area coverage is fixed at 1,000 nautical miles.

FIGURE 8

SYSTEM COST PER POUND OF PAYLOAD ON STATION
VERSUS AIRCRAFT PAYLOAD WEIGHT

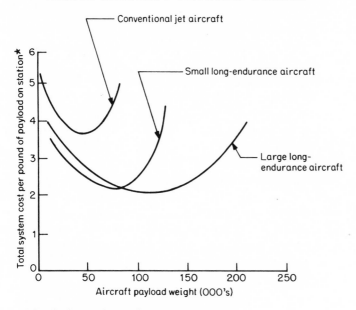

* Synthetic number scale.
NOTE: Area coverage = 1,000 nautical miles.

A Major Difficulty: The Data Problem

What are the main difficulties involved in doing cost analyses of the type described in the previous section? There are many—some bureaucratic, some substantive. Because of space limitations, all of these difficulties cannot be outlined and discussed here. We shall therefore take the most severe—the data problem—and treat it at some length.[20]

In most cases the ability to engage in cost analysis as an integral part of systems analysis studies requires the development and use of

[20] Much of the discussion to follow draws rather heavily on the national security area. This is because the author has had more experience in the Department of Defense than in other governmental agencies. The basic data problems, however, are very similar in all areas, and the methodological and procedural points to be made in this section are applicable to a wide variety of contexts.

cost models. A cost model is a device for generating estimates of the resource impact of future output-oriented program packages in terms of the inputs that would be required to develop, install, and operate these proposed programs over a period of years. The input structure typically involves various categories of facilities, equipment, personnel, supplies, etc., or combinations of these items (maintenance, for example).

For each category in the input structure we must have an estimating relationship (or series of relationships) expressing cost as a function of an appropriate set of cost-generating or explanatory variables.[21] These estimating relationships form the very heart of a cost analysis capability.

Estimating relationships have to be derived on the basis of something. Sometimes that something has to be "experience and judgment" (preferably of an expert). Generally speaking, however, we would prefer that they be developed from statistical analyses of past, current, and near-future data and information. At this point we run headlong into "the data problem." And it is a problem of fundamental importance, because a substantive cost analysis capability cannot exist without an appropriate information and data bank.

Why Is There a Data Problem?

The reader may well wonder why the data problem is so severe. Has not the Government been developing information systems and collecting a huge volume of data in numerous areas for many years? Have not industry and other institutions been doing the same thing? How could there be a "data problem"?

These are legitimate questions. The answers are numerous and varied. Here, we shall try to select a few of the more important ones, with a view to giving the reader a reasonable degree of understanding of why a data problem exists.[22]

---

[21] The cost of a certain type of equipment for the future may be estimated as a function of its performance and/or physical characteristics and estimated production quantity. The cost of equipment maintenance may be estimated as a function of equipment characteristics and projected activity rate.

[22] The points discussed below relate for the most part to technical aspects of the problem. Other factors can be important also. For example, formal information and data systems are sometimes established without sufficient understanding of the relevant organizational and institutional considerations pertaining to the agency in question.

INFORMATION IN THE WRONG FORMAT. Information systems in the Government and elsewhere have indeed generated a tremendous amount of data. In many instances, however, these data are not in an appropriate format to be very useful in a program cost analysis activity serving the long-range planning process.

The main reason for this is that these information systems were established primarily to serve the needs of managers of functional areas of operational activity (maintenance, supply, etc.), of managers responsible for fiscal integrity or fiduciary accounting requirements ("keeping hands out of the till"), of managers concerned with critical resource items across the board (e.g., personnel), of budgeteers concerned with the conventional budget, and the like. In short, the orientation of a large number of past and existing information systems is toward the input side per se, with little or no provision for making meaningful translations reflecting impacts on output-oriented program packages.[23]

THE "MATCHING UP" OR INTEGRATION PROBLEM. The analyst must not only collect historical *cost* data in the right format, particularly when the objective is to derive estimating relationships. He must also obtain information on quantities, physical and performance characteristics, activity rates, and other types of cost-generating variables. The latter must be matched specifically to the cost data points.

Sometimes this is difficult because the information on the cost-generating variables must be extracted from different sets of records than those containing the cost data. And differing sets of records can often have dissimilar bases for reporting—for example, with respect to lot size, time period covered, and the like.

DIFFERENCES IN DEFINITIONS OF CATEGORIES. A different kind of "matching up" problem frequently occurs. This concerns the lack of a one-to-one correspondence between the definition of the content of categories in the input structures set up for program cost analysis purposes, and the definition of analogous categories in the existing data and information collection systems.

[23] Oftentimes the suggestion is made that if the analyst will probe the data base at successively greater levels of detail, he will eventually find the kinds of identifications he needs. Sometimes this is true. On the other hand, one is likely to find that if an information system is structured to deal in terms of, say, "object classes," then going into more detail will simply yield greater amounts of information in the same terms (object classes).

It is not possible to set up *the* preferred input structure which will meet the requirements of cost analyses in support of long-range planning and at the same time be in complete harmony with existing data and information systems at any point in time. Differences in definition of certain categories in the input structure and their counterparts in the existing data base are therefore bound to be present. This creates a data problem for the cost analyst when he is collecting information to serve as the basis for deriving estimating relationships for various categories and subcategories in his input structure. He will often have to make adjustments to the raw data to correct for these definitional differences.

THE INFLUENCE OF TEMPORAL FACTORS. Historical data are, of course, generated over time. This means that numerous dynamic factors will have influences on the information being collected in a certain area. First of all, the information collection systems themselves have a habit of changing over time—for example, the appropriate definition of the content of various categories being used to accumulate the historical data may change as the system evolves. Also, in the case of financial data, price level changes will occur and be reflected in the information being collected over time.

In addition to these types of temporal considerations is the important fact that many government agencies deal with a rapidly changing technology, both with respect to hardware and with respect to organizational and operational concepts. Almost by definition, this means that even with a near perfect information collection system, only a relatively small sample of data can be generated for a given era or class of technology. In the major equipment area, for example, the analyst is lucky if he can have available 15 or 20 good data points for a certain class of hardware. He is more likely to have less than half that number.

By the nature of things, therefore, the analyst is all too often in the world of *very* small samples. As all good statisticians know, this poses real problems in our attempts to develop meaningful *structural* relationships which will permit us to project forward to distant future programs and capabilities.

So much for our listing of problem areas concerning the data base. We repeat that the four points outlined above do not represent a complete enumeration; they should, however, convince the reader that there is such a thing as a "data problem." The question now is: What do we do about it?

Dealing with the Data Problem

At first thought, one might be tempted to say: "If there is a data problem, let's solve it once-and-for-all by establishing *the* information collection system to meet all our needs." People have often made statements like this. Is such a thing feasible?

We think not, for several reasons. Some of the more important of these are the following:

1. Cost analysis problems in support of systems analyses typically vary considerably from one study to another. The requirements for estimating relationships—and hence data and information requirements—are not constant over time, or even for a given small interval of time. In short, the cost analyst who is working in support of the long-range planning process could not specify his data and information needs "once-and-for-all." It would be difficult, if not impossible, then, to establish *the* comprehensive information system.

2. Even if something approaching (1) could be done, we still have to worry about economics. Large information systems—especially those designed for complete enumerations—are very expensive. This poses a systems analysis problem in itself. Would the (large) incremental cost of a new complete enumeration information system be justified in terms of the benefits to be derived—particularly in the context of long-range planning, where high precision in an absolute sense is usually not a prime requirement? The answer is probably "no."[24]

3. In addition to points (1) and (2) is the problem of small samples arising from the fact that many government agencies have to deal with a rapidly changing technology. As indicated previously, this means that in many instances only a relatively small number of observations will be available for a certain era or class of technology. Here, even a near perfect information system cannot increase the sample size.

Where does all this leave us? On the one hand, a strong argument has been advanced for the importance of an appropriate information and data base. On the other hand, trying to solve the problem once and for all does not seem feasible, at least in a *general* sense. Does this mean that the situation is at an impasse?

[24] As will be pointed out later, there are alternatives to complete enumerations on a recurring basis.

The answer is "no." The problem is susceptible to reasonable solution, at least in many instances. Numerous possible alternatives to establishing new complete enumeration information systems may be considered. We shall now outline and discuss briefly examples of a few of the approaches that may be taken to help solve the data problem.

Use of Ad Hoc Sample Surveys

One very interesting possibility which the present author feels has been relatively neglected is sampling, or something akin to sampling. This can be a low cost way of obtaining information that may be very useful in deriving estimating relationships for use in long-range planning studies.

Suppose, for example, that the cost analyst is faced with the problem of developing end-product oriented estimating relationships for some functional area like maintenance or supply in the Department of Defense. Suppose further that the existing cost accounting systems accumulate historical cost data in categories such as labor, material, overhead, etc., and that no provision is made for identifications to end-product packages of military capability (e.g., weapon systems). Conceivably one solution would be to overhaul the entire formal accounting system to accumulate historical cost data in the desired form, in addition to the existing categories needed for purposes of functional management of the maintenance and supply activities. This, however, could be very expensive, and considerable time would have to elapse to permit designing, testing, and implementing of the new accounting system.

An alternative would be to select a few representative locations and to provide for an ad hoc (temporary) "ticketing" system to accumulate costs in terms of weapon systems for a relatively short period of time—say a month or two. The ad hoc arrangement would be supplementary to—and hence would not disturb—the existing formal accounting system. This approach has been used on numerous occasions in the past; and for those cases known to the author, the results have been good—at least for the purpose of deriving estimating relationships for long-range planning.[25] In any event, sampling procedures

[25] The author has conducted simple tests in several instances where complete enumerations were available. The procedure was as follows: Take the complete enumeration as a data base and, using regression analysis, derive an estimating relationship—say $C = \hat{\alpha} + \hat{\beta}X$. Then take random samples of 15 or 20 observations from the complete enumeration and derive similar relationships on the

seem worthy of consideration as an alternative to establishing new complete enumeration systems across the board.

Techniques for Assisting in Handling the Small Sample Problem

We have pointed out that the cost analyst very often finds himself confronted with small samples. Let us consider two examples to demonstrate several things that can be done to help ease the problems arising from having to use data bases containing only a small number of observations from the historical record.

The first is an extremely simple idea, but in some instances it can help a great deal. Particularly in deriving estimating relationships for use in long-range planning studies, the cost analyst should not necessarily restrict himself to the *historical* record in assembling his data base. In many cases he should seriously consider increasing the number of observations by including appropriate data points based on estimates made by experts for the very near future, and/or by taking advantage of certain kinds of qualitative information.

Suppose, for example, we have only four data points available from the historical record (see Figure 9). Suppose further that the analyst must derive an estimating relationship which will help him project out beyond the range of the historical sample (beyond the value X_0 of the explanatory variable). On the basis of the four data points alone, it is not very clear what kind of relationship between C and X should be postulated. For example, the curves AB and CD in Figure 10 would seem about equally plausible. Here is a case where the cost analyst should probe further and attempt to get some sort of additional information (either quantitative *or qualitative*) to help him make an informed judgment.

Suppose that in our hypothetical example the cost analyst, upon further exploration, was fortunate enough to find two more data points in the form of *estimates* for the near future made by reputable experts in the field under consideration. Upon checking out the methods used to make these estimates, the cost analyst decided that it would be appropriate for him to use them as a supplement to his his-

basis of these sample data bases. Then test the resulting estimates of α and β against the values obtained from the complete enumeration to see if there is a significant difference. In the particular cases examined by the author, most of the time no significant difference existed (at the 0.05 level) between estimates of the regression coefficients obtained from the small samples and those obtained by using the complete enumeration as a data base.

FIGURE 9
SMALL SAMPLE EXAMPLE

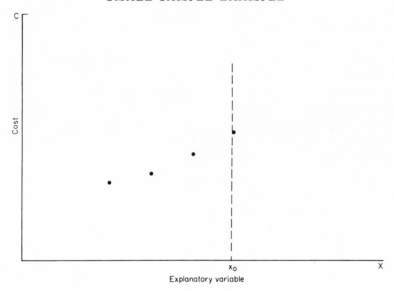

Explanatory variable

FIGURE 10
SMALL SAMPLE EXAMPLE
SOME PLAUSIBLE ESTIMATING RELATIONSHIPS

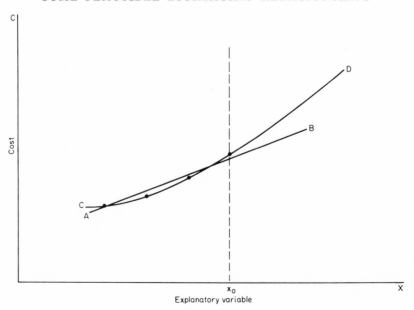

Explanatory variable

torical data base. The result is shown in Figure 11. This would tend to suggest the appropriateness of a linear hypothesis as a basis for projecting out to the vicinity of X_1 in Figure 11.

Let us assume, however, that our cost analyst wanted still further substantiation—if possible. He recalled that in his initial search for an appropriate explanatory variable, he had talked to some engineers who were experts in designing the type of equipment or activity under investigation in this particular case. He decided to consult with them again in the hope of obtaining some thread of qualitative evidence which would help in deciding whether to accept or reject the linear hypothesis. Upon listening to the engineers discuss the structural characteristics of the activity under consideration, the cost analyst became convinced that projections for large values of the explanatory variable X should be made on the basis of a linear relationship between C and X.

This hypothetical example illustrates two points about how one can deal with very small samples: (1) Under certain conditions the size of the sample can be increased by judiciously using estimates for the near future as supplements to the historical data base; (2) it may be

FIGURE 11

SUPPLEMENTING THE HISTORICAL DATA BASE

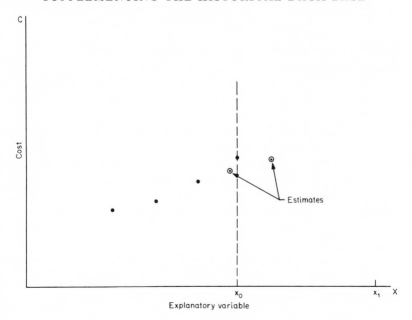

FIGURE 12

DOLLARS PER POUND OF AIRCRAFT WEIGHT
VERSUS CUMULATIVE UNIT NUMBER

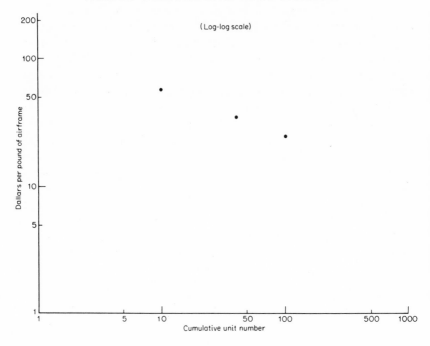

possible to use qualitative information to assist in deciding about what kind of estimating relationship is most appropriate.

As another example, let us consider a case where the sample is very small and we seek to gain additional information by lowering the level of aggregation one notch.

In the area of military major equipment cost analysis, cost-quantity relationships are very important. As the cumulative number of units increases, unit cost usually declines.[26] Suppose that we are interested in a certain type of aircraft airframe (call it X) and that we have only three data points. No other points are available for this particular airframe. The log-log plot of the data base is shown in Figure 12.

---

[26] For a thorough treatment of cost-quantity relationships, see Harold Asher, *Cost-Quantity Relationships in the Airframe Industry,* R-291, Santa Monica, Cal., 1956. Cost-quantity relationships in one form or another are also found in other areas. For example, in the automobile industry unit production costs after launching a new model are considerably higher during the earlier part of the production run than they are later in the model year. These "excess" costs are called "launching costs" in the automobile industry.

Assume now that the cost analysis is part of a systems analysis study in which large numbers of airframe X are being considered: 1000 or more. Should the analyst simply assume a log-linear relationship, connect his three data points, and extend the line out to cumulative outputs of 1000 or more? Most probably not. An experienced analyst knows all too well the dangers of mechanistic extrapolation, for scaling factor reasons and others as well.

Since in our hypothetical example the sample size cannot be increased, what can be done? One possibility is to see if additional information can be obtained by disaggregating. Suppose that our cost analyst goes back to the original data source and finds that additional detail is in fact available. He obtains a breakdown of the total airframe in terms of labor, material, and overhead. A plot of these data is shown in Figure 13. This slight addition to the data base immediately provides useful insights into the projection problem. If we assume log-linear relationships for the components (labor, material,

FIGURE 13

DOLLARS PER POUND OF AIRFRAME VERSUS
CUMULATIVE UNIT NUMBER

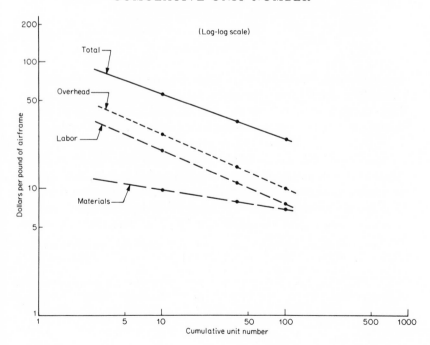

FIGURE 14

DOLLARS PER POUND OF AIRFRAME VERSUS
CUMULATIVE UNIT NUMBER

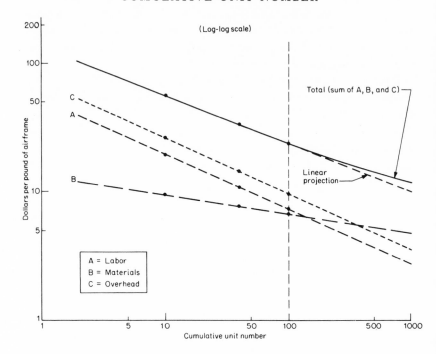

and overhead),[27] it is obvious that on the basis of the available information the total curve cannot be log-linear when projected out to
large cumulative unit numbers because the materials curve has a
significantly different slope than the labor and overhead curves.[28]

If the curves in Figure 13 are extrapolated out to cumulative unit
number 1000, the results are as portrayed in Figure 14. Here it is
clear that the cost analyst has benefited from the information obtained
by disaggregating one level in the data base. Merely extrapolating out
to cumulative output 1000 on the basis of the three original data
points no longer seems appropriate.[29] The difference between the two

---

[27] In general this is not necessarily a good assumption; but we shall use it here
to keep the example simple. The argument is even stronger if the component
curves are assumed to be convex on logarithmic grids.

[28] If the component curves are linear but nonparallel, the total curve (sum
of the components) must be convex on logarithmic grids and must approach as
a limit the flattest of the component curves (e.g., see Asher, *op. cit.*, pp. 70–72).

[29] The difference would be even greater if the component curves were assumed
to be convex.

curves increases still further for cumulative unit numbers beyond 1000.[30]

This example illustrates how going into slightly more detail can help in cases where the cost analyst has to work with a very small sample. A word of caution is in order, however. The reader should not generalize from our example and conclude that in all (or even most) instances the assembly of a more and more detailed data base will, in itself, make for better understanding of the problem.

The Use of Experiments to Broaden the Data Base

Sometimes the cost analyst finds that in a given problem area there is simply a void in the existing formal data base. This is likely to be the case when the planners are considering new proposals for distant future programs or capabilities requiring major equipments and/or operational concepts markedly different from those of the past and the present.

In some instances the existing set of estimating relationships can be used to conduct simulations which will furnish a first approximation to the cost of these proposed new capabilities. In other instances, however, the cost analyst cannot assume that the structural parameters in the existing set of estimating relationships are appropriate for the new activities being considered. He must therefore develop new relationships, or devise techniques for adjusting the present ones. But how does he do this if the necessary data base does not yet exist? One possibility is to see if any experiments are being conducted pertaining to the subject at hand; and if not, to try to initiate such an experiment. Let us consider one example briefly.

A number of years ago, cost analysts were confronted with the task of estimating the cost of the first generation of proposed stainless steel airframes for the mid-1960s. These proposals usually required rather extensive use of stainless steel honeycomb paneling, the production of which would involve a significant advance in the manufacturing state of the art. The historical data base at that time was, of course, confined almost entirely to the experience accumulated in producing aluminum airframes, and little was in the formal records about the fabrication costs of stainless steel honeycomb panels—particularly large panels.

[30] The difference is only about $1.50 per pound at cumulative unit number 1000. At cumulative output 5000, the difference between the linear projection and the nonlinear total curve is about $3.00 per pound.

In the process of talking to the aerospace industry contractors regarding the problems involved in fabricating stainless steel structures, the cost analysts found that one of the companies was conducting a rather elaborate experiment. A special shop had been set up and numerous types of manufacturing operations were being performed on aluminum, stainless steel, and titanium structures. Taking aluminum as the base case, the objective of the experiment was to determine the probable incremental labor costs involved in working the other two materials for a representative sample of various types of manufacturing operations. Armed with these types of data from the experiment, the cost analysts were then in a position to devise techniques for adjusting the historical data base (aluminum experience) so that it would be more appropriate for dealing with the stainless steel airframe problem.

In visits to still other contractors' plants, the cost analysts found that several were experimenting with the construction of stainless steel honeycomb paneling. In sessions with the people conducting these operations the cost analysts obtained a wealth of information (both quantitative and qualitative) about how honeycomb cost might vary with core cell size and shape, shape and size of the panel, number of panel inserts, and the like. As a result, they were able to treat panels as a special cost analysis problem and hence to improve considerably their ability to estimate the cost of stainless steel airframes. The expenditure of the time and travel budget on field work paid off well.

Summary Comment

Rather typically, cost analysts supporting a systems analysis activity spend at least half their time struggling with the data and information problem. In this section we have tried to convey some flavor of the total problem and some notion of the types of techniques that may be employed to solve it. Basically what is required is ingenuity, persistence, and just plain hard work.

Summary

Systems analysis forms the central core of a program budgeting activity. A vitally important part of systems analysis is a cost analysis capability to generate estimates of the resource impact of alternative courses of action being considered for the distant future.

Some of the principal characteristics of a systems cost analysis capability are:

1. An explicit relationship between inputs and outputs, with a strong emphasis on assessing the economic cost of alternative future output-oriented program packages.
2. Explicit treatment of uncertainty.
3. Provision for dealing with scaling considerations.
4. Explicit treatment of problems associated with time.
5. A recognition of the importance of sensitivity analysis, contingency analysis, and *a fortiori* argument.
6. Allocation of a substantial amount of time and effort to the continuous development and maintenance of an appropriate data base.

Establishing and maintaining a cost analysis capability to support systems analysis studies involves numerous difficulties. One of the most troublesome is the data base problem.

Solution to parts of the data problem may be through major overhaul of present formal information systems and through the establishment of new complete enumeration systems. This, however, does not appear feasible as a general solution—at least in the foreseeable future.

Short of such major efforts are numerous alternative possibilities. Some examples are:

1. Use of sampling techniques on an ad hoc basis.
2. Supplementing the existing historical data base by including estimated data points for the near future.
3. Statistical manipulation of the existing data base.
4. Obtaining additional information by conducting experiments.

COMMENT

by EDWIN S. MILLS, *Johns Hopkins University*

Fisher's paper is a contribution to the large and growing literature on cost analysis in the area of national security. There are two ways of writing imaginatively on this subject. One may apply known techniques to practical problems in an imaginative way, or one may introduce an imaginative new technique. Unfortunately, I see neither in Fisher's paper. The latter alternative might, for example, consist of the study of a new production function and of related cost functions, or it might consist of the derivation of a new programing algorithm. No such innovations appear in Fisher's paper and he clearly views his mission as falling within my former alternative. But a contribution of this sort requires extensive empirical analysis so that one can use one's intuition to invent new ways of measuring outputs, trade-offs among inputs, etc. Almost all of Fisher's data are fictitious, and even the nature of the problem is frequently unspecified, presumably for national security reasons. The result is an impression of artificiality similar to the one left by examples in many elementary price theory textbooks.

In the course of his paper, Fisher hints at a number of interesting problems. My main criticism is that he stops the discussion at about textbook level. In addition, although some of the problems have been analyzed and partially solved in the literature, there is an annoying lack of reference to the standard price theory literature in Fisher's paper.

The rest of my comments refer to most of the significant problems raised in Fisher's paper.

The first problem discussed in the section on cost analysis in practice is that of deciding whether cost should be calculated as a function of the rate of output or of cumulative output. Although the former is typically used by economists, the latter has been used in many studies in operations research. Which is appropriate depends on the nature of the situation, and it would have been interesting to have some analysis of the conditions under which each is appropriate.

The second problem, discussed in connection with Figure 4, is that of choosing between two productive processes C and D, when it is uncertain how many units of either will be needed to achieve a certain output. Although the problem is a genuine one, Fisher contributes little beyond the observation that it is rare to find situations, like the one depicted, in which one process uniformly dominates the other regardless of the unknown state of the world.

Fisher's next example is apparently intended to show the effect of the discount rate on the choice of productive technique. Unfortunately, the example chosen shows only that, of two techniques with the same total costs, the one with relatively small near-term costs is preferable at all positive discount rates, although Fisher refuses to accept this obvious implication of his example.

The last example in this section is one in which cost depends on several characteristics of the weapons system in question. It illustrates the point that detailed knowledge may be needed concerning the requirements for particular characteristics if costs are sensitive to the characteristics.

The final substantive section of the paper concerns data problems. This is the more interesting part of the paper and some significant insights are presented. However, much of the section is a disguised discussion of two well-known problems: whether to estimate a cost function directly or to construct it from estimates of an underlying production function; and whether to estimate production functions from statistical data on inputs and outputs or to infer them from engineering and scientific relationships. The answers obviously depend on the precise purpose of the analysis, the assumptions made about factor prices and factor markets, the identifiability of the relationships, and on data availability and reliability. Although special problems obviously arise in the national security area, I do not believe that national security analysts have nothing to learn from the existing literature on these matters.

SYSTEMATIC ERRORS IN COST ESTIMATES FOR PUBLIC INVESTMENT PROJECTS

MAYNARD M. HUFSCHMIDT

University of North Carolina at Chapel Hill

AND

JACQUES GERIN

Consulting Engineer and Planner, Montreal, Canada

Introduction

This paper deals with one aspect of uncertainty in public investment on which very little research has been done—the extent, nature, and causes of error in estimating costs of public investment projects. Although there is general agreement among public investment specialists that cost estimates for project proposals typically fall short of actual costs of projects when completed, this view is based upon fragmentary information, often obtained from superficial comparison of project or program documents and reports.[1]

There is no over-all reporting of cost experience for federal public works; some reports of individual agency experience do exist, but much of the information lies unassembled and unanalyzed in federal, state, and local agency files. More significant for our purpose, even the

NOTE. Special thanks are due to the following for providing information and valuable comments and suggestions on the subject of this paper: G. P. Palo, Manager of Engineering Design and Construction, and members of his staff, Tennessee Valley Authority; Wendell E. Johnson, Chief, Engineering Division, Civil Works, Corps of Engineers, Department of the Army; Harry Shooshan, Deputy Undersecretary for Programs, U.S. Department of the Interior, and Blair Bower, Resources for the Future, Inc.

[1] Cost as used throughout this paper is defined as the money cost of construction and installation of capital facilities of a public works project; it excludes operation, maintenance and replacement costs. The definition does not include opportunity cost considerations. This definition excludes interest during construction (except where otherwise noted) and, with this exception, corresponds to the capital cost information collected by federal water-resource agencies and used as inputs to benefit-cost analyses.

readily available information has not been analyzed in terms of the extent, nature, and probable causes of difference between original estimates and final realized costs.

This paper makes only a small sortie into this largely unexplored field. Time and resources restricted the search to only one sector of U.S. federal investment—water-resource investment, by the Army Corps of Engineers, Tennessee Valley Authority and Bureau of Reclamation. The restricted scope of this study limits our ability to make generalizations. It also points to the need for much additional research on this aspect of public investment.

Extent of Previous Research

Our admittedly sketchy search of sources revealed very little published work on the cost question. This is true even in the field of water-resource investment, which has an extensive literature on benefit-cost analysis. For example, of six major books on water-resource economics,[2] only Eckstein's (1958) gives more than cursory attention to this question, and his discussion is limited to Corps of Engineers cost experience prior to 1951.[3] Altouney made a limited analysis (1963) of Bureau of Reclamation experience based on data collected by the Bureau in 1955.[4] Two of the most useful studies were concerned with cost experience overseas. Healey analyzed 13 water control projects built in India during the period 1946–60,[5] while a Select Committee on Nationalized Industries in Great Britain studied the cost experience of the North of Scotland Hydro-Electric Board in constructing twenty-four hydroelectric power plants.[6] A statistical study by two French

[2] Otto Eckstein, *Water-Resource Development: The Economics of Project Evaluation,* Cambridge, 1958; Roland McKean, *Efficiency in Government Through Systems Analysis, with Emphasis on Water Resources Development,* New York, 1958; John Krutilla and Otto Eckstein, *Multiple Purpose River Development, Studies in Applied Economic Analysis,* Baltimore, 1958; Jack Hirshleifer, James C. De Haven, and Jerome W. Milliman, *Water Supply: Economics, Technology and Policy,* Chicago, 1960; Arthur Maass *et al., Design of Water Resource Systems,* Cambridge, Mass., 1962; Robert H. Haveman, *Water Resource Investment and the Public Interest,* Nashville, 1965.

[3] Eckstein, pp. 149–151.

[4] Edward G. Altouney, *The Role of Uncertainties in the Economic Evaluation of Water Resources Projects,* Institute in Engineering-Economic Systems, Stanford University, 1963.

[5] J. M. Healey, "Errors in Project Cost Estimates," *Indian Economic Journal,* Vol. 12, July–September 1964.

[6] Select Committee on Nationalized Industries, *Report to the House of Commons,* Session Documents, Vol. 7, No. 304, 1956–57, London, H.M.S.O., 1957;

engineers of bias toward cost underestimation rounds out the list.[7] Details on these studies are provided later in the paper.

Scope and Nature of the Analysis

The analysis contained in this paper deals with the cost experience of the three largest United States water-resource construction agencies— the Army Corps of Engineers, Bureau of Reclamation and TVA— from 1933 to the early 1960's. Data on cost experience of the Corps of Engineers were obtained from (1) an analysis made by the Corps in 1951 for the House Committee on Appropriations,[8] and (2) a followup survey by the Corps in 1965.[9] Similarly, Bureau of Reclamation cost experience data came from studies made by the Bureau in 1955 and 1960.[10] Information on TVA experience was provided by the TVA staff.[11]

As an introduction to the analysis, a number of commonly held notions on the occurrence of and reasons for systematic errors are introduced. The actual experience of the three U.S. water-resource agencies is then examined in detail, and the findings are analyzed in terms of the preconceptions or hypotheses which had been advanced

and *Report to the House of Commons on the Electricity Supply Industry,* Session Papers, Vol. 7, No. 116, 1961–62, London, H.M.S.O., 1962.

[7] R. Giguet and G. Morlat, "Les Causes d'erreur systématique dans la prévision du prix des travaux," *Annales des Ponts et Chaussées,* Paris, 122e Année, No. 5, September–October 1952.

Robert Haveman reports (July 1968) that he and Terrell Langworthy have completed a study of cost experience on 86 Corps of Engineers water-resource projects for which construction was started in fiscal year 1956.

[8] U.S. Army, *Annual Report of the Chief of Engineers,* 1951, Part 1, Vol. 3; U.S. Congress, *Investigation of Corps of Engineers, Civil Works Program, Hearings* before and *Report* of the Subcommittee on Deficiencies and Army Civil Functions, Committee on Appropriations, House of Representatives, 82nd Congress, 1st Session, August 1951; U.S. Congress, *The Civil Functions Program of the Corps of Engineers, Report* to the Committee on Public Works from the Subcommittee to Study Civil Works, House of Representatives, 82nd Congress, 2nd Session, December 1952.

[9] Office of the Chief of Engineers, Headquarters, Department of the Army, "Engineering and Design, Project Cost Estimating-Civil Works," Engineer-Circular No. 1110-2-1301, February 3, 1965. A large amount of detailed data not contained in the Circular was provided by Mr. Wendell E. Johnson, Chief, Engineering Division, Civil Works, Office of the Chief of Engineers.

[10] U.S. Bureau of Reclamation, "Analysis of Reclamation Projects," October 1955, cited in Altouney, *op. cit.*; "Analysis of Reclamation Projects," March 1960.

[11] Internal TVA document entitled "Comparison of Estimates with Final Costs: Major Multipurpose and Single-use Projects Constructed by TVA," November 15, 1967, plus supporting materials provided by TVA staff.

earlier. A brief review of information of British, Indian, and French experience is presented. Finally, certain tentative conclusions are advanced and recommendations made for further research on this neglected subject.

Perception of Errors in Cost Estimates

The view most commonly advanced by the expert and the informed layman is that costs of public works projects are consistently underestimated at the time the decision is taken to build the project. Associated with this view is the belief that the variance between estimated and actual costs is often extremely high. Much evidence on specific cases is available to support this view: the Rayburn Office Building on Capitol Hill and the Interstate Highway Program are dramatic examples of this. The reader probably can supply many examples from his own experience.

The following are the major reasons advanced for variations between cost estimates and final realized costs:

1. Changes in general construction price level between that assumed in the project cost estimate and that prevailing during construction of the project.
2. Changes in the size and scope of project between original estimate and final design and construction.
3. Structural modifications and changes in design standards from those assumed at time of original estimate.
4. Changes in the least-cost construction schedule assumed in the original estimate; for example, "speedup" as in World War II or stretch-out arising from budgetary constraints.
5. Occurrence of unforeseen events—strikes, floods—with important cost implications.
6. Inadequate information of certain physical characteristics with important cost implications; for example, insufficient knowledge of dam foundation conditions, including character of soils and rock.
7. Inadequate information on extent and nature of relocations and on land acquisition costs.
8. Unconscious bias toward underestimation of costs arising from estimaters' identification with agency goals for maintaining a construction program.
9. General inadequacies and poor performance in planning and estimating.

In the agency analyses of their cost experience, many of these reasons are often given as explanations of major differences between estimated and actual costs. Detailed analysis of estimated and realized costs for individual projects in the context of the history of design and construction of each project would be necessary to assess the contribution of these factors to cost increases or decreases. No such detailed analyses were made by us; rather, we relied on information provided in published reports or by the federal agencies.

The Cost Record of the U.S. Water Resource Agencies

In the following, the cost experiences of the Corps of Engineers, TVA, and Bureau of Reclamation are summarized and the distribution of "errors" in the three agency programs are compared. Details of the analyses are shown in the text tables and in the Appendix.

Corps of Engineers Experience

A 1951 study made by the Corps at the request of the House Appropriations Committee revealed that the 182 rivers and harbors and flood control projects then current showed a total cost overrun of 124 per cent of the original estimates.[12] The 1951 estimate of cost for these projects was $5.9 billion as compared with the original project estimates totaling $2.6 billion. Because original cost estimates for most of these projects were made in the 1930's, it was to be expected that price increase would account for much of this overrun. In the analysis the Corps explained the overruns as follows: construction price increase, 57.7 per cent; changes in project design, 24.7 per cent; extensions in project scope, 17.6 per cent; changes in local needs and unforeseen conditions, 12.6 per cent; and inadequacies in planning and estimating, 5.8 per cent.

This record of performance came under criticism by the House Appropriations Committee in 1951, a subcommittee of the House Public Works Committee in 1952, and the Task Force on Water Resources and Power of the Second Hoover Commission in 1955. The House Appropriations Committee concluded that investment decisions made by Congress were based on grossly inaccurate cost data. Major reasons advanced by the Committee were the inadequacy

[12] A reminder: cost is defined throughout as construction or capital cost.

of the survey reports, which were too superficial to provide accurate cost information, and the large backlog of projects that imposed a time lag of many years between completion of original survey and start of construction. Thus, cost estimates for the original project were often drastically increased as local conditions changed, new demands arose, and engineering and structural design standards were modified.

These critics strongly recommended that the Corps improve its estimating procedures, curtail new authorizations until the backlog was reduced, and provide a detailed planning report, with refined cost data, at the time when requests were made for funds to start a project.

In 1964, the Corps of Engineers updated its survey of cost experience in an analysis of 184 projects completed during the period 1951–64 (technically, fiscal years 1951–65).[13] This survey revealed that total costs of $3.14 billion exceeded the original project estimates of $2.31 billion by 36.1 per cent. This represented a substantial improvement over the 124 per cent overrun in the 1951 survey. When the original cost estimates were adjusted to account for price changes between time of original estimate and time of actual construction, actual costs were 18.3 per cent less than escalated survey costs. This record is in sharp contrast to the 1951 record which showed actual costs to be 30 per cent greater than escalated survey costs.

Because many of the projects reported in the 1964 analysis had been originally surveyed before 1950, a separate analysis was made by us of sixty-eight projects for which the original survey had been made in 1954 or later. This analysis revealed that the total of actual cost and original estimated costs were less than 1 per cent apart; when price level adjustments were made, actual cost for the sixty-eight projects was 23 per cent below original estimated cost. These data clearly show that the Corps has significantly improved its performance since the early 1950's, when its cost estimating record first came under severe criticism by the Congress.

The Corps left to each of its districts the selection of the precise method for construction price level adjustments. Most districts used the *Engineering News-Record* construction cost index. A single national index is only a crude approximation of actual price changes operative for an individual project. When applied to projects with a long time lag between survey and completion, price index adjustments become very large. For example, *ENR* construction price index adjustments for projects with lags of fifteen to thirty-four years range from 100 per cent to 336 per cent above base-year levels. Such large

[13] Office of the Chief of Engineers, *op. cit.*

TABLE 1

CORPS OF ENGINEERS: SUMMARY OF ESTIMATING PERFORMANCE

	1951 Report	1964 Report Old Projects	1964 Report Recent Projects	Total
Period of record	to 1951	1933–53	1954–65	1933–65
Number of projects	182	116	68	184
Estimated cost, original survey (billions of dollars)	2.64	1.59	0.72	2.31
Escalated cost, original survey (billions of dollars)	4.53	2.91	0.94	3.85
Actual cost (billions of dollars)	5.91	2.42	0.72	3.14
Overruns (per cent of survey cost)				
Original survey cost	124.1	52.6	a	36.1
Escalated survey cost	30.6	−16.8b	−23.0b	−18.3b
Frequency of overruns (per cent of occurrence)				
Original survey cost	n.a.	84	51	72
Escalated survey cost	n.a.	34	29	32

IMPROVEMENT IN PERFORMANCE (CHANGE IN PER CENT OVERRUN)c

	Based on Original Survey Cost	Based on Escalated Survey Cost
1951 to 1964 (old)	57.6	145.0
1964 (old) to 1964 (recent)	100.0	37.0

n.a. = not available. a Less than 1 per cent underrun. b Underrun (actual cost less than estimate).
c Increase in size of underrun is here considered as an "improvement" for purposes of comparison (hence values in excess of 100 per cent). "Real improvements" should be measured as net reduction of error; thus present trends toward overestimation are not real improvements in accuracy.

price adjustments made with a crude index tend to distort the true relationship of price adjustment to other factors contributing to project overruns.

Corps of Engineers estimating performance is summarized in Table 1 below. The total overrun (or underrun) is shown as a per cent of original and escalated survey costs. In addition, the frequency of overruns as a per cent of total number of projects is shown, both for original and escalated survey costs.

The TVA Experience

The TVA has provided data on cost experience of thirty-four projects with costs in excess of $1 million. These projects, many of which were started during the 1930's, include twenty-three multiple-purpose dams and reservoirs, nine fossil fired electric generating plants, one flood protection project, and one water control system. Because many of the projects were built in stages, TVA provided data on sixty-one separate project units.

As shown in Table 2, the actual cost of the thirty-four projects ($2.33 billion) is $130 million below the original estimates of cost

TABLE 2

TENNESSEE VALLEY AUTHORITY

SUMMARY OF ESTIMATING PERFORMANCE

Period of record	1933–66
Number of projects	34
Number of separate estimates	61
Estimated costs (billions of dollars)	2.46[a]
Actual costs (billions of dollars)	2.33
Overrun (per cent of survey costs)	−5.3[b]
Frequency of overruns (per cent of occurrence)	
Independent projects	32.4
Separate estimates	34.4

[a] Wherever possible TVA includes projected price increases in its original estimate. Thus no separate escalated estimates are provided. Interest during construction included for some steam plant cost estimates and final costs. See Appendix Table 5.
[b] Underrun.

of $2.46 billion; this represents a total cost underrun of 5.3 per cent. Approximately one-third of the thirty-four projects, and, similarly, approximately one-third of the sixty-one project units, have experienced cost overruns. In terms of project type, none of the fourteen cost estimates for steam plant units has been less than final costs; total cost underrun for steam plants is 9.3 per cent. In contrast, 45 per cent of the estimates for dams and reservoirs have been less than final project costs; total overrun for this category is 21.7 per cent of estimated cost. Most of these overruns occurred on projects which were built or begun during World War II, when stoppages or accelerated construction was the rule.

Bureau of Reclamation Experience

In common with the Corps of Engineers, the Bureau of Reclamation performance on cost estimation came under critical scrutiny by Congress in 1955. The Bureau report of 1955 has been summarized and analyzed by Altouney, and the analysis of 1955 data presented here is derived from Appendix Table 5 in his report.[14]

Table 3 shows that, for the 103 projects in the 1955 survey, total estimated 1955 cost of $7.3 billion was 177 per cent above the original estimates of $2.6 billion, and almost double the escalated estimates ($3.7 billion) which reflect adjustments for construction price rises between times of original estimates and 1955. (The Bureau of Reclamation uses its own index of construction prices which reflects price changes in the major labor and material inputs to Reclamation projects.) Furthermore almost 90 per cent of all projects showed cost overruns from the original estimate, whether measured on nominal or escalated cost basis. In most cases, the 1955 costs were not final project costs, but were current cost estimates for projects not yet completed.

A subsequent review by the Bureau of Reclamation in 1960 showed a substantial improvement in performance over the 1955 record. Data in the report have been disaggregated to show performance on all projects (128) started between 1935 and 1960, a subset of seventy-nine projects over the same period which excludes units in the Missouri River Basin and Colorado River Storage Projects, and a subset of fifty-four projects surveyed and started since World War II. The seventy-nine projects exclusive of the MRBP and CRSP showed

---

[14] Altouney, *op. cit.,* pp. 102–105.

TABLE 3
BUREAU OF RECLAMATION: SUMMARY OF ESTIMATING PERFORMANCE

	1955 Report	1960 Report		
		All Projects	Exclusive of CRSP & MRBP[a]	Projects Since 1946
Period of record	to 1955	1935–60	1935–60	1946–60
Number of projects	103	128	79	54
Estimated cost: Original survey (billions of dollars)	2.64	3.78	2.51	1.32
Escalated cost: Original survey (billions of dollars)	3.72	4.36	3.02	1.50
Actual cost (billions of dollars)	7.29	6.49[b]	3.43[b]	1.44[b]
Overruns (per cent of survey cost)				
Original survey cost	177	72	36	9.4
Escalated survey cost	96	49	13	−4.1[c]
Frequency of overruns (per cent of occurrence)				
Original survey cost	89	75	67	52
Escalated survey cost	86	63	52	35

IMPROVEMENT IN PERFORMANCE (CHANGE IN PER CENT OVERRUN)

	Based on Original Survey Cost	Based on Escalated Survey Cost
1955 report to 1960, post-war projects	95	104[d]

a CRSP: Colorado River Storage Project. MRBP: Missouri River Basin Project.
b Includes estimate of final cost, as of March 1960, for projects not completed.   c Underrun.
d Underrun is here considered an improvement, hence a value in excess of 100 per cent.

a total overrun of 36 per cent of original estimates, and 13 per cent of original estimates adjusted for price increases. The record for the fifty-four projects surveyed and started since World War II shows a total overrun of 9.4 per cent of original estimates, and an underrun of 4.1 per cent of escalated estimates. The 1960 study includes projects under construction as well as those finally completed. For example, in Table 3, of the seventy-nine projects exclusive of CRSP and MRBP, fourteen were not completed at the time of the study in 1960. Some of these were only at the beginning stage of construction. Similarly, of the fifty-four projects begun after World War II, six were not completed in 1960. Final costs for these projects may be considerably different than the 1960 estimates.

Comparison of Agency Performance

To aid in comparing agency performance on cost estimation, summary data for the three agencies are brought together in Table 4. In terms of both size and frequency of overrun, the TVA has the best record. TVA performance is best, even with the steam plants eliminated from the analysis. With no adjustments for construction price levels, TVA total overrun for dams and reservoirs is 22 per cent of original estimated cost; Corps of Engineers overrun is 124 per cent for projects built or building prior to 1951, and 36 per cent for projects completed between 1951 and 1964; while Bureau of Reclamation overrun is 177 per cent for projects built or building prior to 1955 and 72 per cent for all projects built or building in 1960. In terms of frequency of overruns, 45 per cent of TVA dams and reservoirs experienced overruns; the record for the Corps of Engineers is 72 per cent of all projects completed between 1951 and 1964, and, for the Bureau of Reclamation, 89 per cent of all projects built or building prior to 1955, and 75 per cent of all projects built or building in 1960.

The performance record of both the Corps of Engineers and Bureau of Reclamation is much better on projects for which surveys (and hence cost estimates) were made after World War II. For example, actual cost of sixty-eight Corps of Engineers projects surveyed, authorized and built between 1954 and 1964 was 0.2 per cent *below* estimated costs for the projects. For fifty-four Bureau of Reclamation projects surveyed, authorized and built or building between 1946 and 1960, actual costs were only 9.4 per cent above cost estimates. In the case of each agency, frequency of overruns was slightly over 50 per cent for postwar performance.

TABLE 4

COMPARISON OF AGENCY PERFORMANCE: MAGNITUDE AND FREQUENCY OF OVERRUNS, TVA, CORPS OF ENGINEERS, BUREAU OF RECLAMATION

	Number of Projects	Size of Total Overrun (per cent)		Frequency of Overruns (per cent)	
		From Original Estimate	From Escalated Estimate	From Original Estimate	From Escalated Estimate
TVA:					
Dams	25	21.7	b	45	b
Steam plants	9	−9.6a	b	0	b
Total	34	−5.3	b	34.4	b
Corps of Engineers:					
Flood control:					
1951 report	122	152.9	c	c	c
1964 report, all projects	103	58.5	−7.8	83	42
1964 report, recent projects	30	10.0	−14.3	73	47
Rivers and harbors:					
1951 report	60	99.6	c	c	c
1964 report, all projects	81	27.9	−22.3	58	20
1964 report, recent projects	38	−5.1	−27.2	34	16
Total:					
1951 report	182	124.1	c	c	c
1964 report, all projects	184	36.1	−18.3	72	32
1964 report, recent projects	68	−0.2	−23.0	51	29
Bureau of Reclamation:					
1955 report	103	177.0	96.0	89	86
1960 report, exclusive of CRSP & MRBP	79	36	13	67	52
1960 report, all projects	128	72	49	75	63
1960 report, postwar projects	54	9.4	−4.1	52	35

NOTE: See appendix tables.   a Minus sign indicates underrun.   b Not applicable.   c Not available.

DISTRIBUTION OF ERRORS.[15] An analysis of distribution of errors was made for each agency program. The detailed distributions are shown in Appendix Figures 1 through 6. A summary of the means, modes, medians, standard deviations, and extreme values in terms of per cent of deviation of actual cost from estimated cost is contained in Table 5. Again, the TVA has the best record, with mean, mode and median errors showing underruns, and with a standard deviation of 17.5 per cent. In contrast, best performance of the Corps of Engineers, on projects surveyed and built between 1954 and 1964, shows mean and median errors as overruns and a relatively high standard deviation of 45 per cent. For Bureau of Reclamation projects at least 50 per cent complete by 1960, mean error was 25.8 per cent, median error, 3 per cent, and standard deviation 42 per cent.

Summary of Performance

In summary, the TVA program and recent Corps of Engineers experience (even with no construction price level adjustments for Corps projects) show no consistent bias toward underestimation of project costs. When construction price level adjustments are made for the most recent Bureau of Reclamation program, it too shows no bias toward underestimation. (This assumes that price level adjustments are approximately correct; some information on price adjustments is contained in Appendix Table 4.)

Whatever the measure used (magnitude or frequency of overrun, or distribution of errors), recent estimating performance of the Corps of Engineers and Bureau of Reclamation has improved significantly over performance before World War II and in the 1940's. For the Corps of Engineers, project cost estimates made since 1954 have been significantly better than previous estimates in that total cost overrun as per cent of total program cost has been reduced to 10 per cent without any adjustment for construction cost increases. This compares with a huge cost overrun of 124 per cent according to a 1951 survey of projects whose costs were estimated in the 1930's and 1940's. Similarly, the 9.4 per cent total cost overrun for Bureau of Reclamation projects surveyed since World War II shows a tremendous improvement over the 177 per cent cost overrun revealed in a 1955 survey for projects surveyed in the 1930's and 1940's.

---

[15] The term error as used here is any departure of estimated cost from actual cost.

TABLE 5

COMPARISON OF AGENCY PERFORMANCE: DISTRIBUTION OF ESTIMATING ERRORS, TVA, CORPS OF ENGINEERS AND BUREAU OF RECLAMATION

	Number of Projects	Mean (per cent)	Standard Deviation	Mode (per cent)	Median (per cent)	Maximum Overrun (per cent)	Maximum Underrun (per cent)
TVA (all projects)	61	−1.7	17.5	−5.0	−5.0	53	33
Corps of engineers:							
All projects, 1964 report, escalated estimate	182[a]	−6.18	43	−17.5	−17.5	198	70
Projects since 1954, original estimate	68	+10.66	45	−12.5	+3.4	216	57
Projects since 1954, escalated estimate	68	−9.48	33	−22.5	−14.0	120	70
Bureau of Reclamation, original estimate							
1955 report	103	+163.0	n.a.	+10.0	+100.0	1000	20
1960 report[b]	79	+27.4	58	0.0	+7.0	326	39
1960 report[c]	63	+25.8	42	0.0	+3.0	165	39

n.a. = Not applicable.

[a] Excluding two projects with overruns of 259 per cent and 656 per cent.

[b] All projects exclusive of Colorado River Storage Project and Missouri River Basin Project.

[c] Projects at least 50 per cent complete, excluding two projects with overruns of 251 per cent and 326 per cent.

Although the TVA record has been more consistent throughout the thirty-three-year period of its activity, there is some evidence that its recent cost estimating performance is better than its earlier record.

The Causes of Error

In the agency analysis of cost experience, the deviations of actual from estimated cost are ascribed to various factors, some of which are identical with the nine reasons advanced in the Introduction to this paper. These factors, which may be thought of as proximate causes of error, can be divided into exogenous factors, over which the agency has little or no control, and endogenous factors, which can be modified by improving agency administration.

Proximate Causes

In the Corps of Engineers 1951 survey, about 58 per cent of the $2.8 billion excess of actual over estimated cost was ascribed to price increases and another 22 per cent was traced to authorized project extensions or changed local needs (see Table 1 in the Appendix). These causes are largely exogenous; the agency has no control over general construction price increases, and increases in project size and scope are usually the result of demands arising outside of the agency. The remaining 20 per cent of excess cost, ascribed to structural and engineering modifications, unforeseen conditions and inadequacies in planning, are largely subject to agency control. In analyzing the Corps 1951 survey, a House Appropriations Subcommittee report pointed to the following weaknesses in the Corps' performance:

(a) Price increase arising from structural modifications were over 10 per cent of estimated project cost in one-third of the projects; approximately one-sixth of the projects had price increases exceeding 40 per cent; the largest relative increase was 727 per cent;

(b) unforeseen conditions caused price increases of 10 per cent or more on 38 per cent of the projects; increases of 40 per cent or more showed up on 20 per cent of the projects; the largest increase was 502 per cent;

(c) increased relocation costs were an important factor; for the 182 projects, average increase in relocation costs was 177 per cent; some relocation costs were up to fifty times the original estimate;

(d) increases in land acquisition costs averaged 123 per cent, in part caused by a 42 per cent increase in total acreage required; the largest relative increase of acreage for a single project was 287 per cent;

(e) cost increases ascribed to general inadequacies in planning and estimating (presumably because the increases were otherwise unaccounted for) were in excess of 10 per cent for 28 per cent of the projects; the largest relative increase was 217 per cent.

Much of the cost increase can be traced to the long time lag between project conception in the survey stage and actual construction. This problem of lag was aggravated by World War II; during the years 1941–1945 water resources construction was effectively suspended. Also significant, however, was the fact that project plans and cost estimates were often based on very sketchy information and inadequate analytical techniques. This was particularly true of surveys completed before and during World War II.

Corps of Engineers, 1964 Report

Of the 184 projects reported in this survey, forty-three had actual costs more than 10 per cent in excess of the original estimates adjusted to take account of construction price increases. These excess costs, which amounted to $177 million, were distributed as follows:

Land acquisition	14 per cent
Relocation	31 per cent
Design changes	51 per cent
Higher bid prices than expected	4 per cent

Of fifteen cases of increased land acquisition costs, four were traced to rises in land values and eleven involved changes in project scope. Relocation costs were increased because of increases in project scope and adoption of new legal or administrative criteria and changed design standards, requiring, for instance, rebuilding of roads to higher standards than those of existing roads. One-third of the design changes were ascribed to increases in project scope and two-thirds to geologic and hydraulic conditions different from those assumed at the survey stage.

It is difficult to make a clear separation between exogenous and endogenous factors influencing costs from the sketchy data of the 1964 report. Increase in land values, new legal requirements and changes in project scope are largely exogenous; these factors account for 43 per cent of all reasons cited as causes of increases. On the other hand, design changes probably reflect both exogenous factors, such as new conditions arising from delay between survey and construction stages, and endogenous factors associated with inadequate information at the survey stage.

Tennessee Valley Authority

Examination of the explanations provided by TVA for major cost overruns reveals the following:

(a) Changes in project construction schedules were an important factor, especially during World War II. Some projects, under construction when the U.S. entered the war, were stopped in 1942 and resumed only the after war; construction was accelerated on a few key projects during the war, thus increasing costs; in addition, there were a few instances of schedule stretchout due to delayed or reduced appropriations by Congress;

(b) in some cases, appropriations for construction were made before cost estimates were completed; this was the case for six dams begun in 1936 and for a later project constructed on an emergency basis;

(c) in only a few cases did changes in project scope increase costs significantly; also, there were few situations where costs increased because local conditions were different than anticipated.

BUREAU OF RECLAMATION. For seventy-nine projects (exclusive of project units in the Colorado River Storage Project and Missouri River Basin Program) surveyed by the Bureau of Reclamation in 1960, 55 per cent of the total increase in project costs was ascribed by the Bureau to exogenous price increases. Changes in project scope accounted for 22 per cent; reanalysis of work quantities and unit costs was responsible for another 12 per cent. The remaining 11 per cent was attributed to unforeseen conditions, structural modifications and miscellaneous reasons. Exogenous factors (price increases, changes in project plans) accounted for almost 80 per cent of the increase, but the remaining 20 per cent ascribed to controllable factors provides a significant opportunity for improvement by the agency.

Underlying Factors Influencing Accuracy of Cost Estimates

The underlying factors fall into two broad classes: those related to the project and the timing of survey and construction—type, size, complexity, time lag between survey and construction; and those related to the administrative and institutional framework—nature of pre-authorization surveys, organizational structure, estimating pressures and biases. Major findings with respect to these factors are presented here:[16] details are contained in the Appendix tables.

Factors Related to Projects and Their Timing

PROJECT TYPE. Type of project clearly influences the accuracy of the estimates. As shown in Table 6 and Appendix Table 2, Corps of Engineer flood control projects (levees, channel excavation, flood control reservoirs, local protection works) have a higher total and greater frequency of cost overruns than rivers and harbors projects (dredging, harbor construction, locks and dams including power facilities and multiple purpose dams with power facilities). This inferior performance of flood control projects is maintained when construction price adjustment is applied to original estimates for both rivers and harbors and flood control projects. In terms of project subtypes, frequency of overrun is least for dredging and locks and dams, and greatest for local protection works and reservoirs—flood control and multipurpose. Cost estimation for dredging is relatively straightforward and involves few uncertainties. On the other hand, local protection projects often require land acquisition and extensive relocations in urban settings. Changes in land values are important factors, especially when there is a long time lag between survey and construction. In the case of storage reservoirs, geological and hydrological uncertainties are important elements leading to cost increases. Poor foundation conditions not anticipated at the survey stage can increase costs significantly, as can design changes involving large increases in spillway size occasioned by occurrence of large floods between time of survey and time of detailed project design.

---

[16] The analysis is in single-factor form. Because of small sample sizes, a multi-factor statistical analysis was not undertaken. We recognize that some factors such as size and type of project are positively correlated.

TABLE 6
CORPS OF ENGINEERS
ESTIMATING PERFORMANCE BY PROJECT TYPE[a]

Period	Flood Control[b]		Rivers and Harbors[c]		Total	
	1933–53	1954–65	1933–53	1954–65	1933–53	1954–65
Number of projects	73	30	43	38	116	68
Overruns (per cent of survey cost)						
Original survey cost	88.3	10.0	41.3	−5.1	52.6	−0.2
Escalated survey cost	−5.3	−14.3	−20.8	−27.2	−16.8	−23.0
Frequency of overruns (per cent)						
Original survey cost	86	73	79	34	83	51
Escalated survey cost	40	47	23	16	34	29
Performance coefficient[d]						
Original survey cost	1.03	1.43	0.95	0.67	1.0	1.0
Escalated survey cost	1.17	1.59	0.70	0.54	1.0	1.0

[a] All data from 1964 report.
[b] Includes the following types of projects: levees, channel excavation, flood control reservoirs, local protection works.
[c] Includes the following types of projects: locks and dams, with and without power, multipurpose dams with power, harbor construction, beach replenishment, dredging.
[d] Performance coefficient $= \dfrac{\text{number of overruns in group}}{\text{all overruns}} \div \dfrac{\text{number of projects in group}}{\text{all projects}}$

If coefficient $= 1.0$, group has same share of overruns and of projects;
> 1.0, group has a greater proportion of overruns than of projects;
< 1.0, group has a smaller proportion of overruns than of projects.

TABLE 7

TENNESSEE VALLEY AUTHORITY

ESTIMATING PERFORMANCE BY PROJECT TYPE

	Dams	Steam Plants
Number of estimates	40	14
Original estimate (millions of dollars)	896.1[a]	1565.0
Actual cost (millions of dollars)	915.6[a]	1415.1
Total overrun (per cent)	21.7[a]	−9.6[b]
Frequency of overruns (per cent)	45.0	None
Distribution of errors (per cent)		
Mean	+8.25	−10.71
Mode	+7.5	−12.5
Median	−1.6	−10.4
Standard deviation	18.2	6.1
Maximum overrun	50.0	None
Maximum underrun	33.0	21.8

[a] For 47 estimates including miscellaneous projects related to dams and reservoirs.

[b] Underrun.

Table 7 shows the striking difference between cost estimating experience of TVA with dams and steam plants. The obvious explanation is the relative freedom from estimating uncertainties in the steam plant case. These are summarized for steam plants by TVA as follows:

(1) Area and cost of land for site are fairly well known at the outset;

(2) unforeseen foundation conditions do not greatly affect total costs;

(3) a large percentage of total cost is for equipment (for which cost estimates are fairly firm);

(4) good data are available on past experience for similar projects;

(5) setbacks due to floods or bad weather are improbable;

(6) good prospect of only small changes, affecting cost, between initial planning and final design.

PROJECT SIZE. The data show no conclusive evidence that project size (in terms of total estimated cost) is related to frequency of overruns. Altouney found no evidence of such correlation in his analysis of projects in the 1955 Bureau of Reclamation study.[17] TVA data suggests an inverse relationship between size of project and frequency of overrun, as shown by the following:

Cost Range (millions of dollars)	Number of Projects	Frequency of Overrun (Per Cent)
1.0–9.9	21	57
10.0–49.9	26	27
50.0–216.0	14	14

However, many of the large projects are steam plants and the good record of the large projects is probably more related to the nature of the projects than to their size.

No detailed analysis of influence of size was made for Corps of Engineers projects, but we consider it unlikely that such analysis would show significant correlations that are independent of other factors.

PROJECT TIMING. The timing of project construction in relation to completion of the project survey is important on two counts. When elapsed time between survey and construction is long, increase in construction prices becomes important and actual costs due to this cause alone turn out to be very much larger than estimated cost. For example, using the ENR construction cost index as the measure of price change, a project whose costs were estimated on the basis of 1950 prices would almost double in cost if built in 1965—a time lag of fifteen years. TVA's good record on costs is in part due to the extremely short time lag between completion of survey and start of construction (usually not more than two years). This allows TVA to base its estimates on short-term projected prices.[18]

The second consequence of long time lag concerns changes in project scope and in design standards. Typically these operate to increase project costs. This is shown in the Corps of Engineers data. After adjusting for construction prices, the 119 Corps projects with time lags up to fourteen years have a 28 per cent frequency of overrun, while 38 per cent of the sixty-six Corps projects with time lags of fifteen to thirty-four years have experienced overruns.

Calendar time also appears to be an important factor. Corps of

[17] Altouney, *op. cit.* p. 48.
[18] TVA makes its estimates on the basis of man-hours where possible, and makes separate estimates of projected increases in cost of labor, materials and equipment, rather than applying a single price adjustment factor to a current price estimate.

Engineers and Bureau of Reclamation projects which were surveyed before World War II have poor performance records on costs, as revealed by the 1951 and 1955 studies.[19] In contrast, the record of both agencies is much better for projects with surveys completed since World War II. For TVA, cost overruns were most serious for projects built during World War II, when unusual conditions prevailed in the construction industry.

In summary, time lag between survey and construction is an extremely important factor; fortunately, this factor is amenable to administrative and policy control.

Factors Related to Nature of Planning and Decision Process

There is considerable variation among water resource agencies on the procedure followed in obtaining authorization and appropriations for projects. The Corps of Engineers submits a project or river basin survey report to the Congress (after Presidential clearance) to serve as a basis for *authorization* of the work. The cost estimate prepared at this survey stage is an input to the benefit-cost analysis which Congress relies upon, in part, for making its decision on authorization. Typically authorization acts (Omnibus River and Harbors or Flood Control Acts) are enacted every two years. There may thus be a delay of as much as two or three years between date of cost estimate and authorization of the project. A separate procedure to obtain appropriations for the project must then be followed, which usually involves an additional year or two of delay. Delays of three or four years are common and some projects have even longer lags. Although project costs (and benefits) are updated at the time decisions are made to appropriate funds, the authorization decision is usually the controlling decision on *whether* to proceed with construction. It is not surprising, therefore, that actual costs deviate significantly from the original estimates, especially when the level of precision of cost estimating at the survey stage is considerably less than that appropriate for the engineering design stage.

Bureau of Reclamation procedures are generally similar to those of the Corps in that projects also must proceed through separate authorizing and funding stages. In contrast, the TVA project authorization step is an internal decision of the Board of Directors, usually followed

[19] See footnotes 4 and 8 above.

expeditiously with a request to the President and Congress for appropriations or authority to commit TVA corporate funds. In most cases, the time lag is short and project cost estimates are quite realistic.

The probable influence of authorizing and funding procedures is revealed by a comparison of the standard deviation of estimating errors of TVA and the Corps of Engineers, as shown in Table 5. For TVA projects, the standard deviation of error (as a per cent of estimated project cost) is 18, while for Corps of Engineers projects built since 1954 (which reflect the best record of the Corps) the standard deviation is 33, after price level adjustments have been made.

UNITARY VERSUS DECENTRALIZED ADMINISTRATION. TVA operations are managed from a single headquarters staff with centralized control of planning, estimating, design and construction. TVA has an excellent record of staff continuity allowing the agency to reap the benefits of cumulative experience. In contrast, the Corps of Engineers, with a nationwide program much larger than that of TVA, operates on a decentralized basis with thirty-seven districts and eleven intermediate divisions, which report to the Office of the Chief of Engineers in Washington.

From the standpoint of size of program and geographical scope, TVA project planning and construction (in contrast to its major power operations) is probably comparable to civil works planning and construction in a division of the Corps. TVA cost estimating performance is better than the performance of the Corps as a whole. Yet there are significant differences in performance among Corps divisions. As shown in detail in Appendix Table 3, for projects surveyed and built since 1954, the North Central and South Atlantic divisions had the lowest frequency of cost overruns (15 per cent and 22 per cent, respectively) while the Ohio River, and North Pacific had the highest frequencies (100 per cent).

Because frequency of overrun may also be influenced by project type, a separate analysis was made of projects included in the 1964 report to account for this factor. As shown in Appendix Table 3, the ratio of actual to expected overruns was computed for each Corps of Engineers division, based on the project mix of each division. On this basis, the North Central, North Atlantic and South Atlantic divisions had significantly better performance records than the others, while the Ohio River and North Pacific divisions again had the poorest record. Project mix did not change the rankings significantly.

METHOD OF PROJECT CONSTRUCTION. TVA performs all construction itself by force account while the Corps of Engineers and Bureau of Reclamation rely almost entirely on independent contractors via competitive bidding. It would appear that competitive bidding should lead to more economical construction than force account. But the TVA has made efficient use of force account, because it has had relatively close control of its construction schedule. Within limits it has been able to schedule construction to make best use of its administrative and supervisory personnel. It operates with the relative certainty of well-known labor costs and productivity levels and centralized management.

The Corps of Engineers and Bureau of Reclamation, on the other hand, are subject to both the positive and negative aspects of dealing with independent contractors and independent labor forces. This is likely to result in a highly variable performance, with economies achieved when construction work is slack and bidders are competing vigorously, and higher than normal costs the rule when construction work is plentiful. Although we cannot quantify the importance of this factor in our study, the over-all record of TVA performance indicates that its use of force account has led to important economies.

INSTITUTIONAL BIASES. Planners, designers and estimators are always subject to some environmental pressures in the performance of their work. Can any of these factors affect performance in a consistent fashion, thus leading to an unconscious bias? All three agencies operate within an institutional momentum that provides incentive for doing things, that is, with some oversimplification, to build as many projects as possible. Because economic justification (a favorable benefit-cost ratio) is a necessary condition for obtaining project authorization, there is a definite advantage in maintaining cost estimates as low as possible. The countervailing pressures are the legitimate professional pride of estimators in a task well done. They strive to provide correct information and to be accurate. They are sensitive to the penalties for poor work—criticism of their professional peers, and unfavorable criticism of their agency by Congress and the informed public. It is impossible to gauge accurately the relative weights of these opposing pressures and any judgment would be very rash. It would seem however that the pressures placed upon the Corps of Engineers and Bureau of Reclamation by their relationships with local interests, their greater dependence upon Congressional committees for support and the widespread impact of their programs are at least outwardly much stronger than those imposed upon TVA. All three agencies have a strong professional pride and this factor may well be dominant. The striking improvement in performance by the Corps and the Bureau since 1951 is an indication of this factor in operation.

Secular Changes over Time

The most obvious secular change associated with improvement of performance is the accumulation of experience including increased knowledge of the areas under the jurisdiction of the agencies and increased awareness of the major sources of problems. A second factor, which cannot be measured easily but can be safely assumed, is the improvement in the management of the agencies, the increased professionalization of staffs and improved working procedures. A third factor, which has been particularly important in removing elements of uncertainty at the planning-estimating stage, is the considerable improvement in engineering knowledge and skills that has affected every step of design and construction. Geological and geophysical survey techniques have improved the advance information obtainable at costs within the bounds of preliminary surveys; construction methods provide greater certainty as to the requirements of certain operations (for instance in determining the exact overbreakage required and feasible in rock excavation work). Thus, improved engineering not only increases the effectiveness of construction operations, but, by providing better information, allows for more accurate estimates at the survey stage.

Some Evidence from India, Great Britain and France

In an analysis of thirteen hydroelectric power and irrigation projects built in India during the period 1946–60, Healey found a consistent high bias toward underestimation of costs.[20] As shown in Appendix Table 10, total cost overrun for the thirteen projects was 41.3 per cent of estimated cost. Maximum overrun was 230 per cent and minimum overrun 5 per cent of estimated costs. The very large overruns are ascribed to the following causes in the following proportions:

[20] Healey, *op. cit.*

(a) Poor planning and management, 50 per cent; inadequate or wrong information from preliminary investigations; major changes in project scope due to misinterpretation of project purpose and potential (ignorance of the real production function); considerable mismanagement at site; delays; over supply of equipment; failure to call for tenders;

(b) price increases, 25 per cent; a detailed analysis of cost components show that price increases are not the major factor;

(c) unexplained, 25 per cent—which is probably due to estimating errors.

Healey explains the dominance of poor planning and management as a cause of error by the great difficulty of estimating overhead costs and of implementing proper accounting and management controls in a developing country.

A Select Committee on Nationalized Industries in Great Britain discovered even larger, and more consistently substantial, errors in a 1957 study of the experience of the North of Scotland Hydro-Electric Board.[21] Details are shown in Appendix Table 10. The Committee found two major causes for the large difference (107.5 per cent) between actual and estimated costs: price increases, and the inexperience of the managing authority established after the war. The Committee made a number of administrative recommendations to improve the situation and requested that annual reviews be made of estimates and costs for all projects. The possibility of substantial improvement in procedures is revealed by the results of the Committee's second investigation, in 1962. The improvement is particularly striking in the projects designed between 1951 and 1955 (before the first Committee report but after some 17 years of experience). The overrun was reduced to 6.6 per cent of estimated cost.

A Statistical Approach: France

In 1952 two engineers of Electricité de France published a statistical analysis tending to demonstrate the existence of a bias toward underestimation independent of the optimism or the deliberate attitudes of the estimators.[22] They accept the bias as a fact and seek to remove part of the responsibility for its existence from the shoulders of the estimators. They made two separate analyses of the problem:

[21] Select Committee on Nationalized Industries in Great Britain, *op. cit.*
[22] Giguet et Morlat, *op. cit.*

(a) *Dissymmetry of the probability distribution of errors.* The major factors that cause project costs to be greater than estimates are not independent but related. The engineers who design projects will determine the probability of existence of such factors (for instance unsound rock in a tunnel excavation) and will design so as to minimize the probability of occurrence of costly events. Whenever such events occur, the actual cost of projects will increase so that over the long run the mean value of actual project costs will be larger than the value estimated as most probable.

(b) *Systematic program errors.* The authors postulate a list of possible projects from which only a limited number will be selected and a normal distribution of errors (under- and over-estimates) of mean zero. The projects to be chosen are those which, for equal benefits, are estimated to have a cost lower than a given cut-off cost (y_0) determined by budgetary constraints. These projects will be (1) those with an actual cost (x) equal to the estimated cost (y), (2) those which, because of errors in the estimates, have actual costs greater than estimated costs and (3) (as demonstrated by the authors) some projects which have been overestimated, but which, because of the presence of the limit y_0, have a smaller proportional error than the underestimated projects. Projects which have been overestimated and are expected to cost more than the cut-off budget ($y > y_0$) will not be chosen although their actual cost would have turned out to be less than y_0. Thus, the actual cost of the total program will be greater than estimated and the size of the overrun will be inversely proportional to the percentage of projects to be selected from the list (as determined by the value of y_0).

Although this brief summary does not do justice to Giguet and Morlat's statistical analysis, it is difficult to accept the general validity of their statement. Its validity becomes more evident when considering limit cases: if a very small proportion of the total list is to be selected, those projects with the largest underestimation (for a given level of net benefits) will receive priority; conversely, if the total list is to be implemented, the distribution of errors will be normal, as assumed, and the average error of the estimates will be zero.

Both analyses rely on a number of constraining assumptions that reduce their validity as descriptions of the real world. However as one of the few known attempts to formulate an explanation for the perennial problem of systematic bias it opens new perspectives for research.

Findings and Implications for Public Works Policy and Administration

Our analysis has shown a significant difference among agencies in the accuracy of cost estimates. TVA, with the best record, has more organizational autonomy and a more centralized administration than the other agencies. This leads to the tentative conclusion that organizational and administrative context is the important variable influencing cost estimation performance.

A second finding is that the agencies have achieved very great improvements in estimating performance since the early 1950's. The poor performance of the Corps and the Bureau prior to 1950 can be attributed to the unusual conditions of the 1930's and the immediate postwar years. Agency planning staffs had grown rapidly during the 1930's, had been decimated during the war and were again built up rapidly immediately after the war. Pressures to complete survey reports were strong, and the information required for accurate cost estimates was often seriously deficient. Spurred by the Congressional criticism of the early 1950's, the agencies worked to improve their planning and cost estimating procedures and techniques. Technological change and improvements in engineering design skills have been positive factors also. The results were impressive: recent estimating performance by the Corps and the Bureau has begun to approach the good record of TVA.

The third important finding is that *current* performance of these agencies shows no significant bias toward underestimation of project costs. TVA, which uses projected construction costs and has a short lag period between completion of survey and start of construction, now makes estimates which are typically within 10 per cent of realized costs; recent bias has been toward overestimation. The Corps of Engineers, which typically encounters long time lags between survey and construction and which computes costs on a current price basis, still shows, in its performance since 1954, actual costs running higher than estimated costs. When adjustments are made for price increases, however, this bias disappears. Recognizing the many uncertainties associated with the data, including the crudity of the price adjustments, one can say that *recent* Corps performance (in contrast to earlier performance) shows no obvious bias toward underestimation of real costs.

The fourth point to be made is that recent agency experience reveals persistence of a sizable variance of error, in spite of the great improvements shown over earlier performance. To the extent that this wide spread is not traceable to changes in project scope or purpose, there is opportunity to reduce it through improving planning methods and cost estimating techniques.

The major technical factor which contributes to error in estimation is physical uncertainty; in water-resource projects the most important uncertainties involve geologic structure and hydrologic regime. Estimates at the survey stage must usually be based on incomplete information on these physical aspects. When more complete information becomes available at the design or construction stage, "bad" geologic structure or hydrologic circumstance often impose sizable additional construction cost on the project; rarely does more complete information on these aspects result in a lowering of actual cost from estimated cost. It appears reasonable to conclude that the presence of physical uncertainty carries with it a bias toward underestimation of costs. It is possible to reduce the degree of such uncertainty at the planning stage by increasing the information input, although this will entail extra survey costs.

Although technical uncertainty may be an important factor for a particular class of projects—storage reservoirs, for example—over-all, it appears to be much less important as a cause of error than administrative and institutional factors.

Implications for Policy and Administration

The need for accurate cost estimates as an input to the decision process is obvious. To the extent that cost estimates for an entire program (such as the Interstate Highway program) are below actual costs, the entire schedule will be disrupted in the pressure of a budgetary constraint based on the original estimate. When cost estimates for individual projects fall well below actual costs, the very worthwhileness of the project may be undercut.

The fact that significant improvements in performance can be achieved, as in the water resource examples studied, points to the conclusion that significant payoffs may be possible through study of the planning and estimating process of public works agencies, as a part of over-all management improvement activities. Further, the important role played by institutional structure in the water-resource case points to the need for examining this crucial variable. Some specific suggestions for changes in administration are made below.

THE PLANNING PROCESS. Inadequacies in the planning process seem to be a larger source of error than preparation of cost estimates as such. The superficial nature of the surveys and information used as input to cost estimates has been a major problem. The answer appears to lie in adoption of an approach much like TVA's that a decision to proceed on a project (project authorization) must be taken only on the basis of a reasonably detailed survey. In terms of many public works programs, such as Corps of Engineers civil works, this may involve eliminating the project authorization step, and relying on the appropriation step, as the basis for decision to proceed. In any event, the solution appears to be in more complete and detailed planning before firm decisions to build are taken.

THE COST ESTIMATING PROCESS. Even with reasonably detailed planning and information, uncertainties may still be large at the cost estimating stage. When the cost of additional information to reduce uncertainty is prohibitive, project cost data can be presented in terms of ranges or degrees of accuracy, element by element, and an over-all range of error noted for the project. This prescription is obviously applicable to benefit estimates also, and over-all benefit-cost data could be presented in terms of ranges rather than single-valued estimates. The important information for decision makers is on the differences in range of cost and benefit for individual projects and classes of projects.

More sophisticated use of contingency factors would also provide a means of increasing accuracy of estimates. The presence of large contingency factors, on the order of 20 to 25 per cent, is usually an indication that the information base is inadequate. TVA reports that the contingency factor is considered to cover the following:

(a) Changes in project scope between planning and design stages, including adding minor structures, features and systems not included at the outset;
(b) errors, oversights, and imperfections in estimating methods;
(c) deviations in efficiency of project construction;
(d) variation between estimated and actual cost of equipment and material.

With this concept of contingency, TVA has been able to reduce its contingency factor for large steam plants from a previous range of 10 to 13 per cent to a level of 5 per cent. The point is that contingency factors should not be used as a substitute for detailed cost estimating. The computation of a contingency factor as a residual, element by element, would seem to be a desirable practice.

PRICE CHANGES. It would be most desirable to compute costs on the basis of projected price levels for the labor, materials and equipment components of projects. This is generally the practice of TVA. Where uncertainty as to the date of construction does not permit such procedure, estimates could be supplemented by the addition of a projected price index in order to provide some indication of project costs according to various possible construction periods. Such a scale should however also include the increases in nominal benefits (in fact it would be an adjusted benefit-cost ratio) in order to avoid the fallacy that a delayed project will necessarily be inferior in terms of net gain to the nation. The greatest value of such an index, other than its indication of changes in net benefits, if any, might be simply to acknowledge in advance the influence of the price factor over the estimates in order to "protect the record" of the estimating agency.

CHANGES IN ADMINISTRATIVE STRUCTURE. Improvements in cost estimating could be achieved by fundamental changes in administrative structure in which regional or river basin agencies were given general authority such as TVA has to plan, design, construct and manage a water-resource system subject only to outside control over appropriations. Short of such sweeping change, there could be more centralization of the planning and cost estimating task in the division offices of the Corps of Engineers. Greater competence could be built in a few estimating staffs than now exists in the many districts. More fundamental perhaps is a change in the project authorization procedure which now forces decisions on projects to be made with inadequate information as to cost. The water resource agencies should have general authority to include projects in a regional plan, but actual decision to undertake a project should be deferred until the appropriation stage. Cost estimates made at this time should be reasonably firm because there would be no long delay between completion of the cost (and benefit) estimates and start of the project.[23]

[23] Robert Haveman reports that an analysis by Terrell Langworthy and himself reveals that, for 86 Corps of Engineers projects initiated in fiscal year 1956, *total* costs as estimated at the appropriations stage and as finally realized were remarkably close. A substantial variance existed among projects, however.

Suggestions for Further Research

As stated at the outset, the limitations of this study suggest the need for much further research on this subject. In particular, research is needed on other major public works programs—highways, public buildings, water and sewer systems among others—and at other levels of government—state and local.

In this study, we only touched on the detailed process of cost estimation as carried out by planning and engineering staffs, including such important issues as use of contingency estimates and use of projected construction costs. Studies of this process should be made in detail, perhaps using actual cases and tracing through in detail how the estimates were made and how actual costs varied from estimates on this detailed basis. A study could also be made of the professionals' attitudes toward cost estimation. In our interview with TVA personnel, we noted a professional pride in the agency's good record on cost estimation and a deep concern for doing a good professional job. But detailed studies of attitudes and behavior of professionals are required before one can be definitive about this aspect of cost estimation.

As indicated earlier, our statistical analysis of the available data was quite crude. A multivariate analysis would seem to be indicated, but this should probably be done on a much larger sample than we had available.

Our finding that institutional and management factors probably have a greater effect on accuracy of cost estimates than technical factors should be tested by comparative studies of public works planning. Perhaps the state highway departments are useful places to begin such studies.

Another subject for useful research is to study the relationship between the cost of obtaining additional information and the value of the increased estimating accuracy. Perhaps data can be obtained on cases where lack of information on geologic structure at the estimating stage led to gross underestimation of cost. The cost of obtaining the necessary geologic information to reveal the essential geologic structure (and associated cost) could then be related to the decisions made under the two situations.

In conclusion, it is well to put the problem of cost estimation in its true perspective. In terms of investment decision making, the estimates of money cost of construction are much firmer than are estimates of benefits or consideration of opportunity costs or external costs. But, as we have shown, variations in accuracy of estimates between agencies and even between subdivisions of agencies are very great. It behooves an analyst to know the performance record of the agency whose project he is examining.

We conclude on a note of hope for the many victims and authors of gross miscalculations. John Sawyer, in a paper on "Entrepreneurial Errors and Economic Growth"[24] relates how many of our most important public works would never have been built had it not been for gross errors in the estimates of their costs and benefits. He cites among others the British turnpikes and canals of the 18th century, scores of railroads and canals built in the United States in the 19th century, and more significantly, the Panama Canal, the Welland Canal and the Sault Ste. Marie Canal!

Appendix

TABLE 1

CORPS OF ENGINEERS

CAUSES OF INCREASES IN PROJECT COSTS[a]

Factor	Size of Increase (millions of dollars)	Per Cent of Total Increase	Per Cent of Original Estimate
Price increases	1,887.9	57.7	71.6
Authorized project extension	576.8	17.6	21.8
Changed local needs	134.5	4.1	5.1
Structural and engineering modifications	206.2	6.3	7.8
Unforeseen conditions	279.5	8.5	10.6
Inadequacies in planning and estimating	189.0	5.8	7.1
Total	3,273.9	100.0	124.0

a Data from 1951 report.

24 John E. Sawyer, "Entrepreneurial Error and Economic Growth," *Explorations in Entrepreneurial History,* Cambridge, Vol. IV, no. 4, May 1952.

TABLE 2
CORPS OF ENGINEERS
FREQUENCY OF OVERRUNS BY PROJECT TYPE
1964 REPORT

Type	All Projects			Projects Since 1954		
	Number	Frequency of Overrun (per cent)		Number	Frequency of Overrun (per cent)	
		Original	Escalated		Original	Escalated
Individual types						
1. Levees	17	76	41	0	0	0
2. Channel excavation for flood control	8	75	38	4	50	50
3. Flood control reservoir	48	79	31	5	67	40
4. Local protection	30	94	60	11	91	55
5. Lock and dam, no power	11	55	9	6	17	0
6. Lock, dam and power	3	33	0	0	0	0
7. Multipurpose dam	9	78	22	0	0	0
8. Harbor construction	8	62	12	5	60	0
9. Beach replenishment	1	0	0	1	0	0
10. Dredging	49	57	24	26	35	23
Grouping by major elements						
"Construction" (types 1, 4, 8)	55	83	47	16	81	37
"Dams" (types 3, 5, 6, 7)	71	73	25	21	52	29
"Excavation" (types 2, 9, 10)	58	59	26	31	35	26
Grouping by function (by Corps of Engineers)						
Flood control (types 1, 2, 3, 4)	103	83	42	30	73	47
Rivers and harbors (5, 6, 7, 8, 9, 10)	81	58	20	38	34	16
Total (all projects)	184	72	32	68	51	29

TABLE 3
CORPS OF ENGINEERS
FREQUENCY OF OVERRUNS BY ADMINISTRATIVE
DIVISIONS, 1964

Division[a]	1964—All Projects				1964—Projects Since 1954		
	Number of Projects	Frequency of Overruns (per cent)		R^b	Number of Projects	Frequency of Over-runs[c] Original Estimate (per cent)	R
		Original Estimate	Escalated Estimate				
NED	18	78	38	1.03	10	80	1.57
NAD	16	69	19	.88	7	43	.59
SAD	17	41	6	.71	9	22	.61
NCD	26	38	19	.79	13	15	.39
ORD	17	94	35	1.26	5	80	2.09
MRD	15	87	67	.99	2	100	1.10
LMVD	16	75	50	1.10	6	33	1.17
SWD	21	81	19	1.50	7	86	1.38
NPD	10	30	30	1.33	2	100	1.82
SPD	25	87	44	1.14	7	57	1.32
POD	3	67	67	1.01	0	—	—

NOTE: The table leads to no firm conclusions but to suggestions of real differences between divisions because of the large variations in performance between divisions and the relative consistency of performance within the divisions.

Differences between divisions. The differences between minimum values ("best performance") and maximum values ("worst performance") are considerable for all indicators:

Indicator	Minimum Value	Maximum Value
All projects:		
Per cent overruns (original estimate)	38	94
Per cent overruns (escalated estimate)	6	67
R	0.71	1.50
Recent projects:		
Per cent overruns (original estimate)	15	100
R	0.39	2.09

Consistency within divisions. The same two divisions (South Atlantic and North Central) rank "best" for all indicators; indicators of "poor" performance are less concentrated but Ohio River, Missouri River and North Pacific Divisions rank generally the worst.

Improvement over time. The general improvement noted of more recent projects does not apply consistently to all divisions; indeed, the two "best" divisions perform better in the recent projects and the "worst" fare worse.

These data must be interpreted with care. Some categories are too small to provide significant information, particularly concerning the most recent performance; and a number of significant factors have not been controlled such as date of estimate and duration of project.

a *Divisions and Districts*

NED: New England (no districts)

NAD: North Atlantic (New York, Baltimore, Philadelphia, Norfolk)

SAD: South Atlantic (Wilmington, Charleston, Jacksonville, Savannah, Mobile)

NCD: North Central (Chicago, Rock Island, Detroit, St. Paul, Buffalo)

ORD: Ohio River (Nashville, Pittsburgh, Louisville, Huntington)

MRD: Missouri River (Kansas City, Omaha)

LMVD: Lower Mississippi Valley (Memphis, Vicksburg, St. Louis, New Orleans)

SWD: South West (Albuquerque, Fort Worth, Galveston, Tulsa, Little Rock)

NPD: North Pacific (Seattle, Portland, Walla Walla, Anchorage)

SPD: South Pacific (San Francisco, Sacramento, Los Angeles)

POD: Pacific Ocean (Honolulu)

b R = Ratio of actual to expected overruns, based on original estimates. Controls for the different "project mix" of each division. The expected frequency of overruns in each division is obtained by multiplying the frequency of overruns for each project type by the number of projects of each type in the division.

c Escalated estimate is not analyzed; too few projects for significance.

TABLE 4

CORPS OF ENGINEERS

SIZE OF PRICE ESCALATING FACTOR

Duration of Project (years)[a]	Number of Projects	Size of Price Escalator (per cent)			Per Cent Variation from Mean	
		Mean	Maximum	Minimum	Largest[b]	Smallest[c]
30–34	1	174	—	—	—	—
25–29	11	210	336	68	60	68
20–24	27	197	293	154	49	22
15–19	26	102	281	27	175	73
10–14	48	56	196	12	250	79
5–9	61	28	119	9	337	68
0–4	10	9.8	18	1	84	90

NOTE: Mean, maximum and minimum size of price escalator as a function of project duration (1964 report, all projects).

a Time lapse between original estimate and project completion.

b Per cent difference between largest escalator of group and mean.

c Per cent difference between mean and smallest escalator of group.

TABLE 5

TENNESSEE VALLEY AUTHORITY
ESTIMATING PERFORMANCE

Project	Type[a]	Date of Appro-priation	Com-pletion Date	Original Estimate (thou-sands of dollars)	Final Cost (thou-sands of dollars)	Error (per cent)[b]
Kentucky Dam	DRP	1941	1949	109,167	116,302	+6.5
Pickwick Dam	DRP	1934	1939	32,530	29,701	−8.6
	AGU	1939	1943	4,532	4,327	−4.5
	AGU	1949	1954	8,900	9,129	+2.3
Total				45,962	43,157	−6.1
Wilson Dam	AGU	1939–47	1952	14,947	13,529	−9.4
	Lock	1952	1963	38,000	38,012	+0.1
	AGU	1958	1963	24,000	21,265	−15.8
Total				76,947	72,806	−5.3
Wheeler Dam	DRP	1933	1939	32,117	29,295	−8.7
	AGU	1939	1942	3,572	3,225	−8.6
	AGU	1941	1947	10,085	10,570	+5.0
	Lock	1961	1964	6,000	6,802	+13.3
	AGU[c]	1959	1964	24,500	19,877	−18.8
	Lock	1960	1964	16,000	15,632	−2.3
Total				92,274	85,401	−7.0
Guntersville Dam	DRP	1935	1940	36,335	31,801	−12.4
	AGU	1949	1954	4,400	4,717	+6.8
	Lock	1962	1967	16,500	16,416	−0.6
Total				57,235	52,934	−7.5
Hales Bar	AGU	1940	1949	7,000	8,808	+25.7
	AGU	1949	1955	15,200	14,100	−7.2
Total				22,200	22,908	+3.2
Chickamauga	DRP	1935	1941	43,128	34,368	−20.2
	AGU	1949	1953	4,000	4,228	+5.0
	Channel	1962	1967	1,821	1,675	−8.0
Total				48,949	40,271	−17.8
Watts Bar	DRP	1939 & 1941	1946	38,400	32,977	−14.0

(*continued*)

TABLE 5 (*CONTINUED*)

Project	Type[a]	Date of Appro-priation	Com-pletion Date	Original Estimate (thou-sands of dollars)	Final Cost (thou-sands of dollars)	Error (per cent)[b]
Fort Loudoun	DRP	1940	1946	28,500	34,941	+22.4
	AGU	1941	1950	4,400	4,797	+9.1
Total				32,900	39,738	+20.6
Norris	DRP	1933	1939	31,025	30,508	−1.6
Hiwassee	DRP	1935	1941	19,484	15,923	−18.4
	AGU	1952	1957	5,900	6,384	+8.5
Total				25,384	22,307	−12.3
Cherokee	DRP	1940	1944	31,500	29,765	−5.4
	AGU	1951	1955	7,200	5,536	−23.6
Total				38,700	35,301	−8.8
Ocoee Num-ber 3	DRP	1941	1946	6,600	7,988	+21.2
Appalachia	DRP	1941	1946	20,000	22,559	+13.0
Chatuge	DRP	1941	1946	5,000	7,037	+40.0
	AGU	1952	1957	2,900	2,217	−21.1
Total				7,900	9,254	+17.7
Nottely	DRP	1941	1946	5,000	5,379	+8.0
	AGU	1952	1957	3,200	2,655	−18.8
Total				8,200	8,034	−2.4
Fontana	DRP	1941	1948	47,000	70,421	+50.0
	AGU	1950	1955	3,900	4,310	+10.5
Total				50,900	74,731	+46.4
Douglas	DRP	1942	1945	32,000	40,244	+24.4
	AGU	1942	1950	3,000	2,069	−33.0
	AGU	1951	1955	4,000	2,959	−27.5
Total				39,000	45,272	+16.1
Watauga	DRP	1946	1951	29,500	32,369	+9.8
South Holston	DRP	1947	1952	31,500	31,242	−0.9
Boone	DRP	1950	1955	27,500	27,192	−1.1
Fort Patrick Henry	DRP	1950	1955	13,000	12,420	−4.6
Melton Hill[d]	DRP	1960	1965	34,000	38,489	+13.2

TABLE 5 (CONCLUDED)

Project	Type[a]	Date of Appropriation	Completion Date	Original Estimate (thousands of dollars)	Final Cost (thousands of dollars)	Error (per cent)[b]
Beech River	Water control	1962	1966	6,000	9,238	+53.3
Bristol	Flood protection	1963	1966	2,900	2,175	−24.2
Watts Bar	SP	1940–41	1946	20,000	19,746	−1.5
Johnsonville	SP	1950	1955	98,000	94,284	−3.8
	SGU	1956	1960	83,000	75,705	−8.8
Total				181,000	165,989	−8.3
Widows Creek	SP	1951	1958	103,000	93,826	−8.9
	SGU[e]	1958–60	1967	154,000	132,916	−13.7
Total				257,000	226,742	−11.8
Kingston	SP	1951–53	1961	213,000	198,200	−6.9
Colbert	SP	1951–52	1958	110,500	99,104	−10.3
	SGU[f]	1959	1966	80,000	65,363	−18.2
Total				190,500	164,467	−13.6
Shawnee	SP	1951–52	1959	216,500	213,536	−1.4
Gallatin	SP	1952	1960	85,000	76,051	−10.6
	SGU	1956	1960	73,000	61,864	−15.2
Total				158,000	137,915	−1.3
John Sevier	SP	1952–53	1960	96,000	84,103	−12.4
	SGU	1956	1960	28,000	21,850	−21.8
Total				124,000	105,953	−14.5
Paradise	SP[g]	1959	1966	205,000	178,586	−12.9

[a] DRP = dam, reservoir and powerhouse; AGU = additional generating units; SP = steam plant; SGU = additional steam generating units.

[b] Overrun denoted by +, underrun by −.

[c] Interest during construction included in final cost but not in original estimate.

[d] Interest during construction included in final cost but not in original estimate of power facilities portion.

[e] Interest during construction included for generating unit 8 (original estimate $68 million) in both original estimate and final cost.

[f] Interest during construction included in final cost but not in original estimate.

[g] Interest during construction included in both original estimate and final cost.

TABLE 6: TENNESSEE VALLEY AUTHORITY PERFORMANCE BY PROJECT TYPE, DATE OF APPROPRIATION, AND PROJECT SIZE

Group	Number of Projects	Frequency of Overruns[b]		Performance Coefficient[a]
		Number	Per Cent	
Project type				
1. Dams and reservoirs	21	10	47.6	1.61
2. Additional hydro-generating units	19	8	42.0	1.22
3. Locks	4	2	50.0	1.28
4. Channel dredging	1	0	0.0	0.0
5. Multipurpose water control	1	1	100.0	2.50
6. Flood protection	1	0	0.0	0.0
7. Steam plants	9	0	0.0	0.0
8. Additional steam generating units	5	0	0.0	0.0
All dams (lines 1 and 2)	40	18	45.0	1.30
All steam plants (lines 7 and 8)	14	0	0.0	0.0
Others (lines 3, 4, 5, and 6)	7	3	42.8	1.27
Total	61	21	34.4	1.0
Date of appropriation				
1933–39	8	0	0.0	0.0
1940–44	14	10	72.0	2.09
1945–49	8	5	62.5	1.85
1950–54	15	2	13.3	0.36
1955–59	8	1	12.5	0.38
1960–64	8	3	37.5	1.08
Actual cost of project (in millions of dollars)				
50–260	14	2	14	0.44
10–50	26	7	27	0.77
1–10	21	12	57	1.67

[a] Performance Coefficient =

$$\frac{\text{Number of Overruns in Group}}{\text{Total Number of Overruns}} \div \frac{\text{Number of Projects in Group}}{\text{Total Number of Projects}}$$

[b] Almost 50 per cent of dams have overruns while steam plants have no overruns; the only periods with more than 50 per cent overruns are 1940–44 and 1945–49 (war time and immediately thereafter); the frequency of overruns appears to decline as project size increases. Caution: no cause-effect relationships can be determined; the complementarity of these factors is very high: wartime construction and lower cost ranges are associated with dam construction; recent construction and large size projects correspond to the steam plants.

TABLE 7

TENNESSEE VALLEY AUTHORITY, DISTRIBUTION OF ERRORS

Item	Mean (per cent)	Mode (per cent)	Median (per cent)	Standard Deviation
1 Distribution of all estimates by 5 per cent classes				
1.1 All projects (61 estimates)	−1.76	−5.0	−5.0	17.5
1.2 Dams only (40 estimates)	+0.25	+7.5	−1.6	18.2
1.3 Steam plants only (14 estimates)	−10.71	−12.5	−10.4	6.1
2 Individual distributions, complete projects only				
2.1 Steam plants (9 projects)	−8.02	n.a.	−7.5	5.5
2.2 All dams (23 projects)	+3.40	n.a.	−1.1	14.7
2.3 Dams, except Fontana (22 projects)	+1.45	n.a.	−1.6	11.6
3 Dams only, overruns and underruns				
3.1 Underruns only (13 projects)	−6.87	n.a.	−6.1	5.2
3.2 Overruns only, excluding Fontana (9 projects)	+13.48	n.a.	+13.2	6.1

n.a. = not applicable (projects not grouped by class).

NOTE. Plus sign signifies overrun (actual cost greater than estimate); minus sign signifies underrun (actual cost smaller than estimate). Estimates in Item 1 are grouped by classes corresponding to ranges of errors of 5 per cent; in Items 2 and 3 the projects are distributed individually. Item 1 includes all estimates (61); Items 2 and 3 include estimates for project totals only.

TABLE 8

BUREAU OF RECLAMATION: CAUSES OF INCREASES IN PROJECT COSTS[a]

	Exclusive of CRSP and MRBP[b]			All Projects[c]		
	Size of Increase (millions of dollars)	Per Cent of Total Increase	Per Cent of Original Estimate	Size of Increase (millions of dollars)	Per Cent of Total Increase	Per Cent of Original Estimate
Price increases	507.7	55.5	20.0	1,310.5	48.2	34.7
Changes in project plans	198.4	21.6	7.8	957.9	35.3	25.4
Structural engineering modifications	1.3	0.2	0.1	−16.9	−0.7	−0.4
Unforeseen conditions	69.9	7.6	2.7	87.3	3.2	2.3
Reanalysis of quantities and unit costs	105.8	11.6	4.2	291.4	10.8	7.7
National emergencies	9.3	1.0	0.4	9.6	0.4	0.3
Other	22.4	2.5	0.8	75.7	2.8	2.0
Total	914.8	100.0	36.0	2,715.5	100.0	72.0

[a] Data from 1960 report.
[b] Totaling 79 projects. CRSP = Colorado River Storage Project; MRBP = Missouri River Basin Project.
[c] Totaling 128 projects.

TABLE 9

BUREAU OF RECLAMATION: DISTRIBUTION OF ERRORS

Case	Number of Projects	Mean (per cent)	Standard Deviation	Mode (per cent)	Median (per cent)	Maximum Error	
						Overrun (per cent)	Underrun (per cent)
1955 Report[a]	103	+163.0	n.a.	+10	+100	1000	20
1960 Report[b]							
All projects[c]	79	+27.4	58	0	+7	326	39
All projects except two worst[d]	77	+20.6	38	0	+7	165	39
1960 Report[b]							
Projects at least 50 per cent complete	65	+33.8	62	0	+3	326	39
Projects 50 per cent complete except two worst[e]	63	+25.8	42	0	+3	165	39

n.a. = not available.

[a] Based on original estimate.

[b] Based on original estimates only; exclusive of CRSP and MRBP.

[c] This case comparable with data in Table 3 in the body of the paper.

[d] Projects with overruns of 251 and 326 per cent.

[e] Projects with overruns of 251 and 326 per cent. This case is most significant for purposes of comparison with other agencies.

TABLE 10
ESTIMATING PERFORMANCE: INDIAN AND BRITISH EXAMPLES

Item	India		Great Britain		
	1960[a]	1957[b]	1962i[c]	1962ii[c]	1962 (total)[c]
Period of Record	1946–56	1944–50	1944–50[d]	1951–55	1944–55
Type of Projects	Hydro-power & Irrigation		Hydro-electric Power Plants		
Number of Projects	13	11	5	8	13
Estimated Cost (millions)	Re 6,307	£18,351	£21,400	£33,342	£54,742
Actual Cost (millions)	Re 8,904	£38,100	£51,810	£35,530	£87,340
Overrun (per cent)	41	107	142	6	59
Frequency of Overruns (number)	13	11	5	5	10
(per cent)	100	100	100	62	77
Maximum Overrun (per cent)	230	265	187	29	187
Minimum Overrun (per cent)	5	60	107	–4[e]	–4[e]
Average Overrun (per cent)	74	124	149	6	61

[a] Adapted from J. M. Healey, "Errors in Project Cost Estimates," *Indian Economic Journal*, Vol. 12, July–September 1964.
[b] Adapted from Select Committee on Nationalized Industries, *Report to the House of Commons*, Session Documents, Vol. 7, No. 304, 1956–57, London, H.M.S.O. 1957.
[c] Adapted from Select Committee on Nationalized Industries, *Report to the House of Commons on the Electricity Supply Industry*, Session Papers, Vol. 7, No. 116, 1961–62, London, H.M.S.O., 1962.
[d] Projects in this column completed later than those in previous column.   [e] Underrun.

FIGURE 1
CORPS OF ENGINEERS
DISTRIBUTION OF ERRORS
182 PROJECTS—1933–65

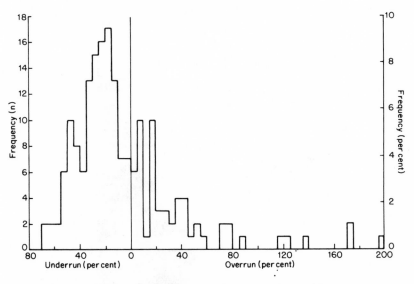

SOURCE: Data from 1964 Report, excluding two projects with overruns of 259 and 656 per cent. Based on escalated survey estimate.

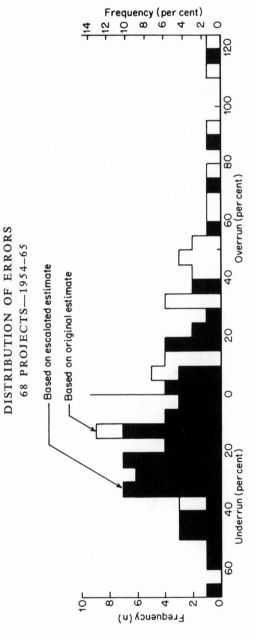

FIGURE 2

CORPS OF ENGINEERS

DISTRIBUTION OF ERRORS

68 PROJECTS—1954–65

Based on escalated estimate

Based on original estimate

SOURCE: Data from 1964 Report.

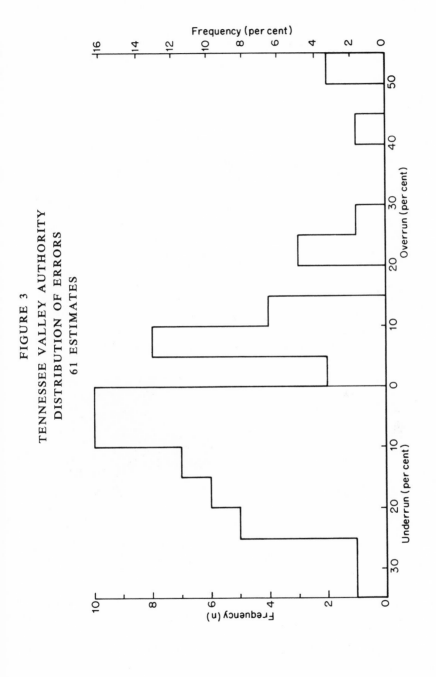

FIGURE 3

TENNESSEE VALLEY AUTHORITY

DISTRIBUTION OF ERRORS

61 ESTIMATES

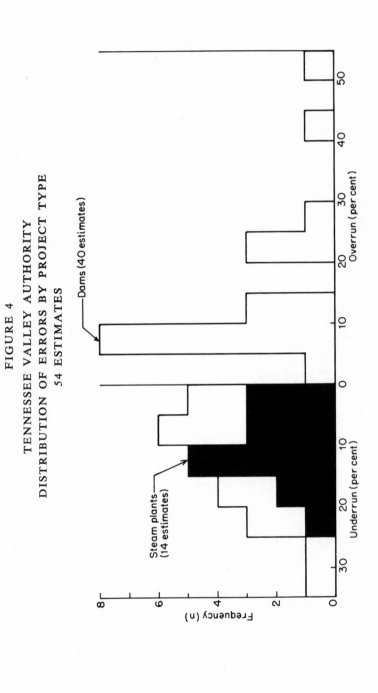

FIGURE 4

TENNESSEE VALLEY AUTHORITY

DISTRIBUTION OF ERRORS BY PROJECT TYPE

54 ESTIMATES

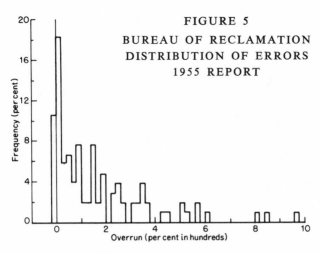

FIGURE 5
BUREAU OF RECLAMATION
DISTRIBUTION OF ERRORS
1955 REPORT

NOTE: Adapted from Edward G. Altouney, *The Role of Uncertainties in the Economic Evaluation of Water Resources Projects,* Institute in Engineering-Economic Systems, Stanford University, 1963. (Based on 103 projects; original estimate.)

FIGURE 6
BUREAU OF RECLAMATION DISTRIBUTION OF ERRORS
1960 REPORT

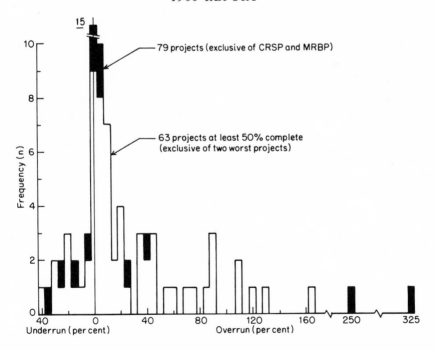

NOTE: Based on initial authorization cost.

EXTERNALITIES IN PUBLIC FACILITY USE: THE CASE OF HIGHWAY ACCIDENTS

WILLIAM VICKREY
Columbia University

That accidents are an important incident to the use of public high-ways is no secret; how important is often not fully realized, nor has attention been given to the relation of such accidents to the manner in which individuals pay for highway use.

A great deal of work has indeed gone into the measurement of benefits from accident reduction resulting from better highway design or various forms of accident prevention activity. But it remains by and large true that the average user of the highways has relatively little appreciation of the impact of his activity on accidents in general, nor has there as yet been much discussion of appropriate means of bringing this cost home to him. In a sense, this is but another aspect of the externality problem involved in traffic congestion, but an aspect which has unique features worthy of detailed examination.

The National Safety Council estimates the cost of highway accidents in 1966 as follows:[1]

Property damage	$ 3.3 billion
Wage loss	2.6
Medical expense	0.6
Total direct loss	6.5
Insurance administration	3.5
	$10.0 billion

Not included is any allowance for "pain and suffering," whether or not reflected in the award of damage in excess of the direct cost, nor any public agency costs, such as those of police and courts (to the extent not covered by legal fees), nor any indirect costs from incon-venience to employers, etc.; nor is it clear that the claimants' expenses of collection are included. As a general order of magnitude, however,

[1] National Safety Council, *Accident Facts,* 1967.

the minimum figure for costs is substantially in excess of total gasoline tax revenues ($7.4 billion in 1966), and an inclusive figure would rival the total amount of governmental expenditure on highways.[2]

The degree to which this cost is borne by highway users in their capacity as such is difficult to determine with any accuracy from the data available. One obvious mode of payment is through various forms of insurance. Total automobile insurance premiums earned in 1967 came to $8.9 billion and loss claims incurred to $5.4 billion, which would seem to take care of a good deal of the $6.5 billion of loss.[3] However, payments by insurance companies included in many cases a considerable amount for damages in excess of the direct monetary cost, and in other cases must be discounted considerably to allow for costs incurred by claimants in presenting their claims. On balance, there remains a very substantial amount of loss uncompensated for by such insurance. In a sampling study of Michigan personal injury accident cases related to accidents occurring in 1958,[4] it was found that out of an estimated total aggregate loss for the state for the year of $178 million, only $85.2 million in reparations was received by the victims from all sources, of which $17.5 million came from the victims' own automobile insurance, and $46.7 million from tort claims, insured and uninsured. In addition, there was an expectation of future compensation payments amounting to $8.4 million, not broken down as to source, bringing the total received from all outside sources to $93.6 million, leaving $84.5 million of the loss to be borne by the victims individually. In a very rough average sense, then, it can be estimated on the basis of this sample and the various outside figures that, of the losses suffered directly by traffic accident victims, 38 to 40 per cent are compensated from automobile-related sources, i.e., automobile insurance or judgments against tortfeasors; 48 to 50 per cent are borne by the victims themselves (including in this figure an estimate of the cash surrender value of life insurance policies liquidated to provide benefits), and 11 to 13 per cent are provided from sources unrelated to the use of automobiles, such as sick leave provisions, pensions, social security, health insurance, and the like. When to this there is added the uncompensated losses experienced by bicyclists and pedestrians, the cost of providing courts for the adjudication of cases, and the cost of various forms of public assistance, subsidized

[2] An estimate of $12 billion for 1967 is given in *The Economist* (London, 1968, p. xxi); it is not clear how inclusive this figure is intended to be.

[3] Best's Fire and Casualty aggregates and averages, July 13, 1967.

[4] A. F. Conard *et al., Automobile Accident Costs and Payments,* Ann Arbor, Mich., 1964.

hospital care, or other services tendered to victims of motor vehicle accidents and financed from nonmotor vehicle sources, it is apparent that there is a gross subsidy to motor vehicle users of the order of at least $1 billion and quite possibly as high as $2 or $3 billion, financed in ways that have no restraining influence on motor vehicle use.

But this is on the basis of gross averages, and as so often in the case of transportation, gross averages conceal as much as, if not more than, they reveal. If efficient decisions are to be made as to the amount of motor vehicle traffic to make use of, it is the marginal and not the over-all average cost that is of concern, and the object is to bring the decision-maker face-to-face with the differentials between the marginal costs of the alternatives under consideration at the time of decision. While there is very little good statistical information on the relation between increments of traffic and increments of accidents, something can be deduced from considerations of general principles.

According to the National Safety Council, some 22,300 of the 53,000 motor vehicle accident deaths, or 42 per cent, occurred in collisions between two or more cars. It is reasonable to presume that, in most cases where two cars collide, the accident would not have happened if either car had not been there, and that the foregoing of the trip by either vehicle would have eliminated the entire cost of the accident. In effect, then, the entire cost of the accident is a part of the marginal cost, *ex post,* of both trips. Bringing the marginal cost of such accidents home to the potential motorist would involve providing that in the event of an accident, each motorist, lacking insurance, would be required not only to bear the cost of his own damages, but pay a penalty equal to the damages suffered by the other. If the two motorists wish to purchase insurance against the eventuality, they should be required to pay premiums sufficient not only to compensate the two motorists for the damages sustained, but in addition pay into the public treasury a sum equal to the damage claims. That is to say, motorists should be required to buy enough insurance to cover the risk of accident and pay a tax of 100 per cent of the premium (or at least 100 per cent of that portion of the premium used to pay claims).

Matters are, of course, not quite as clear-cut and simple as this example suggests. There is, for example, the phenomenon of the accident looking for a place to happen, as with the maniac who persists in passing on blind curves, until such time as a fatal encounter removes his genes from the driving population by Darwinian selection. Keeping the potential victim of one fatal collision from the scene would then merely shift the accident to another later occasion. A similar consideration applies in somewhat modified form to the driver of a car with a suddenly developing defect: if a tire blows out and causes a collision with another car, keeping the other car out of the way might only substitute a fixed object for the car, though in this case the probable damages would be considerably reduced. On the other hand, not all accidents recorded as noncollision, or collision with a fixed object, are free from interaction effects: in many cases the car that hits a fixed object (or a pedestrian!), or rolls over in the ditch, has swerved to avoid a more serious collision with another car that has got off scot free.

On a larger level, one can consider, in the abstract, the relation between increments in traffic density and increments in the number of encounters that give rise to the possibility of a collision. On an unseparated highway, for example, the number of times a car making a given trip will pass cars coming in the opposite direction will obviously be proportional to the density of the opposing traffic flow, so that the total number of such encounters will vary as the square of the traffic density. With very low density of traffic, these encounters will constitute the main occasions at which collisions between two cars are possible. (Even where density is somewhat higher, so that the accident potential involved in following or overtaking cars going in the same direction becomes significant, such occasions also tend to increase in frequency according to the square of the traffic flow.) But as density increases to still higher levels, opportunities to overtake drop off; on the one hand, this reduces the number of occasions for accidents to take place during overtaking, and average speeds are reduced. On the other hand, the temptation to overtake under hazardous circumstances increases, and possibilities for accidents due to multiple interaction increase, as when the slowing down of the first car in a sequence of closely following cars forces each subsequent car to brake somewhat more sharply than the preceding car until finally a car finds itself unable to brake in time and collides with the car in front. There is also the increased possibility that one collision will involve still other cars. As traffic flow increases still further, however, movement is likely to be slowed to the point where accidents, when they occur, cause relatively little damage.

Unfortunately, the available statistics are not entirely appropriate for the derivation of the marginal cost of accidents per trip. Indeed, a superficial look at some of the data might tend to cast doubt on the entire analysis. For example, data by states on deaths per vehicle-mile show a strongly inverse relation to density of traffic: the highest death rates are found in the Southern and mountain states, where traffic densities are generally low, and the lowest in the Northeast and in California, where densities are relatively high. With respect to two other measures, the number of bodily injury claims per 100 vehicles and the number of property damage claims per 100 vehicles, the reverse relation exists: the highest rates are found in the high-density states. And if one looks separately at the death rates in one-car and multiple-car accidents, according to some figures at least, the one-car death rate shows a strong negative association with traffic density while the two-car death rate shows an equally strong positive association.[5]

It is clear, indeed, that there are not only a number of types of accidents, differing in their economic implications and etiology, but there are a number of traffic situations that present substantially different relationships between the volume of traffic and the cost of accidents. For analytical purposes we may distinguish (a) the solo accident, involving only the motorist himself and having substantially no externality effects, except insofar as the victim may then draw on community services or obtain nonautomobile insurance compensation; (b) the auto-nonauto accident, in which injury is done to pedestrians, cyclists or wayside property; and (c) the auto-auto collision. The following types of ambients may similarly be distinguished: (i) the low-density road, usually of at most two lanes where interactions are almost entirely of the crossing or meeting variety, with overtaking relatively unimportant, with the number of occasions for auto-auto accidents varying very nearly as the square of the traffic flow; (ii) the moderate density, nondivided highway, with some constraint imposed on drivers by the presence of preceding cars; (iii) the high-density, nondivided highway, characterized by extensive queuing conditions, substantial amounts of close following, passing maneuvers executed in the face of oncoming traffic, and the like; (iv) heavy urban traffic, with frequent signalized intersections; (v) divided lane highways under free flowing conditions, with interactions largely in overtaking, or with cars stopped by emergency or entering or leaving; (vi) heavy traffic in divided lane highways, with interactions involving chiefly following, lane-changing, entering and leaving.

Unfortunately, the data that might show precisely how accident rates vary with traffic volume for different conditions are not easy to come by. One indication is given by data in Table 1 showing data for

5 J. L. Recht, *Multiple Regressions Study of the Effects of Safety Activities on the Traffic Accident Problem,* Chicago, National Safety Council, December 1965. See especially equations 5, 6; but *per contra* see also equations 41, 42!

TABLE 1

AVERAGE AND MARGINAL ACCIDENT RATES, CALIFORNIA FREEWAYS, 1960–62

Average Daily Traffic Class (000's)	Number of Segments	Accidents per Million Vehicle Miles	Average Daily Traffic per Lane (000's)	Accidents per Million Lane Mile Days	Increments in Total Accident Rate	Increments in Traffic Density	Marginal Accident Rate per Million Vehicle Miles	Ratio of Marginal to Average Accident Rate	Million Vehicle Miles
(x)	(n)	(q)	(h)	(Q)	(ΔQ)	(Δh)	(m)	(r)	(V)
FOUR-LANE FREEWAYS									
0–7.0	1	1.04	1550	1612	1612	1550	1.040	1.000	55
7.0–10.0	3	1.51	2225	3360	1748	675	2.590	2.031	97
10.0–15.0	18	0.86	3400	2924	–436	1175	–.371	–.313	1269
15.0–21.5	18	0.95	4725	4489	1565	1325	1.181	1.300	970
21.5–31.6	32	1.18	6350	7493	3004	1625	1.848	1.735	2306
31.6–46.5	20	1.45	9600	13920	6427	3250	1.977	1.503	2051
46.5–68.0	8	2.03	13525	27456	13536	3925	3.449	1.982	491
68.0–100.0	1	2.46	17100	42066	14610	3625	4.030	1.795	107
Over 100.0	0	—	—						
Total or average	101	1.25	6675					1.455	7346

16.0–15.0	0	—	—					1.000	44
15.0–21.5	1	1.02	3467	3536	3536	3467	1.020	.917	338
21.5–31.6	8	1.00	4417	4417	880	950	.927	1.00	1292
31.6–46.5	18	1.00	6617	6617	2200	2200	1.00	1.568	2341
46.5–68.0	19	1.20	9133	10960	4343	2517	1.725	1.387	4424
68.0–100.0	23	1.41	13917	19623	8663	4783	1.811	1.690	2509
100.0–120.0	12	1.70	18267	31054	11431	4350	2.628	1.618	578
Over 120.0	4	1.89	21683	40981	9927	3417	2.905		
Total or average	85	1.40	11200					1.455	11526

0.0–31.6	0	—	—					1.000	196
31.6–46.5	3	1.04	5262	5472	5472	5262	1.040	.399	879
46.5–68	11	.86	7225	6213	741	1962	.378	2.041	1155
68–100	12	1.30	10738	13959	7746	3512	2.205	1.033	1865
100–120	8	1.31	13538	17735	3775	2800	1.348	1.875	3185
Over 120	14	1.73	18612	32199	14464	5075	2.850		
Total or average	48	1.43	12225					1.596	7280

$$Q = hq; \quad m = \Delta Q/\Delta h; \quad r_i = 2m_i/(q_{i-1} + q_i); \quad \bar{r} = \left[\sum_{i=1}^{n-1} \tfrac{1}{2}(r_i + r_{i+1})V_i + r_n V_n \right] \Big/ \sum_{i=1}^{n} V_i$$

California Freeway segments[6] classified by traffic density and number of lanes: marginal accident costs seem to exceed average accident costs by about 50 per cent over-all, though there is considerable variation in the relationship. There seems to be some tendency for the average rate to decline with increased traffic for very low levels of traffic, leading to a marginal accident rate below the average. This may simply be an artifact resulting from the prevalence among the low-volume segments of segments recently opened to traffic, where temporary exits and entrances and the lesser familiarity of the traffic with the road would influence the accident rate, or it may represent a beneficial effect of a low level of traffic in keeping drivers alert, warning of curves at night, and minimizing the chances of going in the improper direction. In any case this range of traffic flows accounts for only 3 per cent of the total freeway traffic. Freeways in turn accounted for 15.6 per cent of fatal accidents and 17.3 per cent of all accidents.

Other indications that there may be a positive relation between traffic density on a given roadway and the accident rate per vehicle-mile are found in the higher insurance premiums charged in high-density areas and in data showing that limited access freeways have lower accident rates than do older facilities.[7] It is at least possible that a good deal of this accident reduction can be related to the reduction in the traffic/capacity ratio that comes about with the construction of extremely high-capacity facilities.

In a sense, the excess revenues generated by charges for marginal accident propensities in excess of the average cost of all accidents would constitute a contribution towards the rental value of the highways. In this respect accidents are simply a form of congestion cost. In a world of constant returns to scale, these excess accident premiums would contribute to a fund which, when combined with other congestion charges, would just suffice to finance the optimum roadway system. This may perhaps be clarified by imagining that highways are sufficiently divisible so that a number of parallel highways can be operated serving each corridor, each highway operated by an entrepreneur in perfect competition with the others, on the basis of a toll which with free entry will tend to be set at a level just covering the costs of the entrepreneur. If c is the cost of roadway per unit of width

[6] Richard A. Lundy, *Effect of Traffic Volumes and Number of Lanes on Freeway Accident Rates,* California Division of Highways, Traffic Department, July 1964, Table 4, p. 9.

[7] See Table 2.

TABLE 2

SUMMARY OF ACCIDENT RATES ON THE

CALIFORNIA STATE HIGHWAY SYSTEM, 1964–66

(ACCIDENTS PER MILLION VEHICLE-MILES)

	Total Including Property Damage Only	Fatal and Bodily Injury	Fatal
Rural Areas			
Freeways	1.00	.47	.045
Other	2.48	1.13	.091
Total	2.06	.94	.078
Urban Areas			
Freeways	1.61	.68	.022
Other	5.61	1.91	.042
Total	2.84	1.06	.028
All Areas			
Freeways	1.48	.63	.027
Other	3.70	1.43	.072
Total	2.52	1.01	.048

or capacity w, q the flow of traffic, and p the toll, we then have, for each highway, $pq = cw$. If $h = q/w$ is the density of traffic relative to capacity, $p = cw/q = c/h$, and if we suppose that the various roads are operated under various tolls and various densities to suit the relative preferences of the users as to price versus quality, tolls will vary inversely with the density of traffic; otherwise profits or losses would induce changes in the pattern.

We may suppose that the users, in addition to the toll paid to the firm providing the highway, also pay a premium $r(h)$ for insurance against accident during each use of a highway at density h, the rate generally increasing with h to reflect the higher accident rate on highways operated at higher traffic densities. (It makes no difference, for present purposes, whether the insurance is on a liability basis or on a direct compensation basis.) Put $v_i(h)$ for the value placed by the user on the ith use when that use is at density h, defined as the total price (toll plus premium) that the user would be willing to pay for use under those conditions rather than foregoing the use entirely. Then $(dv_i/dh)dh$ is the change in the value of the ith use resulting from an increment in traffic density dh produced by an increment of traffic $dq = wdh$ on the roadway in question. If we assume that the variety of roadways available approximate to a continuous spectrum, then for any use i that in equilibrium uses a roadway with a density h, a toll $p(h)$ and an insurance premium $r(h)$, we must have $(dv_i/dh) = (dp/dh) + (dr/dh)$; otherwise the user would find it to his advantage to move either to a less congested road where the toll would be higher and the insurance premium lower, or to a more congested road where the reverse would be true, depending on the sense of the inequality. In the former case he would value the gain in quality plus the reduction in premium more than the increase in toll, and conversely in the latter case.

Thus, although different uses of the same roadway may have different values, the differential between the value of each use at a particular density h, and the value of that use at adjacent densities, given by dv_i/dh, must be the same for all uses i which use the same road (or any other road operating at the same density h). Accordingly, the impairment of the value of service to users of a roadway having a volume of traffic q and a density h caused by an increment of traffic dq resulting in an increase of h by $dh = dq/w$ is given by

$$
\begin{aligned}
mdq &= q(-dv/dh)dh \\
&= q[-(dp/dh) - (dr/dh)](1/w)dq \\
&= (q/w)[-d(c/h)/dh - dr/dh]dq \\
&= h[ch^{-2} - (dr/dh)]dq \\
&= [p - h(dr/dh)]dq
\end{aligned}
$$

whence $p = m + h(dr/dh) = m + [d(rh)/dh - r]$.

In other words the toll is equal to the sum of the short-run congestion cost suffered by others, m, plus the excess of the short-run marginal accident cost, $d(rh)/dh$, over the average accident cost, r.

Of course, in practice there are generally substantial economies of scale in rural highways at least; urban streets may be characterized by diseconomies of scale. The extent that the roadway system as a whole shows decreasing or increasing returns to scale would be reflected in the generation of a surplus rent or a deficit condition.

The chief difference between accident externalities and other forms of congestion cost lies in their pattern of variation among roads of different characteristics and the degree of economy or diseconomy of scale encountered. In the case of the usual notion of congestion cost, the importance of this factor at very low levels of traffic is such that it is usual to consider the marginal public cost of travel on such roads as consisting almost entirely of the wear and tear element, which has been estimated at 0.1¢ per mile for paved roads, as contrasted with 1.8¢ per mile for gravel and 3.3¢ per mile for earth roads (to indicate very rough orders of magnitude).[8] If, however, one gives full weight to the data indicating that high death rates, at least, are associated with low traffic volumes, then it seems likely that a charge approximating 1¢ per mile would be appropriate[9] as representing the accident cost of travel on low-density paved roads, with perhaps a lower figure for the less risky dirt and gravel roads. Since, however, only a relatively small mileage is driven, in the United States at least, on unpaved roads, and most of this is portions of trips involving paved roads as well, the problem of adjusting charges to cover costs on the unpaved roads can probably be neglected. What this means is that while, on the basis of congestion and maintenance costs alone, traffic on low-density paved roads would be considered to have a marginal cost well below the level of the gasoline tax, consideration of the accident element makes it possible to suppose that the marginal cost and the tax rate are much more closely in line in this instance. Moreover, in terms of accident costs, the economies of scale in low-density highway construction appear to be much less drastic than for other costs: if traffic is doubled and road miles are doubled to maintain the same density of traffic per mile of road, intersections are quadrupled, and, to the extent that intersections are an accident hazard, economies of scale are offset.[10]

Where traffic density is higher, it is difficult to say very much about the marginal accident cost of traffic, except that it is likely to vary considerably according to circumstances. If a general system of congestion charges is installed, records enabling the cost of accidents to be included in the congestion charge may either by that time have been developed or may be developed as a byproduct of the congestion-charge system. However, there are no immediate prospects for any such general congestion levy, and it becomes appropriate to ask what

[8] See Allan A. Walters, *The Economics of Road User Charges,* International Bank for Reconstruction and Redevelopment, Washington, D.C., 1968.

[9] In 1966, total accident costs were $10 billion for 935 billion miles of travel, or 1.07¢ per vehicle mile (National Safety Council, *op. cit.,* p. 59). Although accident rates are lower for lower density roads, this can be offset by the allowing for higher death rates per accident, for the probable excess of marginal cost over average cost, and for pain and suffering and indirect costs not included in the $10 billion figure. On balance 1¢ seems reasonable.

[10] In California in 1966, 32.4 per cent of all accidents and 23.7 per cent of fatal accidents occurred at intersections. (Department of California Highway Patrol, *Report of Fatal Injury Motor Vehicle Traffic Accidents for 1966,* p. 54.)

methods of paying for accidents can be suggested as more conducive to economical allocation of resources, and to more equitable compensation of victims.

The bill of indictment against the present tort liability insurance system is a long one. Many victims obtain inadequate compensation or none at all, as a result of the difficulty of proving fault, the insolvency of the tortfeasor, inability to identify the guilty party, lack of or inadequacy of insurance coverage, or improvident settlement under pressure. A few fortunate victims obtain multiple compensation from two or more sources. Contentious victims of minor accidents often obtain nuisance settlements in excess of their losses, while victims having major losses appear to be substantially undercompensated even where compensation is paid. The costs of the system are exorbitant, the overheads of various kinds amounting to more than the net amounts received by the claimants. The process of pursuing a claim is often demoralizing, and inhibits early rehabilitation efforts. Many insurance companies claim that the business is an unprofitable one in general; much of the underwriting is done on the one hand by shoestring operators who often fail to meet their obligations and on the other by large companies or associated groups wishing to maintain a full-line offering.[11] Unlike most other forms of insurance, claimants are generally not the company's own policyholders, which creates an atmosphere in which adjusters often press hard for inadequate settlements, especially of the larger claims. The contingent fee system, considered unethical in many other countries, is in the United States the dominant arrangement for the prosecution of claims, and is considered by many to be a substantial source of abuse. Still another feature peculiar to the United States is that the claimant is not, at least in legal theory, ordinarily entitled to recover his legal expenses explicitly in addition to his losses, even in cases of demonstrable contumacy on the part of the defendant. There is thus no adequate penalty imposed on insurance companies for going to court with a weak case.

These and other considerations have led to repeated attempts at reform, including the enactment of financial responsibility laws in many states, compulsory liability insurance in a few, the "workmen's compensation-type" plan in effect in Saskatchewan, and the "Keaton-O'Connell" type of plan recently passed by the lower house in Massachusetts but subsequently defeated. The main features of this latter

[11] Cf. "Auto Insurance Pot Boils Over," *Trial Magazine,* Oct./Nov. 1967, pp. 12–13.

plan are that losses between a given lower limit and some defined upper limit are to be compensated on a compulsory hazard-insurance basis without regard to fault, while victims retain the nominal right to prosecute claims for smaller amounts on the basis of fault, on the supposition that few will incur any very substantial expense in doing so, and to prosecute claims on the basis of fault for the excess over the amount awarded on the nonfault basis.

For present purposes, however, what is important is that all of the proposals except the Saskatchewan plan retain the current methods of writing automobile accident insurance. While the settlement costs might go down considerably with the elimination of fault determination as an issue in the bulk of cases, too much should not be expected from this, since the amount of the compensation to be paid would still require adjudication or negotiation. There would still remain in any case the underwriting costs, which tend to be particularly heavy in view of the complexity and inaccuracy of the rating methods adopted by the various companies in attempting to adjust premiums to various circumstances deemed to have a bearing on the individual risk being underwritten. And policies would still be written basically in terms of insuring a car for a given period, a basis that almost inevitably seriously distorts the economics of the situation.

Three types of decisions are, in fact, involved in the generation of automobile accidents: the decision whether to maintain a car (or a second or third one); the decision whether to make a given trip by car and, if to make it, by what route and at what time; and the decision as to what degree of caution to exercise while driving. While one could argue that drivers would exercise more appropriate caution if held strictly accountable, without the possibility of insurance, for accidents in which they were involved (even for accidents in which they were not negligent in the legal sense), it is almost universally agreed that it is better to accept a degree of "moral hazard" in inducing a certain relaxation of caution by insuring, rather than accept the consequences of serious impoverishment of unlucky individuals through lack of insurance. Many writers in the field, particularly those advocating the abandonment of the fault concept, claim with some degree of plausibility that, for most individuals, moral responsibility, the threat of the uninsurable unpleasant effects of accidents, and the threat of penalties for traffic regulation infractions provide enough of an incentive for safe driving that the addition of the threat of uninsured liability for damages caused would have relatively little incremental effect. In some cases, the threat of increased insurance rates for risks with bad past records may also operate as an additional incentive, though this seems to be more of a deterrent against the presentation of small claims than an incentive for added caution. In any case, for present purposes this aspect of the problem can be considered relatively unimportant. About the most that one could consider doing in this direction would be to require all insurance policies to have a substantial deductible to be borne by the insured in the event of liability.[12] It is one of the many anomalies of auto accident insurance that where the insured is adjudged at fault, the full amount of the settlement is paid by the insurance company, whereas in collision coverage an innocent victim of an accident not involving demonstrable fault on the part of another party is often required to bear the burden of a deductible.

In any case the payment of the insurance premium bears primarily on the decision whether to maintain an additional car, and only to a minor extent, if at all, on the decision whether or not to make a particular trip.

To be sure, most underwriters attempt, in determining premiums, to take some account of whatever information is available on the mileage that the insured car is expected to cover during the term of the policy. It is clear, however, that this provides very little deterrent to the use of the car for marginal trips, since this usage is unlikely to induce an increase in the premium rate, and since, in most instances, the policyholder will be unaware of the degree to which information on mileage driven, even if made available to the underwriter, would affect the insurance premium. The most likely place for this kind of influence to operate is in decisions relating to the journey to work, where the character of the usage can be fairly well defined and taken into account. At best, however, this influence is likely to be small, particularly as underwriters cannot, in a competitive market, offer large rate differentials on the basis of largely unverified representations.

Indeed, it is precisely in those cases where the maintaining of an additional car is a close decision that the premium is most likely to overstate the risk substantially: a car that can barely be afforded is likely to be a car that will add much less to total mileage driven and to risk exposure than would be indicated by the added premium that the underwriter will find it necessary to charge. Thus, the manner of

---

[12] Ideally, one might require the size of this deductible to vary with the resources of the insured.

assessment of insurance premiums is likely to result in a more intensive use of a smaller stock of active cars than would be economically most efficient. It is not clear whether the number of car-miles thus generated would be greater or less than would occur under a more accurate assessment of accident costs: this would depend on the relative elasticities at various points and either result is theoretically possible. But even if the impact of the time-related premium on the active stock of cars were large, the cars added to the total stock as a result of more accurate adjustment of insurance premiums would increase total travel relatively little. It therefore seems likely that this added mileage would be more than offset by reduced intensity of use of the existing stock.

The inefficiency induced by the time-related pattern of insurance premiums might not of itself be sufficient to warrant a change in the practice, but in the light of the widespread dissatisfaction with the present system, for other reasons, it may be an appropriate time at least to explore possibilities for change.

A most appropriate and, as far as collection is concerned, convenient way of assessing the major part of the cost of accidents against motor vehicle users might be a supplement to the gasoline tax. Regional differences in accident cost rates could be reflected in differential tax rates, and while some inequity and inefficiency would be engendered by the opportunity to fill up in the low-tax areas, this problem on the whole seems minor compared to the widespread inequities in the present situation or in any time-based premium approach. It might be best to ignore state and local dividing lines and collect part or all of the tax on the basis of the point of retail sale. This would permit the rate to be graduated more smoothly and would minimize the disturbances to competitive relationships that tend to occur where the tax varies in substantial jumps across a political boundary.

The main difficulty with this approach is that while it takes care of collection, it fails to provide a mechanism for the distribution of compensation to its victims. This is no problem in a place like Saskatchewan, where insurance is already a government monopoly, and it would indeed be an easy means of achieving a substantial improvement in equity and efficiency for Saskatchewan to replace its periodic premium system partially or totally with an increment to its fuel tax. This would have the substantial advantage of extending coverage almost automatically to out-of-state cars driven in Saskatchewan; the only problem then remaining would be to provide coverage, possibly through conventional private coverage, for Saskatchewan cars being driven elsewhere.

One might, indeed, consider the superiority of the gasoline tax (and possibly also tire taxes) as a means for assessing accident costs, not only in terms of equity and efficiency in allocation, but also in terms of cost of collection (as compared with the cost of selling insurance individually) to be great enough to warrant, if necessary, the establishment of some form of monopoly organization to take care of the awarding of benefits to claimants out of the funds thus provided. It should not be thought, however, that workmen's compensation procedures provide an adequate precedent in themselves for such a scheme: victims of industrial accidents constitute a relatively homogeneous group to which uniform standards can be applied fairly readily, while traffic accident victims cover the entire range of economic status, and it may be that a more flexible, pluralistic approach is needed to deal with the range of cases they present. The Saskatchewan plan has been neither a complete failure nor such an outstanding success as to compel imitation; and what works reasonably well with a relatively homogeneous population might develop difficulties in a more industrialized and heterogenous area. But despite all the difficulties that might develop under such a monopoly or state board, it is hard to imagine a situation more unsatisfactory than the existing one.

Nevertheless, the prospects for developing such a public or quasi-public instrument are not bright, particularly as insurance interests, in spite of their loud wails of anguish at the losses they claim to be suffering from the existing business at regulated rates, are sure to mount vigorous opposition to any such proposal. It may be necessary, therefore, to seek some way by which assessment through the gasoline tax can be combined with private enterprise claim settlement.

One way would be simply to establish a state fund derived from suitable surcharges on fuel taxes, registration fees, drivers' license fees, and possibly tolls and congestion charges, where these are in effect, and then allow insurance companies to bid for the job of taking care of accident claims relating to the operation of suitably packaged sets of automobiles registered in the state, possibly including in each package some suitably defined obligation with respect to accidents in the state involving out-of-state vehicles. It would even be possible to include in such a scheme a differential in the surcharge on drivers' licenses to produce much the same effect as that produced by the higher premium rates now generally enforced against younger drivers. However, it seems unlikely that such a result, accepted with considerable protest even when imposed by private companies impelled by the competitive drive for better underwriting results, would persist in explicit legislative enactment. In any case, there seems to be no reliable way of varying a premium according to the amount of driving done by a particular driver, as distinct from the mileage a particular car is driven.

A major difficulty with such a plan, at least in the Northeastern states, where a large volume of short-haul interstate traffic exists, is that unless a roughly similar plan were adopted simultaneously by a number of contiguous states, avoidance of the insurance surcharge through preferential purchase of fuel out of state would present a fairly serious problem, especially where state lines run through areas with high premium rates.

One procedure that might get around this difficulty, though it would produce others, would be to hold a mass shotgun wedding between oil and insurance companies, by requiring each oil company, as a consequence of the sale of its gasoline for highway use, to assume an appropriate share of the liability for all accidents involving the automobile using its gasoline. The cost of the accidents would then be included in the price of the gasoline, which the oil company could vary with location, and, in the case of credit card sale, with the rating accorded the particular vehicle. Such a scheme would of course require some means of determining whose gasoline a car was using at the time of an accident. One means would be to require the maintenance of a vehicle log, showing the gallons, mileage, outlet, and brand of each fuel purchase, possibly backed up by a similar log maintained by the service station, showing the vehicle license number. Where credit cards are used the record would be relatively automatic. Another method might be the addition of some quantitatively determinable tracer compound to the product of each oil company, so that subsequent analysis of the fuel of a car involved in an accident could establish the company or companies liable for the damages. To facilitate the analysis, a removable sampling cartridge could be installed in the fuel line at relatively slight cost. Still another method might involve the application of a seal to the gas tank cap. Or a combination of methods could be used.

It would even be possible to develop such a form of insurance as a voluntary method, which would involve obligating the vehicle operator to buy his gasoline almost entirely by credit card. There seems to be no essential reason why the incremental accounting and selling costs involved should be any higher than the costs involved in the commission system; the scheme should be especially attractive to vehicle owners running a low annual mileage. It might be difficult, however, to develop the scheme in a form that would meet the requirements of the compulsory insurance states.

The problem of identifying the underwriting party would be simpler if the liability were attached to the sale of tires, since the brand here is obvious. The main difficulty with this is that tire use can occur at a great distance from the place of sale, so that no substantial geographical discrimination is possible and adoption on less than a nationwide scale would hardly be feasible. Moreover the insurance element in the price would have to be as much as two or three times the present retail price, which would be likely to have serious distorting effects. Unless a substantial rebate were available on the turning in of used carcasses, depending on the weight of tread rubber remaining, the high cost of tires might induce uneconomical and dangerous use of tires worn thin. On the other hand, the liability for accidents would encourage tire manufacturers to promote safer tires. There would be strong and perhaps even excessive incentives to watch tire inflation and wheel alignment very closely, and hard cornering and high speed travel would be appropriately costly. There would be a slight favorable side effect in that travel on gravel and dirt roads would be more costly in terms of tire wear, which is in keeping with the higher maintenance costs of such roads. Use of tire taxes as a vehicle for payments for the marginal costs of accidents and congestion occasioned by highway users seems on the whole more appropriate for underdeveloped countries, particularly where little vehicular traffic across frontiers takes place, than for a federation of fifty states jealous of their independence of action.

But whatever is done with insurance, there will remain substantial elements of gross externality not covered by such insurance, calling for some form of payment by highway users in addition to insurance premiums. One element, resulting from the diseconomies-of-scale element according to which increased density of traffic on a given road increases the average cost of accidents per vehicle-mile, can perhaps best be treated conceptually as a kind of rent to be charged for the use of a limited resource, applicable, where economies of scale in the production of roadway capacity permit, to the improvement of the roadway network, but often, as in the case of core city streets, considered only as a rent paid in relation to the inherent scarcity of urban land.

A second externality element consisting of contributions from outside the motor vehicle economy for the succor of victims and alleviation of damage inflicted by vehicular traffic, can well be considered as warranting a net additional charge on highway users to be levied apart from any highway trust funds and used as a general revenue. A third, somewhat similar element, would arise from the fact that compensation paid victims is seldom equal to the full cost, inclusive of all elements of pain and suffering endured by the victims. While it may be possible to come up with some not too outrageous estimates of what this added cost should be evaluated at in the aggregate, it may be impossible to come up with the comparable breakdown of this figure for individual cases, and undesirable to pay actual compensation on this scale even if it could be done, in view of the moral hazard that might thereby be generated. But the fact that the full compensation is not, and possibly should not be paid to the individual victim does not affect the desirability of assessing the full loss against the activity responsible for it, if that activity is to be held to an optimal level.

COMMENT

by MARTIN J. BAILEY, *University of Rochester*

The first reading of this paper, with its suggestion to let the oil companies pay the costs of all highway accidents, suggested the conclusion, "Vickrey scores again!" As we all know, Vickrey belongs to a small, elite group who have kept the economics of public policy from becoming hopelessly dull. Moreover, he belongs to a still smaller group who are nearly always right. That public authorities have always rejected his proposals merely adds luster to his other accomplishments.

However, a second reading raises questions. Although his proposals this time have most of their usual attributes, it isn't clear that they are right. At best, they fail to follow from his own analysis and evidence. First, he discusses costs borne by third parties: sick leave provisions, pensions, social security, health insurance, unallocated court costs, public assistance, subsidized hospital care, and so on. These classes of external costs apply to all types of accidents, and deserve to be considered as a group, rather than piecemeal. A perfectly discriminating, Pareto-optimizing solution to the announcement effects of these subsidies would be to discontinue them. That may not be the right thing to do, but it highlights the point that these subsidies deserve to be considered as a distinct subject.

Second, merely having the gasoline companies pay accident costs doesn't meet the problem. In the light of Vickrey's own argument about the excess of marginal cost over average cost, they should in addition pay something, perhaps an equal amount, into the highway fund.

Third, whereas traffic time delays undoubtedly rise monotonically with volume, so that a net excise tax is appropriate for each trip, it is not clear that accidents also rise monotonically. Vickrey's own reasoning and evidence say they do not. He notes that total fatalities decline with volume, because a decline in single-car fatal accidents more than offsets a rise in multiple-car fatal accidents. (Evidently the extra traffic gets in the way and so protects the prospective single-car accident victim.) This decline in fatalities may be enough to offset, or outweigh, the rise in accident property damage and bodily injury with higher traffic volume. Moreover, Vickrey notes that above a certain degree of congestion serious accidents most likely stop altogether, and accident rates, property damage, and so on, probably decline. If so, the effect of more trips on accident rates points to a tax on trips only up to that volume at which these rates reach a maximum. At higher volumes there should instead be a subsidy.

Figure 1 shows the average traffic accident rate as a function of volume as the curve AR. The curve MR is marginal to $AR,$ and shows the additional accidents per unit of additional traffic. In the left-hand portion of the figure, up to the volume V_1, MR is higher than AR; the difference is the appropriate rate of tax to charge so that a motorist, in contemplation of a trip, bears its full marginal cost. This difference is given by the vertical lines that shade this portion of the figure. However, at volumes higher than V_1 the line MR is below AR; the difference is the appropriate rate of subsidy to induce more trips and push down the accident rate.

FIGURE 1

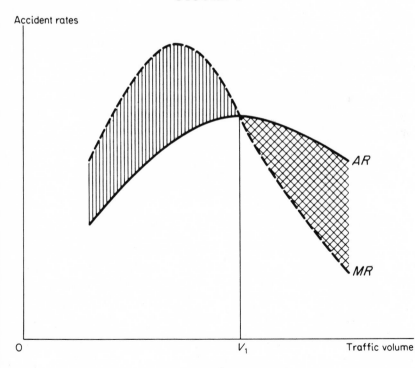

Unfortunately, we lack hourly data on accident rates, speed, and volume, to measure these effects exactly. With such data it would be possible to work out the right rates of tax for all circumstances to correct for the combination of time delay effects and accident rates effects.

THE VALUE OF OUTPUT OF
THE POST OFFICE DEPARTMENT

JOHN HALDI

Haldi Associates, Inc.

Introduction

Postal traditions are quite old. The early Greeks and Romans had regular mail systems for communicating with distant military commanders or government officials, and the familiar mailbag is said to have originated with the Phoenicians, predating even the Greeks and the Romans. The American colonies had a privately operated postal service by the early sixteen hundreds, and from 1712 until the Revolution regular postal service was provided by a wholly owned subsidiary of the British Post Office. The United States Post Office was established by Benjamin Franklin in 1775, nearly one year before the Declaration of Independence was signed. It was one of the initial agencies of the government, and it has been a government agency ever since. The Post Office is thus the nation's oldest public enterprise. As such, it enjoys a rich history of which it can be justly proud.

With a government-protected monopoly on carrying the mail, the Post Office has grown to be quite large. In the fiscal year ended June 30, 1967, expenditures totaled $6.3 billion, revenues were $5.0 billion, its labor force averaged more than 700,000 full- and part-time employees, its net investment in plant and equipment was estimated to be $800 million, and the volume of mail handled was over 78 billion pieces—almost 400 pieces for every man, woman and child in the United States.

The postal system is a widespread network; the United States had 33,121 individual post offices in 1966. At the same time the bulk of postal operations is highly concentrated in and between our large

NOTE. Valuable comments and criticisms were received from a number of people, especially William Sullivan, Arthur Edens and Emerson Markham of the Post Office Department, and Lewis Gaty of Swarthmore College. The author assumes sole responsibility for all opinions expressed here.

metropolitan areas. The 317 largest post offices, which constitute less than one per cent of all post offices, accounted for over 67 per cent of all postal revenues in 1966. Looked at from the other end of the scale, 86 per cent of all offices accounted for less than 7 per cent of all revenues. Summary data on the distribution of revenues by size of office are given in Table 1.

The principal mission of the Post Office is, of course, to receive mail from senders and deliver it to addressees. However, the Post Office also provides a number of auxiliary services. Some of these are mail-related: for example, special delivery, registered mail, certified mail and parcel post insurance. Nonmail special services provided by the Post Office include the sale of postal money orders, administration of civil service examinations, assistance in taking the census and, until recently, the postal savings system. In terms of man hours expended or revenues received, all special services taken together amount to less than 6 per cent of total Post Office revenues. Because these special services ars so diverse and relatively so small, this paper will exclude them from further consideration and will focus exclusively on the value of ordinary mail service.

One facet of mail service, *international mail,* will not be discussed in this paper. International mail constitutes a small part of the total mail picture. In 1966 it accounted for less than 4 per cent of postal revenues and less than 0.8 per cent of total mail volume.

TABLE 1

1966 POSTAL RECEIPTS, BY SIZE OF OFFICE

Class of Post Office	Number of Offices	Per Cent	Receipts[a] (millions of dollars)	Per Cent
First—large	317	0.9	3,066.9	67.6
First—small	4,307	13.0	1,175.4	25.9
Second	7,125	21.5	207.2	4.6
Third	12,971	39.2	75.2	1.7
Fourth	8,401	25.4	11.0	0.2
Total	33,121	100.0	4,535.7	100.0

SOURCE: U.S. Post Office Department, *Cost Ascertainment Report,* Washington, D.C., 1966, p. 89.

[a] Excludes value of money orders sold.

Throughout this paper *the postal production function will be treated as fixed,* an assumption which fits the existing situation well. For years the technology observed throughout the postal system has remained virtually static[1] and questions concerning the possibility of shifting the production function would constitute a legitimate and interesting field of inquiry. Indeed, Congress does perennially inquire whether the Post Office is installing enough new equipment and spending enough money on research and development. Some sharp critics of the Post Office contend that existing technology offers substantial potential for mechanizing mail handling and reducing costs. These critics submit that increased mechanization is prevented chiefly (1) by interference from Congress and labor unions and (2) by the fact that postal managers have virtually no incentive to reduce costs. Milder critics are less sanguine about existing technology, but they are dissatisfied with the Post Office's research effort, and they, too, sense that Post Office management has virtually no incentive to make economically correct decisions regarding capital-labor substitution. The problem of how to give proper incentives to managers of large government enterprise is obviously very important, as students and critics of the Post Office have frequently pointed out. However, such questions are a digression from the main purpose of this paper, which is a discussion of the valuation and pricing of postal services under existing technology.

It should be pointed out that the above questions were under intensive study by the President's Commission on Postal Organization during the time this paper was being prepared. Questions concerning the best organizational form for the Post Office are not considered here because of the complexity of the subject and because the study by the Presidential Commission was known to be underway. The Commission's report, which was not released in sufficient time to integrate into this study,[2] concludes that Post Office management is severely hampered by the present organizational form, and the Commission recommends that the Post Office cease to be a cabinet agency of the government and instead become a government-owned corporation more or less like TVA. The Commission's report[3] and the four separate contractor reports (published separately as appendices to the study) are

[1] Except for developments in air transportation, which the Post Office was in no way responsible for, but which the Post Office has taken advantage of.

[2] An addendum at the end of this paper gives a summary comparison of the conclusions of this paper and the Postal Commission's report.

[3] *Towards Postal Excellence,* Report of the President's Commission on Postal Organization, Washington, D.C., June 1968.

recommended reading for anyone interested in studying postal problems in depth.

This paper will address itself to the following issues: *First,* should the Post Office continue to be regarded as a "natural monopoly," or should the government allow private firms to offer regular mail service in competition with the Post Office? *Second,* how would postal services be priced under competitive conditions? To provide a substantive basis for discussing these issues, it will first be necessary to explore the nature of the Post Office as it now exists.

Postal Rates and Mail Volume

The Post Office now divides all postal rates into four classes. The basic distinctions between these four classes are summarized in Table 2. The apparent simplicity of Table 2 is, however, a bit deceiving. Within these four classes Congress has authorized a number of further distinctions and subclassifications, most of which have the effect of giving substantial discounts to particular mailers or to certain

TABLE 2

DISTINGUISHING CHARACTERISTICS OF THE
FOUR BASIC MAIL CLASSES

Class of Mail	General Description
First	Private correspondence (sealed) plus post cards. First class mail receives priority in handling and shipping. The privacy of first class mail is considered inviolate, and mail is forwarded (or returned) as often as necessary to make final delivery.
Second	Newspapers, magazines and similar publications which may be presumed to possess some news or literary value.
Third	Mostly advertising matter—commonly called "junk mail"—plus certain small parcels or other miscellaneous items weighing less than one pound.
Fourth	All parcels or packages weighing more than one pound and not exceeding the upper size limits.

types of mail. As a consequence, the Post Office really has twenty-six —not four—different rate classes.

Some of the distinctions in the rate structure are based on sound economic principles. *First,* the form in which mail is turned over to the Post Office can significantly affect the collection, sorting and processing costs of the Post Office. Large bulk mailings which the sender presorts, bundles by Zip code and then delivers direct to the Post Office loading dock will unquestionably reduce handling costs of the Post Office. *Second,* parcels, magazines or similar bulky items have much greater weight per piece than do letters or circulars. The cost of shipping letters long distances is small compared to other handling costs, but this is not true for bulky items. Hence for these latter items the rate structure should and properly does take account of weight and distance shipped. *Third,* the addition of low-priority items to the mail system enables the Post Office to even out its work flow and utilize more fully its work force, plant and equipment. Despite the validity of these three economic factors, it ought to be recognized that economic principles are of limited assistance in explaining the existing rate structure. The determining forces are undoubtedly as much political as economic.

A striking feature of the rate structure is the extent of the differential between various classes of mail. Among the four classes of mail the highest charge is on first class, the lowest on second class. Rates for third and fourth class mail fall between these two. To illustrate the extent of the extreme differences that exist, if magazines paid first class rates the cost of mailing a typical issue of *Time* would be about 54–60 cents, an increase of between 1,700 and 1,900 per cent over current rates.

The preceding example may give a slightly unfair picture of the extremes of the existing rate structure. As stated previously, magazines do not require the same handling as letters, and from a mail-handling point of view the two are not strictly comparable. To appreciate the difference in rates for items with similar mail-handling characteristics, let us compare (1) a 32-page magazine weighing 4 ounces and consisting of 50 per cent advertising, with (2) a 32-page advertising piece also weighing 4 ounces. Assume both are distributed nationally in large quantities, both are bundled by Zip code and are taken by the mailer to the Post Office for distribution. The charge for mailing the magazine would range between 1.1–2.25 cents per copy, depending on the distance mailed, whereas the advertising piece would cost 4.0 cents per copy to mail to any address in the United States.

TABLE 3
RATES ON SECOND CLASS MAIL[a]

Classification	Rate (cents)
Within county of publication (newspapers):	
Weekly	1.3 per lb.
—minimum	0.2 per copy
Local city delivery rates:	
More often than weekly	1.0 per copy
Less often than weekly, 2 ozs. or less	1.0 per copy
Less often than weekly, over 2 ozs.	2.0 per copy
Outside county of publication	
Regular publications:	
Editorial portion	3.0 per lb.
Advertising portion:	
Zones 1–8 (see schedule)	4.6–15.0 per lb.
Minimum	1.1 per piece
Classroom publications	60% of regular rates
Nonprofit publications	
Editorial	1.9 per lb.
Advertising:	
Zones 1–8 (see schedule)	2.3–3.5 per lb.
Transient rate	5.0 first 2 ozs.
	1.0 ea add'l oz.
Entry fees:	
Original entry	$30.00–$120.00
News-agent entry	$25.00
Reentry or additional entry	$15.00–$50.00

[a] PL 90-206, December 16, 1967, authorized certain step-increases in these rates, to become effective on January 1st of 1969 and 1970.

The rates for most of the subclasses within second and third class mail are shown in Tables 3 and 4. These tables illustrate the complexity of the rate structure as well as the variation in rates within a given class of mail.[4]

Subclassifications within the second and third class rate structures give significant discounts to authorized nonprofit organizations. Tables 3 and 4 illustrate the extent of these discounts for second and

[4] Tables 2 and 3 show major rate classifications but omit some detail contained in the complete schedule.

TABLE 4

RATES ON THIRD CLASS MAIL[a]

Classification	Rate (cents)
Single pieces:	
Circulars, merchandise	6.0 first 2 ozs.
	2.0 ea add'l oz.
Keys and identification devices	14.0 first 2 ozs.
	7.0 ea add'l 2 ozs.
Bulk mailings:	
Regular:	
Circulars, etc.	22.0 per lb.
—minimum	3.6 per piece
Books, catalogs, etc.	16.0 per lb.
—minimum	3.6 per piece
Nonprofit:	
Circulars, etc.	11.0 per lb.
—minimum	1.4 per piece
Books, catalogs, etc.	8.0 per lb.
—minimum	1.4 per piece
Annual bulk mailing fee	$30.00

[a] PL 90-206, December 16, 1967, authorized a second step-increase in these rates, to become effective on July 1, 1969.

third class mail. In the fourth class rate schedule discounts are given to books and records, and even bigger discounts are given for such mailings to and from libraries, schools and other educational institutions. As there is no indication that the cost of handling mail for nonprofit organizations is any different than that of other mail with similar handling characteristics, the rate differences simply reflect discrimination in favor of certain mailers. It is highly doubtful whether these rate differentials could be justified in terms of differences in the elasticity of demand. It is much more likely that they have no economic rationale whatsoever and instead represent an intentional subsidy or transfer payment to those institutions or organizations which benefit from the lower rates.

Table 5 gives data on mail revenues and the volume of mail handled. It also provides additional perspective on the rate structure. Table 5 contains 1966 data, the last year for which complete informa-

TABLE 5
POSTAL REVENUES AND VOLUME, BY CLASS OF MAIL, 1966

	Revenues (millions of dollars) (1)	Pieces (millions) (2)	Revenue per Piece (cents) (3)	Revenue per Pound (cents) (4)
First class mail:				
Regular	2,333.9	40,421.8	5.8	180.97
Airmail	186.5	1,780.5	10.5	231.70
Air parcel post	90.5	47.7	189.9	86.34
Total, first class	2,610.9	42,250.0	15.2a	178.16a
Second class mail:				
Magazines	74.5	3,380.9	2.2	4.06
Newspapers—daily	27.0	1,894.0	1.4	3.74
Newspapers—other	5.9	840.1	0.7	3.18
Nonprofit publications	8.3	2,300.3	0.4	2.03
Classroom publications	1.5	108.1	1.4	2.82
Other second class revenues	9.1	110.2	—	—
Total, second class	126.3	8,633.6	1.5a	3.92a
Controlled circulation	18.9	347.0	5.46	13.54
Third class mail:				
Single-piece rate	200.9	3,347.7	6.0	56.50
Bulk rate, regular	436.2	14,101.1	3.1	32.89
Bulk rate, nonprofit	36.9	2,856.3	1.3	28.41
Fees	7.6	—	—	—
Total, third class	681.6	20,305.1	3.4a	37.62a
Fourth class mail:				
Parcels	784.3	767.7	102.16	15.54
Catalogs	31.1	103.6	30.02	8.07
Special rate (39 USC 4554a)	53.9	202.8	26.56	7.23
Special rate (39 USC 4554b)	1.5	16.1	9.28	1.85
Total, fourth class	870.8	1,090.2	79.87a	14.00a
All otherb	663.6	3,005.6	—	—
Total	4,972.0	75,631.5		

SOURCES: *Survey of Postal Rates,* House Document No. 106, Washington, D.C., 1967; and U.S. Post Office Department, *Cost Ascertainment Report,* Washington, D.C., 1966. Revenue from certain items with different rates, such as post cards, airmail postcards, etc., has been merged into the larger classification.

ᵃ Average.

ᵇ Includes reimbursement for franked government mail, international mail, special services (registry, insurance, etc.) and other miscellaneous revenues.

---

tion was available. The revenue figures are therefore based on 1966 rates and do not reflect the current rate schedule, which went into effect January 7, 1968. The figures in Table 5 show that first class mail (including airmail) is the backbone of the postal system in terms of either *revenue* or *pieces handled*. In 1966 first class mail accounted for 56 per cent of basic mail revenue and 56 per cent of all pieces handled.[5]

The rate structure shows the maximum which mailers are allowed, but of course not all pieces of mail weigh the maximum allowed. The great differences in rates *actually paid* for various classes of mail are reflected most strikingly in columns 3 and 4 of Table 5, which show, respectively, *revenue per piece* and *revenue per pound*. On a *per piece basis* the average postage on a regular first class letter (5.8¢) is over 2.5 times more than the postage on a typical magazine (2.2¢); the postage for a typical advertising brochure (3.1¢) is about 1.5 times more than for a typical magazine. If all first class letters weighed exactly one ounce, in 1966 the Post Office would have received only 80 cents per pound for first class mail. In fact, it received $1.81 per pound. Thus on a *weight basis,* the Post Office realized from first class letters about 45 times more than from magazines, which paid 4 cents per pound. Advertising material, at 33 cents per pound, paid about 7.5 times more than magazines. These figures give some indication of the extent of the subsidies Congress is willing to pay in order to have magazines and newspapers distributed via the mail.

The postal rate structure reflects a number of different concepts. For first class mail, rates are based on the presumption that the service rendered has a high value to users and that enough should be charged to attempt to eliminate the deficit incurred on other classes of mail. In other words, first class rates reflect a "value of service" concept administered by a benevolent monopolist who fails to take full advantage of the inelasticity of demand. For the editorial content of periodicals and for publications of nonprofit organizations, the information which these presumably convey to the public is used to ration-

---

[5] The category "Controlled circulation" following "Second class mail" is really a subclassification of second and third class mail, but it is reported separately by the Post Office because these periodicals pay substantially higher rates than do other second class mailers.

alize the substantial loss (or subsidy) which is intentionally incurred. The advertising portion of periodicals has a rate formula which depends on both weight *and distance,* but the *maximum* charge for magazine advertising is less than the *minimum* charge for an equivalent amount of bulk third class mail. Hence an element of subsidy also underlies the advertising portion of periodicals.

The rates for fourth class mail are also based upon weight and distance. For parcels the Post Office charges fees related to both distance and weight because (1) the law requires that revenues cover at least 96 per cent (and not more than 104 per cent) of the cost of handling parcels and (2) competition from firms such as United Parcel Service makes demand for this service somewhat more elastic. This competition precludes the Post Office from charging uniform fees which do not vary with weight or distance shipped. For if it did attempt to levy a uniform rate which would just cover all expenses then, since the Post Office does not have any monopoly on parcel shipments, private firms would almost surely undercut the Post Office on short-haul lightweight business and let the Post Office carry only long-haul heavy business at a substantial loss. The Post Office has avoided this situation by establishing a zone-rate structure for parcel post.

In addition to the various rate concepts discussed above—value of service, subsidy to provide information to the public, and weight-distance—second and third class bulk mailers also pay an annual permit or "entry fee." These permit fees are quite low in relation to the regular postage paid by most bulk mailers, but they do add a trace of a two-part tariff to the rate structure.

Nature of the Demand for Postal Services

About three-fourths of all mail originates in business firms, and a large portion of all mail is also addressed to business firms. A breakdown of first class mail by originator—business and institutional versus individuals—is shown in Table 6.

It is worth noting that although all first class mail is considered "private correspondence," in fact only a fraction consists of actual letters. A significant portion of first class business mail consists of items like bills, credit cards or dividend checks. Each month banks, telephone companies, gas and electric utility companies, department

TABLE 6
ORIGINATORS OF DOMESTIC MAIL
(PER CENT)

Originator	Class of Mail				
	First	Second	Third	Fourth	All Mail
Business or Institutional	75	100	96	80	80
Individual	25	0	4	20	20
Total	100	100	100	100	100

SOURCE: U.S. Post Office Department, results of a number of unpublished surveys.

stores, oil companies, etc., send millions of statements through the mail.

On normal workdays the mailing habits of business cause the Post Office to be faced with a serious peak-load problem. Throughout the day secretaries type and prepare letters and automatic equipment prepares bills, dividend checks, etc. Most of this mail is deposited in chutes and mail boxes towards the end of the working day, between 3:30 and 5:30 P.M. Half of all originating first class mail is received at the Post Office between 4 and 7 P.M. The distribution of the arrival of first class mail at the Post Office throughout the day is shown in Figure 1. Between the hours of 5 and 9 P.M., consequently, a typical post office presses all available manpower into sorting the mail and preparing it for transportation to the area of final delivery. Between 8 and 10 P.M., most of the outgoing mail is dispatched to the airport or train station. Then a relative lull sets in until sometime around 3 or 4 A.M., when mail from other post offices starts arriving for final delivery. Again, from about 4 to 8 A.M., the Post Office is pushed to capacity as it prepares all the incoming mail for final delivery. By 9 or 10 A.M., the large work spaces of the Post Office are again mostly idle, with only skeleton crews on hand to process mail from the occasional late-arriving train or plane. Most of the 4 to 7 P.M. peak-loading problem is of course attributable to business firms since they originate so much of the mail.

The fact that so much of the first class mail from business firms consists of "bulk" items like bills suggest that the Post Office could

FIGURE 1

ARRIVAL OF ORIGINATING-OUTGOING FIRST CLASS
MAIL AT MAIN POST OFFICE

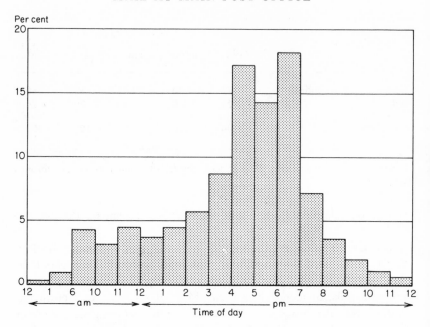

SOURCE: Post Office Department, Bureau of Operations, *NIMS Program Report*, PFY 1968, Quarter III.

probably use the price mechanism to promote more efficient use of its plant and equipment. Under competitive conditions one expects that prices will fall during periods of excess capacity and lower marginal cost. This has the desirable effect to both society and the individual firm of utilizing excess capacity and "spreading the overhead." The Post Office could easily adopt the competitive "solution" to its problem of excess capacity by offering discounts or rebates to any first class mailer who would bring large quantities of mail to the Post Office between, say, 10 A.M. and 12 noon, Monday through Friday. To take advantage of such a discount, many business firms would be required to hold overnight the bills or invoices which they prepare during the day. Under the existing rate structure they have absolutely no incentive to do so. However, there is every reason to expect that large mailers would react quite favorably to discounts of, say, 2–5 per cent because even though postage for an individual piece is usually small in relation to the value of the contents mailed, the total cost of postage represents a significant expense to many firms.

SECULAR GROWTH OF DEMAND. Mail volume has grown every year since World War II. For the years 1946–1966 the over-all growth rate averaged about 3½ per cent per year. Every class of mail did not change uniformly, however. Mail of the first two classes increased at about the same rate as the over-all average, but third and fourth class mail exhibited markedly different behavior.

Since 1953 the advertising portion of third class mail, which comprises the bulk of all third class mail, has increased at a compound rate exceeding 4 per cent per year. The regular parcel post portion of fourth class mail, on the other hand, experienced a sharp downtrend after 1951. The chief causes of this decline were higher rates plus Congressional limitations on size and weight of parcels, which diverted many parcels to private carriers. In contrast to the decline in ordinary parcels, the volume of books and records rose sharply, undoubtedly reflecting the markedly lower rates for these items.

PRICE ELASTICITY. Although brief, this review of secular growth indicates that demand has grown somewhat faster in those classes or subclasses where rates are lower. From this it would appear that mailers are indeed conscious of postal rates and respond to rate differentials and changes in rates with a fairly elastic demand. However, econometric studies of the demand for mail services show that:

Growth in mail volume can be "explained" almost exclusively in terms of changes in population and real GNP.

After allowing for the effect of population and real GNP, *the demand for mail services appears to be highly price inelastic,* indicating that existing substitutes for mail service are rather imperfect.

Changes in the rate differential between first and third class mail has resulted in a measurable shift in the distribution of the total volume between these two classes, and here there appears to be some cross-elasticity and substitution.[6]

[6] Baratz (1962, pp. 4–12) goes into considerably more detail on the studies and the economic rationale underlying these conclusions. Virtually all econometric studies of the demand for postal service have originated within the Post Office Department, as a consequence of the Post Office Department's obvious interest in forecasting mail volume.

An examination of the available substitutes for mail service reinforces the conclusion that the demand is probably price-inelastic. To begin with, first class mail is protected from direct competition by the so-called Private Express Statutes. These laws give the Post Office authority to prevent any person or any firm from regularly carrying or distributing private correspondence. The Post Office enforces these laws at all times, going so far as to prevent large companies from carrying intracompany correspondence between different plants on a regular basis.[7] With all competition of this sort totally eliminated, the remaining substitutes for mail service currently are:

Private messenger
Telephone
Private Wire
TWX
Western Union

Each of these has the advantage of being somewhat faster than mail service. Except for local telephone calls, however, the cost of each of the above substitutes is considerably higher than the 6 to 12 cents charged for most letter mail. But local phone calls are probably used right now in preference to the mail. Given the cost of dictating and typing a letter, it seems unlikely that many letters are written when a local phone call would suffice.

Certain major components of first class mail will be subjected to future competition from recent inventions now being developed. This may increase the elasticity of demand somewhat. Most important will be the advent of the so-call "checkless society." This is to be accomplished by electronic devices which will enable people to pay their bills by wire—over the telephone lines perhaps. Also under development by the Xerox and Magnavox Corporations is a device that will transmit letters, maps, charts, etc., over long distance telephone lines. Although the cost of this latter device will probably be somewhat more than six cents per page, it will enable business firms to transmit exact facsimiles. This is something which existing substitutes do not now permit, and the cost for such printed messages could well turn out to be lower than private wire, TWX, or Western Union.

The readership of virtually all magazines is widely dispersed geographically. A great many magazines cater to special interest groups, ranging from specialized trade groups to automobile, sports or fashion

[7] See, for example, the article on page 1 of the *Wall Street Journal,* June 5, 1967.

enthusiasts. Some national newspaper and magazines, such as *Christian Science Monitor, Wall Street Journal, Newsweek* or *Time* can usually be procured at convenient newsstands. These latter publications face considerable competition from television and radio. Moreover, every magazine must compete for reading time of its target audience. Hence the demand for magazines may be somewhat price-elastic. Nevertheless, the second most economical method of distributing magazines to subscribers would probably be far more expensive than mailing. Since postage accounts for only 15 to 20 per cent of the regular subscription price, demand for mail service by magazine publishers is probably inelastic over a price range considerably in excess of present rates.

One fairly recent development by large national periodicals is worth noting. Several large mailers now use facsimile typesetting to print regional editions simultaneously in a number of locations. This practice probably developed independently of postal rate considerations. Nevertheless, it probably results in saving the Post Office a certain amount of extra transportation cost since the second class rate structure does not reflect the full incremental cost associated with moving bulk mail over long distances, especially distances exceeding 1,000 miles. If the rate structure were changed so as to reflect true cost differentials, more magazines might publish regional editions.[8] Encouraging such practices where cost considerations warrant could not worsen over-all economic efficiency, and it might yield some improvements.

Third class mail is the principal method by which many advertisers reach highly selected audiences. The chief alternative to direct mail advertisers seems to be first class mail rather than other media. Though first class mail is more expensive, it is said to receive more attention from the addressees. Hence demand by third class mailers may be elastic, but the Post Office itself provides the competition.

The parcel post portion of fourth class mail has more competition from the private sector than any other type of mail. This competition consists chiefly of United Parcel Service, Railway Express, Air Express and less-than-carload-lot freight forwarders. It has lobbied long, vigorously, and with some success to place weight and size restrictions on parcels carried by the Post Office. As noted earlier, this is the only

---

[8] Or they might use nonpostal transportation to the area of final delivery, if some more economical private arrangement could be made. It is reported that many publishers take out "multiple-entry permits," which the Post Office has only recently permitted, and by this means they do attempt to minimize their transportation costs.

class of mail which has shown a year-to-year decline in volume since World War II. Thus the price elasticity of parcel post is probably greater than for any other type of mail. But parcel post constitutes only 15 per cent of total revenues and 1.4 per cent of total pieces mailed. Hence parcel post is not important enough to affect the over-all conclusion that elasticity of demand for mail service is probably price-inelastic, at least around the existing price level.

Postal Costs

Mail-handling technology is a highly labor-intensive activity. This fact is vividly illustrated in Figure 2, which shows that during the last decade labor costs have actually become an *increasing percentage* of

FIGURE 2

LABOR COSTS AS A PER CENT
OF TOTAL POSTAL COSTS
1926–65

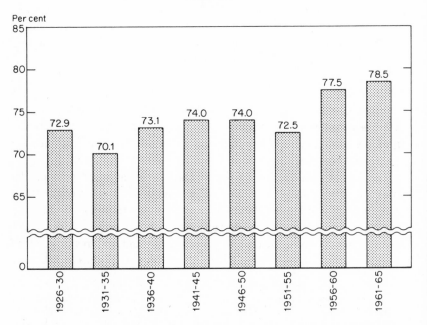

SOURCE: U.S. Post Office Department, *Annual Report of the Postmaster General,* 1966, Financial Supplement, p. 80.

all expenditures by the Post Office. For thirty years prior to 1955 labor costs averaged around 73 per cent, but since 1955 labor costs have increased to a current rate of around 80 per cent.

The definition of labor costs used to calculate the percentages in Figure 2 includes direct salaries *plus* fringe benefits. Labor cost also includes a 10 per cent differential for night work, plus overtime rates paid for weekends and time over forty hours. The 10 per cent differential for night work represents a sizable expenditure because a large number of man-hours are consumed after 6 P.M. on account of the peak-load problem discussed previously. Actions or policies which alleviated this problem would thus have immediate and direct payoff to the Post Office.

Direct payments to common carriers for transportation services have, during the years 1926–65, varied between 14 and 24 per cent. This is shown in Figure 3. The combined total of labor and transporta-

FIGURE 3

TRANSPORTATION COSTS AS A PER CENT
OF TOTAL POSTAL COSTS
1926–65

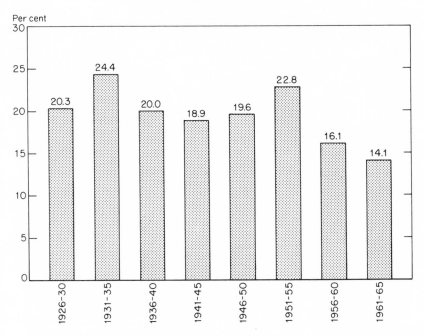

SOURCE: Same as Figure 2.

tion cost has been fairly stable, averaging just under 94 per cent for the last forty years.

Capital spending by the Post Office was almost exclusively on new *buildings* prior to 1920. After 1920 the Post Office began investing in trucks and other vehicles for moving the mail, but prior to 1945 the Post Office spent virtually nothing on *mechanization and equipment* for handling the mail.

Since 1945 spending for mechanization has increased, but it still represents a small percentage compared with other industries. In the last 14 years, for example, mechanization and equipment spending has accounted for just about 1 per cent of total expenditures, as Figure 4 shows. Spending on mechanization is low either because the capital equipment presently available does not yield many worthwhile economies, or because Post Office management has little incentive to install

FIGURE 4

MECHANIZATION AND EQUIPMENT AS A PER CENT
OF TOTAL POSTAL EXPENDITURES
1954–67

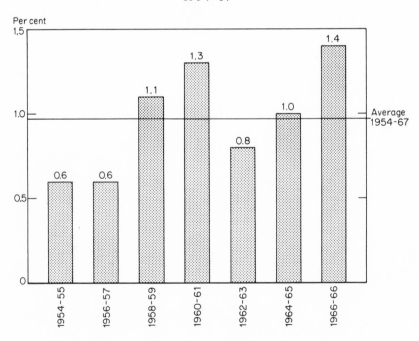

SOURCE: Internal data supplied by the U.S. Post Office Department.

cost-saving equipment.[9] Regardless of the reason, the Post Office shows no evidence of mechanizing at either a rapid or an expanding rate.[10]

Public protection of monopoly is usually predicated on the assumption that significant economies of scale exist out to and beyond the point of current operation. For the Post Office, however, the validity of this assumption appears to be somewhat dubious. Short-run marginal cost may be low for minimal increases in mail volume, but it appears that *marginal cost increases sharply with substantial increases in volume.* This is demonstrated each Christmas when the Post Office is temporarily forced (1) to authorize a significant amount of overtime at premium rates, and (2) to add untrained employees who at first are less productive than regular employees. The supervisory staff is not adequate to train or supervise so many new employees at once, and, by the time these added employees become trained, the Christmas season is over. Since labor accounts for 80 per cent of all postal costs, the increased unit-labor costs offset any savings that occur elsewhere in the system.[11] In view of the fact that postal technology is so labor-intensive, the fact that the short-run marginal cost curve is U-shaped should not be considered unusual or unexpected.[12]

Long-run cost behavior is more difficult to ascertain. Direct evidence on this question is unfortunately lacking. Productivity is known to vary between facilities, and as a general rule productivity is greater in smaller offices than in larger offices. But it is impossible to infer the long-run cost curve of the entire postal *system* from this sort of evidence. In the long run all costs are variable by definition and the Post Office is presumed able to adjust capital and labor in whatever way is

[9] The Post Office is said to have made a substantial number of pre- and post-mechanization cost studies which show that mechanization does not pay. It is not clear whether the results of these studies represent a shortcoming in technology, failure by management to capture potential cost savings, or simply poor techniques in estimating payoff from mechanization.

[10] Statements that Congress and labor unions have seriously impeded worthwhile mechanization appear to be inaccurate. This is not to deny that both groups wield important influence. However, to date Post Office management has not recommended any large-scale mechanization program for either of these two groups to thwart or resist.

[11] Other costs also rise at Christmas. For example, extra trucks are rented at higher short-term rates. It is not too important whether total "trucking" costs increase proportionately or less than proportionately with the increase in volume because they represent such a small part of the total costs.

[12] In a few of the most modern facilities it is said that short-run productivity increases (and marginal cost declines) with increases in volume. The number of facilities where this occurs is so few, and is expanding so slowly, however, that it does not affect the over-all conclusion concerning the entire postal system.

optimal for accommodation of increased mail volume. The question, therefore, is: Given an increase in mail volume and sufficient time to make all desired adjustments, what would the Post Office do and will the resulting unit cost be less than today's average cost? It turns out that the answer depends upon (1) the composition or *mix* of the increased volume, and (2) whether mail service will be allowed to decline or the current level of service will be continued.

For some insight into this problem of long-run cost, let us examine the behavior of postal costs along the program lines adopted in the planning-programing-budgeting (PPB) system. The programs and 1966 costs are shown in Table 7. The Post Office defines its programs along *functional* lines, as can be seen from Table 7. These functional cost categories provide a convenient way of assessing how long-run costs are likely to vary with changes in *workload* or *output of postal service*.

Acceptance, Category I, contains two principal activities: (1) selling stamps and (2) picking up mail along collection routes. Virtually all costs in the acceptance category are assignable to first class mail. For example, stamps are used almost exclusively on first class mail. Practically all mail picked up in collection boxes is first class since (1) mailers deliver all second class and all bulk third class mail directly to the loading dock, and (2) the public mails parcels at the Post Office

TABLE 7

1966 POST OFFICE COSTS, BY PROGRAM
CATEGORY

Program Category	Amount (millions of dollars)	Per Cent
I. Acceptance	510.5	9.1
II. Processing	1,542.7	27.5
III. Delivery	2,367.3	42.2
IV. Transportation	863.9	15.4
V. Other	325.3	5.8
Total	5,609.7	100.0

SOURCE: Percentage breakdown obtained orally from the Post Office Department and applied to total accrued cost figure found in *1966 Cost Ascertainment Report,* p. 16.

itself. To some extent acceptance costs do not vary with changes in workload. Only with large increases in first or fourth class mail by the general public, such as now occurs only during the Christmas season, would the Post Office find it necessary to increase window services in order to alleviate severe queuing problems.

Mail Processing, Category II, is composed solely of costs incurred *at major processing facilities.* These are usually sizable establishments in principal cities. The main post office in Chicago, for example, has about 15,000 full-time employees who do nothing but sort and process mail. In a major processing facility *originating mail* typically goes through the following distinct operations:

Operation	Mail Affected
1. Edging-stacking	"Loose" first and third class
2. Facing-cancelling	Nonmetered first and third class
3. Sorting	All mail not presorted and bundled by Zip code area

Despite all research and development efforts to date, mail processing in today's Post Office remains highly labor-intensive. Facing-cancelling is the only operation which has been more or less mechanized. Sorting of mail, which accounts for most of the costs in Category II, is done almost entirely by hand.[13] The principal capital costs associated with the sorting operation are (1) annual depreciation of the "cases," which probably amounts to between one and three dollars per man, and (2) the cost of the building itself. Observers have speculated that only Chinese agriculture is more labor-intensive.

Processing costs clearly vary with changes in workload. However, since so much second and third class mail is presorted and handled as bundles rather than as individual pieces, the extent of the variation in total processing cost will depend on the "mix" of any increased volume. But if the mix remains unchanged and the Post Office has to sort additional mail *with the same service now given existing mail,* then it is safe to say that processing costs will either increase proportionately or more than proportionately. In order to handle permanent increases in mail volume, the Post Office will have to hire additional workers, and additional facilities will also be required since major postal facilities are already jammed to capacity during peak periods.

---

[13] The chief exception is parcels, where various mechanical devices are employed to help speed the sorting operation.

Delivery, Category III, comprises about 42 per cent of all postal costs. Delivery cost is the only *common cost* of major significance in the postal system. Special interest groups such as second and third class mailers have focused attention on the relationship between workload and delivery cost. These groups traditionally maintain that the entire cost of delivery should be charged to first class mail on the grounds that delivery costs would be unchanged if there were no second or third class mail. In other words, they claim that delivery costs are not workload-related. But under no circumstances is their argument entirely correct.

A carrier is given eight hours to (1) sort and prepare for delivery of all mail on his route, (2) go from the Post Office to his route, (3) make delivery to all patrons on the route, and (4) return to the Post Office. Only items (2) and (4) can be treated as entirely invariant with regard to the amount of second and third class mail. On average, sorting and preparation of mail for final delivery require over two hours of a carrier's time. This part of a carrier's job is obviously workload-related, and the time which it requires will unquestionably increase as per capita mail volume increases. Similarly, the number of stops which a carrier must actually make will, on a statistical basis, increase as the per capita volume of mail in the system increases. It is undoubtedly true that delivery costs do not vary proportionately with increases in the volume of mail handled, but neither are they totally invariant.

Available data are sparse, but on net balance it is reasonable to assume that the delivery portion of the postal system exhibits some economies of scale. That is, if the volume of mail for delivery over the existing route structure increased, delivery costs probably would not increase proportionately. Where carriers do not have a full load, the cost of increased mail is chiefly the additional time required to sort and prepare it for delivery. But as over-all volume increases, a point is reached where a carrier cannot sort or deliver any more. Then, given to time to adopt long-run alternatives, the Post Office can make various adjustments, each of which involves some increase in costs.

Increase the number of trucks depositing mail at storage boxes along the carrier's route; or

Shorten existing routes; or

Supply the mailman with a vehicle (or a bigger vehicle).

Thus long-run delivery costs are a function both of workload and the total number of patrons for which delivery service must be provided.

TABLE 8

POST OFFICE PAYMENTS TO COMMON CARRIERS

FOR TRANSPORTATION, 1966

	Amount (thousands of dollars)	Per Cent
Railroad service	317,109	46.3
Airmail service:		
Domestic	96,312	14.1
International	106,322	15.5
Water service:		
Domestic	4,545	0.7
International	10,585	1.5
Star Route service	115,035	16.8
Other	34,748	5.1
Total	684,656	100.0

Source: U.S. Post Office, *Cost Ascertainment Report,* Washington, D.C., 1966.

Transportation, Category IV, is composed of (1) all costs of transferring mail (bundling, loading, unloading, etc.) from one processing facility to another and (2) payments to common carriers. The first functions are related directly to workload, and their cost will vary proportionately with changes in the volume of mail.

A breakdown of 1966 payments to common carriers is shown in Table 8. Payments to some carriers vary directly with the amount of mail shipped, but others do not. Airlines are usually paid on the basis of ton-miles shipped; hence this portion of transportation cost varies directly with weight and distance. But domestic airmail service accounted for only 14 per cent of all carrier payments.[14] In 1966 almost half of all carrier payments were still being made to the railroads. Bulky items such as parcels, magazines, catalogs and circulars figured heavily in this railroad traffic. Payments to railroads are sometimes variable (as occurs when the Post Office pays by the linear foot for a partial carload), but frequently they are semivariable (this occurs when the Post Office rents the entire car). Regardless of whether the

[14] Air carriers will receive a somewhat larger portion as all long distance first class mail is shifted to airlift.

Post Office rents entire railcars or pays by the linear foot, it buys rail services on a "cube basis," not on a weight basis. Thus when railcars are less than full the Post Office can handle additional mail at no additional transportation cost. In the absence of any data or studies on economies of scale in the transportation function, one can only speculate. It is my suspicion, however, that if all "lumpiness" occasioned by these semivariable or semifixed costs were smoothed out on a cost-quantity diagram, the resulting curve would show that payments to private carriers for transportation exhibit either slight economies or constant returns to scale for the entire postal system.

Looking beyond the postal system, extra mail may increase social costs somewhat less as more of our existing transportation capacity is utilized. In this event, however, virtually all savings (if any) arising from this source would accrue to the airlines and railroads, and would not be reflected in the Post Office's cost function.

LONG-RUN COST BEHAVIOR: SUMMARY. The preceding review of the behavior of various categories of postal costs, summarized in Table 9, enables some inferences to be drawn about the extent of economies of scale in the postal system. In the absence of better data, it seems reasonable to conclude that within the context of existing technology the postal production function exhibits some economies of scale. These economies do not result from any large-scale technology but simply from increasing the utilization of underutilized overhead

TABLE 9

LONG RUN COST BEHAVIOR IN THE POST OFFICE

Category	Per Cent of Total Cost	Extent of Economies of Scale
I. Acceptance	9	Significant
II. Processing	27	Probably none; perhaps slightly increasing costs
III. Delivery	42	Some
IV. Transportation	16	Probably none; perhaps a few
V. Other	6	Unknown; these costs mostly not workload-related
Total	100	Some, but not extensive

which must exist in order to provide service to the entire postal system. But such excess capacity as exists does not occur uniformly throughout the system. Excess capacity is most notable in delivery service to the less densely settled areas of the country. Also, residential carriers probably have some excess capacity, especially along delivery routes in the suburbs where there are no apartment houses. This result agrees generally with Baratz (1962, pp. 30–33), who has analyzed certain available data and has also conducted an extensive survey of the literature on this subject.

If the postal production function does not exhibit significant economies of scale, as surmised here, an important policy issue arises: Should the Private Express Statutes be repealed? Repeal would end the Post Office's monopoly on first class mail and would allow private firms to offer competitive mail service, if any firm so desired. A likely result of such repeal is that some large firms would carry their own intrafirm mail between plants and between cities. As noted previously, this form of private mail service is from time to time detected and stopped by postal authorities. In addition to this form of competition, private firms might also attempt to compete with the Post Office in and between major cities, especially on business delivery routes.[15]

Since all realizable economies of scale were reached long ago in the high density portion of the postal system, competition probably would not increase social costs. The Post Office admits to a 12 per cent profit on gross income from first class mail.[16] If this is true, *the return on*

[15] Private competition has been observed at various times in our history (especially in the 1840's, 1860's and 1930's), and on more than one occasion this competition has been instrumental in bringing about significant reductions in postal rates as well as increased service. For more detail see Kennedy (May 1957).

[16] Since 1926 the Post Office has regularly determined the cost of handling each class of mail, and the profit or loss on each class of mail, by means of the *Cost Ascertainment System* which allocates to the various classes of mail every cost of the Post Office, including the salary of the Postmaster General, his furniture, etc. In the Cost Ascertainment System costs are charged directly to the responsible class of mail wherever possible (such direct charges account for 17 per cent of total cost) and all other costs (83 per cent of total cost) are allocated on the basis of extensive samples taken during the year. Such fully-allocated costs are not useful for questions concerning incremental cost or economies of scale. Their usefulness for rate-making determinations is also dubious.

A better procedure would be to charge each class of mail with its direct costs *plus all traceable indirect costs,* leave all nontraceable costs in an unallocated overhead account, and then debate the extent to which each class of mail should cover its own cost and contribute to the unallocated overhead. For further discussion of the Cost Ascertainment System, see Kennedy (June 1957).

investment would be rather high since investment is so low. Hence private firms which efficiently catered only to the low cost portion of the market would probably prosper. Of course, if the Post Office suffered a substantial loss of its first class mail volume, the postal deficit would then increase further, at the expense of the general taxpayer. But there is no economic argument why first class mailers should subsidize other mailers. The likely outcome of allowing private firms to compete with the Post Office would thus be a number of income transfers, but not a marked change in social efficiency.[17] Competitive "waste" from duplicate postal services in major cities would probably be no greater than the "waste" involved in "duplicate" grocery stores in suburban neighborhoods. Over a long-run period consumer benefits from competition probably far exceed any short-term waste. Hence it would appear that on economic grounds the Private Express Statutes should be repealed.

Pricing for Economic Efficiency

If we assume that all benefits of the postal system are appropriable either to mailers or addressees, then, with the usual Pareto Model as a yardstick, competitive prices should reflect the cost of the service rendered. The postal rate structure deviates from this norm in several significant ways. To appreciate better the deviations which exist, the postal system will be examined both by function and by class of mail. Let us begin with the functional approach.

ACCEPTANCE. As previously discussed, most of the expense associated with entering mail into the system is properly chargeable to first class mailers. But among first class mailers the Post Office spends considerably more providing acceptance service to some than to others. For many mailers, such as individuals and small firms, the Post Office incurs the cost of selling stamps and picking up mail from boxes all over the downtown and suburban areas. A great number of large first

---

[17] Private postal firms with strong economic incentives to reduce costs might very well bring about marked shifts in the postal production function. Certainly the production possibilities curve could not shift much less than it has over the last 200 years. As noted in the introduction, however, this paper treats all shifts in the production function as exogenous.

class mailers, though, put postage on their mail with a meter [18] and then truck it to the rear door of the post office. Mail delivered in this manner circumvents both the edging-stacking and facing-cancelling operations inside the post office and goes directly to the sorting area. Some large mailers may even presort all their "bulk" first class mail. They do this at little cost to themselves by having their computer address all pieces in one Zip code area before addressing mail to another Zip area. Mail arriving at the post office in this condition can go directly into mail bags for shipment to the office of final delivery.

Were postal rates established competitively, then any mailer following the above practices would almost certainly be "rewarded" with a discount commensurate with the cost which he saves the Post Office. Any such discount would of course be a positive inducement to large mailers to carry out those mail handling functions which they can do more efficiently than the Post Office. By not adopting a "bulk rate" for first class mail and instead charging everyone the same rate, the Post Office is not only practicing price discrimination, it is also missing an excellent opportunity to use the price system to reward and promote activity which would result in greater over-all social efficiency.

The efficiency gained from presorting is obvious, and the Post Office is very much aware of it. Note, for example, that the Post Office *requires* second class mail to be presorted and bundled by Zip code, and in order to induce bulk third class mailers to presort their mail, the Post Office uses the price system in exactly the manner advocated here for first class mail. That is, third class mail *not* presorted and bundled by Zip code is charged individual piece rates rather than the bulk rate. The *minimum* differential between the single piece rate and the bulk rate is 2.4 cents per piece (refer to Table 3 for more detail), a discount from the single piece rate of over 40 per cent. The differential between piece rates and bulk rates is so great it may even exceed the Post Office's additional cost of sorting individual pieces. This use of the price system is obviously effective—over 80 per cent of all third class mail was sent at the bulk rate in 1966 (see Table 4).

Inasmuch as the Post Office purports to be more of a benevolent monopolist than an exploitative monopolist, it is difficult to explain why it refuses to do more to encourage and reward metering, presorting and bundling of first class mail while at the same time it adopts

[18] It has been estimated that it costs the Post Office as much as fifty times more to take in revenue of, say, $500 million from sale of stamps than from postage meters.

such strong inducements in the third class rate structure. True, the Post Office is fond of claiming that it treats all first class mailers equally, and that the "individual citizen" is able to post a single letter for six cents, just the same as the large mailer. However, individuals can—and do—post single pieces of third class mail, but when this occurs the Post Office is rather callous about equal treatment or equal rights for the "individual citizen."

It is also interesting to note, incidentally, that the "equal treatment" attitude perpetrates a sort of myth (within the Post Office Department, at least) that all individuals do indeed pay exactly six cents for their stamps. This ignores the very obvious fact that a great number of six cent stamps are bought and then resold through vending machines in drug stores, hotels and elsewhere for more than six cents apiece. Clearly the public is willing to pay a price for the sort of convenience which the Post Office does not and cannot offer, but which certain entrepreneurs are willing to supply. The stamp resale market renders an important and valuable service to both the public and the Post Office by increasing the convenience and accessibility of stamps; yet the Post Office refuses to give official recognition to this fact by taking any action—such as offering discounts on large quantities of stamps which would encourage the practice.

PROCESSING. First class mail receives top priority in sorting and dispatching. This is as it should be, considering the premium paid by first class mailers.

Within second class mail it is interesting to observe that various publications receive two rather different levels of service, *regular* and *expedited handling* (the latter being so-called *red-tag* service), despite the fact that all "for-profit" publishers pay according to the same rate schedule. Red-tag service is given to newspapers, news magazines and other magazines considered to have "time-value." Newspapers alone account for about 38 per cent of all second class mail, and when this is added to the volume of news magazines, it results in about 50 per cent of all second class mail receiving expedited handling. Among all magazines a few thus receive priority handling and service equivalent to that given first class mail, but *at no extra cost* and despite the rather sizable loss which is attributed to second class mail. This priority service almost surely has direct out-of-pocket costs associated with it. An individual post office hires sufficient workers to enable it to process and dispatch on average all originating priority mail in time to meet established departure schedules for planes and trains. As the volume of priority mail increases, the number of workers necessary to process this mail within fixed time limits will also increase.

Expedited handling has other incremental costs, too. Second class mail receiving red-tag service is transported and sorted on railway post office (RPO) cars, along with first class mail (where RPO service still exists). RPO cars are now reputed to be the most expensive method of sorting and transporting mail in the entire postal system, and mail trains on high density runs such as New York-Washington have multiple RPO cars. If red-tag service were eliminated the Post Office could conceivably save money by reducing the number of RPO cars. It would appear that magazines receiving red-tag treatment are given a service which far exceeds the rate charged, much less its value. Were mail services offered competitively this sort of price-service combination would almost surely not exist.

Regular or nonpriority second class mail and all third class mail are sorted and processed only after preferential treatment has been given to priority mail. Under normal operating conditions most of this deferred mail is sorted and sent on its way within 24 hours after being received at the Post Office. From this point on the postal system does not subject such mail to any more intentional delays. This means that second and third class mailers receive substantial discounts from first class rates for only slight delays in processing.[19] In general, this "deferred service" is as *predictable* as first class or priority service (a very important point to many bulk mailers) and it is almost as good. Conceivably the discounts in the rate structure could reflect different elasticities of demand, but it is much more likely that second and third class rates are simply a result of political lobbying. There is no compelling reason why prices which achieve political equilibrium should be the same prices as those which achieve competitive equilibrium.

TRANSPORTATION. Virtually all ordinary first class mail which moves over 200 miles is now sent via "airlift" or "deferred air." For ordinary airmail the Post Office pays the airlines about 30¢ per ton-mile, and for airlift it pays about 18¢ per ton-mile. The essential

[19] This is not to say that mail should be intentionally delayed until the difference in service reflects the difference in rates charged. Planned delays of more than 24 hours would neither be desired by mailers nor practical for the Post Office. Major postal facilities are built to handle mail in a *flow,* and storage space is minimal throughout the entire facility. A deferred class of service with intentional built-in delays of more than 24 hours would probably increase the Post Office's cost by requiring additional storage space to be leased or constructed.

difference between ordinary airmail and airlift is that airlines can refuse to accept airlift mail if they have passengers or higher-paying air-freight, whereas the airlines are obliged to take all ordinary airmail on a first priority basis. Thus those mailers who pay the airmail premium receive *guaranteed* service whereas others take their chances. From time to time the two services will vary, but probably more than 80 per cent of all long-distance ordinary first class mail is delivered on the same day it would have been delivered had it been sent via airmail.

It is sometimes suggested that because of transportation costs the Post Office should charge more for long-distance first class letters. However, this suggestion ignores two important facts: (1) the cost of administering such a differential rate structure would probably be high; and (2) transportation is but a small percentage of the total cost of handling first class mail. This latter point can be readily illus-trated. Referring back to Table 4, note that in 1966 the average revenue per pound of airmail letters was $2.32. The Post Office paid the airlines about 37¢ per pound to send regular airmail from New York to San Francisco, or less than 15 per cent of the total revenue. Similarly, on ordinary first class letters the Post Office received on average about $1.81 per pound and it paid about 20¢ per pound (only 11 per cent of revenue) to airlift mail from New York to Los Angeles. For shorter distances, such as Chicago-Miami or Chicago-San Fran-cisco, the transportation cost would be less; and under the higher postal rates which went into effect in January 1968, these percentage figures will be reduced even further.

Third class mail, like first class mail, is charged a flat rate per piece regardless of distance shipped. Price discrimination is significantly greater in the third class category, however, since transportation costs account for a greater share of revenues. Referring to Table 4 again, the Post Office received about 33 cents per pound for regular bulk third class mail, which on a weight basis represents only 18 per cent of the amount received for regular first class mail. Although surface trans-portation cost is less than airlift, it is not 82 per cent less. Hence, the ratio of transportation cost to revenue is greater, which suggests that for bulk third class mail the Post Office should probably adopt a weight *and distance* rate schedule like those for second and fourth class mail. Such a rate schedule would be relatively easy and inexpen-sive to administer since under existing regulations all bulk third class mail is delivered to a loading dock for checking in by regular postal employees. If postal services were offered competitively, such a rate schedule would probably evolve in the natural course of events.

DELIVERY. Each day carriers sort and deliver all first, second and third class mail which they receive for the patrons on their routes. At this point in the system no mailer and no class of mail receives preferential handling. This is probably as it should be as there are no cost savings nor is there any other economic rationale for setting aside and delaying delivery of any mail once it is in the hands of the carrier, except on those rare occasions when a carrier has more mail than he can physically handle. Different patrons do, however, receive a marked difference in both the quantity and quality of delivery service. Business routes receive at least two deliveries a day, but all residential routes in the United States receive only one delivery a day.

Moreover, among the totality of residential routes *the cost and service given to various types of residences differ markedly.* Strange as it may seem, the Post Office has never established a set of residential delivery standards based on an equal-cost concept, on an equal-service concept, or on any other economic criterion. Mail is delivered direct to the door of many families, which is by far the most "luxurious" and expensive service provided by the Post Office. Houses in many older suburbs and in virtually all newer suburbs receive only curb delivery, which costs the Post Office considerably less than door delivery. And, in apartment houses, delivery service probably costs the Post Office less per customer than any other type of residential service. The cost differences are indeed striking. The Post Office may spend up to ten times more providing door service to an individual home than it spends delivering mail to a family living in an apartment house. Under competitive conditions where people pay according to value received, suburban families would probably receive some minimal level of service (curb delivery perhaps), and they would be charged a monthly or yearly fee for incremental service above the minimum. Mailers would pay only the postage required for "minimal delivery." Mailers probably do not care, after all, whether the addressee's mail is delivered to a curbside box or to his door, so long as it is delivered promptly to a location which is reasonably convenient and secure.

The suggestion to charge addressees for certain delivery services is not as novel as it may sound. Incremental pricing schemes which reflect differences in value rendered to individual customers are accepted as standard practice with our regulated monopolies. The telephone company, for example, provides "minimal" service with a standard black instrument. The customer pays extra for additional service in the form of color telephones, lighted dials, different shapes, pushbuttons, etc. In view of the political controversy generated by the sizable postal deficits in recent years, it is somewhat surprising that the Post Office has never been held accountable for not giving postal patrons a choice between door and curb delivery, with the customer paying an additional fee for the cost of the additional service. On occasion the National Association of Home Builders has mounted sizable campaigns to generate political pressure sufficient to force the Post Office to give more door delivery service in new suburbs. The Post Office has resisted these pressures, but an equally simple and more expedient way of dealing with such pressures would seem to be use of the price mechanism along the lines recommended here.

PARCEL POST. The preceding discussion of functions omitted any reference to fourth class mail because parcel handling is almost a separate subsystem within the over-all postal system. Parcels, because of their odd sizes, shapes and weight, are always sorted and handled separately from other mail. Long-distance parcels are usually shipped via rail on a space-distance basis, and in all major cities parcels are delivered by separate delivery trucks, independent of the regular route carrier. Only in small cities and on rural routes, which account for a small and declining percentage of all mail, are parcels delivered along with other mail. Because of the law which says that parcel post must be self-supporting, and because of competition from the private sector, the basic parcel post system is structured along fairly rational economic lines. Exceptions do exist, however. Congress has on occasion yielded to political pressure from private firms and placed some peculiar weight-size limitations on the parcels which the Post Office can handle.[20] These competitive restraints act chiefly to the detriment of the consumer and should probably be repealed.

Within the fourth class rate structure, substantial discounts are given to library and educational materials, books, records or catalogs on the ground that these items somehow promote the "public service" more than do other parcels. There is no apparent economic rationale whatsoever for these discounts, and in a competitive system they almost certainly would not exist. Among other things, these differential rates

[20] Small post offices (second, third and fourth class post offices) can accept larger and heavier parcels than can large (first class) post offices, despite the fact that they are less well-equipped to handle such parcels. The reason for this anomalous restriction is that Railway Express and United Parcel Service do not offer any parcel service to the smaller communities served by the smaller post offices, and Congress is reluctant to deprive these sparser areas of such service.

result in income transfers from retail book stores and record outlets to book clubs and record clubs which sell direct to consumers through the mail.[21]

FIRST, SECOND, AND THIRD CLASS MAIL. Mail with different handling characteristics, different costs and different priority requirements would receive differential treatment and pricing under competitive conditions. The interclass differentials in the current rate structure are based in part on such considerations, but more on the political power of the press and the lobbying ability of third class mailers, plus a "public value of information" concept which Congress attaches to dissemination of news and literature. To achieve competitive pricing most of these distinctions should be substantially reduced or totally eliminated.

Intraclass differentials in the second and third class rate structures also contain many noneconomic distinctions which are now enshrined with all the virtue which Congress and the Post Office Department accord to long-standing tradition. One major distinction is between *qualified nonprofit institutions* and ordinary private firms or individuals. Qualified nonprofit organizations are given sizable discounts in the name of "public service." One familiar result of this discount is the large volume of mail from nonprofit organizations soliciting gifts or donations. Under normal competitive conditions discounts on this type of mail would not exist. In fact, they probably would not even exist under conditions of regulated monopoly, since nonprofit institutions generally do not receive discounts on their telephone or light bills.

SUMMARY. The Post Office is a government agency occupying a monopolistic or quasi-monopolistic position. As one might expect, the postal rate structure reflects a number of significant departures from competitive pricing. Even after the shortcomings of the Cost Ascertainment System have been taken into account, it is fair to say that a great many mailers and addressees are not charged in proportion to the costs incurred on their behalf.

[21] The annual subsidy on this class of mail, based on the Cost Ascertainment System, is $63 million. An interesting study by McLaughlin (1968, p. 54), which is a pioneering attempt to apply cost-effectiveness analysis to the Post Office, points out that if one's primary interest is in promoting "culture," $63 million would have bought: "1. A 100 per cent increase in the number of books purchased annually by libraries, or; 2. Ten thousand elementary school teachers (an increase of 1 per cent over the current number), or; 3. Ten thousand four-year college scholarships (at $1,650 per year), or; 4. Sixty-six major symphony orchestras (an increase of 260 per cent)."

Generally speaking, first class mail is overpriced and most other mail is underpriced. On net balance, the total cost of mail service exceeds the revenues received by a substantial amount. The Post Office has yet to establish any experience with the new higher rate structure, which became effective in January 1968, but in 1967 total costs exceeded revenues by over 20 per cent.

Because the postal system is so widespread (every business firm and virtually every home in the country is both a sender and receiver of mail), the net result of a more allocative pricing system is difficult to calculate. A great number of income transfers would certainly result. But in addition it is almost certain that a pricing system which better reflected the cost differences occasioned by different types of mail would cause certain mailers to adopt practices which would result in greater social efficiency. It is true that the Post Office recognizes some of these potential efficiencies and attempts to achieve them either by regulation or by inducing large mailers to adopt socially desirable practices out of "good will." But adoption of a "competitive" rate structure would appear to be a far simpler and less expensive method of correcting any social inefficiencies associated with the postal system. Unfortunately, as so often occurs when resource allocation problems interact with Congress, competitive pricing does not draw much political support.

Externalities

The preceding discussion assumed that all benefits from postal service are distributed directly to individuals or organizations in proportion to the amount of mail they send or receive. This assumption needs critical examination.

For over 200 years postal service has tended to be a government monopoly in every country of the world. Why? Do governments confer postal monopolies on themselves primarily to raise money, or because postal systems contain some extensive externalities or public goods elements omitted from the previous discussion, or simply because of an historical tradition which has roots elsewhere? The answer to the first part of this question is straightforward. Governments do not run postal systems for purposes of indirect taxation because postal receipts rarely cover postal expenditures in any country of the world. Quite the contrary; the citizenry must generally be taxed to whatever extent is necessary to cover the postal deficit.[22]

Historical development is certainly one important factor in explaining our government postal monopoly. The British Post Office became a public monopoly in 1609 primarily in order that the government might control and censor all correspondence entering and leaving Great Britain.[23] The U.S. Post Office was patterned on the British model. But over the last 200 years, attitudes concerning government censorship of the mail have completely reversed. Both the U.S. and British Post Offices now go out of their way to accord complete privacy to first class mail. However, like the famous Cheshire Cat who disappeared but left his grin behind, the government monopoly remains long after the original rational disappears.

In addition to historical precedent, is there any economic rationale to help explain government ownership of the Post Office? Does the postal system, considered as a whole, contain some externalities or public goods elements which justify either government monopoly or the extensive subsidies which the Post Office receives? Indeed, in years past the Post Office has from time to time been used by Congress to promote various transportation programs generally regarded as possessing certain public good characteristics. The development of *Post Roads,* such as the old Boston-New York Post Road (which actually ran from Boston to Florida), was furthered by the Post Office. Less widely recognized but also true is the fact that Post Office pilots pioneered night flying. Later, after the Post Office switched to commercial airlines for its airmail requirements, Congress for many years used the Post Office as a convenient means of subsidizing air carriers in order to develop the industry. However, Post Office support of government-sponsored transportation programs is strictly historical. Within the Federal Government, responsibility for major support of all transportation programs except maritime now lies with the recently formed Department of Transportation and its constituent agencies.

Turning to the current postal deficit, which exceeded one billion dollars in 1966, one can inquire whether any portion of this is assignable to any generally recognized economic externalities. The postal deficit falls broadly into two categories: (1) subsidies or losses

---

[22] In some countries the postal system is operated in conjunction with other publicly run businesses, such as the telephone company, and profits from the telephone system are used to offset postal deficits.

[23] See Kennedy, May 1967, p. 94.

The Analysis of Public Output

attributable to *public service* as defined in the Postal Policy Act of 1958, and as amended in 1962; and (2) other revenue deficiencies not covered under the Postal Policy Act. Following these distinctions, the presentation of the postal deficit is usually based on (1) the Postal Policy Act and (2) the Cost Ascertainment System which, as previously mentioned, fully allocates all Post Office costs except those attributable to *public service*. A breakdown of the 1966 deficit is given in Table 10.

TABLE 10

THE 1966 POSTAL DEFICIT

(MILLIONS OF DOLLARS)

	Public Service[a]	Postal Deficit or Surplus
First class mail	—	116.3
Second class mail		
In county publications	67.2	—
Nonprofit and classroom publications	116.5	—
Regular publications	—	−236.3
Other, incl. controlled circulation	—	−9.9
Third class mail		
Single piece rate	—	−32.2
Bulk rate, regular	—	−269.5
Bulk rate, nonprofit	99.5	—
Fourth class mail		
Parcel and catalogs	—	−22.6
Special rate	75.2	—
Government mail	0.4	7.1
Free for the blind	2.9	—
International mail	0.3	−16.3
Special services (COD, insured mail, special delivery; money orders)	55.0	—
Nonpostal services for other agencies	24.5	—
Part of the cost of operating of rural post offices and rural routes	105.5	—
Deficit	547.0	462.4

SOURCE: 90th Congress, 1st Session, House Document No. 106, *Survey of Postal Rates,* Washington, D.C., April 17, 1967, p. 60.

[a] As defined in the Postal Policy Act of 1958, as amended in 1962.

Whenever one starts with the premise that all postal costs should somehow be allocated to the various classes of mail, then, regardless of whether one uses the Cost Ascertainment System or some other allocation system, any deficit will always be attributed to particular classes of mail.[24] Thus the second column of Table 10 assigns all of the regular operating deficit to the various classes of mail. And any other system which fully allocates all costs will inevitably make the deficit appear as a subsidy to one group of mailers or another. Hence any such system cannot reveal any evidence on the existence of public goods or external economies.

The *public service* portion of the deficit reflects all arguments accepted by Congress for subsidizing mail service. In the first column of Table 10 the various classes of mail have been assigned $362.0 million of the public service deficit, $79.5 million is assigned to special and nonpostal services, and $105.5 million is attributed to rural postal service. The $362.0 million deficit assigned to various classes of mail arises from knowingly and deliberately carrying certain mail at a discount from the general rate structure and below cost—that is, by accepting mail from various nonprofit institutions (an alumni magazine, for example) for less than similar mail from profit making organizations (an ordinary magazine, for example). The method of computing this part of the public service deficit has been sharply criticized, but the critics would simply shift part of the public service deficit to the other column in Table 10. Hence this portion of the public service deficit offers no evidence of public goods or externalities. It simply reflects subsidies or transfer payments, paid for by the general taxpayer, to those mailers whom Congress feels it is in the public interest to subsidize.

It can be argued that the various institutions to which Congress has given postal subsidies in the public interest—for example, schools, libraries and churches—create a variety of nonmarket benefits which far exceed any subsidy which they receive from the Post Office. But questions of whether these institutions deserve to be subsidized by the government, or the extent to which they deserve to be subsidized, or whether they should be subsidized directly instead of via the Post Office, are not relevant to a discussion of whether the postal system itself contains any externalities or public goods. That is, the postal system cannot be presumed to contain any elements of public goods

---

[24] Thus when one's concern is with externalities, the usual technical criticisms of the Cost Ascertainment System are not relevant to the discussion, as these almost always aim simply at reallocating total cost. For this reason these criticisms will not be discussed here.

just because it serves customers which may exhibit such characteristics.

This conclusion also applies to two other items shown in Table 10: "Special services" and "Nonpostal services for other (government) agencies." Any deficit attributable to these two items reflects transfer payments to the mailers or users involved, and not external economies or public goods inherent in the postal system itself.

One major item in Table 10 not related to "class of mail" is the public service cost of operating rural post offices and rural routes. This item arises in part because the Post Office has from time to time proposed that a number of rural post offices be closed and equal service be provided by alternative means but at substantially lower cost. It is not known whether such moves could or would reduce costs by the amount shown in Table 10. This item appears in Table 10 in part because Congress has resisted this "efficiency approach" and has instead substituted the "public service" concept. Hence, part of the public service deficit attributed to this item is something of an "employment subsidy" for rural postmasters, and not a public good.

The other part of the deficit under this item is attributed to delivery service on sparsely settled rural routes. At the present time the Post Office gives delivery service along rural roads which average three patrons for each two miles. When the density is less than this, then anyone wishing to have his mail delivered must erect a mailbox along the nearest road which has delivery service. In this connection it should be noted that under current delivery standards the Post Office makes no attempt to carry mail to the property line of every rural patron. Nevertheless, it does deliver mail in areas where the population is relatively sparse, and it is generally acknowledged that the cost of this delivery service exceeds any reasonable assignment of the revenues received from such mail.

Were we to depend solely on competitive firms to supply postal service, it is reasonable to assume that rural areas would either receive less service than now, or else they would be forced to pay more for the existing level of service. It is also reasonable to assume that as the population density of rural areas increases above the minimum required for delivery service, the cost of providing such service will also increase, but far less than proportionately.[25] That is, there are probably substantial economies of scale associated with rural delivery service along existing routes. In a sense, then, rural postal service,

[25] Conversely, as the rural population continues to decline, this will probably have an adverse effect on the Post Office's attempts to reduce its deficit.

which is a small and declining portion of the total postal system, exhibits a characteristic associated with a "mixed" public good.

In conclusion, the vast majority of the postal system does not exhibit the usual characteristics associated with public goods. For example, if existing users attempt simultaneously to increase their consumption of mail service, total postal costs will rise substantially. Similarly, if new users or patrons are added to the system, costs will also rise. And postal services can be extended or withheld from patrons on an individual basis should there be any reason or desire to do so. Only in delivery service to rural areas are economies of scale so large as to approach on rare occasion a pure public good. Whether this part of the system justifies the extensive monopoly given the Post Office is a moot question indeed.

Addendum: The Report of the President's Postal Commission

The Commission's report, including the four appendices published separately (hereafter, the "Report"), was released too late for systematic referencing and integration into this paper. However, a few observations and comparisons will be given here.

In terms of coverage, the Report treats all major topics discussed in this paper and it covers several other subjects as well. By far the most important problem studied in the Report—and omitted here—is the possibility of downward shifts in the cost curve through greater technological and managerial efficiency. Regarding this subject, the Commission concludes that existing management procedures are unduly cumbersome and complex, particularly rate-setting and construction of major new facilities. The Report estimates that total cost of the existing postal system could be reduced by as much as 20 per cent through greater efficiency resulting from improved management procedures. Based chiefly on this finding the Commission strongly recommends changing the Post Office from a government agency to a government-owned corporation.

The Report contains a large amount of useful data, much of it being the result of original surveys done by private contractors. Both this study and the Report draw, of course, on the same basic data or observed "facts." Hence, many observations or conclusions are similar. Thus:

1. Business firms are the chief source of mail, but the Report also gives data showing that the household sector is the major recipient.
2. Demand for postal services is generally price-inelastic.
3. The Post Office should be regarded principally as a business-type enterprise, which collects revenues and gives services for the fees charged. The Commission recognizes that some types of mail— notably news media—may deserve subsidization in the "public interest." However, the Commission did not recognize or endorse any public goods arguments concerning the postal system.
4. Labor costs dominate all other factors involved in the supply of postal services. Moreover, and regardless of what one may have read concerning new postal machinery, the Commission concludes as I do, that the Post Office gives no evidence of modernizing or automating at a rate which will significantly alter the capital-labor ratio in the foreseeable future.
5. Rate schedules should be substantially revised, and in the general directions indicated here. The Commission recommends that rates be based more on economic criteria and less on political considerations. It should be noted, however, that although the Report makes a number of rather specific observations concerning the adequacy or inadequacy of various rates, the Report says nothing about charging addressees or patrons who regularly receive a level of delivery service which costs substantially more than alternative forms of adequate delivery service (e.g., door delivery instead of curb delivery).

Finally, the reasoning which leads the Commission to favor continuation of the existing postal monopoly is worth commenting on, inasmuch as the Report and this study reach opposite conclusions on the basis of many similar observations or assumptions:

a. Despite the inadequacies of the Cost Ascertainment System, the Report acknowledges that delivery to central business areas is "low cost" and that the Post Office earns a substantial "profit" or contribution to overhead on this part of the system. The Report accepts the conclusion that if it were not for the Private Express Statutes vigorous competition would most likely arise in this area. (The Report refers to such competition as "cream-skimming.")
b. Although not stated explicitly, the Report appears to recognize that present mail volume long ago passed the point of discernible

economies of scale in downtown or central business delivery areas. Thus the Report does not appear to disagree with my conclusion that in such districts one or more competitors could coexist with no significant decrease in social efficiency.

c. A survey taken by one of the Commission's contractors indicates that many large business firms would prefer to have available, and would be willing to pay a premium for, a particular type of mail service not now offered—labeled by the Report "urgent"— and which would virtually guarantee next-day delivery. Similarly, for "non-urgent" first class mail (of which there appeared to be quite a bit) these same mailers would prefer a lower rate over "next day delivery." Thus this survey indicates that many large mailers would prefer to have first class mail offer different price-service options rather than attempt to achieve next-day delivery for *all* first class mail.

d. The Report acknowledges that large postal facilities are generally overcrowded, sometimes grossly. These facilities are probably operating at a point of increasing marginal cost. Moreover, the Report implies that given the 10-year period now required to plan and construct major new facilities, this situation is likely to get considerably worse before it improves. Effective competition would alleviate this overcrowding and could thus increase over-all economic efficiency. Moreover, effective competition might result in more innovation in the means by which mail is processed (it is certainly unlikely that competition will lead to any less innovation than in the past!).

e. As noted previously, the Report and I agree that repeal of the Private Express Statutes would most likely result in competition in and between the major central business districts. Moreover, we also agree that private firms are not likely to offer much competition in rural or suburban areas where the Post Office has some element of "natural monopoly." Instead of competing, private carriers would most likely use the Post Office to deliver any such mail which found its way into their delivery systems. Thus the Report and this study both conclude that private firms would have little incentive to increase social costs by competing inefficiently and uneconomically.

f. In those central business areas where private firms would most likely compete, the Report and I both agree that the private firms would attempt to offer large mailers lower rates or more desirable service on first class mail. Moreover, we both agree that the Post Office could possibly lose a substantial part of this segment of first class mail. Many large mailers could be expected to switch from the Post Office to private firms because they would receive a preferred service, or lower cost. The Report acknowledges that private firms are likely to capture enough of this business (i) to make it financially rewarding for them, and (ii) to affect significantly and adversely the revenues of the Post Office.

g. The Report and I both agree that competition would reduce or eliminate much of the contribution to overhead now paid by large first class mailers. In turn, this will either increase the postal deficit or it will force rate increases on those classes of mail which continue to use the Post Office in preference to private carriers.

Thus, while the Report and this study agree on the seven foregoing points, considerations of social efficiency and concern for consumer preferences lead me to favor repeal of the Private Express Statutes whereas concern over financial viability of the Post Office leads the Commission to favor retention of almost all of the existing postal monopoly.

References

1. Baratz, Morton S., *The Economics of the Postal Service,* Washington, D.C., 1962.

2. Kennedy, Jane, "Development of Postal Rates: 1845–1955," *Land Economics,* Vol. 33, pp. 93–112.

3. ———, "Structure and Policy in Postal Rates," *Journal of Political Economy,* Vol. 65, June 1957, pp. 185–208.

4. U.S. Post Office Department, *Cost Ascertainment Report,* Washington, D.C., 1966.

5. Report of the President's Commission on Postal Organization, *Towards Postal Excellence,* Washington, D.C., June 1968.

6. McLaughlin, John Francis, "Analyzing Benefits of a Postal Subsidy: Special Fourth-Class Rate Mail," *Massachusetts Institute of Technology,* May 1968, unpublished term paper.

COMMENT

by WILLIAM M. CAPRON
Harvard University (formerly with the Brookings Institution)

Those of us who have applauded the recent "push" to build systematic analysis into the process of government decision making, which many of us feel is at the core of the effort begun in 1965 to establish a planning-programing-budgeting system on a governmentwide basis, are grateful that there is a Post Office Department. At least this is true of those of us who have been actively engaged in promoting this effort to improve the kind and quality of information available to those who must make decisions on government policies, programs, and budgets.

The reasons those interested in promoting the use of analysis are glad that postal service is a federal activity lies in the fact that, at least at first glance, this seems to be an activity which is sold to users in the market place and in which there are not significant externalities, with all, or almost all, of the benefits accruing to the individual users of the service. As a result the analyst does not have to grapple with formidable problems of social benefit estimation. Nor need he be concerned in a major way with income redistribution.

Not only does the "payoff" side of the analysis of the Post Office operation look to be relatively straightforward, but the production function seems to be susceptible of measurement and specification. Thus the analyst can hope to come up in relatively short order with "hard" analyses which can point to specific improvements in the operation of this federal activity. And for those interested in establishing the credibility and usefulness of a widespread application of systematic analysis, some quick payoff applications are very welcome. It is no secret that there are legions of skeptics throwing cold water at the corporal's guard of PPBS enthusiasts.

Alas, it turns out that my statement above that the benefit estimation problems are simple and straightforward is an overstatement. As Mr. Haldi's paper reminds us, the Congress has traditionally used the postal service as a device to subsidize activities considered to be in the public interest. Rather than providing direct subsidies to defray distribution costs of newspaper, magazine, and book publishers—to say nothing of junk mail advertisers—the Congress has chosen to "jigger" the rates charged to certain classes of mail and groups of users. The result, as Haldi makes clear, is that rates and costs in some cases bear little relationship to each other. Moreover, since useful analysis requires that we recognize that the Post Office is not producing a single service, but several distinct services, in an important way this is a case of joint production and we are faced with a difficult problem of cost allocation. Those familiar with business cost and production function analysis will not need to be told that joint production poses a serious challenge to the analyst.

I thoroughly agree with Mr. Haldi's implication that the public would be much better served if the Post Office could rationalize its pricing structure to a "competitive" basis. Regarding the subsidy issue, there are three separate questions which need to be faced in this connection and it is important to distinguish each from the others: First, should an activity be subsidized in order to achieve some legitimate public purpose? Second, if so, should the subsidy be in the form of below-cost mail service? And, third, if we answer "Yes" to both of the foregoing questions, should the subsidy come from the general taxpayer via the appropriation process, or from other users of mail service via below-cost prices to the nonsubsidized user and above-cost prices to other users? I am prepared to accept a "Yes" answer to the first question above with regard to at least some mail service users now subsidized. I am skeptical that a persuasive case can be made for a "Yes" answer to the second question, though tradition is so strong that subsidy of *distribution* cost of an activity may have to be accepted. But, on the third question, it seems very hard indeed to believe that some users of mail service should subsidize others. In other words, *if* we are to subsidize some postal users, as an economist I am certain that this should be done out of general Treasury funds—though I will be forced to qualify this view below.

I have no quarrel with Mr. Haldi's identification of the many anomalies in the present structure of postal rates, and the inefficiencies which this structure encourages and abets. At least conceptually—if not politically—the present rate structure could be rationalized so that there was a correspondence for particular users between what they pay and the costs incurred in providing that service, while maintaining the Post Office as a regular department of government. However, a Presidential Commission which is to report shortly has been investigating the possibility of transforming the Post Office Department into a public corporation—or the creation of some other organizational format which will free the postal service from annual and detailed Congressional appropriation and oversight and give management a good deal of discretion. From a practical standpoint I hope that the Commission recommends such a change, for I think there are at least two important advantages which *might* be gained by such an institutional modification. In the first place, the corporation and its management might be (and should be, in my view) given the authority to proceed with the rationalization of the postal rate structure, discussed above.

In connection with the recommendation of the Kappel Commission that the Post Office be reorganized as a government corporation under which management would have far more discretion, I need to enter a *caveat* to my previous discussion of the subsidy issue. Although I still believe that, conceptually, subsidies should come from general Treasury funds, I must recognize that there may be an overriding institutional-political argument to the effect that if the subsidy is relatively small (it is suggested by some that the subsidy amounts to a small percentage of total cost) and if we can gain a good deal of freedom for the management of the postal service by an institutional arrangement which takes the postal system out of the annual Congressional appropriation process, then it *may* be worth paying the price of requiring the rates to reflect price discrimination in favor of those classes of users the Congress deems deserving of subsidy. But I wouldn't pay this price if (1) the subsidy were significant (from either the subsidizers' or subsidized view) *or* (2) if Congress insisted on setting the absolute level of rates to be charged subsidized users. (The alternative, which might be acceptable, would be a Congressional determination that the subsidy be a certain fixed percentage of cost of providing the service, leaving management free to set the over-all structure and level of rates within this constraint.) This point is an illustration of the need, which sometimes faces us, to depart from the dictates of sound economic analysis in order to gain important institutional and procedural changes, given the facts of the workings of our political processes. In other words, some sacrifice of the niceties of economic reasoning may be necessary to make much more important economic gains possible.

The second potential gain from the creation of a more independent and autonomous institution to run the postal service is that the management might be in a position to achieve substantial economies through improvement in the production process, and they might be somewhat better able to resist—where resistance is appropriate—

the demands of the postal workers union. It is a commonplace in Washington to note that that union has one of the best track records on the lobbying circuit between the Capitol and the White House. A side effect of the present political coupling of Congressional decisions with regard to civil service pay rates with postal worker pay rates has meant that it has been politically much more difficult to achieve the kind of adjustment of civil service pay scales necessary to attract and retain the kind and quality of people necessary to discharge effectively federal responsibilities.

My one serious question about Mr. Haldi's analysis lies in his suggestion that we might actually transform the postal service into a competitive market. He seems to me to give a qualified endorsement to repeal of the Private Express Statutes, which "would end the Post Office's monopoly on first class mail and allow private firms to offer competitive mail service." He bases this position on his conclusion— again carefully qualified—that economies of scale are not significant in the production of the postal service. It seems to me possible that Mr. Haldi has gone astray because, in his attempt to estimate (or at least infer) the shape of the long-run cost curves, he has confined himself to costs borne by the Post Office itself. Before I can agree with him that a competitive market structure would not introduce significant inefficiencies, from society's standpoint, I think we need to consider the *total* cost functions involved in the sending, receipt, and "assimilation" of materials distributed through the postal system. And this requires that we look not only at Post Office Department costs involved in the system but also at costs borne by users. Moreover, he has not yet persuaded me that the scale economies *internal* to the Post Office are minor. Haldi does recognize, for example, that there are "some" scale economies in connection with the delivery function. I suspect that if one considered business firms and individuals who receive mail and the cost to them the "some" would be "somewhat" larger. Do we really want three, four, or more "mail deliveries" coming to our doors? While obviously postal service is nothing like telephone service in that there is not the same compelling requirement that we all be (literally) wired into the same system, nonetheless it seems to me that there are real "convenience" advantages—which translate into cost advantages—in having a single postal delivery service at least for first class mail. It is worth noting in this connection that estimates have been made which indicate that we today do pay a price for supporting a system of competitive home milk deliveries. The advantages of competition in this case may outweigh the added

costs of several milk trucks traveling down each street. And the customer has the option of performing the delivery function himself by purchasing milk at the grocery store. At least for local mail delivery, the customer also has this option—one that few select since, even today's relatively inefficient mail system does provide a service at very low price "per unit."

I also wonder if senders of mail, and particularly business firms (which as Haldi points out are the dominant consumers of mail service), would not suffer increased costs if they were sending their outgoing mail through a number of separate postal services (e.g., bulk mailing with Zip code sort would be more cumbersome and produce smaller gains in efficiency). Of course, it is possible to conceive of an industry structure of a number of local monopolies for each kind of service. But such a system would certainly add something to total costs, if for no other reason than that a fairly elaborate system of recordkeeping would be necessary in order to keep track of transactions among these local monopolies. Moreover, it is not at all clear to me that a system of decentralized local monopolies is really going to have the competitive incentives to improve service and reduce costs at which the Haldi proposal is aimed at achieving.

Thus it seems to me at least possible that the economies of scale in the total system are a good deal more significant than those Mr. Haldi finds internal to the Post Office Department (even if we accept his judgment that internal scale economies are modest). I should hasten to add that I am perfectly willing to accept a suggestion that there may be much more room for the private and competitive provision of certain specialized services now provided by the Post Office Department. We already have a real-life example of this in the shipment of packages. The parcel post system does face competition from private firms (or "rivalry," if one is a purist about the term "competition"). Indeed, in this instance one questions the way the Congress has tied the hands of the Post Office Department, limiting the size of package it may accept in the parcel post system. I would be willing not only to see these restrictions dropped so that the rivalry between the Post Office, on the one hand, and United Parcel, Railway Express, etc., could be given freer rein, but I would be willing to see the Private Express Statutes repealed or at least drastically modified so that private firms could attempt to enter various parts of the total postal service market. But, as I speculated above, I am not at all sure that such entry would be very effective or widespread *if the Post Office Department (or a public corporation taking its place) is per-*

mitted to adjust its rates to reflect the costs of various types of service.
My disagreement with Mr. Haldi is not flatfooted. Postal service is
certainly not like telephone service (as I noted above), in that in the
case of postal service there is not a clear-cut and dominant public
interest in having a single interlinked system (forced by the technology
and economies of the system), and I recognize together with Mr.
Haldi that competition increases the possibility that innovations will
be developed which would provide better and more efficient postal
service.

Before I close let me note the recent report by the British National
Board for Prices and Incomes on post office charges.[1] One is struck
by the strong similarities between the British and American postal
systems. For example, the distribution of costs among the various
functions seems to be very much the same in the two countries, and
they are also wrestling with an irrational rate structure. In fact, the
report was undertaken in response to a proposal by the Postmaster
General that rates be increased *and* modified. The specific modification
proposed is the establishment of a "two-tier letter service." The
present British first class mail system recognizes two categories, defined
on the basis of *contents,* not quality and speed of service. Printed
matter (e.g., newspapers, magazines, etc.) is handled at a much lower
rate than letters. Under the new proposal, first class mail of whatever
content will get priority handling (e.g., delivery virtually guaranteed
the day after posting anywhere in the country) while second class
material may be deferred. The major rationale for this shift will
sound very familiar to anyone who has read Mr. Haldi's paper: it is
expected that the two-tier system will permit a smoothing-out of the
work load over the twenty-four hour period, significantly reducing
the present requirement for nighttime—i.e., premium pay—work.

It is my understanding that the British report was written, at least
in part, by an economist known to many of us—Ralph Turvey. I
think those who know Turvey will agree that this suggests that the
report deserves a careful reading. I was therefore struck by one of the
findings of this study because it buttresses a question that I wish to
put to Mr. Haldi: Because of the "joint product" character of producing postal services, how reliable are the presently available attempts
to allocate costs by function and by type of service? The British report
questions the usefulness for decision purposes of the very meticulous

[1] *Post Office Charges,* Report No. 58, National Board for Prices and Incomes,
March 1968, Her Majesty's Stationery Office, London, Great Britain.

and exhaustive allocation of costs currently made by the British Post Office on the grounds that there are enough joint costs and overhead elements involved to suggest that the allocation of total costs can only be done by rather arbitrary rule-of-thumb techniques (e.g., in the British case the salary of the Postmaster General is completely allocated to the various services and functions). The specific issue is the relevance of the cost allocations to decisions about *pricing policy* (e.g., a system of cost allocation designed for *cost control* by management may not be useful for pricing decisions, especially in a joint production situation).

I began by suggesting that those of us who hope to see systematic analysis more widely used in illuminating public decisions welcomed the existence of the postal service as a federal function because it at least seemed to offer a set of problems more directly and immediately susceptible to the kinds of analysis we economists think we know how to do. And I think that this expectation is supported to a degree by Mr. Haldi's paper and some of the work which I understand has been done in the Post Office Department over the last couple of years—when this output is compared with the typical run of the Program Memoranda and analyses produced by other agencies. (It is not accidental that some of that work has been useful and good nor that Mr. Haldi chose this subject for his paper: he was instrumental in aiding the Postmaster General and his key associates in understanding the value of, and in beginning to use, analysis.) However, the honesty and modesty with which he presents this paper indicate that even in the case of Post Office activity problems of data availability and of analysis are formidable and that much hard work is still to be done. His paper also underlines the pervasive importance of the institutional, political, and "social value" environment and the need for the analyst to understand this environment if his work is to be relevant.

INDEX

Acceptance costs, 358–359, 364–366

Accessibility
and highway construction, 87–88
and public projects, 90

Accident costs. *See* Highway accidents, costs of

Accident rates. *See* Highway accidents

Ad hoc sample surveys, in cost analysis data, 254–255

Ad hoc "ticketing" system, 254

Adaptive responses to demoralization costs, 119–120, 119n, 126
aggressive, 119, 123n

Administrative costs of compensation payments, 121–122, 125–126, 131, 135

Administrative structure
errors in cost estimates related to, 289, 297, 301t–302t
of Post Office, 341

Advisory Task Force on CATV. *See* Task Force

Aerospace industry, cost analysis in, 261–262

Air carriers, 361n

Air Express, 353

Air pollution, 215
caused by public projects, 88, 92
and equilibrium, 14
federal government control of, 213–214
See also Environmental changes caused by public projects

Air traffic control system, production functions of, 223

Aircraft, problems in cost analysis of, 248, 258–261

Airmail, 367–368

Allocation. *See* Resource allocation

Altouney, Edward G., 268, 268n, 275, 275n, 286–287, 287n, 315n

Antisubmarine warfare system. *See* ASW system, cost analysis of

Appraised value. *See* Property value

Army Corps of Engineers. *See* Corps of Engineers

Arrests, as output measure, 46

Arrow, Kenneth, 126n

Asher, Harold, 258n

ASW system, cost analysis of, 247–249

Attributability test, 94, 96t–97t

Automobile industry, "launching costs" of, 258n

Automobile insurance, alternate forms of, 332–334. *See also* Automobile insurance costs

Automobile insurance costs
and decision making process, 329–330
determination of, 330–331
and highway accidents, 318–319, 328

Baltimore, relocation study in, 75, 83–85, 103

Baltimore Highway Project, 69n

Baltimore Urban Design Concept Team, 69n

Baratz, Morton S., 351n, 363

Bargaining
for collective goods, 214
costless, 7, 7n
and game theory, 8–9
in perfectly competitive price system, 5
unrestricted, 8–9
See also Bargaining costs

Bargaining costs
and game theory, 7n
and monopoly, 6
and Pareto efficiency, 10–12
See also Bargaining

Benefits of public improvements, 90–91

Bergson, Abram, 128n

Berry, Brian J. L., 144n

Bicyclists, highway accidents and, 318

Black power separatism, 216

Bloc-grant schemes, 139
Boucher, W. I., 232n
Bower, Blair, 267n
Braybrooke, D., 219n
Break, George F., 176n
"Break-even point," 235
Breton, Albert, 143n, 210, 210n, 218n
British National Board for Prices and Incomes, 386
British Post Office, 373, 386–387
Brock, William, 139n
Buchanan, James M., 120n, 128n, 140–141, 141n, 145n, 153n, 161
Bulk mail, 343, 349–350
Bundy report, 185
Bureau of the Census, 163ff
   study of relocated households, 77–78, 102
Bureau of Reclamation, 269
   causes of increases in project costs, 308t
   errors in estimating costs of, 275, 276t, 277
      compared with other water resource agencies, 277–281
      and decision making methods, 288, 290
      distribution of, 309t, 315n
      and project size, 287
      proximate causes of, 283–284
Bureaucracies
   and data collection, 225
   growing demands upon, 217
   partisan adjustment among, 224
   and suboptimization, 226n
Business firms
   and mail services, 379
   and public project construction, 80, 88, 90
   uncompensated losses of, 107
   See also Residential and business location model

Cable television, 117
California, automobile accidents in, 322t–323t, 324, 325n, 327n
Campbell, Alan K., 175n
Capacity, excess, 363

Capital spending by Post Office, 356–357
Capital-labor substitution in Post Office, 341
Census Bureau. See Bureau of the Census
Central place theory, 144, 144n
Centralization, 182, 210, 211
   and collective decision making, 32–35
   and World Trade Center Problem, 133–134
   See also Decentralization
Chase, S. B., Jr., 108n
Christaller, Walter, 144, 144n
Christian Science Monitor, 353
Churches. See Community facilities
Cities
   exploitation by suburbs of, 66–67
   in federalism model, 144
   role of local government in problems of, 31
   shortage of low-cost housing in, 76
   See also City planners; City services
City planners
   and public projects, 99
   and World Trade Center problem, 118–119
City services, suburban consumption of, 67
Civil costs, in government expenditure estimates, 168
Coase, Ronald, 122n
Collective action, 4, 18–20. See also Collective decision making system; Decentralization
Collective decision making system
   efficiency of, 64
   establishment of, 32–35
Collective goods. See Public goods
Collective redistributive function, 36–43
Colorado River Storage Project, 275, 277, 283
Committee for Economic Development, 215
Commodities. See Public goods
Common carriers, Post Office payments to, 361t

Community facilities, effects of public projects on, 87, 111
Community values, uncompensated loss of, 128
Commuting costs, effect of public projects on, 82–83
Compensation
  criteria for paying, 137–138
  for demoralization costs, 119–128
  determination of amount of, 92–95, 96*t*–97*t*, 98, 112–113, 131
  to displaced renters, 77–78
  failure to pay. *See* Uncompensated losses
  for highway accidents, 328–329, 335
  "imperfect," 124
  and justice, 107–108
  for losses due to home financing arrangements, 109–110
  and losses offset by benefits of public improvements, 90–91
  and pricing signals, 134
  for relocation costs, 75–78
  and risks of property ownership, 91–92
  and "simple" net gains, 126*n*
  for spillover costs of television interference problem, 134–135
Compensation laws, basic principle of, 70
Competition, Post Office efficiency and, 352–354, 363–372, 379–380, 382–386
Competitive equilibrium, 3, 5
Conrad, A. F., 318*n*
Congestion cost, 324–328
Congress. *See* United States Congress
Constant-cost assumption, 145
Construction costs, 76, 88, 103. *See also* Public projects, losses caused by
Construction schedules, errors in estimating costs and, 283
Consumers coalition, 6
Consumption of public goods, 47–49
  aggregate, 3, 3*n*
Consumption bundles, choice of, 3, 4
Contingent contracts, competitive equilibrium and, 10

Contingent fee system, 328
Contract method of financing, 73–74
Convictions, as input or output measures, 46
Corps of Engineers, 268, 269
  causes of increases in project costs of, 299*n*
  errors in estimating costs by, 271–272, 273*t*
    compared with other water resource agencies, 277–281
    distribution of, 311, 312
    overrun frequency by administrative division, 301*t*–302*t*
    and planning and decision making methods, 288–291, 294
    and project size, 287
    by project type, 284*t*–285*t*, 300*t*
    proximate causes of, 281–283
    and size of price escalating factor, 302*t*
Cost
  and decentralization, 33, 34
  definition of, 267*n*, 271*n*
  of highway accidents. *See* Highway accident costs
  of Post Office. *See* Postal costs
  of public goods, 217
  of public investment projects. *See* Public investment projects, errors in estimating costs of
  of substitutes for mail service, 352
  of transmitting information, 12–13
  of urban highways and urban renewal. *See* Displacement costs; Public projects, losses caused by
  See also Acceptance costs; Automobile insurance costs; Civil costs; Commuting costs; Congestion costs; Cost analysis; Delivery costs of Post Office; Demoralization costs; Disequilibrium costs; Displacement costs; Dollar costs; Federal expenditures; Government expenditures; Highway costs; Incremental costs; Modification costs; Overhead costs; Processing costs; Produc-

Cost (*Cont.*)
  tion costs; Psychological costs;
    Public costs; Resource costs;
    Spillover costs; State expenditures; Transaction costs
Cost analysis
  capabilities of, 237–238
  and characteristics of programs, 265
  conceptual framework for, 233–237
  and cost as function of rate of output or cumulative output, 264–265
  and data problem, 249–250
  differences in definitions of categories, 251–252
  influence of temporal factors, 252
  information in wrong format, 251
  integration problem, 251
  solutions for, 253–262
  errors in. *See* Public projects, errors in estimating costs of
  and estimating relationships, 250
  fixed effectiveness framework for, 242–244
  of major military equipment, 258–261
  and national security, 264–265
  principal characteristics of, 263
  and sample problem, 255–261
  in terms of time-phased cost streams, 242–247
  useful output of. *See* Cost functions
  and varied system characteristics, 247–249
Cost analysis models, 237–238
Cost Ascertainment System, 363*n*, 371, 371*n*, 374, 375*n*, 378
Cost function, 239–244
Cost-plus contracts, 11
Crime rates, as police output measure, 46
Cyert, R. M., 115*n*

Data problem. *See under* Cost analysis
Date appropriation, cost estimates and, 306*t*
De Haven, James C., 268*n*
Deaths, traffic density and, 320–321, 324

Decentralization, 182, 210, 211
  and collective decision making, 32–35
  and cost estimates, 289
  efficiency of, 64
  and public output production, 34, 34*n*
  growing demands for, 217
  progress of, 185
  and provision of public services, 216
  and size of jurisdictional unit, 34–35
  See also Centralization
Decision making
  centralized vs. decentralized, 133–134
  and cost analysis, 235, 235*n*
  and errors in cost estimates, 288–291
  and highway accidents, 329–330
  and need for strengthened adversary system, 225–227
  partisan incrementalism approach to, 219–221
  systematic approach to, 220–224, 228–230
  and systems analysis, 232
  use of data and analysis in, 225–226
Defense expenditures, 190, 192–194
Deliverability of compensation, 94, 96*t*–97*t*
Delivery costs of Post Office, 360, 362*t*
  and equal-service concept, 369–370
  and pricing efficiency, 369–370
Demand
  nature of, choice of decision making method and, 222, 228
  for postal services, 378
  by business firms, 348–351
  secular growth of, 351–354
Democracy, income distribution and, 19. *See also* Federalism models
Demolition. *See* Displacement costs
Demoralization costs, 115, 119–128
  compensation for, 134
  of World Trade Center television interference, 129–133
Department of Defense. *See* United States Department of Defense

Department of Housing and Urban Development. *See* United States Department of Housing and Urban Development

Design changes, errors in estimating costs related to, 282, 294

Detroit Supervisors' Inter-County Committee, 184

Disadvantaged families
and net gains of World Trade Center, 132
reaction to spillover costs of public projects, 125–128

Discounts
and choice of productive technique, 265
and cost analysis, 234–236, 245–246
on mailing rates, 344–345, 350–351, 367, 367n

Diseconomies of scale, 217
and size of political unit, 33, 34, 33n–34n
and urban renewal and highway projects, 109–111
See also Economies of scale

Disequilibrium costs, transaction costs and, 17–18

Displacement costs, 109–111
caused by uncertainty and delay, 79–81
cost of maintaining property after appraisal, 81
cost of paying for alternative locations, 75–78
cost of seeking alternative locations, 75
declines in property value, 80–81
deterioration of neighborhood quality of life, 80
difficulties of measuring, 92–94
disruption of established relationships, 71
due to home financing arrangements, 73–74
due to taking of real property, 73
higher operating costs at alternative locations, 78–79
imposed upon households in surrounding areas, 82–88

changes in relative accessibility, 87–88
disruption of local communications, 82–83
higher taxes, 82
increased competition for low-income housing, 83–87
reduction of efficiency of community facilities, 87
reduction of employment opportunities, 82–83
reduction of services, 82
resulting from adverse environmental changes, 88
resulting from construction process, 88
spillover of deterioration, 83
kinds of, 72t–73t
losses of rental income, 81
moving costs, 78
and nonwhite families, 83–85
of renters, 77–78
and retail establishments, 107
tests for determination of, 94–98

Distributional issue, 128–129, 128n
and allocative efficiency, 108–109, 108n

Dollar costs, 235–236

Dostoevski, Fëdor, 29

Downs, Anthony, 123n, 130n

Dredging, cost estimating for, 284

Drugs. *See* Narcotic and drug abuse

Eckstein, Otto, 268, 268n

Economic efficiency. *See* Efficiency

Economic theory
and cost analysis, 233–234
and Pareto efficiency, 8
value of, 3

Economies of scale, 263
and cost analysis, 241–242
and fiscal equivalence, 217
and highways, 326–327
by local government, 63–64
and postal service, 357, 362–364, 383–384
and size of political unit, 33, 34, 33n–34n
See also Diseconomies of scale

Edens, Arthur, 339n
Education, government expenditures for, 175t, 177t, 178, 180t, 181
Effectiveness analysis, 242
Efficiency, 222
  and adaptive responses to non-compensation, 123n
  in allocation, 141
  and compensation for spillovers, 119–128
  and decentralization, 33–35
  of decision making methods, 221
  and design of World Trade Center, 130, 130n
  and externalities among political jurisdictions, 34–35
  of Post Office, 350, 364–372
  and systematic decisions, 230
Electricité de France, 292–294
Emigration, income distribution and, 37–38. *See also* Migration
Employment opportunities, effect of public projects on, 82–83
End-product-oriented estimating relationships, 254
Engineering News-Record, 272, 274
  construction cost index, 287
Enthoven, A. C., 235n
Environmental changes caused by public projects, 70, 88
  compensation for, 92, 98
  See also Air pollution; Water pollution
Equal service concept, 366, 369–370
Equilibrium
  competitive, Pareto efficiency and, 3–6
  game theory concepts of, 10
  imperfectly competitive, 6–10
  and risk, 10–13
  and standard lighthouse example, 14
Errors in estimating costs. *See* Public projects, errors in estimating costs of
Estimating relationships, 250
  for long-range planning studies, 255
  and simulations, 261
  for small sample example, 256t
Evaluation of society, 27–30

Exclusion, 2
  and failure of futures markets, 16–17
  fiscal equalization as substitute for, 154–155
  and lighthouse example, 15
  See also Exclusion costs
Exclusion costs, transaction costs and, 17–18
Explicit land prices, 59–61
Externalities
  among political jurisdictions, 34–36
  cost of, 55–58
    and use of city facilities by suburban dwellers, 47–49, 47n
  current analysis of, 1–3
  illustrations of, 13–16
  and land prices, 60–61
  and market failure, 15–17, 28–29
  and nonoptimal market behavior, 13–16
  and optimal distribution of population, 51–53
  and Pareto-efficiency, 24–30
  and personal decisions, 65
  political, 32–33
  and postal deficit, 373–377
  in public facility use. *See* Highway accidents
  and size of jurisdiction, 217
  and spillover costs, 122–123
  See also Demoralization costs; Interjurisdictional externalities

Fabricant, Solomon, 170n
Fair market value, 73, 76, 102–103
  determination of, 95
  and impending demolition, 80
  and psychological costs, 92
Federal agencies, programs of, 183t
Federal aid
  to education, 178–181
  and government expenditure estimates, 170
  and provision of public services, 217–218
  for public health and welfare, 178–181
  See also Federal grants

Federal budget. *See* Federal expenditures; Program budgeting
Federal expenditures, 198*t*
  on grant programs for regional planning, 183*t*
  shares of aggregate governmental activity, 169*t*, 170, 171*t*
  and tax credits and subsidies, 186–188
Federal fiscal equalization. *See* Fiscal equalization
Federal government
  and adversary system, 226
  future increases in financing role of, 181
  program budgeting for. *See* Program budgeting
  See also Federal aid; Federal expenditures; Federal grants; Government expenditures
Federal grants, 158, 182, 183*t*, 184, 190*t*, 191, 191*t*, 211
  average annual growth rates of, 191*t*
  and fiscal equalization, 159–161
  to local governments, 182, 184–185
Federalism models
  constant cost, full mobility model, 143–148
  fiscal equalization as substitute for exclusion rights in, 154–155
  with impure public goods, 160–162
  with impure public goods under state provision, 150–157
  increasing cost, Ricardian model, 148–150
  and inefficiency in state provision of public goods, 155–157
  policy implications of, 157–158
  with pure public goods, 159–160
  two-state, 146–148
Financial responsibliity laws, 328
Fire protection, local expenditures per capita on, 175*t*
First class mail
  and acceptance service, 364–366
  arrival at main post office, 350
  and business firms, 349–351
  future competition with, 352
  See also Mail classes; Post Office

Fiscal equalization
  attitudes toward, 139–143
  and economies of scale, 217
  efficiency basis for, 139–142
  equity arguments to support, 139–140
  in federalism models
    constant cost, full mobility model, 143–148
    with impure public goods, 160–162
    with impure public goods under state provision, 150–157
    increasing cost, Ricardian model, 148–150
  and public goods, 142
  as substitute for exclusion rights, 154–155
  and tax transfers, 139–141
  See also Fiscal policies
Fiscal policies
  responsibilities for fragmentation of, 224, 229
  implication of federalism model for, 157–158
  trends in, 194–196, 218
Fiscal surplus
  and impurely public goods model, 151
  and population movement, 155–157
Flood control projects, cost overruns for, 284
Force structure cost model, 238*n*
Forest Service, production functions of, 223
Forte, Francesco, 145*n*, 153*n*
Foundation conditions, estimating errors and, 284
France, errors in cost estimates in, 292–294
Franklin, Benjamin, 339
Free enterprise system, risks of property ownership in, 91–92. *See also* Federalism models
Freedom of movement, 153
Fried, Marc, 73*n*
Freight forwarders, 353
Friendly, Fred W., 118, 118*n*
Futures markets, failure of, 16–17

Game theory approach, 7, 7*n*
  and bargaining, 8–9
Gasoline tax, accident costs and, 331–332
Gaty, Lewis, 339*n*
Geologic information, cost estimates and, 298
Gerelli, Emilio, 155*n*
Ghettos, 216
Giguet, R., 269*n*, 292*n*, 293–294
Glazer, Nathan, 216*n*, 217*n*
GNP
  and allocation efficiency, 141
  in federalism model, 143
  government expenditures as per cent of, 209*t*
  and Post Office volume of mail, 351
Goals, social versus bureaucratic, 133–134
Goodell, Charles, 139*n*
Goods and services
  civil purchases of, 169*t*, 170
  defense and nondefense government purchases of, 174*t*
Government activities
  contracted out, 65–66
  and resource allocation, 18–19
Government efficiency. *See* Optimal government theory
Government employees, number of, 169*t*
Government expenditures, 207*t*
  absolute changes in shares of, 168*t*
  aggregate, 164*t*, 198*t*, 199*t*
    federal and state-local percentage measures of, 200*t*
  by alternative measures, 206*t*
  average annual growth rates of federal and nonfederal, 173*t*
  between 1902 and 1966, 163–171
  current and prospective developments, 182
  and new levels of local government, 182, 184–185
  on defense and nondefense purchases, 174*t*, 174–175
  definition of, 165
  direct, 204*t*

federal government's share of, 208*t*, 210–211
  federal and nonfederal functions of, 171–172, 174–175
  on goods and services substituted for defense purchases, 190
  gross and net measures of, 186*n*
  and high-cost urban functions, 175–176
  on human capital, 176–181, 203*t*
  as per cent of GNP, 209*t*
  percentage shares by level of maintenance and development of, 202*t*
  trends in, 194–196
  See also Federal expenditures; Intergovernmental expenditures; Local expenditures; State expenditures
Government grants. *See* Federal grants
Governmental insurance trust system, 165, 165*n*
Grant-in-aid programs. *See* Federal grants
Great Britain, errors in cost estimates in, 292, 310*t*
Great Depression, 177
Gross national product. *See* GNP

Harriss, C. Lowell, 165*n*
Haveman, Robert H., 268*n*, 269*n*, 297*n*
Hayek, F., 28
Healey, J. M., 268, 268*n*, 291, 291*n*, 292
Health and hospital expenditures, 179*t*
  federal, state, and local shares of, 178, 180*t*, 181
  nonfederal, 177*t*
  per capita local, 175*t*
Heller, Walter H., 139*n*
Heller-Pechman scheme, 139*n*, 190
Heterogeneity, income distribution and, 35
Highway accident costs, 317–319, 327*n*
  deaths, 320–321, 324
  and oil companies, 333, 336
  payment of, 336–338
  and state fund concept, 332–333

and supplement to gasoline tax, 331–332

and traffic conditions, 321, 322*t*–323*t*, 324–328, 331

See also Automobile insurance; Highway accidents

Highway accidents
on California freeways and state highways, 322*t*–323*t*, 324, 325*n*
causes of, 319–320
and fault concept, 329–330
and insurance coverage, 328–329
alternate forms of, 332–334
and traffic density, 336–338
See also Highway accident costs

Highway tolls, 325–326

Highways, expenditures on, 175*t*, 180*t*

Hirshleifer, Jack, 268*n*

Hitch, Charles J., 220, 236, 236*n*, 237

Home financing arrangements, displacement by public projects and, 73–74, 109–110

Home rule
and interjurisdictional externalities, 35–36
and size of political unity, 33–35

Homogeneity
and income distribution, 35
of local communities, 32, 32*n*

Hospitals. *See* Health and hospital expenditures

House Appropriations Committee, 269, 271–272, 281

House Public Works Committee, 271–272

Household indifference maps, convexity of, 3–6

Households, residential. *See* Low-income households; Residential households

Housing markets
compensation and, 98, 103
and demolition, 83–87

Housing and urban renewal, expenditures on, 175*t*, 180*t*, 181. *See also* Public projects

Human capital expenditures, 176–181, 195

Identifiability test, 94, 96*t*–97*t*

Immigration. *See* Migration

Impurely public goods, in federalism model, 150–157

Incentives
for comprehensive regional planning, 182, 183*t*, 184
for private builders, 104
for private industry, 186–188

Income
aggregate, 43
and compensation costs, 137–138
in federalism model, 143–144
and migration patterns, 158*n*
See also Income distribution; Income redistribution; National income; Per capita income

Income distribution
and collective redistribution function, 36–43
and decentralization, 34–35
desirable, 4
and displacement costs, 89–90
efficiency issues involved in, 224, 229–230
ideal, 27–28
and notions of justice, 26
and Pareto efficiency, 25
See also Income redistribution

Income redistribution, 19
and role of government, 67–68
and social services, 158*n*
See also Income distribution; Tax transfers

Income transfers from retail book and record stores to book and record clubs, 370, 371, 371*n*

Increasing returns, 6–7, 7*n*

Incremental costs, assessment of, 238

India, cost estimate errors in, 291–292, 310*t*

Individual-choice behavior, 149, 151

Information
and cost estimates errors, 270
economic value of transmitting, 12
format for, 251
See also Information costs

Information costs, transaction costs and, 17–18

Input categories
definitions of, 251
in residential location model, 45–46
Institutional biases, cost estimates and, 290–291
Insurance. *See* Automobile insurance
Insurance companies, equilibrium rate and, 10–11
Intergovernmental expenditures, 165–166, 165*n*
for education, health, and welfare, 179*t*
and optimal local government, 63–64
state-to-local, 167
Intergovernmental revenues, 165
Interjurisdictional externalities
model of residential location with, 44–59
and optimal local government, 43–59
Internal Revenue Service, 229
production functions of, 223
International affairs, federal and non-federal expenditures on, 167, 172*t*, 173*t*, 174, 204*t*, 205*t*
and Pareto efficiency, 8
International mail, 340

Javits, Jacob, 139*n*
Johnson, Wendell E., 267*n*, 269

Kahn, C. Harry, 187*n*
Kappel Commission, 383
"Keaton-O'Connell" type plan, 328
Kennedy, Jane, 363*n*, 373*n*, 380
Knight, Frank H., 28, 153, 153*n*
Krutilla, John, 268*n*

Labor costs of Post Office, 354–356, 378
and mail processing mix, 359
Labor-land ratio in federalism model, 159
Laird, Melvin, 139*n*
Land, in federalism model, 143
Land acquisition, errors in cost estimates and, 282

Land prices, explicit. *See* Explicit land prices
Land values
and accessibility of metropolitan area, 88
effects of public projects on, 90
and estimating errors, 284
See also Fair market value; Property value
Langworthy, Terrell, 269*n*, 297*n*
"Launching costs" of automobile industry, 258*n*
Leibenstein, Harvey, 128*n*
Libraries, local expenditures per capita on, 175*t*
Life insurance policies, highway accidents and, 318
Lindblom, C. E., 219, 219*n*
Lindsay, John V., 116, 118–119, 118*n*, 136
Liquor stores, government expenditures on, 165
Local autonomy, 182
Local communications, disruption by public projects of, 82
Local government expenditures, 198*t*
in areas surrounding condemned area, 81–82
between 1902 and 1966, 164*t*
compared with federal expenditures, 211
for education, health, and welfare, 179*t*
on high-cost urban functions, 176*t*
per capita, in metropolitan and non-metropolitan areas, 175*t*, 175–176
projected and hypothetical, 189*t*
as shares of aggregate governmental activity, 169*t*, 170, 171*t*
trends in, 195
See also Local governments
Local governments
associations of, 184
federal grants-in-aid to, 191*t*
federation of, 215–216
future of, 182, 184
new levels of, 182, 184–185
number of, 215–216

welfare evaluation of, 31*ff*
See also Local government expenditures
Logrolling for collective goods, 214, 214*n*
Losses caused by public projects. *See* Public projects, losses caused by
Low-cost housing, public projects and, 99–101
Low-income households
in Baltimore, 83–85
and cable television, 117
and displacement losses, 83–87, 108–109
and public housing, 86*n*
rough estimates of, 101–105
and uncompensated losses, 99–101
Low-income housing
access to, 84–85
availability of, 85–87
competition for, 83–87, 110–111
See also Public housing
Low-income neighborhoods, effects of public projects on, 73–78
Lundy, Richard A., 324*n*

Maass, Arthur, 268*n*
McLaughlin, John Francis, 371*n*, 380
McKean, Roland N., 220, 236*n*, 237, 268*n*
McNamara, Robert, 220, 221, 231
Magazines, postal subsidies and, 381–382
Magnavox Corporation, 352
Mail. *See* First class mail; Mail classes; Parcel post; Parcels; Post Office; Second class mail; Third class mail
Mail classes
and acceptance costs, 364–366
distinguishing characteristics of, 342
effects of rate differential between, 351–354, 371
by originators of domestic mail, 349*t*, 349–350
postal revenues and volume by, 346*t*, 347–348
Mail processing costs, 359
Mailer, Norman, 216*n*

Majority rule
and allocative process, 19
and welfare maximization, 32
Management. *See* Administrative structure
Marginal cost
of additional moves to suburbs, 52–54
definition of, 240
of Post Office, 357
ratio of business in suburb to business in city, 62
Marginal mover, 52–53
Margolis, Julius, 128*n*
Market economy, effect of differential information on, 11–13
Market failures, 2
and externalities, 16–17, 28–29
and social norms, 20
and transaction costs, 17–18
Market value, fair. *See* Fair market value
Markets
nonoptimal behavior of, externality and, 13–14
universality of, 3–6
Markham, Emerson, 339*n*
Maryland State Roads Commission, 69*n*
Massachusetts, automobile insurance in, 328–329
"Matching up" problem, 251
Maxwell, James A., 167, 167*n*
Measurability test, 94, 96*t*–97*t*
Mechanization of Post Office, 341, 356–357, 357*n*
Medical costs of highway accidents, 317
Mental health, "program packages" for, 238
Mera, Koichi, 157*n*
Michelman, Frank I., 115, 115*n*, 119, 119*n*, 120, 120*n*, 125*n*, 127*n*, 128*n*, 130*n*, 131*n*, 135
Michigan, insurance statistics for, 318
Mieszkowski, Peter M., 193*n*
Migration
and central government grants, 158

Migration (*Cont.*)
and differential fiscal surpluses, 155–156
and efficiency of public goods provision, 159–161
and exclusion rights, 154–155
in federalism models, 148–149, 148n, 151–155, 160–162
and fiscal policies, 157
and income distribution, 37–38
of low-income households, 76
to metropolitan area, 38
to suburbs, 162
and tax transfers, 141
and taxes, 160
Military major equipment cost analysis, 258–261
Mill, John Stuart, 29
Milliman, Jerome W., 268n
Missouri River Basin Program, 275, 277, 283
Models
of cost analysis, 237–238
of effects of externality on nonoptimal market behavior, 13–14
of monopolistic competitive equilibrium, 7
of perfectly competitive market, 29–30
of political process, 18
of residential and business locations, 61–63
of residential location with interjurisdictional externalities
and character of resource misallocation, 58–59
and equilibrium population distribution, 53–58
and optimal distribution of population, 51–53
specification of, 44–51
of tax system and income distribution, 36–37
See also Federalism models
Modification costs, 20
Money costs. *See* Dollar costs
Monopoly
advantages of, 5, 6

and economies of scale, 357, 357n
incorporation into general equilibrium system, 7
reasons for existence of, 6
See also Postal monopoly
"Moral hazard," 11
Morality, fundamental principle of, 26
Morlat, G., 269n, 292n, 293–294
Moving costs, 78, 95
Musgrave, Richard A., 141, 141n, 142, 145n
"exclusion principle" of, 14

National Advisory Commission on Civil Disorders, 100
National Aeronautics and Space Administration, 238
National Association of Home Builders, 370
National Bureau of Economic Research: Universities-NBER Committee Conference, 141
National defense
and collective decisions, 65
and cost analysis, 247–249
and government expenditure estimates, 167, 172t, 173, 174, 204t, 205t
National income, tax transfers and, 140–141
National income accounts, 163ff
shares of, 201t
National Safety Council, 317, 317n, 319
National security. *See* National defense
Natural resources, expenditures on, 175t, 180t, 181
Narcotic and drug abuse, "program packages" for, 238
Negative income tax, 19, 193, 193n
Negroes
and displacement losses, 108–109
effects of public projects on, 84–85
and federal grants, 162
Neighborhood deterioration, effects of public projects on, 80–81, 83, 98
Neighborhood subunits, 185, 185n–186n

Net gains of public projects, 126, 132
Net negative impact test, 94, 96t–97t
New York City
   decentralization in, 185
   PPBS effort in, 221
   See also World Trade Center problem
Newspapers
   and postal subsidies, 381–382
   and pricing efficiency of Post Office, 366–367
Newsweek, 352–353
Night work wage differential, 355
Noise, public project construction and, 88, 92
"Noise level" of cost analysis, 246
Nonbuyers, pricing and, 14
Nonconstruction costs of public projects. *See* Displacement costs; Public projects, losses caused by
Nonconvexities, competitive equilibrium and, 5
Noninherent riskiness test, 94, 96t–97t
Nonmarket allocation of externalities, 1
Nonmeasurability of displacement losses, 93–94
Nonprofit organizations, discounts on mail rates of, 344–345
Nonpublic goods production, partisan pressures and, 223, 229
Nonwhite families, effects of public projects on, 84–85, 99–101. *See also* Low-income households; Negroes
North of Scotland Hydro-Electric Board, 268n, 292
Novick, David, 231n

Office of Economic Opportunity, 226
Oil companies, accident costs and, 333, 336
Older persons, effects of displacement on, 76
Olson, D. G., 120n, 122n
Olson, Mancur, Jr., 213n, 218n
Opportunity costs in systems analysis studies, 235–237

Optimal local government, 32
   and constituent composition and the collective redistributive function, 36–43
   criteria for, 35
   goals of, 65–66
   and interjurisdictional externalities, 43–59
   and optimality of public sector, 32
   and residential location model, 44–49, 61–63
      with explicit land prices, 59–61
   and scale economies, 63–64
   and size of "home rule" unit, 33–36
   and size of jurisdiction, 66
Out-of-state automobiles, 331–332
Output
   and decentralization, 34
   in federalism model, 145
   of members of coalition, 9
   and program budgeting, 232
   in residential location model, 45–46
   See also Public output
"Output-oriented entities." *See* "Program packages"
Overhead costs, errors in cost estimates and, 292
Overtime, 355, 357

Palo, G. P., 267
Panama Canal, 299
Parametric cost models, 237–238
Parcel post, 348, 353–354
   and Post Office pricing efficiency, 370–371
Parcels
   and competitors with Post Office, 353–354
   and mechanization of Post Office, 359n
   Post Office charges for, 348
Pareto efficiency
   and competitive equilibrium, 3–6
   of compulsory insurance, 11
   of externalities, 1, 24–30
   and imperfectly competitive equilibrium, 8
   and income distribution, 27–28
   and Pareto-optimality, 24–25

Pareto efficiency (*Cont.*)
  and production in coalitions, 9
  and size of political jurisdictions, 34
  and utilitarianism, 26
  See also Pareto inefficiency; Pareto
    optimality
Pareto inefficiency
  and ethical standards, 12
  and externalities, 2–3
  and monopolistic competitive equi-
    librium, 7–8
Pareto optimality
  and collective goods, 213
  and collective services, 218
  and distributional equity, 107
  and federal action, 162
  in federalism models, 150, 151
  of fiscal transfers, 154–155, 154n
  of migration, 160, 161n
  and Pareto-efficiency, 24–25
  and public services, 216
  and welfare maximization, 32
Parks and recreation, local expenditures per capita on, 175t
Partisan incrementalism, 219–221
Peak load problem, 350, 355
Pechman, Joseph A., 139n, 187, 193n
Pechman Task Force Report, 139n
Pedestrians, highway accidents and,
  318
Per capita costs, consumption of interjurisdictional public goods and,
  48–49
Per capita income
  in federalism model, 144
  and immigration to suburbs and
    cities, 37–38
  and tax system, 36–37
Perfectly competitive market model,
  29–30
Permit fees, 348
"Pig-principle," 24
Pigou, A. C., 153, 153n
Planning
  and errors in cost estimates, 282
  "pure requirements" approach to,
    232
  See also Decision making

Planning, Programing, Budgeting System. *See* PPBS
Police districts, mini, 216
Police services
  as input or output measures, 46
  local expenditures per capita on,
    175t
Political behavior, economic theory
  and, 3
Political decision making, in residential
  location model, 45
Political externalities
  and selection of highway sites, 100
  and size of jurisdiction, 66
Political jurisdictional units
  clusters of public functions, 33, 33n–
    34n
  consolidation of, 63–64
  and delegation of power, 32–35
  externalities among, 34–35
  size of, 34
    and benefits of public goods, 217–
      218
Politico-economic models, 18
Pollution. *See* Air pollution; Water
  pollution
Population distribution
  in federalism models, 148, 148n
  and income distribution, 36–42
  optimal, 51–53
Port of New York Authority, 136, 137
Post Office
  benefits of analysis of, 381–382
  competitors with, 352–354
  cost of operating. *See* Postal costs
  deficits. *See* Postal deficits
  and demand for postal services, 348–
    354
    secular growth of, 351–354
  development and growth of, 339–
    340
  and excess capacity, 349–351
  expenditures for, 172t, 173t, 174,
    204t, 205t
  history of, 166, 372–373
  monopoly by. *See* Postal monopoly
  organization of, 341–342
  and permit fees, 348

postal revenues and volume by class of mail, 346t
rate structure. *See* Postal rates
Report of President's Postal Commission, 377–380
services of, 340
supervisory staff of, 357
technology of, 341
waste in, 221
Postage meters, 365, 365n, 366
Postal costs
and capital spending, 356–357
and economies of scale, 357, 357n
and labor costs, 354–356
as a per cent of total costs, 354
long-run, 357–364
and acceptance costs, 358–359, 362t
and delivery costs, 360, 362t
and mail processing costs, 359, 362t
and transportation costs, 361–362, 362t
mechanization and equipment as a per cent of total, 356
and Report of President's Postal Commission, 377–380
transportation costs, 355–356
Postal deficit, 373–374, 374t
attributable to public service, 375–376
attributable to rural delivery service, 376–377
Postal monopoly
and President's Postal Commission, 378
reasons for, 372–373
Postal Policy Act, 374
Postal production function, 341
Postal rates
and competition, 363–364, 363n, 364n
concepts affecting, 347–348
efficiency of
and acceptance costs, 364–366
and delivery costs, 369–370
and mail classes, 371
and parcel post, 370–371

and processing costs, 366–367
and transportation costs, 367–368
and growth of mail volume, 342–348, 351–354
on second class mail, 344t
on third class mail, 345t
Postal receipts by size of office, 340t
Postal subsidies, 375, 381–386
PPBS system, 220, 221
criterion for application of, 230
in foreign affairs area, 226
and postal costs, 358–362
Pred, Alen, 144n
Premiums for lower and higher-valued homes, 103
President of the United States, 231–232
President's Commission on Postal Organization, 341–342, 377–380
Presorting of mail, 365
Price changes, errors in cost estimates and, 274, 281, 292, 294, 297
Price elasticity
of demand for magazines, 353
of demand for Post Office services, 351–354
Price systems, 6–7
role of state in, 18
Prices
and competitive equilibrium, 3, 5
and cost, 7
and costs of transmitting information, 12–13
and nonbuyers, 14
See also Price elasticity; Price systems; Pricing mechanism
Pricing mechanism
and organization of Post Office, 350–351
and traffic problems, 158n
Principal-agent relations, 12
and codes of professional ethics, 20
Private cost of moving to suburbs, 54
Private Express Statutes, 363, 364
repeal of, 384–386
Private postal firms, 364n
Problem solving, interactive analytic process and, 226–227. *See also* Decision making

Processing costs, Post Office efficiency and, 366–367
Production in coalitions, 9
Production costs, transaction costs and, 17
Production function
  and data availability, 223, 229
  and efficiency estimates, 222–223
Professions
  Pareto inefficiencies in, 12
  partisan adjustment among, 224
Profit on first class mail, 363–364
Program budgeting
  definition, 232
  inception of, 231–232
  See also Cost analysis; PPBS system
"Program packages," 238, 239
Property damage, highway accidents and, 317
Property ownership, inescapable risks of, 91–92
Property rights
  and allocation of scarce resources, 153
  in federalism models, 149
Property taxes
  explicit, 60
  and move to suburbs, 49–51
  and public improvements, 92
Property value
  declines in, 80–81
  diffused and locally concentrated impacts upon, 91–92
  in highway and urban renewal areas, 81, 100
  See also Fair market value
Protective adaptive responses to demoralization costs, 119, 120n
Psychological costs of displacement, 92, 93
Public agencies, neighborhood subunits of, 185
Public assistance, highway accidents and, 318
Public costs, taxes and, 49–51
Public enterprises, in government expenditure estimates, 166
Public facilities
  and compensation, 98

used by suburban dwellers, 47–49, 47n
Public finance, allocative efficiency of, 140–143
Public goods
  beneficiaries of, jurisdictional boundaries and, 212–218
  "catchment areas" of, 217
  effects of inefficiency in state provision of, 155–157
  in federalism models, 145–147
  and fiscal equalization, 142
  impurely. *See* Impurely public goods
  and national product accounting, 145n
  partisan pressures for production of, 223, 229
  tax-pricing of, 145
  See also Externalities
Public housing, 76, 86n
  and government expenditure estimates, 166
  See also Low-income housing
Public investment projects. *See* Public projects
Public output
  per capita effective demand for, 45
  in residential location model, 46
  used by suburban dwellers, 54–58
  See also Output; Public projects
Public policy
  and theory of general equilibrium, 6–7
  and uncompensated costs, 105
Public projects
  causes of increases in costs of, 299t, 308t
  cost analysis study of, 269–270
  errors in cost estimates of
    causes for, 270–271, 281–291
    and construction method, 290
    data available on, 267–269
    extent of previous research on, 268–269
    in France, 292–294
    in Great Britain, 292
    in India, 291–292

and institutional biases, 290–291
and policy findings and implications, 294–297
and project scope, 283, 292
and project size, 270, 281, 297, 306*t*
and project timing, 287–288
and project type, 284, 285*t,* 286, 300*t,* 306
and secular changes over time, 291
suggestions for further research on, 298–299
and unitary versus decentralized administration, 289
in U.S. water resource agencies. *See* Bureau of Reclamation; Corps of Engineers; TVA
losses caused by, 69–70, 72*t*–73*t*
and compensation. *See* Compensation
displacement losses, 71, 73–79
and distinguishing between real resource losses and redistribution losses, 89–90
indirect losses to surrounding areas, 81–88
and project size, 119–128
and uncertainty and delay, 79–81
See also Displacement costs
Public services
contracted out, 65–66
and effects of public projects, 82, 90–91
and urban-suburban relations, 213
Public utilities, government expenditures on, 165
Public welfare programs, 177
expenditures for, 175*t,* 177*t,* 178, 179*t,* 180*t,* 181, 193
Public Works Committee Report, 101–105
Public works policy, 294–297. *See also* Public projects
Publishers, postal subsidies and, 381–382
Pure exchange economy, 13–16

Quade, E. S., 232*n*
Quality of life, effect of public-project area designations on, 80

Racial discrimination, displacement by public projects and, 84–87
Railway Express, 353, 385
Ralston, August, 120*n,* 122*n*
RAND Corporation, 231*n,* 238*n*
Rate structure of Post Office. *See* Postal rates
Real property losses, displacement by public projects and, 73
Recht, J. L., 321*n*
Redistributional losses compared with resource losses, 89–90, 108–109
Red-tag service, 366–367
Regional councils, 184
Regional government, 184–185
Regional planning, federal grant programs providing incentives for, 182, 183*t,* 184
Relationships, relocation and, 71
Relocation
and errors in cost estimates, 282
excess costs of, 95
and World Trade Center problem, 132
See also Displacement costs
Rent controls, 132*n*
Rent subsidies, 102
Renter households, displacement and, 77–78, 102, 104
Rents, displacement and, 84, 102, 104
Residential and business model, 61–63
Residential households, and losses caused by public projects. *See* Public projects, losses caused by
Residential location function, 50–51
introduction of relative land prices into, 59–61
Residential location model, 59–61
Resource allocation
and collective action, 18–19
efficiency in
and compensation, 134–135
and distributional equity, 108–109, 108*n*

Resource allocation (*Cont.*)
Pareto-efficient, 10, 13–16
Pareto-optimal, 212–215
and rationing process, 15
in response to uncompensated spillovers, 128–129
and size of jurisdiction, 66
solutions for problems in, 65–66
and tax transfers, 140–141
and trade with others, 5
and transaction costs, 2
and uncertainty, 10–11
with unrestricted bargaining, 9
Resource cost functions, in residential location model, 46
Resource costs
and excess suburbanization, 58–61
of public output, suburban population and, 47–48
Resource losses compared with redistributional losses, 89–90, 108–109. *See also* Resource misallocation
Resource misallocation, 58–61
and business location, 61–63
Retirement systems, 165*n*
"Revealed preference," 28–29
Reverse externalities, 47, 47*n*
Ricardian model, 159
with impurely public goods, 150–157
Risk
and equilibrium, 10–13
and insurance companies, 10–11
and optimal allocation, 11
Robinson, Warren C., 188*n*
Rothenberg, Jerome, 120*n*, 128*n*, 210, 210*n*
RPO (railway post office) service, 367
Rural population, decline in, 376*n*
Rural route delivery, 376–377

Sacks, Seymour, 175*n*
Samples. *See* Ad hoc sample surveys; Small sample problem
Samuelson, Paul A., 141, 141*n*, 142
San Francisco, reorganization of government in, 185
Saskatchewan plan, 328, 331–332
Sault Ste. Marie Canal, 299

Savings, consumption of interjurisdictional public goods and, 48–49
Sawyer, John E., 299, 299*n*
Schelling, T. C., 226*n*
School boards, mini, 216
Schools, "overloading" costs of, 111. *See also* Community facilities; Education, government expenditures for
Schultze, Charles, 214*n*, 219*n*
Scott, Anthony D., 140, 140*n*
Second class mail
and periodicals, 353
and pricing efficiency, 366–367
rates on, 344–345, 344*t*, 348
See also Mail classes
Segregation, 216. *See also* Racial discrimination
Select Committee on Nationalized Industries, 268, 268*n*, 292, 292*n*
Services. *See* Public services
Sewerage and sanitation, local expenditures per capita on, 175*t*
Shannon, John, 193*n*
Shooshan, Harry, 267*n*
Shopping centers, access to, 90
Significance test, 94, 96*t*–97*t*
Sirkin, Gerald, 133*n*
Slayton, William L., 101*n*
Small sample problem, techniques for handling, 255–261
Smith, Adam, 6
SMSA population, in model of residential location, 44–45
Social costs. *See* Costs
Social insurance, 165*n*
Social norms
and collective action, 20
evaluation of, 29–30
Socrates, 29
Space research and technology, federal and nonfederal expenditures on, 204*t*–205*t*
Spillover costs
reactions to unanticipated and anticipated, 125
of World Trade Center, 118, 118*n*
and demoralization costs, 119–128

distributional considerations, 128–129

Staats, Elmer B., 234n

Stamps, sale of, 265n

"Standard" and "substandard" housing, 77

State expenditures, 198t
  between 1902 and 1966, 164t
  compared with federal expenditures, 211
  impact of federal aid programs on, 192
  projected and hypothetical, 189t
  as share of aggregate governmental activity, 169t, 170, 171t

State governments, federal grants-in-aid to, 191t

Steiner, Peter, 125n, 130n, 133n

Stores. *See* Business firms; Community facilities

Stubblebine, W. C., 120n

Synoptic view, 226

Systems analysis. *See* Cost analysis

Suboptimization, 226, 226n

Subsidization
  and optimal local government, 63–64
  to private builders, 104
  See also Federal grants

Suburban population, use of city facilities by, 47–49, 47n

Suburbanization, 66–67
  and collective redistributive function, 37–38
  excess, 58–61
  and optimality, 43–59

Suburbs, move to. *See* Suburbanization

Sullivan, William, 339n

Supervisory staff of Post Office, 357

Task Force, 130n, 131, 133, 136

Task Force on Water Resources and Power of Second Hoover Commission, 271

Taussig, Michael K., 187n–188n

Tax collection in Latin America, 221

Tax credits, 196

Tax prices
  of public goods, 147n

of "rich" and "poor," 156
  in two-state federalism model, 147

Tax reduction policy, 193

Tax transfers
  criticisms of, 140–142
  in federalism model, 154–155
  and fiscal equalization, 139–141
  as government expenditures, 165
  and provision of public goods, 155n

Taxes
  in areas surrounding public projects, 81–82
  collection of, 66
  in federalism model, 144–145, 159, 159n, 160n
  and immigration and emigration, 38–40
  and income redistribution, 36–42
  and move to suburbs, 66–67
  See also Property taxes; Tax collection; Tax prices; Tax reduction policy; Tax transfers

"Taxpayer's surplus," 147

Telephone calls versus postal services, 352

Telephone company, equal service concept of, 369–370

Television interference problem. *See* World Trade Center problem

Temporal factors, cost analysis data and, 252

Tennessee Valley Authority. *See* TVA

Third class mail rates, 345t, 345, 348. *See also* Mail classes; Postal rates

Tiebout, Charles M., 141, 141n, 142, 185n

Time, 353

Time preference assumptions, 245
  and cost analysis, 234–236

Time-phased program costs, 242–247

Tinbergen, Jan, 220

Tire taxes, accident costs and, 332, 334

Tobin, James, 193n

Tort claims, 318

Traffic, effects of urban renewal on, 82. *See also* Traffic density

Traffic density
  externality problems involved in, 317

Traffic density (*Cont.*)
and highway accidents, 320–321,
336–338
and highway construction, 158*n*
and public projects, 88
Transaction costs
identification of, 2
and market failure, 2, 17–18
and production costs, 17
Transfer payments, government expenditure estimates and, 170
Transportation
government support of, 373
as input or output measures, 46
"program packages" for, 238
Transportation costs of Post Office,
355–356, 361, 362*t*, 367–368
Tullock, Gordon, 128*n*, 210, 210*n*
Turvey, Ralph, 386
TVA, 269
errors in cost estimates of, 274–275,
303*t*–305*t*
compared with other water resource agencies, 277–281
distribution of, 307*t*, 313, 314
and planning and decision making
methods, 288–291, 294
and project size, 287
and project timing, 287–288
by project type, 286
by project type, size, and date of
appropriation, 306*t*
proximate causes of, 283
TWX, 352

UHF directional transmitters, television interference problem and,
117–118
Uncertainty, 263
explicit treatment of, 234, 234*n*
Uncompensated loss
concentration among low-income
minority groups, 99–101
and demoralization costs, 119–128
distributional considerations, 128–
129
from highway accidents, 318–319
responses induced by, 120–121

rough estimates of, 101–105
solutions for problem of, 105–106
Underdevelopment, social norms and,
20
Unemployment compensation, resource
allocation and, 141
United Parcel Service, 353, 385
United States Congress
attitude toward PPBS, 220
and errors in cost estimates, 290,
294
and parcel post regulations, 370
and Post Office, 373, 381–382
and postal subsidies, 347, 375
United States Department of Defense,
226
and ad hoc sample surveys, 254–255
cost streams, projections of, 235
planning in, 236–237, 236*n*–237*n*
and program budgeting, 231
"program packages" of, 238
United States Department of Housing
and Urban Development, 77
United States Post Office. *See* Post
Office
United States water resource agencies,
comparison of cost estimate performance of, 277, 278*t*, 279, 280*t*,
281. *See also* Bureau of Reclamation; Corps of Engineers; TVA
Unpaved roads, accident costs on, 325
Urban areas. *See* Cities
Urban highway construction. *See* Public projects
Urban renewal. *See* Housing and urban
renewal; Public projects
Urbanization, government expenditures
and, 195
Utility functions, 19

Value judgments
and compensation, 107–108, 138
and move to suburbs, 52
of social scientists, 24
Vertical integration, transaction costs
and, 2
Veterans' services, government expenditure estimates and, 172*t*, 174

Vietnam War, 196
and government expenditures, 188–194
Vining, Rutledge, 144n
Violence, uncompensated losses from, 100
Voter, as principal or agent, 19

Wages
of government employees, 169
highway accidents and loss of, 317
Wall Street Journal, 352–353
Walters, Allan A., 327n
War Production Board, program budgeting in, 231
Wars, indirect costs of, 167
Water pollution, 215
Wealth, redistribution of. *See* Income distribution; Tax transfers
Weapon systems, cost analysis of, 254
Weisbrod, Burton, 123n
Welfare. *See* Public welfare; Welfare criteria; Welfare economists; Welfare recipients
Welfare criteria, individualistic, 32
Welfare economists, 89–90
Welfare recipients, collective redistributive function and, 36–42
Welland Canal, 299
Western Union, 352
Wildavsky, A., 219, 219n
Williamson, Oliver E., 120n, 121n, 122n, 136–138
Wilson, James O., 73n, 77n, 101n
World Trade Center problem
and centralization versus decentralization, 133–134
and demoralization costs, 129–133
issues involved in, 115–116
solutions to, 134–135, 136–138
Task Force report on, 116–117

Xerox Corporation, 352

Zeckhouser, Richard, 213n